MORALITY, NORMATIVITY,
AND SOCIETY

MORALITY, NORMATIVITY, AND SOCIETY

DAVID COPP

New York   Oxford
OXFORD UNIVERSITY PRESS
1995

Oxford University Press

Oxford   New York
Athens   Auckland   Bangkok   Bombay
Calcutta   Cape Town   Dar es Salaam   Delhi
Florence   Hong Kong   Istanbul   Karachi
Kuala Lumpur   Madras   Madrid   Melbourne
Mexico City   Nairobi   Paris   Singapore
Taipei   Tokyo   Toronto

and associated companies in
Berlin   Ibadan

Published by Oxford University Press, Inc.,
200 Madison Avenue, New York, New York 10016

Library of Congress Cataloging-in-Publication Data
Copp, David.
Morality, normativity, and society / David Copp.
p.   cm.
Includes bibliographical references and index.
ISBN 0-19-507879-9
1. Social ethics.   2. Social norms.   3. Ethics.   I. Title.
HM216.C673   1995
303.3'72—dc20   94-12013

1 3 5 7 9 8 6 4 2

Printed in the United States of America
on acid-free paper

For Marina

Preface

The main idea of society-centered moral theory first occurred to me almost fifteen years ago, during a hike with Ken Ferguson in the mountains near Vancouver. Since then I have benefited from the encouragement and criticisms of many people. I want to thank them all, although I cannot hope to mention them all by name.

I began developing the ideas in this book while on sabbatical leave from Simon Fraser University. The Social Sciences and Humanities Research Council of Canada assisted me with a leave fellowship, and the philosophy department at the University of British Columbia gave me its hospitality. In addition to this sabbatical leave, my department and the dean of arts at Simon Fraser were understanding enough to grant me several years of leave of absence to enable me to pursue my work elsewhere and to accept fellowships during the academic years 1983–1984 and 1988–1989. The S.S.H.R.C. awarded me a research grant and stipend during 1983–1984. I spent 1984 through 1987 in the philosophy department at the University of Illinois at Chicago, enjoying their collegiality and stimulation. Their Campus Research Board helped me with a short research leave. The generosity of the Research Triangle Foundation enabled me to spend the academic year 1988–1989 at the National Humanities Center in North Carolina. I have also been helped by research grants from the Committee on Research at the University of California, Davis. I want to thank all of these people and institutions for their generosity.

Some parts of the book have appeared elsewhere. I first proposed the central idea of chapter 2 in "Normativity and the Very Idea of Moral Epistemology," which was published in the 1990 Spindel Conference supplementary volume of *Southern Journal of Philosophy* (Volume 29, 1990). A portion of chapter 4 abbreviates the argument in "Contractarianism and Moral Skepticism," which was in Peter Vallentyne, ed., *Contractarianism and Rational Choice: Essays on Gauthier* (copyright © 1991 by Cambridge University Press). Another part of chapter 4 is an abbreviated and revised version of "The 'Possibility' of a Categorical Imperative: Kant's *Groundwork*, Part III," which appeared in James E. Tomberlin, ed., *Philosophical Perspectives*, Volume 6, 1992. Chapter 7 is an abbreviated version of "The Concept of Society," which was in *Dialogue*, Volume 31, 1992. Chapter 9 is a significantly revised version of "Reason and Needs," which appeared in R. G. Frey and Christopher W. Morris, eds., *Value, Welfare and Morality* (copyright © 1993 by Cambridge University Press). I am grateful to the publishers of these essays for permission to use them here.

I owe a special debt to Richmond Campbell, who encouraged me from the beginning and gave me comments on early drafts. I am grateful too for the help I received from my colleagues in the three philosophy departments I have belonged to over the years. Most recently, my colleagues Philip Clark, Michael Jubien, Jeffrey C. King, and Paul Teller gave me valuable suggestions as I brought my work to completion. Walter Sinnott-Armstrong and several anonymous referees generously read the entire manuscript and gave me tough criticisms, without which this work would have been much poorer.

Among the people I want to thank are J. G. Bennett, Michael Bratman, David Braybrooke, Bryson Brown, D. G. Brown, Charles Chastain, Rachel Cohon, Steven Davis, Gerald Dworkin, John Martin Fischer, Patricia Greenspan, Anil Gupta, Russell Hardin, Gilbert Harman, Tom Hill, Jr., Marcia Homiak, Ali Akhtar Kazmi, Richard Kraut, Anton Leist, Barry Loewer, David Lyons, Christopher Morris, Kai Nielsen, Peter Railton, Geoffrey Sayre-McCord, Nicholas Sturgeon, Mark Timmons, Raimo Tuomela, Peter Vallentyne, R. X. Ware, Alison Wylie, and David Zimmerman. I have indicated in the footnotes places where I can remember having followed someone's specific suggestion or remark.

Twenty or more of my students read versions of the manuscript in graduate seminars I gave at the University of Illinois at Chicago, the University of California, Davis, and Stanford University, where I visited in 1992. Walter Sinnott-Armstrong used the manuscript in a class of his at Dartmouth in 1993. Three discussion groups read parts of the manuscript, at various stages of its development between 1981 and 1992. I presented parts of several chapters to more than twenty audiences. In all cases, I benefited from the resulting discussion and criticism, and I am grateful to the members of these audiences and groups for their comments and their patience with early approximations to my current ideas.

I am deeply grateful to my wife, Marina Oshana. Her suggestions and encouragement, and especially her friendship, were of immense help to me in the completion of this project.

Davis, California   D. C.
August 1994

Contents

MORALITY, NORMATIVITY, AND SOCIETY

1

Introduction

This book presents a picture of morality, its nature, its justification, and its role in society. The picture is meant to explain the conditions under which our moral claims are true. It is also meant to explain the sense in which moral claims are normative—the sense in which they guide our choices. There are two main ideas. First, a moral claim is true only if a related moral standard or norm is justified. Second, society needs to have a social moral code as part of its culture in order to enable us to get along together in our social life. It is because of this need that certain moral standards are justified and hence that certain moral claims are true.

There are, then, two main components to the picture. There is a cognitivist theory of normative language, the "standard-based theory," which provides a general account of the truth conditions of normative propositions. And there is a theory of the justification of moral codes and standards, the "society-centered theory." There are other components as well. This introductory discussion is a preliminary sketch, meant to orient the reader and to explain how the components fit together.

There are many different kinds of normative claims, including claims of morality, etiquette, and epistemology. Normative claims include those regarding which things are right or wrong, virtuous or vicious, justified or unjustified, polite or rude. They contrast with non-normative claims, such as the claim that the cat is in the cupboard and the claim that snow is white.

The standard-based theory is designed to explain the distinction between the normative and the non-normative by explaining what the normativity of a claim consists in. The theory depends on the idea of a *standard*. As I explain in chapter 2, standards are norms or rules, expressible by imperatives.[1] According to the theory, normative claims express propositions which entail, nontrivially, that relevant *standards* have an appropriate *status*. The nature of this status depends on the kind of normative claim in question. In the case of moral claims, the status is itself normative; moral propositions are true only if corresponding moral standards are appropriately *justified*.

1. Compare Gibbard, 1990, p. 46.

3

It should be said that the theory distinguishes between "paradigmatic" and "non-paradigmatic" normative propositions and explains the latter in terms of the former. It is the paradigmatic propositions which entail (nontrivially) that a standard has a relevant status.

The standard-based theory implies that normativity is "internal" to moral propositions, in that paradigmatic moral propositions entail nontrivially that a related moral standard is justified. But nothing about anyone's actual motivations need be entailed by a moral proposition, or by someone's believing a moral proposition. Hence, the theory is "externalist" in one familiar sense. In chapters 2 and 5, I explain that there are two aspects of moral "conviction," namely, *belief* in a moral proposition and *subscription* to a moral standard. Subscription normally goes together with belief in a corresponding moral proposition, but it is not guaranteed to do so. One can in principle subscribe to a standard without believing a corresponding proposition. Subscription to a standard entails a tendency to comply with it, or to support compliance with it. Motivation is therefore "internal" to the state of subscribing to a moral standard even though it is "external" to the state of believing a moral proposition.

The society-centered theory is intended to explain the conditions under which a moral standard would be relevantly justified. Justification here is not merely a matter of deriving a standard from the basic standards of a moral view. For these basic standards could lack any justification, and if so, then the derived standard might also fail to be justified. Consider, for example, a rule prohibiting the lending of money at interest. Most readers would view it as unwarranted, or at least as lacking sufficient justification in our actual circumstances to be morally binding.

The main body of the book, chapters 5 through 11, presents and defends the society-centered theory. According to the theory, a moral code is justified in relation to a society just in case the society would be rational to select it as its "social moral code." Several amendments to this initial formulation are introduced in chapters 6 and 10.

The combination of the standard-based theory with the society-centered theory supports versions of moral realism, naturalism, and relativism. Before I explain this, however, and explain the society-centered theory more fully, it is worth emphasizing that the two theories are independent parts of the overall model I am proposing.

On the one hand, the society-centered theory is compatible with other theories of normative judgment, including non-cognitivist theories, which deny that moral claims express propositions. A non-cognitivist theory would view moral claims as *prescribing* something, such as a course of action, or as *expressing* an attitude of the speaker toward something. One could combine such a theory with the society-centered theory of moral justification. This would be to combine a *non-cognitivist* semantic theory for moral claims, according to which moral claims are not candidates for truth or falsity, with a *non-skeptical* theory of moral justification, according to which certain moral standards are justified. Of course, I do not mean to say that such a combination would be plausible.

On the other hand, the standard-based theory is compatible with other theories of moral justification. The standard-based theory says that a paradigmatic moral proposition entails that a relevant moral standard is appropriately justified. But the idea that an appropriate justification would be *society centered* is not part of the theory of normativity. It is an idea for which I argue separately in the rest of the book. First, one could hold instead that *no* moral standard has or could have an appropriate kind of justification, which is the thesis I call "moral skepticism." Or, second, one could propose a different theory of justification from the society-centered theory.

As for the first option, I briefly discuss moral skepticism in chapter 3. Skepticism implies that typical moral beliefs are false, for, given the standard-based theory, if there are no appropriately justified moral standards, then there are not any true paradigmatic moral propositions. Skepticism implies that there are, in fact, no moral duties or requirements, no moral virtues or vices, no moral reasons, and no moral goods or bads.

As for the second option, there are many non-skeptical moral theories that differ from the society-centered view. Immanuel Kant worried about the view that duty is "a vain delusion and a chimerical concept," and he described certain people as ridiculing "all morality as being a mere phantom of human imagination."[2] Kant aimed to answer this skeptical doctrine with an account of morality that is quite different from the society-centered theory, but the skepticism that worried him, about categorical imperatives, is at root the same as the skepticism that denies there are any justified moral standards.[3]

Chapter 4 uses the conceptual scheme introduced in the book to classify a variety of non-skeptical theories, such as Kant's theory and certain forms of naturalism and contractarianism. Any one of these theories could in principle be viewed as supplying an account of the justification of moral standards, and be combined with the standard–based theory. I believe, however, that none of them is successful.

Because the standard-based theory and the society-centered theory are independent in the way I have explained, a reader who rejects one might accept the other. Yet each contributes to the plausibility of the other. A semantics of moral judgments cannot be defended satisfactorily except in the course of developing an otherwise satisfactory account of the overall nature of morality. The society-centered theory provides such an account and therefore contributes to the defense of the standard-based theory. Then again, the standard-based theory enhances the plausibility of the society-centered theory, by adding to it an account of moral truth, knowledge, and argument. Hence, even though the two theories are logically independent, it is best to evaluate the position as a whole.

The plausibility of the society-centered theory depends on a distinction between moral standards and other kinds of standards, such as standards of aesthetics and epistemology. Chapter 5 introduces "the attitudinal conception of morality," according to which a standard is a person's moral standard just in case she subscribes to it as a moral standard. Similarly, a moral code is a sys-

---

2. Kant, 1785, Ak 402 and 407, respectively, in the Prussian Academy pagination.
3. See Copp, 1992a.

tem of standards that is subscribed to as a moral code. The goal of the chapter is to explain this. In part, a person who subscribes to a code as a moral code wants it to play the role of "social moral code" in her society. There is, therefore, a conceptual link between the notion of a moral code and the notion of society.

A series of chapters lays out and defends the remaining key elements of the society-centered theory. Chapter 7 explains the concept of a society. Some readers will be skeptical about the very existence of societies. More plausibly, many philosophers have doubts about the notion that a society can make a choice and that its choices can be evaluated for rationality. These are some of the most important theoretical doubts one might have about society-centered theory. And there are moral doubts. A society-centered view might seem to treat individual human beings, and their needs and interests, as of essentially no consequence in morality. All that counts, it may seem, is the social whole, and so, it may seem, a morality justified by my lights would require the members of a society to live their lives in service to the society as a whole.

I would not have written this book if I did not think that I could adequately meet these objections. But before I attempt to answer them, I try, in chapter 6, to motivate the effort by presenting arguments that support the plausibility of a society-centered approach. I believe that the failure of society-centered theory would leave skepticism holding the field, for I think that no other theory of moral justification is viable. This should be some motivation for attempting to make the approach work. I also think the theory is intuitively plausible, when described sympathetically. I believe it is common sense to think of morality as justified by the fact that society needs it in order to facilitate cooperation, to enable us to deal with conflict in a non-destructive manner, to give us a sense of security, to enable culture and friendship to develop and flourish, and so on. Society-centered theory is a theoretical development and generalization of these common ideas.

The theory requires defense of the notion of societal choice, and I undertake the defense in chapter 8. I attempt to make plausible that a society prefers one option over another if the members of the society are nearly unanimous in preferring the first to the second. I do not mean to suggest that societies are especially solicitous of the preferences of their members. I intend to state what constitutes societal preference and choice.

Chapter 9 is an investigation of the notion of rational choice, or of "self-grounded" reasons. This is a topic with a massive literature of its own. There are special difficulties for me, both because I do not accept a standard account and because I want to make claims about societal choice. As for the second point, I argue in chapter 8 that an adequate account of rational choice for the individual case could be extended to an account of rational societal choice. If I accepted a standard account, according to which the rational choice for an agent would be, roughly, the choice that would best satisfy the agent's overall system of preferences, then, given my account of societal preferences, society-centered theory would lead to an analogue of ideal moral code utilitarianism. But because I do not accept a standard account, I need to develop my preferred account and explain its consequences for society-centered theory.

The needs-and-values theory that I defend provides a central role for a concept of basic needs. Any agent has a reason to ensure its ability to meet its basic needs. And I argue in chapter 10 that any society needs some moral code to have currency in it. Ignoring many complications, the moral code that would *best* serve the needs of a society is the code that the society would be most rational to choose, and it is the moral code justified for the society.

Chapter 10 discusses some normative implications of this overall view. I argue that meeting societal needs depends on meeting the needs of individual persons. Because of this, my "needs-based," society-centered theory supports duties and virtues that we can expect to serve the needs of individual people. Indeed, I argue, it gives support to a form of egalitarianism about the meeting of basic needs. It also gives support to a form of virtue theory. Yet it does not underwrite all of our everyday moral views. The point of the theory is to give an account of the justification of moral standards, and there is therefore the possibility that it may in some cases speak with a different voice from intuition.

The combination of the society-centered theory and the standard-based theory implies a form of moral relativism. It implies that any paradigmatic moral proposition entails that some moral standard is justified in relation to a relevant society. And it permits different standards to count as justified in relation to different societies. However, the bite of this form of relativism is softened by my account of the concept of a society, for societies may overlap and be nested within one another. Chapter 10 explains the key implication of this idea, and chapter 11 defends this form of relativism against standard objections.

The overall theory also supports moral realism and moral naturalism. Moral *realism* can be understood as the thesis that certain moral claims express true moral propositions.[4] That is, certain moral claims express propositions that accurately represent the way things are.[5] The standard-based theory implies that a necessary condition of the truth of a paradigmatic moral proposition is that some moral standard be justified, and the society-centered theory explains under what conditions a moral standard would be justified. Taken together, these theories support moral realism, for, as I argue in chapter 11, some moral standards are in fact justified, and this means that some moral propositions are true. Given the needs-and-values theory, moreover, moral "facts" are "natural" facts, in a recognizable sense. Ignoring irrelevant complications, a moral standard is justified just in case its currency would enhance the ability of the

---

4. Geoffrey Sayre-McCord says moral realism is the thesis that (1) moral claims, when construed literally, are literally true or false, and (2) some are literally true (1988, p. 5).

5. As Sayre-McCord argues, a *moral* realist would offer the same theory of truth for moral propositions as she offers for the nonmoral propositions that she holds to be literally true. She claims that at least some moral claims express propositions that are true in the sense given by this theory. Sayre-McCord remarks that it does not much matter which theory is relied on. See Sayre-McCord, 1988, pp. 5–6. Yet realism may become uninteresting on "deflationary theories" of truth. Compare Horwich, 1993.

relevant society to meet its needs. And it is an empirical matter whether the currency of a given standard would enhance a society's ability to meet its needs.

My overall position implies that there are moral reasons, but it implies that there are reasons of various other kinds as well. For example, there are epistemic reasons if any epistemic standards are appropriately justified. Nothing in my view guarantees that people will have reasons of any interesting nonmoral kind to be moral. Whether a person has a self-grounded reason to comply with the moral code justified in relation to her society depends on her own needs and values. In a morally well-ordered society, of course, people would be raised to have values that give them reason to be moral, but not all of us live in well-ordered societies.[6] I argue in chapter 11 that the failure to show that everyone has a sufficient nonmoral reason to be moral is not an objection to society-centered theory.

Armed with this overview of my argument, let us turn to the details. I fear that unless morality fits the mold of reason by serving the needs of society, the skeptic is correct to say that the concepts of duty and virtue are delusory and chimerical, and that morality is "a mere phantom of human imagination."

6. The term "well-ordered society" comes from Rawls, 1971.

2

A Cognitivist Theory
of Normative Judgment

Moral claims are normative. In this chapter, I present a theory that is intended to explain what their being normative consists in.

Among moral claims are claims to the effect that something is morally right or wrong, good or bad, virtuous or vicious, just or unjust. There is not, however, a special terminology that distinguishes moral claims from claims of other kinds.[1] In some cases, we use quite specific and subtle terms of appraisal, or metaphors. We speak of "thoughtless" actions, "vicious" persons, and the like. In some cases, moreover, we rely on the context to indicate that we are making a moral claim. It can therefore be a matter of debate whether a claim is moral in nature, but I assume that this is not a problem for us, since we can work with clear cases.

All moral claims are normative. In this respect, they differ from typical nonmoral, empirical claims. Meteorological claims, such as the claim that there is a blizzard in Yellowknife, are not normative. Some would describe this difference between moral claims and meteorological claims by saying that the former are "action-guiding" or "prescriptive" while the latter are "descriptive."

There are familiar theories that attempt to explain the normativity of moral claims by reference, ultimately, to the motivations or reasons of relevant agents. The "standard-based theory," which I introduce in this chapter, explains normativity in a quite different way, by using the idea of a standard. Propositions are "the sorts of things that are true or false." They are expressed by typical declarative sentences.[2] Standards, by contrast, lack truth value. As I explain below, a standard is a norm or a rule, expressible by an imperative. The theory says

1. See McDowell, 1985, p. 123, n. 2.
2. Salmon and Soames, 1988, p. 1. I intend my view to be (largely) neutral among theories about truth and about the nature of the bearers of truth value. Readers who think that sentences of certain kinds are the bearers of truth values may find some of my ways of speaking misleading, but they may not be in fundamental disagreement with me. My theory says that a sentence used to make a moral claim expresses a proposition. To simplify, I sometimes write that a moral claim itself expresses a proposition, and I sometimes write that claims and sentences are true when they express true propositions.

that the sentences we use to make normative claims express *propositions* about relevant *standards*.[3] In central or "paradigmatic" cases, the proposition expressed by a *moral* claim entails that some relevant *moral* standard is justified.[4] This is so in virtue of the truth conditions or content of the proposition expressed by a moral claim.[5] And this is what explains the normativity of the proposition.

Many kinds of nonmoral claims also express normative propositions. For instance, epistemological statements to the effect that a certain belief is justified are normative, as are propositions to the effect that a given action was rational or prudent. There are, however, different types of normativity. Propositions about the proper use of language are normative, for example, but in standard cases they are not normative in the way that moral propositions are normative. The standard-based theory is a unified theory of normativity.

In paradigmatic cases, type-one normative propositions entail nontrivially that a relevant standard has an appropriate currency. For instance, the proposition that it is ungrammatical to split an infinitive entails that to split an infinitive is to abridge certain standards of English usage, which have the relevant kind of currency among users of English. Type-two normative propositions are more deeply normative, for paradigmatic propositions of this kind entail that the relevant standard has a standing that is itself normative. A paradigmatic type-two normative proposition entails nontrivially that a relevant standard is appropriately *justified*. It entails, not that the standard *has been* justified, but that it has a relevant normative *status*. For instance, the proposition that one ought not to argue ad hominem entails that to argue ad hominem is to abridge a warranted standard of argument. And a proposition expressed by a paradigmatic moral claim entails that a corresponding moral standard is relevantly justified. Of course, standards of these different kinds do not have precisely the same status; they are not justified in virtue of the same considerations.

I begin by arguing that moral claims are normative and that they express propositions. In the course of the argument, I explain that the distinction between non-normative and normative claims is not a "fact/value distinction." I then explain the notion of a standard, develop my account of the two types of normative propositions, and argue that moral claims express type-two propositions. To avoid the appearance of circularity, I argue in various places that the standards I invoke in explaining the content of normative propositions can be expressed, in principle, without using any normative terms.

3. Others have attempted to explain the normativity of some moral propositions by invoking notions similar to that of a standard. See Brandt, 1979 and 1985. Castañeda attempted to analyze statements about what a person ought to do as statements about the justifiability of *practitions* (Castañeda, 1963, 1974; see Wong, 1984, pp. 26–36; also Bratman, 1983). Wong attempted to analyze them as statements concerning the rules of adequate moral systems (1984, chapter 4). Gert views morality as a system of rules (1988).

4. I explain the distinction between moral standards and standards of other kinds in chapter 5.

5. That is, as I shall say, the entailments are "nontrivial." The need for this qualification was brought home to me by John Fischer and J. G. Bennett.

The Normative and the Non-Normative

The idea that moral claims are normative is best taken as given. A philosopher might claim not to know what it *means* to say moral claims are normative, meaning that he has no theory or analysis of normativity, or he might deny a particular theory of normativity. But I do not see any ground for denying that moral claims are normative. It is important, nevertheless, to consider a variety of arguments that may seem to blur, or to undermine the philosophical significance of, the distinction between normative and non-normative claims. The main target of these arguments is the so-called fact/value distinction.

The fact/value distinction is a putative distinction between "factual" claims and "evaluative" claims. I assume that a claim is "evaluative" just in case it is normative,[6] and a claim is "factual" just in case it expresses a proposition. A "fact" is simply a true proposition. This is safe to assume since it is a fact that p just in case the proposition that p is true.[7] We do not need to involve ourselves in the metaphysics of facts.

There are different theories of truth, but we do not need to choose among them here. I assume that a true proposition is one that accurately represents the way things are. But the important point is to use the same theory of truth in connection with moral propositions as one uses in connection with propositions that are taken to be true in an exemplary and literal sense, such as propositions about the weather. It does not matter which theory this is, with the possible exception of a "deflationary" theory, such as a theory according to which to say something is true is merely to reiterate it.[8]

The idea that there is a fact/value distinction is, then, the idea that the distinction between the factual and the non-factual coincides with the distinction between the non-normative and the normative. I claim these distinctions do not coincide. As I argue in this section, there is a philosophically useful distinction to be drawn between normative and non-normative claims. But, as I argue in the next section, normative claims are factual. They express propositions. Hence, there is a distinction between the non-normative and the normative, but it does not map onto a distinction between the factual and the non-factual.

So-called non-cognitivists are the main advocates of a fact/value distinction. According to non-cognitivism, a person's claim is normative if, in making it, he expresses a characteristic attitude toward something, or prescribes something, such as an action. "Non-cognitivism" can be characterized roughly as the thesis that normative claims do not express propositions.[9] It would be more accurate,

---

6. As the term is ordinarily used, however, some "evaluative" claims are not normative, and some normative claims are not "evaluative." For example, although the claim that one must tell the truth is normative, it is not, strictly speaking, evaluative. Also, although a description of my car as "battered and slow" would typically amount to an evaluation of my car, it is not normative.

7. See Frege, 1988, p. 51.

8. See Sayre-McCord, 1988, p. 6, especially n. 13. See also Wong, 1984, p. 14; Wiggins, 1988, p. 148. For a deflationary theory, see Horwich, 1993. For a general discussion, see Blackburn, 1984, pp. 224–60.

9. "Non-cognitivism" is the standard term, but "non-propositionalism" is more descriptive.

however, to characterize it as the thesis that the *normative content* of a normative claim is not expressed by any proposition, for some sentences have both normative and non-normative content. It follows that normative claims are nonfactual insofar as they are normative. Non-cognitivism is committed to a fact/value distinction. It is committed to the thesis that a claim is non-normative insofar as it is factual and it is non-factual insofar as it is normative.

As I indicated, I oppose the idea that there is a fact/value distinction because I hold, against non-cognitivism, that normative claims express propositions. Some philosophers oppose the fact/value distinction, however, by attempting to undermine the distinction between normative and non-normative claims. For this reason, I will consider three lines of argument that call into question the distinction between the non-normative and the normative.

The first trades on the fact that scientific theorizing is governed by norms of scientific method. It may seem to follow from this that there is not a clear distinction between normative and non-normative theorizing, that theoretical activities cannot be sorted into mutually exclusive normative and non-normative kinds. One may be tempted to draw the further conclusion that normative and non-normative claims are too tightly intertwined to be usefully distinguished.

Hilary Putnam claims, for example, "The practices of scientific inquiry upon which we rely to decide what is and what is not fact, presuppose values." He points out that our conception of epistemic rationality is normative.[10] Alan Gewirth says that science is explicated or defined "by reference to certain methodological requirements or norms." They are "norms as to the methods by which to solve problems and resolve controversies," and they have "a similar logical status" to "the principles of ethics." He concludes that science and ethics can both be described as cognitive with equal justice.[11]

Arguments of this kind rely on the fact that scientific reasoning makes use of norms, both norms that are specific to science and norms of logic and epistemology. As Allan Gibbard has pointed out, however, the fact that our reasoning and practices of scientific inquiry are guided by norms does not show that the conclusions we reach are themselves normative. In Gibbard's words, "The justification of factual beliefs is a normative matter, but that does not turn factual beliefs into normative judgments."[12] It does not mean that all propositions are normative.

The second argument depends on the claim that the concept of truth is itself normative.[13] If this is so, a true factual claim is itself one with a normative status, and it may seem to follow that the distinction between normative and non-normative claims is illusory. But this clearly does not follow. To call a proposition true may be to make a normative claim about it, but it does not follow that every true proposition is itself normative. To call a belief justified is to make a normative claim about it, but it does not follow that every justified belief is

10. Putnam, 1981, pp. 128, 136. Quoted by Gibbard, 1990, at p. 31–32.

11. Gewirth, 1960, pp. 318–21.

12. Gibbard, 1990, p. 34.

13. Consider the theory that truth is "warranted assertability." Michael Kubara urged me to discuss this argument. See, for example, Darwall, Gibbard, and Railton, 1992, p. 153, n. 87.

itself normative. Moreover, it is implausible that truth is a normative concept. To say that a proposition is true is not to make a normative claim about it.

The third argument may appear to show that the distinction between normative and non-normative claims is not a deep difference of kind. The argument turns on a distinction drawn by Bernard Williams between "thick" moral concepts or properties, such as those of *treachery*, *loyalty*, *usury*, and *courage*, and "thin" moral concepts or properties, such as *rightness* and *goodness*. Williams claims that the thick concepts have non-normative content, for, as he says, their application is "determined by what the world is like (for instance, by how someone has behaved)."[14] The key premise in the argument is John McDowell's claim that the normative content of a proposition involving a "thick" concept is inseparable from its non-normative content.[15] Suppose then that the truth of a non-normative proposition about a person's behavior settles that, for example, the person has been disloyal. Now if the latter is a normative claim, and if its normative content cannot be separated from its non-normative content, then the normativity of a claim cannot in general be due to some distinguishable component or characteristic of its content. There is not a difference in kind between the content of normative and non-normative claims.

One might deny that the so-called "thick concepts" are normative.[16] But I want to argue instead that the normative content of a proposition involving a "thick concept" *is* separable in principle from its non-normative content.

McDowell argues that although "evaluative classifications," such as *loyal*, correspond to genuine kinds that are "there in the world," the relevant kinds cannot be "externally characterized in non-evaluative terms." He argues that a thick concept and its extension, and the extension of the associated term, can be mastered only by someone who has understood the concerns of the community that uses the concept, as shown by the community's "admiration or emulation of actions [and so on] seen as falling under the concept."[17] We cannot determine who is properly classified as "loyal" unless we understand the normative concerns that lead people to categorize people as loyal or disloyal. Because the extension of a thick concept cannot be characterized in non-evaluative terms and can be mastered only by someone with a relevant normative perspective, McDowell holds that its normative and non-normative elements cannot be separated.

This argument is not persuasive. On McDowell's view, normally competent people who have understood the normative concerns of a community that uses a thick concept could master the extension of the concept and of the associated term. If so, they could go on to use the term in making non-normative claims by canceling its standard normative implications. For example, a medieval historian could say that a particular banking practice "fell within the extension of

14. Williams, 1985, pp. 129, 140–45. It is not clear what Williams means by "determined." There is a sense in which the application of the *thin* normative concepts is also "determined by what the world is like (for instance, by how someone has behaved)."

15. McDowell, 1981, pp. 144–45.

16. See Brower, 1988.

17. McDowell, 1981, pp. 144–45. See also McDowell, 1979.

the medieval concept of 'usury.'" She could add that calling the practice a case of "usury" would have implied a negative evaluation of it, given the moral perspective of the medieval community. In saying this, the historian would not be using the concept of usury in the standard way. Rather, she would be referring to the concept in order to coin a co-extensive non-normative concept, the concept of being in the extension of the relevant community's concept of "usury." Call this the concept of "quasi-usury." A "quasi-thick concept" is a non-normative concept that can be used to pick out the extension of the corresponding thick concept. It can be used to identify the non-normative element in the semantics of the thick concept.

According to the standard-based theory, the normativity of propositions involving thick concepts is to be explained by reference to relevant, putatively justified, moral standards. Quasi-thick concepts can be used to define the content of these standards. For example, on the supposition that loyalty is a normative concept, loyalty can be understood as, roughly, a steadfastness of character that meets moral standards governing character. The standards governing character call for quasi-loyalty.

McDowell holds that the properties picked out by the thick concepts are analogous to "secondary qualities."[18] But there is nothing here to undermine my claim that, in principle, the extension of a thick concept can be picked out by means of a non-normative quasi-thick concept. Nor does McDowell's view undermine the distinction between normative and non-normative properties. On the contrary, it is an attempt to explain the distinction, an attempt that I think is inadequate. It is insufficiently general, for the "thin" normative concepts, such as the concept of goodness, also pick out normative properties. And it does not distinguish the normative status of morally significant properties, such as cruelty and loyalty, from the status of morally doubtful properties, such as usury.[19]

Some may worry that one cannot draw a clean distinction between the normative and the non-normative without relying on the doubtful analytic-synthetic distinction. But there is no need here to claim that any propositions are analytic. I am making a proposal in semantic theory, which is to be judged by its fruitfulness.[20] I claim it is useful in a semantics of the language to draw a distinction between normative and non-normative sentences and claims, and to explain it on the basis of a distinction between normative and non-normative propositions. Accordingly, I offer my account as a hypothesis about the nature of normativity in language and thought.

18. McDowell, 1985. The idea is this: The property of loyalty cannot be explained except in terms of the virtuous person's propensity to respond appropriately to certain manifestations of steadfastness of character. In the case of a normative property, unlike an ordinary secondary quality, the response of a person with the relevant sensibility is *merited*. McDowell, 1985, pp. 117–20.

19. People whom our tradition counts as virtuous may have a particular way of seeing instances of quasi-cruelty and quasi-loyalty, but, if so, people who would be seen as virtuous in another tradition would have a particular way of seeing instances of quasi-usury. The standard-based theory would distinguish the status of the different properties on the basis of whether the corresponding standards are justified. See Darwall, Gibbard, and Railton, 1992, pp. 152–65.

20. See Gibbard, 1990, pp. 31–32.

Certain sentences are normative in their literal meaning. Examples are the sentences "It is morally admirable to eat the gall bladder of a slain enemy" and "Alice is despicable." The standard-based theory explains the normativity of such sentences on the basis that they express normative propositions. It is worth mentioning that in some contexts, a sentence that is literally normative can be used to make a non-normative claim. For instance, suppose that, in the course of describing the moral sensibility of a tribe living in a remote jungle, an anthropologist says, "It is morally admirable, here, to eat the gall bladder of a slain enemy." In saying this, she would not be making a moral claim, for the context would make it clear that she was merely reporting the group's standards, which she does not view as justified. Taken literally, the sentence she uses expresses a (type-two) normative proposition, but she is using it to express a proposition that is not normative (in this way). It is also worth mentioning that, in appropriate contexts, a non-normative sentence can be used to make a normative claim. Suppose, for instance, that I say, "Alice ran right into the line of fire, which made it possible for her friends to escape." Although my sentence is not literally normative, in many contexts I would be taken to have said that Alice was loyal and courageous.

Moral Claims as Expressing Propositions

The distinction between the normative and non-normative could be accepted by a non-cognitivist who denied that there are normative propositions. Accordingly, I now turn to the question whether moral and other normative claims express normative propositions.

I believe that they do. As a foil for my position, I will dicuss a non-cognitivist theory recently proposed by Allan Gibbard, which he calls "norm-expressivism." According to this theory, moral claims (on a "narrow" conception of "morality") are claims about the rationality of feelings of guilt and anger. They do not express propositions about these feelings, however. Rather, a *person* who says that something someone did was morally reprehensible *herself* expresses, roughly, her "acceptance of norms" that permit "the agent to feel guilt over having performed the action, and . . . others to feel angry at him for having performed it."[21] And the person does not merely express her acceptance of such norms; she expresses her acceptance of higher-order norms that require their acceptance.[22]

I favor a cognitivist theory because I think cognitivism is more natural and more simple than non-cognitivism. I will consider four types of reasons why this is so: reasons having to do with our moral practice and discourse, reasons having to do with our moral intuitions, methodological reasons, and reasons that derive from the ubiquity of the normative.

21. Gibbard, 1990, pp. 7 and 44, respectively. Gibbard introduces "broad" and "narrow" conceptions of morality on pp. 40–41. For another recent non-cognitivist theory, see Blackburn, 1984, chapter 6.

22. Gibbard, 1990, p. 169. This sentence is my gloss on a discussion of normative objectivity that occupies several chapters in Gibbard's book.

First are reasons that derive from moral practice and discourse. If someone does something in apparent ignorance of its being wrong, we may in some situations think she ought to have *known* it was wrong. We think of people we disagree with as being *mistaken*. We view ourselves as having moral *beliefs*, and we view certain things as matters of moral *knowledge*. We may express our agreement with someone's moral claim by saying, "That's true." We conduct moral arguments by giving reasons, as if we thought truths were at stake. All of this is familiar.

Second are reasons having to do with our moral intuitions. David Brink points out that we think the blameworthiness of a person who acted wrongly depends on whether or not he knew, or ought to have known, that he was acting wrongly.[23] There are things that are so obviously bad that people ought to know they are wrong, and it is a sign of morally bad character not to know that such things are wrong. It therefore seems to be part of our moral view to think that one can know that certain things are right and other things are wrong.

Taken together, these considerations suggest that it is natural to us, as we engage in moral thought, to have beliefs that commit us to the existence of moral propositions. We might call this the "natural participant attitude."[24] Cognitivism, then, is the natural position.

A non-cognitivist would try to construe the relevant features of our moral discourse and practice in ways that are consistent with non-cognitivism. For example, "That's true," if said by me in response to a moral claim made by you, could be construed as a way of reiterating what you said. But strategies of construal lead to the third class of reasons in favor of cognitivism, methodological reasons.[25]

At stake are issues in metaphysics and philosophy of language, as well as in ethics. It is desirable to have our theories be as simple and unified overall as possible, subject, of course, to the constraint that we want to be able to explain the phenomena. But strategies of construal lead to complexity and disunity since different accounts must be given of the semantics of a variety of sentence types and a variety of terms, depending on whether the context is a moral context. I will illustrate these considerations with Gibbard's theory, but my arguments do not turn on the details of his position.

Sentences that would standardly be used to make moral claims can be embedded in larger sentential contexts, such as in the antecedent of a conditional sentence. For example, the sentence "Swimming is wrong" is embedded in the conditional, "If swimming is wrong, someone will stop us." It would not be plausible to hold that a person who asserts this conditional is expressing her acceptance of any norms about swimming, for the embedded sentence about swimming is unasserted; it is not used to make a moral claim. Yet, a proper

---

23. Brink, 1989, p. 27.

24. This is, I suspect, part of what David Wiggins had in mind when he spoke of the "inner view" and the "participant perspective." See Wiggins, 1988, pp. 135–37; see also J. L. Mackie, 1977, pp. 30–35.

25. I am grateful to Jeffrey C. King for helping me to think about methodology in philosophy of language.

theory should assign the same meaning or content to a sentence in an embedded context as it assigns to it in an unembedded context. P. T. Geach called this "the Frege point." It poses a problem for non-cognitivist theories, for standard non-cognitivist accounts are designed to deal with unembedded contexts, where sentences are used to make moral claims.[26]

Unless this problem can be met, non-cognitivism will be unable to account for the validity of certain instances of *modus ponens*. For example, there is a valid argument from the claim that if swimming is wrong, someone will stop us, and the claim that swimming is wrong, to the conclusion that someone will stop us.[27] A proper theory must account for the entailment of this conclusion by the premises. And if moral claims do not express propositions, then entailment cannot be explained in the standard way, in terms of the preserving of truth.

Gibbard aims to explain entailments involving normative statements using a semantics of "factual-normative worlds." The theory is complex, but the basic idea is simple. Consider a sentence p that contains normative terms. The normative terms in p can be replaced with corresponding phrases, such as "permitted according to normative system n," and the like. The result is a non-normative sentence, $p*n$, which corresponds to p relative to an arbitrary normative system n. It expresses a proposition about the content of n. Then, for example, a set of sentences, one of which embeds p, is said to "entail" p just in case the corresponding $p*n$ set entails $p*n$.[28] This semantics handles the Frege point, for it assigns the same content to a normative sentence whether or not it is embedded in a larger context.

Yet problems appear in other places. Gibbard's account implies that various sentential contexts in which a sentence p can be embedded are ambiguous, with their semantics depending on whether p is normative. A cognitivist theory could avoid this kind of complexity. For example, if p is *not* normative, a sentence of the form *S knows that p* expresses a relation between S and the proposition expressed by p. Similarly, a sentence of the form *It is possible that p* expresses a proposition about the proposition expressed by p. And a sentence of the form, *If p then q*, expresses a proposition concerning a relation between the propositions expressed by p and q. But if p *is* normative, matters are otherwise, for p does not express a proposition. A variety of complex constructions give rise to problems, since it appears that a non-cognitivist theory must treat them differently, depending on whether an embedded sentence is or is not one that would standardly be used to make a normative claim.[29]

26. See Geach, 1965, esp. pp. 463–64; and also Geach, 1958; Searle, 1969, pp. 136–41. Gibbard discusses the issue at Gibbard, 1990, pp. 92–102. See Frege, 1988, pp. 37–38.

27. See Geach, 1965, p. 463.

28. Gibbard, 1990, pp. 86–89, 94–102. For simplicity, I speak of entailment as a relation among sentences.

29. Suppose p is normative and q is not. Then consider sentences of the form *It is possible that p and q*, and *S believes that p and q*. In these cases, different treatments will be required of a single occurrence of the constructions *It is possible that* and *S believes that*. This was pointed out to me by Jeffrey King.

At best, then, Gibbard's way of dealing with the Frege point adds an unwanted complexity and disunity to our semantics, our logic, and our psychology of belief, complexity that would not be needed by a cognitivist account of normative claims. By comparison, the standard-based theory is simple.

There is a fourth argument in favor of cognitivism. A variety of claims are normative, including not merely moral claims and claims about rational choice, but also epistemological claims of various kinds and claims about the meaning of words.[30] If our semantics of moral claims is non-cognitivist, then if normative claims are to be given a unified treatment, the semantics for all normative claims must be non-cognitivist. But then it cannot be simply true or false whether "chair" means chair, for this would be a normative claim, which would imply in part that "chair" ought standardly to be used only of chairs. And it cannot be simply true or false whether *S knows that p*. Even in cases in which *p* is not normative, *S knows that p* is normative, for (I assume) it implies something to the effect that *S is justified in believing that p*, or *S is not violating any warranted epistemic norm in believing that p*.[31] And these sentences would not express propositions on a non-cognitivist account of them. A person would, at least in part, be expressing her acceptance of a norm, in saying something of the form *S knows that p*. The complexities of non-cognitivism would need to be incorporated into a semantics at a wide variety of places, given the variety of normative claims. One could avoid some of the complexity by combining a *non-cognitivist* theory of type-two normative claims with a *cognitivist* theory of type-one normative claims.[32] At best, however, this would be a partial solution, and it would imply a disunified account of normativity.

For all of these reasons, I think that cognitivism is the natural position about the semantics of normative claims. Nevertheless, my standard-based theory can be viewed as a kind of compromise with non-cognitivism. As we will see, it implies that non-cognitivists are correct to think that attitudes other than belief and entities other than propositions must be invoked in a full account of moral conviction.

I do not think that anyone would propose a non-cognitivist theory if he thought a cognitivist theory could give a plausible account of the normative aspect of moral and other normative claims. Indeed, the standard objection to cognitivism is that it cannot explain normativity. Gibbard argues, for example, that cognitivist theories "miss a general element of endorsement—an element an expressivistic analysis can capture." This element of endorsement is, he thinks, the "specially normative aspect" of moral claims.[33]

Of course, I claim that the standard-based theory *does* capture the "norma-

30. Kripke, 1982, p. 37. Gibbard discusses the idea that "norms infuse meaning" at 1990, p. 35.

31. If *p* is normative, then *S knows that p* is doubly normative, for it entails *p*, and so its assertion would express one's acceptance of the norms that would be expressed by assertion of *p*.

32. Gibbard seems to hold that claims about meaning are *not* normative and that there *are* "facts of meaning" (1990, pp. 23, 35). He does not explicitly consider the alternative I suggest in the text: a cognitivist theory of type-one normative claims.

33. Gibbard, 1990, pp. 10 and 22. In the passage where he says this, he is discussing judgments about rationality, but he would presumably say a similar thing about moral claims.

tive aspect" of moral claims. In the case at least of a paradigmatic moral claim, the *normative aspect* is that it expresses a proposition which implies nontrivially that there is a relevant justified moral standard. One who makes a paradigmatic moral claim implies that the relevant standard is justified, and in this sense she endorses it.

One might object that even if moral and other normative claims express propositions, I have not yet shown that these propositions are normative. I have not yet shown that the normativity of these claims is explained by the nature of the propositions they express. Perhaps the property of being normative is a property of the *sentences* used to make normative claims or of the *speech act* of making a normative claim, rather than of the propositions expressed in making normative claims. Or perhaps, although these propositions are normative, this is merely *contingent*; for example, perhaps the normativity of a proposition which is believed by a person depends on whether the person is relevantly motivated. These views are "externalist" in the sense that, according to each of them, the normativity of a claim is not explained in terms of an essential property of the proposition expressed by the claim. But each of these views seems to imply, implausibly, that even if Alice did something that was wrong, there need not be anything normative that is true of what Alice did. For it is possible that the proposition that what Alice did was wrong should be true even if no one believes it, even if no one has used any sentence to express it, even if no one has performed any relevant speech act, and even if no one has any relevant attitude toward what Alice did. But, of course, if what Alice did was wrong, there is something normative that is true of what Alice did. Because externalist views cannot explain this, cognitivism about normative claims leads to a theory in which normativity is an essential property of the propositions expressed by normative claims.

The Concept of a Standard

Central to the standard-based theory is the concept of a standard. A standard specifies a criterion against which one can in principle judge or appraise our actions, states of our psychology, states of our character, social institutions, and so forth. Norms and rules are standards, as are ideals and conceptions of the virtuous. Commonsense morality includes a variety of standards, such as standards calling for loyalty to friends, honesty, and fairness, and standards prohibiting cruelty, theft, and double-dealing. It includes standards concerned with our actions, our desires, and our character. There are also nonmoral standards: epistemological ones, standards of etiquette, legal standards, and so on.

Standards have the following important characteristics: (1) A standard is not a proposition, but (2) it specifies that certain conditions are to be met by things of a certain category, perhaps under certain conditions, and (3) it is something to which things (the things in question) can conform or fail to conform and with which (if the thing in question is an agent) an agent can comply or fail to comply. These three characteristics are individually necessary and jointly sufficient for something to be a standard.

Gibbard's non-cognitivism employs the notion of a *norm*, which seems similar to my notion of a standard. He says that a norm is "a possible rule or prescription, expressible by an imperative."[34] This proposal might well serve as a definition; a *standard* is anything that is expressible by an imperative. In certain contexts, standards may also be conveyed by indicative sentences, as I will illustrate, but any standard can be expressed by an imperative.

The notion of a standard is needed in the semantics of imperatival sentences that express commands, such as "Shut the door." Just as the corresponding indicative sentence expresses the proposition that you will shut the door, this sentence expresses the command (for you) *to* shut the door. The command specifies that the addressee is to shut the door, it is something the addressee can conform to and comply with, and it is not a proposition, since it has no truth value. Hence, it is a standard.[35]

Consider now sentences that express proposed rules for a game or some other practice, or proposed provisions of a legislative scheme. Suppose, for example, that I propose adopting the rule that graduate students are to take an examination in ethical theory. I write a set of proposed rules that includes this sentence: "Students take an examination in ethical theory before they are admitted to candidacy." In this context, the sentence expresses a standard.[36] To be sure, in a different context, the same string of words would be used to express the proposition that students take an examination in ethical theory. The rule obviously must be distinguished from this proposition. The relevant professors adopt the rule, not the proposition. Prudent students comply with the rule, not the proposition. The adoption of the rule will bring it about that the proposition is true, if the students comply with the rule. But it is not as though the professors adopt the *proposition* and, by adopting it, make it true. Their reason for adopting the rule obviously is not that they think the *rule* is true, or that they want to make it true. Indeed, rules are not a sort of thing that can be true or false. Once they adopt it, a proposition *about* the rule becomes true, the proposition that the rule is binding on graduate students. The view that rules are propositions would have difficulty explaining what is going on in cases of this sort, in which a rule is adopted.

As we have seen, then, the notion of a standard is required in an adequate semantics of a variety of non-normative sentences. This means that an adequate semantics of the language would give to standards a role comparable to the role it gives to propositions. There is, of course, room to debate the semantics and metaphysics of standards, as there is room to debate the semantics and metaphysics of propositions, but I do not need to take a position on it here. The notion of a standard is not peculiar to the semantics of normative claims; because of this, the standard-based theory is entitled to take the existence of standards as primitive or as a given.

34. Gibbard, 1990, p. 46; see also p. 70.
35. Frege said that a "command" has a "sense," but he denied that commands express "thoughts" (1988, p. 37). For relevant arguments, see R. M. Hare, 1952, pp. 4–16.
36. I read it as being in the imperative mood. To a reader who takes it to be indicative in mood, it is an example of an indicative sentence that can be used to convey a standard.

The distinction between standards and propositions can be marked in a number of ways. Propositions are evaluated semantically as true or false, whereas standards are evaluated as to the nature of their "standing." Acceptance of a proposition is a matter of believing it, whereas acceptance of a standard is, as I shall say, a matter of "subscribing" to it—of intending to conform with it or to support conformity with it. To account for these differences, a semantical theory would construe propositions and standards differently. A standard could be viewed as a function from "initial" situations to situations in which it is conformed to; on this view, for any situation in its domain, a standard tells us what would have to be the case in order for it to be conformed to. For example, the rule of chess, that the bishop moves only diagonally, tells us, for any given position in the game, which subsequent positions involving a change in position of a bishop are in conformity with the rule. On this construal, a rule with an "open texture" would be seen as a partial function, which would fail to tell us anything about certain states of affairs.[37] A variety of other accounts have been given of the distinction between standards and propositions.[38]

I shall suppose that the set of all standards includes all conceivable standards. This means that there are an indefinite number of standards. It also means that standards may be spurious, just as propositions need not be true. For example, there is a standard that calls for clapping your hands before combing your hair. It obviously has no authority or standing, and, because of this, it may seem peculiar to call it a standard. Bear in mind, then, that I will be referring to certain things as "standards" that might better be called merely "putative" standards.

Conformity to a standard is a matter of meeting the conditions specified by a standard as those that are to be met. If a standard specifies how one is to act, then conformity is a matter of one's behavior. Certain standards purport to direct or assess our character or our motives or emotions. In these cases, conformity is a matter of having appropriate psychological states.

Compliance is *intentional*.[39] This does not mean that, in order to comply with a standard, one must have the standard explicitly in mind or that one must know exactly how it would be formulated. For example, a person can comply with a legal rule without being an expert in the law. But the person must be aware of the rule and aware that it applies to himself, and he must conform, or bring about what counts as conforming, partly because he believes that it counts as conforming. For example, I might have the headlights of my car adjusted in a certain way because I believe there is a law about headlights and that my hav-

37. I owe the idea of treating rules as functions of this kind to Bryson Brown (in personal communication).

38. Castañeda (1963, 1974) proposed that there is a characteristic relation that serves as the copula in all standards or "practitions." We might call it the "is to" relation. For discussion, see Bratman, 1983; Wong, 1984, pp. 26–36. R. M. Hare proposed a semantics of "neustics" and "phrastics" that could be used to explain the distinction between standards and propositions (1952, pp. 17–31). I am grateful to Michael Bratman, Jeffrey C. King, and the members of my seminar at Stanford in the fall of 1992 for helpful discussion of these ideas.

39. See Sumner, 1987, pp. 63–64.

ing them adjusted in this way will bring me into conformity with the law. In this case, if I succeed in conforming, I am also complying with the law even if I do not know exactly what the law requires. I am complying as long as I am intentionally conforming, regardless of the further details of my intentions.

Two Types of Normative Propositions

Certain standards have a kind of de facto standing in that they have "currency" in a given group. But other standards have or seem to have an "authority" or "justification" that is itself normatively significant. I shall explain that paradigmatic type-one normative propositions are true only if the standards to which they appeal have a de facto standing, whereas paradigmatic type-two propositions are true only if the relevant standards have an appropriate *normative* standing or justification.[40] Leaving aside the non-paradigmatic cases, which I discuss later, I hold that a normative proposition is true only if some relevant standard has a relevant standing of one of these kinds. Until the section on non-paradigmatic normative propositions, I work with paradigmatic propositions.

Type-one normative propositions appeal to standards that have currency in a relevant collective. Consider claims of etiquette or law, for example. If it is true that double-parking is unlawful, then there must be in the appropriate jurisdiction a rule of law that prohibits double-parking. If it is true that belching is impolite, then there is a rule in the local code of etiquette that calls on people not to belch in public. In order for it to be the case that double-parking is unlawful or that belching is impolite, the standards in question need only have currency or be "in force" in whatever sense is relevant in the cases of law and etiquette, respectively. It may seem that the standards need not be justified in any interesting sense.

A statement counts as a paradigmatic type-one normative proposition just in case two conditions are met. First, a nontrivially necessary condition of its being true is that some relevant standard have currency in a relevant group, institution, society, or other collective. Second, it is not the case that a nontrivially necessary condition of its being true is that some relevant standard have a normative status—that it be appropriately justified. The second condition ensures that the distinction between type-one and type-two propositions is exclusive.

The kind of standing that is required of a standard, in order for a corresponding paradigmatic normative proposition to be true, depends on the kind of claim in question. In some cases, there is room to dispute precisely what kind of standing is involved. It would take me beyond my present concerns were I to explore these issues in any detail, but I should mention disputes in philosophy of law about the conditions under which legal rules are valid. Positivists hold, in essence, that for any given legal standard, there is a conjunction of empirical propositions, none of which is itself normative, such that the standard is valid just in case that conjunction is true. According to positivism, propositions of law are

---

40. I am not aware of any other kinds of paradigmatic normative propositions.

type-one normative. But natural law theory maintains that certain normative conditions must be satisfied as a necessary condition of a legal standard's being valid.[41] According to certain versions of natural law theory, the validity of a legal standard entails nontrivially that some standard is morally justified. Hence, for example, double-parking would be unlawful only if some relevant standard, perhaps a constitutional standard, had an appropriate moral justification. On this kind of view, legal claims express type-two normative propositions.[42] I will nevertheless follow the idea of positivism that propositions of law are type-one normative.

It is not required that a person subscribe to a standard, or be otherwise motivated to comply with it, in order to make normative judgments relative to it. The examples of law and etiquette illustrate this idea. An anarchist can truthfully assert that double-parking is unlawful, and an iconoclast can truthfully assert that belching is impolite. Their statements will be true just in case the relevant conventional rule systems have appropriate content. Of course, an iconoclast would be unlikely simply to say that belching is impolite, for doing so would imply conversationally, even if it would not logically entail, that she herself subscribes to the relevant standards of etiquette. These observations support a kind of "externalism": One may believe a type-one normative proposition without subscribing to, or otherwise being motivated to conform to, any relevant standard.

Type-two propositions are normative in a deeper sense than are type-one propositions, for they appeal to standards taken to be justified rather than to standards that are taken merely to have currency in a relevant collective.[43] A statement counts as a paradigmatic type-two normative proposition just in case a nontrivially necessary condition of its being true is that some relevant standard have a relevant normative status—that it be appropriately justified. Propositions about the rationality of choices, actions, and beliefs are type-two normative.[44] And I shall argue in the next section that moral claims are type-two normative.

We can evaluate standards on the basis of criteria specified by higher-order standards. For example, at some point, a rule was introduced into baseball that

41. I do not claim that my usage of the terms "positivism" and "natural law" is the same as the standard usage in the literature. My discussion ignores many complications.

42. Ronald Dworkin's view seems to imply that propositions of law are type two. He says "propositions of law are true if they figure in or follow from the principles of justice, fairness, and procedural due process that provide the best constructive interpretation of the community's legal practice" (1986, p. 225).

43. From this point on, in fact, I will often refer to type-two normative propositions simply as normative without qualification.

44. I have in mind claims such as that it is rational to aim to satisfy one's desires, or it is rational for a layman to accept the results of the established science of the day. So-called hypothetical imperatives are also type-two normative. But sentences that express them can also sometimes be read as expressing non-normative propositions. For example, the sentence "If you want a university education you ought to finish high school" can be taken to express either the non-normative claim that finishing high school is a prerequisite to attaining a university education or the normative claim, which is supported by the empirical claim I just mentioned, that the desire to attain a university education is a reason for finishing high school.

prohibited players from doctoring the ball. This rule forbade the spitball, among other things. We can easily imagine fans debating whether the game was improved by introducing the rule, invoking standards they may or may not be able to articulate for judging the game. So we see that there can be higher-order standards for evaluating the suitability of first-order standards for some specified role. Of course, normative propositions of baseball are type-one normative. Their truth depends only on the fact that relevant rules are incorporated into the official rules of baseball, but the example illustrates justification in relation to higher-order standards.

A standard qualifies as justified just in case it meets criteria of justification specified by a relevant higher-order standard. There is obviously a threat of regress here, which I discuss in the next chapter. Here I want to stress that the criteria that must be met by a standard, as a condition of the truth of a corresponding paradigmatic type-two proposition, depend on the kind of proposition at issue. Epistemological standards must be justified in order for corresponding paradigmatic epistemological propositions to be true, and moral standards must be justified in order for corresponding paradigmatic moral propositions to be true. But different criteria are relevant to the justification of standards of the different kinds. It is unclear, moreover, what precisely are the criteria of justification for standards of these kinds. This is a matter for philosophical debate.

Indeed, it can be a matter of debate whether a given claim or type of claim expresses a type-one or type-two normative proposition. I have already mentioned normative propositions of law. A second example is propositions of aesthetics. Of course, nothing prevents me from judging paintings in the light of my own aesthetic standards, but an aesthetic claim expresses a true proposition about a painting only if some relevant aesthetic standards have a standing in virtue of which they are appropriate to use in evaluating paintings in a way that other standards would not be. It is unclear whether propositions of aesthetics are type-one or type-two normative.

I shall now argue that moral propositions are type-two normative. A paradigmatic moral proposition is true only if relevant moral standards meet relevant criteria of justification. The precise content of these criteria is argued in later chapters.

Moral Propositions as Type-Two Normative

It is trivial that there is a standard that prohibits slavery, but there are also standards that permit it.[45] If slavery is indeed morally wrong, as we believe it to be, then some standard that prohibits it must be *justified*.

Suppose that the moral code with currency in our society permitted slavery. Suppose, indeed, that I am the only one who believes slavery to be wrong and

---

45. I speak of things that are "prohibited," "required," and "called for" by standards. I will explain these locutions in terms of what would be the case if a standard were conformed to.

that no one else subscribes to any prohibition on slavery. Of course, there is an indefinite number of imaginable prohibitions on slavery, and because I am morally opposed to slavery, I presumably subscribe to some of them. But I believe slavery wrong, so I must take it that there is a *justified* prohibition on slavery. Otherwise, the prohibition I accept might have no other standing than the fact that I accept it. I would have to concede that if I were to be brainwashed so that I ceased to subscribe to any prohibition on slavery, the standards prohibiting slavery might be of the same standing as any arbitrary or eccentric standard, such as a standard mandating the enslavement of anyone who is red-haired. Given this concession, I could not intelligibly take it to be true that slavery is wrong.

Slavery would be wrong even if the conventional moral code in our society condoned it or did not contain or imply any prohibition on it. It would be wrong even if no prohibition on slavery had any social standing and even if no one subscribed to any such prohibition. But there are an indefinite number of standards that condone and even enjoin slavery, as well as standards that prohibit it. The prohibitions on slavery in virtue of which slavery is wrong must therefore have some property that the conflicting standards do not have. They must presumably be warranted, authoritative, or justified. The standards that condone slavery, by contrast, are not justified. If it is true that slavery is wrong, its wrongness depends on, and is in virtue of, the fact that some relevant standard that prohibits slavery is justified.

I hold then that the truth of a proposition to the effect that something is morally wrong depends on, and is in virtue of, the fact that some relevant standard is appropriately justified. This is what explains the normativity of claims of this kind; they are type-two normative. Analogous arguments lead to the conclusion that claims to the effect that something is morally required or morally right are also type-two normative. They are true only if some relevant standard is appropriately justified.

It is not part of my goal to give a full account of the truth conditions of any moral claim. I am attempting merely to explain what it is that makes them normative. Still, it may be useful to propose truth conditions for propositions to the effect that an action *A* is morally wrong.

Let me say that a standard "calls for" a person to do *A* in a given circumstance just in case, if the person failed to do *A* in that circumstance, he would thereby fail to conform to the standard. Let me also point out that although a moral code is a *system* of standards, a code can also be regarded as itself a standard, for it can be construed as specifying a complex criterion for the appraisal or judging of actions and persons. Now, following an idea of John Stuart Mill's, I propose that an action is wrong only if an agent ought to be sanctioned for doing it, at least prima facie.[46] In particular, he ought to be sanctioned by his own conscience. More precisely, my proposal is as follows: A person's doing *A* would be morally wrong in a given circumstance just in

46. See Mill, 1863, chapter 5, paragraph 14. I discussed Mill's theory in Copp, 1979b. Also see Lyons, 1976.

case the moral code justified for that circumstance is such that (1) it calls for the person not to do *A* in that circumstance and (2), if the person were to do *A* in the circumstance, then assuming the person's action did not meet "excusing conditions" specified in the code, the code would call for the person to regret having done *A*. Of course, I read this as entailing that *there is* a relevant justified moral code.

Propositions to the effect that something is morally good imply that there are justified standards concerning objects of desire. Consider, for example, the proposition that friendship is morally good. It implies that the desire to seek or to maintain friendships meets justified moral standards regarding the things to choose or desire.[47] Propositions to the effect that something is a moral virtue imply that there are justified standards pertaining to character. The proposition that kindness is a virtue implies that appropriate and justified standards for character call for people to be kind.[48]

These proposals may seem controversial, both morally and conceptually. First, it may be viewed as a substantive and controversial moral issue whether regret is ever appropriate when one has acted wrongly. I think on the contrary that if a moral code does not include standards calling for regret under certain circumstances, then it does not treat any actions as wrong. But the more important point is that this proposal about regret is not part of the standard-based theory itself. The standard-based theory does not imply anything about the content of the standards that are at issue. It does not foreclose any controversial normative issues.[49]

Second, it may seem that there need be no conceptual error in accepting a moral or other normative claim while denying that any relevant standard has a relevant status. Of course, I claim otherwise. In the moral case, I claim it would be a conceptual or semantic error to accept a moral claim yet to deny that any moral standard is justified. But this would not be a *shallow* error which would show that the person who made it lacked ordinary competence with moral concepts. On the contrary, it would be an interesting philosophical error.[50]

I cannot hope to discuss all of the many kinds of claim that can be construed as moral, but I do want to assert that all moral claims are type-two normative. To complete my argument, I need to address certain apparent counterexamples, such as the proposition that ruthlessness is no virtue. Before doing so, however, it will be useful to introduce the notion of a moral "property."

47. For similar proposals see Rawls, 1971, p. 399; Kagan, 1989, pp. 60–61. My remarks in the text concern the idea that friendship is *morally* good.

48. Gregory Trianosky speaks of standards of vice and virtue (1986, pp. 26–40).

49. If it did foreclose such issues, it might be liable to a version of G. E. Moore's "open question argument." See Moore, 1903, pp. 10–21, esp. 10–12. Gibbard uses similar reasoning, and he cites Moore (1990, pp. 10–12; see p. 11, n. 9). I discuss the argument in chapter 11.

50. There is a sense in which the meaning of a sentence is the proposition it expresses. In this sense of "meaning," however, the meaning of a sentence is not in general transparent to people who know how to use it. Hence, a competent speaker of the language may not recognize that the sentence "Kindness is a virtue" expresses a proposition which entails that some moral standard is justified.

Naturalism and Normative Properties

The property of being morally wrong is, roughly, the property an action has when the justified moral code calls for it not to be done and also calls for regret if it is done. A standard specifies that certain conditions are to be met by some objects or "calls for" the objects to meet the conditions. Hence, if a moral standard is justified, there is the property of being "called for" by a justified moral standard. Let us say that this is a moral property. I hold that a necessary and sufficient condition for the existence of a moral property is the existence of a justified moral standard.

Given this account of moral properties and the analogous account of normative properties in general, one might suspect that the standard-based theory is committed to properties that, in the words of J. L. Mackie, would be metaphysically "queer" and "utterly different from anything else in the universe."[51] The issue here reduces to a worry about the idea of a justified standard. Is this idea suspect? Would the property of *being justified* be "utterly different from anything else in the universe"? It would not be, if it were a "natural" property.

I assume that a theory that postulates normative facts or properties counts as a form of naturalism only if it claims or implies that these facts or properties are *empirical*.[52] A paradigmatic type-one claim entails that a relevant standard has a kind of de facto standing, as, for example, the norms of etiquette have a sociological status in virtue of which claims of etiquette can be true. This idea is obviously compatible with naturalism. But the standard-based account of type-two claims does pose a problem, for it says that a paradigmatic type-two claim entails that a relevant moral standard is *justified*. It remains to be seen whether there is a set of empirical conditions, the satisfaction of which by a standard both constitutes and is necessary and sufficient for the standard's being justified. If there *is* such a set, then the standard-based account is compatible with naturalism. I return to this question in chapter 11.

Suppose, however, that the standard-based theory turns out *not* to be compatible with naturalism—suppose it entails that (type-two) normative facts are *not* empirical. What should we conclude? What would *follow* is that either the standard-based theory is false, or no (paradigmatic) type-two normative claim is true, or the facts in virtue of which (the true) type-two normative claims are true are not empirical.[53] It would be hasty to draw either of the first two conclusions unless we could defend the proposition that *all* facts are empirical, and this proposition seems clearly to be false. If it were true, then it would be a fact that all facts are empirical, and this fact would *itself* be empirical. Yet it surely

51. See Mackie, 1977, pp. 38–42. Tiffany Diggs pressed this objection.

52. That is, the propositions in question are knowable (by humans) only a posteriori, or through experience. And a property is empirical just in case the proposition that it is instantiated is knowable only through experience. See Kant, 1781, Introduction, B2–3; Bradley and Swartz, 1979, p. 150. Kitcher (1992) construes naturalism as rejecting the a priori.

53. That is, to illustrate the middle case, one could hold that a standard is justified only if it has a relevant non-empirical property, but there is no such property. Hence no paradigmatic type-two proposition is true.

is not an empirical fact that all facts are empirical. There are facts of logic and mathematics, for example, and the issue whether they are empirical is conceptual or philosophical, not empirical. Therefore, some facts are not empirical.

Philosophy can be viewed as proposing explanations that are to be assessed for their fruitfulness. But I am not prepared to say that an adequate philosophical explanation would not postulate anything non-empirical. So I am not prepared to say that the standard-based theory is unacceptable unless moral properties turn out to be empirical by its lights.

Non-Paradigmatic Normative Propositions

To this point, I have restricted my discussion to *paradigmatic* type-one and type-two normative propositions. For completeness, this somewhat technical section introduces the idea of a *non-paradigmatic* normative claim.

A variety of normative propositions do not entail that any standard has any relevant standing. They are not normative in the paradigmatic sense I have explained so far, but they are normative in an extended sense. Consider, for example, the proposition that forthrightness is not impolite. It is normative, and since it is a proposition of etiquette, I would classify it as type-one normative. But it is not inconsistent with the proposition that no standards of etiquette have any currency at all in any relevant social group. Similarly, the proposition that ruthlessness is no moral virtue is a normative moral proposition, yet it is not inconsistent with the proposition that there are no justified moral standards at all. To deal with examples of these kinds, I need to amend my definitions of the two types of normative claims. I claim that all moral propositions are type-two normative, but some of them are non-paradigmatic. Non-paradigmatic normative propositions contain a paradigmatic proposition in one of the ways I will explain.

Begin with type-one claims. Call a proposition a "paradigmatic" type-one normative proposition just in case its content or truth conditions are such that (1) it is true only if some relevant standard has a currency in a relevant collective and (2) it is not the case that it is true only if some standard has a relevant justification or other normative status. There are propositional operators, such as *it is possible that* and *it is believed that*, which can operate on a type-one proposition to yield a new proposition. The new propositions count as type-one normative. Hence, given that the proposition that it is unlawful to park in front of a fire hydrant is type-one normative, I will say that the proposition that it is possible that it is unlawful to park there is also a type-one proposition. Propositions can be combined by means of logical connectives, such as disjunction. If a type-one proposition is connected in some such way with another proposition, then I will classify the resulting proposition as type-one normative. Hence, the proposition that either it is unlawful to park there or the sun is shining is a type-one proposition.

In summary a proposition is type-one normative just in case it is a paradigmatic type-one proposition, the result of connecting a type-one proposition with other propositions, or the result of an operation on a type-one proposition. Consider, then, the proposition that forthrightness is not impolite. The proposition that forthrightness is impolite is a paradigmatic type-one proposition, so its denial is also type-one normative, although it is not paradigmatic.

Turn then to type-two normative propositions. Call a proposition a "paradigmatic" type-two normative proposition just in case its content or truth conditions are such that it is true only if some relevant standard has a relevant normative standing. Now I say that a proposition is type-two normative just in case it is a paradigmatic type-two proposition, the result of connecting a type-two proposition with other propositions, or the result of an operation on a type-two proposition.

Propositions to the effect that something is morally wrong are paradigmatic type-two normative. So are propositions to the effect that something is a moral virtue, that something is morally good, that something is morally bad, and that something is a duty. Since these moral propositions are paradigmatic type two, I will call them "paradigmatic moral propositions."

Given my account, and given that the proposition that ruthlessness is a moral virtue is type-two normative, the proposition that ruthlessness is *no* moral virtue is also type-two normative, although it is not paradigmatic. For similar reasons, the following are also classified as type-two normative, although not as paradigmatic: There is nothing morally wrong with singing. Either the sun is up or singing is morally bad. There is no duty to bring aid. There are no duties at all. Competition is permissible. Everything is permitted.

I would construe a proposition to the effect that some action *A* is morally permitted as equivalent to the proposition that it is not the case that there is a moral duty not to do *A*. The proposition that there is a moral duty not to do *A* is a paradigmatic type-two normative proposition, and so its denial is also type-two normative. Its denial is equivalent to the proposition that *A* is morally permitted, and so the latter is also type-two normative.

On this account, then, a proposition to the effect that some action is morally permitted is normative, even though it is consistent with the thesis that there are no adequately justified moral standards at all. I call this thesis—that there are no adequately justified moral standards—"moral skepticism." It could also be called "moral nihilism." As the example illustrates, I am classifying some propositions as normative moral propositions even though they imply nothing that a moral skeptic would need to deny. But the main point is the characterization of the central cases. A moral skeptic is committed to denying the truth of any *paradigmatic* moral proposition.

Given my account of normative properties, it is easy to see why paradigmatic type-two propositions are the interesting normative propositions. It is a (nontrivially) necessary condition of the truth of a paradigmatic proposition that some relevant standard be relevantly justified, and it is therefore a necessary condition of the truth of a paradigmatic proposition that there be a normative property. This cannot be said of propositions that are not paradigmatic. There is, then, a sense in which a non-paradigmatic normative proposition lacks normative import: It is not a (nontrivially) necessary condition of the truth of such a proposition that a relevant standard have a relevant standing. In this sense, a non-paradigmatic *moral* proposition lacks normative import, and in a corresponding sense, it also lacks *moral* import: It is not a (nontrivially) necessary condition of the truth of such a proposition that there be a moral property or that a moral standard be justified. This explains why a moral skeptic could accept the truth of a non-paradigmatic moral proposition.

Rule Skepticism

John McDowell has proposed two lines of argument that might plausibly be thought to undermine my doctrine that there is always a moral standard in the background of a moral claim. The first is a group of arguments from claims about the virtues and about the thick moral concepts. The second is more general and flows from a general skepticism about rule following.

The more general argument is motivated by arguments in Wittgenstein's *Philosophical Investigations.* Saul Kripke and McDowell both present versions of it, and there is, of course, the version found in the *Investigations.*[54] I do not intend to discuss it in detail here, for I believe I can show that the argument simply is not relevant to moral philosophy any more than it is relevant to mathematics.

Very briefly, the argument works as follows. Consider the instruction "Add 2." We are inclined to think that the meaning of this expression determines that the series, 2, 4, 6, . . . , would correctly be extended indefinitely by adding 2 to the previous member of the series. Its meaning determines how one *ought* to go on. Yet what could constitute the instruction's having one meaning as opposed to some other meaning? And what could constitute one's understanding its meaning? For example, the instruction could instead pick out the "quus 2" function, which is like the "plus 2" function except that after 1000, the correct extension of the series is 1000, 1004, 1008, . . .[55] Or a person might take it to mean the "quus 2" function rather than the "plus 2" function. There seems to be no property of the instruction that determines its proper interpretation, and there seems to be no property of the person who putatively understands it that determines how he ought to go on. The issue is supposed to be quite general. It seems that no property of an expression or of a person who understands it could determine what the expression means or what the person takes it to mean.[56]

McDowell thinks it follows from these considerations that it is a philosophical prejudice to suppose that what goes on in reasoning, including but not limited to moral reasoning, must be explicable in terms of the reasoner's being guided by a formulable universal principle.[57] Any such principle itself stands in need of interpretation, just as the instruction "Add 2" stands in need of interpretation. He says we should "resist the prejudice, and respect Aristotle's belief

54. Kripke, 1982; McDowell, 1984; Wittgenstein, 1953.
55. McDowell, 1979, p. 337; he cites Wittgenstein, 1953, section 185.
56. McDowell, 1984, pp. 328–29; Kripke, 1982, pp. 272–73, 294.
57. McDowell, 1979, p. 339–41.

that a view of how one should live is not codifiable." A virtuous person makes reliable judgments as to what he should do, but this is to be explained by attributing to him "a conception of how to live." It is not to be explained by attributing to him a grasp of a universal principle.[58]

If the skeptical argument poses a problem about moral rules, however, it is because it poses a general problem about meaningfulness, and the general problem implies corresponding problems not only about rules but also about concepts. We know there is a solution to the problem, for we know there is meaningful language. Whatever the solution is, it vindicates our ability to have specific concepts and to follow specific rules.

Furthermore, if, as McDowell himself supposes, we can attribute to a virtuous person a certain conception of how to live, rather than any of the alternative "quus-like" conceptions a person could have in principle about how to live, then we are also free to suppose that there is a standard that expresses his conception of how to live.

McDowell realizes that the argument does not cast doubt on the idea that there is a "plus function" in mathematics which determines that 1000 plus 2 equals 1002, not 1004.[59] Since this is so, then by parity of reasoning, the argument does not cast doubt on the idea that there is a standard or rule that captures each given conception of how to live. This means the argument does not cast doubt on the possibility of codifying the virtuous person's conception of how to live. We can therefore ignore rule skepticism in thinking about the nature of moral rules.

Despite this, of course, McDowell may be correct that moral reasoning is not a matter of being guided by universal principles. He is surely correct that a virtuous person may respond immediately to a situation by making a moral claim, without consciously applying any moral rule.[60] We often hear an account of something someone did and judge right away that it was wrong, without making any conscious application of moral principles or rules. Nor do we in general apply rules of English usage in making claims about proper usage. We often can recognize immediately an instance of improper usage. It seems, therefore, that a person can make a moral judgment without having in mind, or reasoning in terms of, an articulated rule.

Yet McDowell claims that a virtuous person's views about how to behave *cannot* be codified in a rule about virtuous behavior. The principles we cite in moral argument are only generalizations that hold for the most part. A virtuous person's reliability in making correct moral judgments is to be explained, not by postulating that she grasps and follows a principle, but in terms of her conception of how to live, and this conception cannot be understood except from within her way of seeing particular situations.[61]

58. McDowell, 1979, p. 342.
59. He thinks it casts doubt on the idea that following such a function is a matter of having a mathematical competence that is like the "inexorable workings of a machine." McDowell, 1981, p. 151.
60. McDowell, 1979, pp. 332–33, 337.
61. See McDowell, 1979, pp. 336–37, 342, 345–46; 1978, p. 21.

None of this constitutes an argument against the standard-based theory. The standard-based theory is an account of the semantics of normative claims. It is not about the psychology of normative reasoning and judgment or about the epistemology of the virtuous person, and it does not entail that we have the ability to formulate rules that capture the different views about how we should act. The standard-based theory does not imply that a person who believes that a given sentence is ungrammatical would be able to articulate a standard that the sentence fails to meet. The theory does not imply that anyone who has a normative belief must be able to articulate a relevant standard.

Moreover, the theory does not entail that there must be a rule that codifies a person's view about *how we should act*. The theory says that moral propositions about actions entail that *there is* a relevant justified moral standard. Yet, for all that I have said, this standard might not be directly concerned with action. Virtue theorists could be correct in thinking that the most basic or fundamental justified moral standards directly concern states of character rather than actions, and, in this sense, the justified moral code might be a morality of virtue rather than of duty. For example, the proposition that what Carol did was disloyal must entail that some moral standard is justified, but the standard may not codify the way in which a loyal person would act.

It may seem, however, that if McDowell is correct that it is not possible to characterize the extension of a thick concept in non-normative terms, then it may not be possible, even in principle, to formulate a standard that corresponds to a thick concept without using that very concept. This would introduce a kind of circularity that might seem objectionable.[62] In any event, I argued before that, for each of a community's thick moral concepts, there is a non-normative quasi-thick concept that is co-extensive with it. We can use this quasi-concept to formulate the relevant standard. For instance, the standard pertaining to loyalty calls for a steadfastness of character that amounts to quasi-loyalty. This would seem to eliminate any worrisome circularity.

Accordingly, once McDowell's arguments are properly understood and evaluated, and once my view about moral standards is properly understood and qualified, I think the standard-based theory of normative propositions emerges unscathed.

Internalism, Externalism, and Moral Reasons

Cognitivist theories of moral judgment typically assume that normativity is to be explained in terms of *motivation* or *reasons*. That is, they assume that the normativity of moral judgment is to be explained in terms of a relation between moral propositions, or the state of accepting a moral proposition, and our motivations or reasons. In this sense, the theories are motivation-based or reason-based.

Motivation- and reason-based theories are either internalist or externalist. "Internalist" theories hold that normativity is "internal" to moral judgment;

---

62. McDowell, 1981, pp. 144–45. See also McDowell, 1979.

they seek to explain normativity by postulating a necessary link between moral judgment and the existence of nonmoral reasons or motives to be moral. "Externalist" theories also seek to explain normativity in terms of a link between moral judgment and reasons or motives, but they hold that the link is contingent. Different theories postulate a different kind of link to reasons or motives. For example, certain versions of internalism hold that it is a necessary truth that if a person believes that he is morally required to perform a given action, then the person is motivated to some degree to perform the action.[63]

Against externalist theories, I have already argued that the normativity of a claim needs to be explained in terms of an essential property of the proposition it expresses. It needs to be explained in terms of the content of the proposition it expresses.

Internalist *reason-based* theories are not sufficiently general. Propositions about the reasons people have are normative, and their normativity needs to be explained. It would obviously be unhelpful to attempt to explain the normativity of moral propositions by citing the existence of *moral* reasons. But even if one were to attempt to explain the normativity of moral propositions by citing the existence of nonmoral reasons, this would leave unexplained the normativity of propositions about these nonmoral reasons.

The standard-based theory offers an account that applies to claims about reasons as well as to other normative claims. In general, I propose, there is a K reason to make a given choice just in case (1) there is a K standard that calls for the choice and (2) the standard has the relevant K standing.[64] There are epistemic reasons just in case there are justified epistemic standards governing our beliefs, for example, and there are moral reasons just in case there are justified moral standards that call for certain choices.

This leaves internalist *motivation-based* theories. They also are not sufficiently general, for they cannot plausibly be extended to explain the normativity of type-one claims, such as claims of law, etiquette, and language, and nonmoral type-two claims, such as claims of aesthetics and epistemology. The standard-based theory provides a unified account of normative propositions of all kinds.

Instead of going into detail regarding my objections to motivation- and reason-based theories, however,[65] I want to point out that the standard-based theory

63. For a discussion of forms of internalism and externalism, see Brink, 1989, pp. 37–43.

64. If there is a K reason to do something, there is a K reason to do the things that are means to doing it and, perhaps, the things that are "necessary enablers" of doing it. Hence, if a K standard "calls for" something, it "calls for" things that are means to, or necessary enablers of, that thing. Walter Sinnott-Armstrong introduces the idea of a "necessary enabler" (1992, p. 400).

65. Brink distinguishes the following versions of internalism (Brink, 1989, pp. 40–41). "Agent" internalism holds that the concept of morality is such that the proposition that an agent has a moral obligation entails that the agent has a (reason or) motive to act accordingly. "Appraiser" internalism holds that the concept of morality is such that a person who makes a given moral judgment has a (reason or) motive to perform the kind of action judged favorably. And "hybrid" internalism says that the concept of morality is such that an agent who judges that he has a given moral obligation has a (reason or) motive to act accordingly. But first, consider the propositions that private property is unjust and that kindness is a virtue. Since these propositions neither refer to an agent nor entail anything about obligations, it appears that agent and hybrid

represents a compromise position. The standard-based theory holds that *normativity* is internal to a moral proposition, for it holds that a paradigmatic moral proposition is true only if some moral standard is justified. This feature of it will appeal to internalists. But the theory denies that normativity is to be explained by postulating an internal relation between moral judgment and motives or nonmoral reasons, and this feature of it will appeal to externalists.

To be sure, some theories regarding the justification of moral standards do imply that it is a necessary condition of a standard's being justified that certain agents are (or would be) motivated to comply with it, or that they have (or would have) reasons to comply. For example, a Kantian view would imply a necessary connection between the truth of a moral judgment and the reasons and motivations of "fully rational agents." Hence, the standard-based theory is *consistent* with a kind of internalism. But internalism about reasons or motives is not *required* by the theory. The theory is neutral between internalism and externalism about reasons and motives.[66]

The distinction between moral propositions and moral standards allows me to distinguish two senses in which one can have a moral "conviction." On the one hand, a person can *subscribe* to a moral standard. As I shall explain in chapter 5, this entails having the intention to conform to the standard or to support conformity with it. It therefore entails being motivated to some degree to act appropriately. It does not entail believing that the standard is justified. On the other hand, a person can *believe* a moral proposition to be true. If the proposition is paradigmatic, this commits the person to believing that a corresponding moral standard is justified, but it does not entail that the person subscribes to a corresponding standard.[67] It does not entail that the person is at all motivated to act appropriately. It turns out, on my theory, that an internalist position is correct about the relation between subscription and motivation, but an externalist position is correct about the relation between belief and motivation. This is another respect in which my theory represents a compromise between internalism and externalism.

Let me illustrate my claim that believing a moral proposition neither entails, nor is entailed by, subscribing to a corresponding standard. First, consider a moral skeptic who is morally opposed to capital punishment; that is, she subscribes to a moral standard that prohibits capital punishment. It does not follow that she believes capital punishment is morally wrong. Indeed, given her

---

theories cannot explain their normativity. And since neither proposition refers to an action-type, it appears that appraiser theories also cannot explain their normativity. Perhaps the definitions of these types of theory could be amended to deal with the examples. But second, since theories of all three types make claims about the concept of morality, they say nothing about the normativity of nonmoral claims. It seems unlikely that the concept of etiquette is such that we are motivated to avoid doing things that are, or that we judge to be, impolite, or that the concept of aesthetics is such that we are motivated to avoid watching movies that are, or that we judge to be, bad.

66. My remarks about internalism and externalism in the introduction were oversimplified.

67. A standard "corresponds" to a moral proposition just in case it is a standard that the proposition entails (nontrivially) to be justified.

skeptical view that no moral standard is relevantly justified, she must deny that capital punishment is wrong. Second, suppose that Alice believes moral standards are justified in virtue of being prescribed by God. Suppose she believes that God has prescribed against abortions. It does not follow that she intends to comply with this prescription. Indeed, it is possible that she intends to have an abortion should she become pregnant. If so, she may have the belief that abortion is morally wrong even though she does not subscribe to any standard that prohibits abortion.

Certain internalist positions can be interpreted as holding that a person does not have a "sincere" moral conviction that p, where p is a paradigmatic moral proposition, unless her state of mind combines both belief that p and subscription to the corresponding standard. I have no objection to this way of thinking as long as it is kept in mind that moral belief itself does not logically entail subscription to a standard. It is possible to fail to see this because a person who makes a moral claim does imply *conversationally* that she subscribes to the corresponding standard.[68] The making of a moral claim is typically an expression both of belief and of subscription to a moral standard. As I explain in chapter 11, we normally subscribe to standards we view as justified.

According to my position, a paradigmatic moral proposition to the effect that a person ought to make a given choice entails that there is a *moral reason* for her to make that choice. Yet it does not follow that she has a "self-interested" or "self-grounded" reason to make the choice. In chapter 9, I present a theory of self-grounded reasons that I call the "needs-and-values" theory. It implies, roughly speaking, that a person has a self-grounded reason to comply with a moral standard if she subscribes to it in a way that places it among her values. But as we have seen, a person who believes a moral proposition may not subscribe to the corresponding standard, and so, on the account I will give, she may have no self-grounded reason to comply with it or to support compliance with it.[69]

This reveals another respect in which my view represents a compromise. An internalist position is correct about the relation between moral subscription and self-grounded reasons, but an externalist position is correct about the relation between moral belief and self-grounded reasons.

People normally are raised in a way that leads them both to subscribe to the moral standards of their community and to view them as justified. When moral culture is effectively taught, there is a warranted expectation that people *do* have motives and reasons to comply with the standards that their moral beliefs commit them to viewing as justified, for normally people *do* subscribe to these standards. It is important, then, that the moral standards of the community be

---

68. Grice has developed a theory of conversational implication (1989, pp. 22–40).

69. A person who believes a moral proposition is committed to there being a *moral* reason to conform to the corresponding standard (or to support conformity with the standard). Hence, a person who acknowledged all the reasons she is committed to believing there to be would acknowledge a moral reason to conform to (or to support conformity to) the standard. Yet she might not have a self-grounded reason to do what she acknowledges *there is* a moral reason for her to do. For related discussion, see Korsgaard, 1986.

justified ones and that moral education be effective. In a well-ordered society, people would subscribe to *justified* moral standards. They would be motivated and have self-grounded reasons to comply with these standards or to support compliance. Moral education and socialization to justified moral standards cement the connection between moral belief and truth, and moral life.[70]

Conclusion

In this chapter, I have proposed a new cognitivist theory of normative judgment. I will soon turn to the other major component of my overall position, the society-centered theory. It proposes a criterion, satisfaction of which is necessary and sufficient for a moral standard to count as justified.

In chapter 3, however, I examine an argument to the effect that *no* moral standards are justified, and in chapter 4 I explore various alternatives to the society-centered theory. I have already mentioned the example of the Kantian theory. I do not think that this theory is successful or that any of the other theories I will discuss in chapter 4 is successful, but a discussion of them will help to clear the ground for my own approach.

70. See Wong, 1984, pp. 64–65.

3

Normative Skepticism:
A Regress Argument

The standard-based theory presents us with several questions, the most important of which is, Under what conditions would a moral standard qualify as justified? In this chapter, I present a skeptical argument that brings into stark relief the difficulty of this question. The argument puts the problem in a much wider context, however, by calling into question not only the existence of justified moral standards but also the existence of relevantly justified standards of any kind.

In simplest form, the argument relies on the fact that a proposition to the effect that a standard is justified is *itself* type-two normative. According to the standard-based theory, a paradigmatic type-two proposition is true only if some standard is relevantly justified. But the latter proposition, that a standard is justified, is itself a paradigmatic type-two proposition and is therefore true only if some standard is relevantly justified. This is so in a trivial way, of course. But it is also true in a more threatening way, which leads to a regress argument. Moreover, as we shall see, there are forms of the argument that do not depend on the standard-based theory. Because of this, the argument is not merely a threat to this theory. It is a threat to the idea that, unlike the many arbitrary normative standards we can imagine, there are some standards that are authoritative, justified, certified, or valid.

A Skeptical Regress Argument

All paradigmatic type-two normative propositions, including those in epistemology and the theory of rational choice, as well as those in ethics, entail that some standard is relevantly justified. The argument I am about to consider purports to show that no standard of any kind is relevantly justified.

Where I write of the "relevant" normative status for a standard of a kind K, I mean the normative status that *some K* standard must have—according to the standard-based theory—if any paradigmatic normative proposition of kind K is true.

Therefore, if the argument does show that no standard of any kind is relevantly justified, it follows that no paradigmatic type-two normative proposition is true.

In what follows, and throughout the rest of the book, I frequently will drop the qualifier "paradigmatic." The reader should bear in mind that, unless I indicate otherwise, I am discussing the paradigmatic cases.[1]

A general version of the argument can be stated as follows: Consider the proposition that (for some kind K) a standard S of kind K is justified. In order to qualify as justified, S must meet some appropriate criteria of justification, criteria specified by a more general or higher-order standard S', which speaks to the evaluation of standards relevantly similar to S. For example, if S is an epistemic principle, then S' is a principle relevant to the evaluation of epistemic principles. But there are any number of standards, most of which are arbitrary and contrived. If S qualifies as justified on the basis that it meets criteria specified by a standard S', then S' must itself qualify as justified. Otherwise, too many standards would qualify as justified. One would only need to postulate a standard S' that is met by the original standard, and then the original standard would qualify as justified, no matter how arbitrary or contrived it and S' might be. Hence, the claim that S is justified implies that a standard S'—which specifies criteria relevant to the justification of standards similar to S—is itself justified. S' must, of course, be a more general or higher order standard than the standard S whose justification was initially at issue. And now we see the threat of a vicious regress, for S' must be justified relative to a still more general or higher-order standard, a standard that is itself justified, and so on. Unless this regress can be stopped, the claim that some standard of kind K is justified appears to be ungrounded.

In what follows, I will refer to this argument and to instantiations of it as the *basic* regress argument. Given the standard-based theory, we can derive a second argument, the *normative truth* regress argument. According to that theory, a paradigmatic normative proposition P entails that some standard S is justified; that is, it entails a second normative proposition, to the effect that some S is justified. This proposition entails in turn that a standard S', which bears on the evaluation of standards similar to S, is justified; that is, it entails a third normative proposition regarding the status of a more general or higher-order standard. This third entails a fourth normative proposition, and so on. There may be no way to stop this regress, and, if not, the idea of normative truth may evaporate. The argument may lead in this way to the conclusion that there are no true paradigmatic normative propositions.

The basic regress argument appears to support a blanket skepticism about normative *standards*, the thesis that there are no relevantly justified standards at all. Henceforth, I will refer to this thesis as "normative skepticism." The normative truth regress argument appears to support the different thesis that there are no true paradigmatic normative propositions. This thesis about nor-

---

1. Also, for variety, I will sometimes refer to moral propositions as moral "claims" or "judgments."

mative truth does not follow from normative skepticism taken by itself. One would also need to invoke the standard-based theory of normative judgment. Of course, I am assuming here that the standard-based theory is true. But a normative skeptic, or a skeptic about standards of a kind *K*, could deny it.

Moral skepticism is the thesis that *there are no relevantly justified moral standards.*[2] Given the standard-based theory, of course, it follows from moral skepticism that no paradigmatic moral claim is true.[3] If the very idea of a moral standard being justified has no content, then it is not even possible that a paradigmatic moral claim be true.

Moral skepticism must be distinguished from non-cognitivism. As we saw, non-cognitivism rejects the standard-based theory, for it asserts that moral claims do not express propositions. But this does not mean it is committed to denying that any moral standards are justified. A non-cognitivist theory might assert that no proposition is expressed by a claim to the effect that this or that moral standard is or is not justified. But it would not follow that no moral standards are justified. It would merely follow that the claim that no moral standards are justified does not express a proposition. Hence, non-cognitivism does not entail moral skepticism.[4] Similarly, a non-cognitivism about all normative claims would not entail normative skepticism.

The basic regress can be instantiated in an argument that appears to support moral skepticism. Consider capital punishment, for example. The standard that speaks against executing this particular prisoner can be derived from a standard that speaks against judicial executions in general. The latter may perhaps be derived in turn from still more general standards. But the most general standards in a person's moral view are not derived from any other moral standards, and our problem arises with respect to these most general standards. Are the most general standards justified? If not, then derivations of less basic standards from more basic and general ones do not relevantly justify the less basic ones; that is, the derivations do not establish that the less basic standards have a status that enables them to underwrite the truth of corresponding moral claims, such as, in the example, the claim that it would be unjust to execute this prisoner. Perhaps the most general moral standards can be justified in relation to a meta-ethical standard that pertains to the evaluation of moral standards, in which case the derived standards can also be justified in relation to this standard. But if so, this meta-ethical standard must also qualify as justified relative to a still higher order standard, if any moral standard is to count as relevantly justified.

The regress does not become a problem in ordinary moral argument, where we take most of our moral view for granted. But in a philosophical context in which the issue is to explain the normative status required of a moral standard

2. Notice that the skeptic need not deny that the moral standard that requires us to perform actions that are right is adequately justified. Let us say her thesis is that no substantive moral standard is appropriately justified. I was helped here by J. G. Bennett.

3. A skeptic need not deny that everything is permissible or that what is right is right or that there are no duties. But these are non-paradigmatic propositions, and, as explained in the preceding chapter, they lack normative and moral import.

4. Non-cognitivism is compatible both with moral skepticism and its denial.

in order for a corresponding moral proposition to be true, we need to be able to explain what status the most general moral standards would have, if corresponding general moral propositions were true. What, if anything, distinguishes the most general moral standards in our moral view from the most general standards in, say, a Nietzschean moral view? Given an account of the concept of overman, specific Nietzschean standards can be derived from the general Nietzschean standard that calls on people to exhibit the characteristics of an overman. Yet we think that these standards are not relevantly justified, for we think it is not true that being an overman is a virtue, and we think specific Nietzschean moral claims (such as that Stalin's ruthless behavior exhibited high standards of virtue) are not true. The regress argument suggests that our own most general moral standards have no different status from the Nietzschean standards.

Assumptions behind the Regress

The basic argument can be viewed as having the following structure: On the assumption that a standard of kind K is justified, for any kind K, it follows that there is an infinite regress of justified standards. Moreover, the regress is vicious; that is, there are decisive theoretical objections to any assumption that entails such a regress. Hence, there are decisive objections to the assumption that there is a justified standard of kind K.

An attempt to escape the argument must therefore attack either (1) the claim that the regress follows from the assumption that some standard is relevantly justified or (2) the claim that the regress is vicious.

Let us begin with the claim that a regress follows from the assumption that there is a justified standard. The argument for this depends on the thesis that if a standard of kind K is justified, then it is justified relative to, or on the basis of its satisfying, some other justified standard, a more general or higher-order standard that is appropriate for evaluating standards of kind K. This thesis can be viewed as the conjunction of four more specific claims. Let us consider them one at a time.

First is the claim that if a standard S is justified, it is justified relative to some standard S'. I think that we have to accept this. A standard could hardly qualify as justified unless it met some criteria or other, criteria relevant to the evaluation of standards of its kind. These criteria are captured by a standard that could be specified, at least in principle. After all, for any criteria that could conceivably be imposed on things of a given kind, there is a standard that putatively imposes the criteria on things of that kind. Hence, the concept of a standard and the concept of justification ensure that a standard can qualify as justified only if it satisfies the criteria specified by some standard. In effect, that is, the property of being justified is a relational property; for a standard to be justified is for it to be justified relative to a standard.

Second, given that a standard S can be justified only if it is justified relative to some standard S', S' must itself be justified. I think that we have to accept this claim as well. There are any number of quite arbitrary standards. Hence, the mere fact that S meets criteria specified by S' cuts no ice. Or, assuming S is of kind K, the mere fact that it meets criteria specified by S' for the evaluation of standards of kind K can hardly show S to be justified. The standard S' must itself be relevantly justified.

The remaining two conjuncts of the thesis are less clearly correct; that is, it is less clear that S' and S must be distinct and that S' must be more general than, or of a higher order than, S. Perhaps a standard could qualify as justified without satisfying the criteria specified by some *other* standard; perhaps some standards are self-certifying or self-justifying. This would be a foundationalism of standards. Or perhaps a standard could qualify as justified without satisfying a more general or higher-order standard; perhaps the set of justified standards forms a mutually supporting network that is not hierarchical. This can fairly be described as a coherentist picture.

I do agree that some standards are *self-supporting*. Consider, for example, the standard that a standard is to be subscribed to if it can be expressed in English in fewer than twenty words. Given that I have just expressed it in nineteen words, this standard meets the criterion it specifies. But the mere fact that a standard S meets the criterion specified by some standard S' is not sufficient for S to be justified. S' must itself be justified, as we have already seen, even if S and S' are identical. Hence, the existence of self-supporting standards does not fundamentally alter our situation. Even if S meets the criteria of justification that it itself specifies, we must still look further in order to find a justification for S.

Perhaps it will be objected that some standards are *self-evidently* justified, without being *self*-justifying. Consider, for example, the epistemic standard that calls on us to have beliefs that we are called on to have by justified epistemic standards. This standard may be self-evidently justified, but it lacks normative import in an obvious sense; even though it is justified, there may be no beliefs we are called on to have by any justified epistemic standard; there may be no proposition we are called on to believe. This standard and others of its kind are uninteresting, and I do not think that any interesting standards are self-evidently justified. Furthermore, given what I have argued, even if a standard is self-evidently justified, it is justified relative to *some* standard, and if it is not *self*-justifying, then it is justified relative to some *other* standard. Hence, we are back where we started, facing the regress.

Nor do I think that coherentism is a viable option. To simplify, let me suppose that coherentism is, in this context, the thesis that a standard of a kind K is justified if and only if it is a member of a coherent and mutually supporting set of beliefs and standards, all the members of which would be accepted in specified K-ideal circumstances by some given person or group. This position only moves our problem back one step. It proposes a K-coherentist standard that must be met by standards of kind K. We need to ask whether this standard is justified, and our problem arises again at this level. If the standard is *not* justified, then coherentism is at best doubtful. And if the standard *is* justified, it must either be self-justifying or justified in terms of some other standard. It plainly is not self-certifying (unless K-ideal circumstances are specified in a way that trivializes the standard, robbing it of normative import).[5] Hence, if it is justified, it is justified in relation to some other standard, and we are back where we started.

One might object that the K-coherentist standard may be justified relative to a generalized coherentist standard and that, if it is carefully formulated, the generalized standard may be justified in virtue of satisfying itself. The generalized standard would be to the effect that a standard is justified if and only if it is a member of a relevant network of beliefs and standards. This new standard could itself meet the criteria it specifies because it could itself turn out to belong to a relevant network of beliefs and standards. But, as we have seen, the fact that a standard meets its own criteria is not sufficient to qualify it as relevantly justified. Consider again the standard that a standard is to be subscribed to if it can be expressed in English in fewer than twenty words. This standard meets the criterion it specifies, but it plainly has no standing whatsoever, except as a contrived example in this book. Hence, the generalized coherentist standard needs to be justified, and we are back where we started once again.

One might reply that the generalized standard would not be part of a relevant network of beliefs and standards *unless* it were justified in relation to the beliefs and standards in the network; that is, a standard's being relevantly justified is a necessary condition of its membership in a coherent network, given what is meant by "coherence." So understood, the generalized standard may be self-evidently justified, but it cannot help us to avoid the regress problem. The proposal implies that a standard must be justified to be eligible for membership in a coherent network. That is, membership in a coherent network is not the criterion a standard must meet to qualify as justified. Rather, containing only justified standards is the criterion a network must meet to qualify as coherent. This means we need to look elsewhere to find criteria of justification for standards.

My conclusion is that, except in uninteresting cases, a standard cannot qualify as justified unless it satisfies criteria specified by some distinct and more general or higher-order justified standard. I therefore do not think the regress can be avoided, except in these uninteresting cases.

Is the Regress Vicious?

If the regress cannot be avoided, we can escape the skeptical conclusion of the regress argument only if the regress is not vicious. I shall now attempt to show that the regress is not vicious.

Recall that to assert that a standard is justified is to speak of its *status*, not to report the result of a *process* of normative investigation. A standard is justified when it has a particular normative status, regardless of whether anyone has

---

5. Consider, for example, the view that a standard of kind K is justified if and only if it is a member of a coherent and mutually supporting set of beliefs and standards, all the members of which would be accepted by a given person or group in circumstances in which all and only *justified* standards and beliefs are accepted by that person or group.

verified its having that status. An infinite sequence of *events* of justification would be an impossibility, but there is no barrier to the existence of an infinite hierarchical structure of standards, with standards of each order satisfying the standards of the next higher order. Therefore, the regress does not pose a problem.[6]

To hold this is not to adopt the implausible infinitist position that a standard's satisfying a standard, which itself satisfies a standard (and so on without end), is what qualifies it as justified. The infinitist position is implausible because it does not rule out the existence of more than one hierarchical structure of standards of a given kind, where the first-order standards in the different hierarchies conflict with one another. Consider, for example, a hierarchy of epistemological standards that begins with a first-order standard mandating that one reject all propositions inconsistent with those affirmed in the Bible and that continues by mandating at each higher level that one accept the standard at the next lower level. There is a similar hierarchy for every book that purports to have been divinely inspired, and these hierarchies of standards may be compared with the similar hierarchy that begins at the first level with a standard mandating that one reject all propositions inconsistent with those affirmed in the works of Bertrand Russell. (Perhaps I should mention that Russell was an atheist.) This set of examples shows that an infinite hierarchy of standards, with standards of any given level satisfying the standards of the next higher level, could still be quite arbitrary. The fact that a given standard falls within such a hierarchy seems to show nothing whatsoever about its status as warranted or unwarranted.

Yet I am not proposing that we adopt the infinitist position in order to escape normative skepticism. According to the infinitist position, the fact that a standard has a place in an infinite hierarchy of standards is sufficient to show it to be justified. But the point I am insisting on is that the fact that a standard has a place in an infinite hierarchy of standards is *not* sufficient to show it *not* to be justified.

It may be useful to compare the regress arguments I have been discussing with a regress argument that is standardly discussed in epistemology. The latter, which I will call "the epistemic regress argument," is generated by two assumptions: First, any proposition we are justified in believing must be supported by an inference from other propositions we are justified in believing. Second, no belief can be appealed to as a premise anywhere in its own complete justification. Given these assumptions, if a person is justified in any belief, there is at least some other proposition that she is justified in believing; if she is justified in believing it, there is at least some additional proposition that she is justified in believing; and so on. Hence, to be justified in believing anything, one must be justified in believing an infinite number of propositions. Because this is impossible, it is impossible to be justified in believing anything.[7]

6. Consider this analogy: Perhaps there is one theorem of geometry only if there is an infinity of theorems. But this is not a vicious regress. To say there is an infinity of theorems is not to say there is an infinity of theorems that have been *proven* to be such.

7. See, for example, Lehrer, 1974, pp. 155–56, 13–16.

This regress argument differs in important ways from the regress arguments I have been discussing, which we can call "the new arguments." First, the new arguments address the normative status of standards and the truth of normative propositions, rather than the epistemic status of beliefs. The arguments do imply that there are no justified epistemic standards and that there are no true normative propositions in epistemology. But, unlike the epistemic regress argument, they are not exclusively concerned with epistemic standards and claims. Second, the epistemic regress turns on an assumption to the effect that the justification of belief is inferential; that is, it turns on an assumption about the content of a standard that expresses criteria for the justification of belief. The new arguments imply that this standard is not justified. They therefore undermine the epistemic regress argument.

The most important difference between the new arguments and the epistemic regress argument is the following: The new arguments postulate a regress of *statuses*, whereas the epistemic argument postulates a regress of inferential *performances* and *psychological states*. The epistemic argument is concerned with the justification *persons* can have in believing a proposition, and it depends on the claim that a person is not justified in believing something unless she believes it on the basis of an inference from other propositions she is justified in believing. It seems impossible for a person to perform an infinity of inferences or to have an infinity of beliefs. This is the nub of the issue. But the new regress arguments are concerned with the status a *standard* can have of being justified. The arguments lead to the conclusion that a standard has this status only if an infinity of standards have it. But, I am claiming, it is not impossible for an infinity of standards to have this status. This is how I propose to escape the regress.

My solution to the new regress problem does not yield a solution to the epistemic regress problem. To escape the epistemic regress, one might deny that the justification of belief is always a matter of performing an inference. That would be to block the claim that there is a regress. My strategy with respect to the new regress problem, however, is to deny that the regress is vicious, not to deny that there is a regress.

In the next two sections, I propose a general model for the philosophical justification of a kind of standard. Then I will explain why normative skepticism is not seriously on the agenda.

A Challenge for a Theory of Justification

Even if the regress is not vicious, the basic argument poses a challenge: What would a viable account of the justification conditions of moral standards, or of any other kind of standard, look like? Briefly, a viable theory regarding standards of a given kind K would identify a property that could be possessed by K standards and propose that K standards that have the property count as relevantly justified. The theory would have to explain why such standards count as justified by defending the claim that K standards that have the property do indeed ground true paradigmatic normative propositions of kind K.

The problem of defending a theory of justification conditions arises with respect to standards of many different kinds, including moral standards, epistemic standards, aesthetic standards, and standards of rational choice. I assume that a plausible account of the justificatory conditions for standards of one kind would differ in general from the account for standards of another kind. For example, a theory about the justification conditions of epistemic standards would identify a property possessed by certain epistemic standards and argue that standards that have the property can ground true epistemic claims. Similarly, a meta-ethical theory would aim to identify a key property that is possessed by relevantly justified moral standards. There is no reason to expect that the theories would identify the same property as the key property of both epistemic and moral standards. The different kinds of normative standards need to be considered one at a time.

I assume, moreover, that there may be certain kinds of standards that lack any relevant justification. This would mean that all paradigmatic type-two claims of those kinds are false. Indeed, I suspect that aesthetic standards may lack relevant justification. If so, then paradigmatic normative aesthetic claims are false, unless they are construed as type-one normative rather than as type-two normative.

Any theory about the justification conditions of a kind of standard would rest ultimately on standards regarding philosophical theory and argument. This may seem to show, once again, that we face a climb up an infinite hierarchy of justification, for our standards regarding theories and arguments could, of course, be assessed themselves, at least in principle. But we generally assume that they are justified. Our theorizing must end at some point. We stop climbing at the point where we think we can see far enough, the point at which we stop asking for more in the way of justification.

We also sidestep the climb by changing direction. In the moral case, we present a theory as to the justification conditions of moral standards, in effect proposing a standard that the original standards must meet in order to qualify as justified, and then we defend the theory by invoking general epistemological and philosophical criteria. We do not embark on an infinite program of defending standards in terms of meta-standards. Rather, we propose a meta-standard for the evaluation of moral standards. Then, rather than going on to propose a meta-meta-standard, which would not be to the point, we proceed to evaluate the theory in which the meta-standard is proposed by invoking standards that apply to philosophical theories in general.

Perhaps it will be objected that, for all we know, these standards are not justified. If we stop theorizing before we know that they are justified, then, perhaps, we are not justified in holding that any standards of any kind are justified. Notice, however, that this objection is epistemological rather than metaphysical. The regress arguments I have been discussing in this chapter concern the metaphysical issues of whether there are any justified standards and whether there are any true normative propositions. I have not been concerned with epistemological issues as such. Moreover, the objection does not raise a special problem for the standard-based theory. *Any* account of our theorizing must concede that we stop theorizing before we have addressed every question that can be raised. I see no reason to accept an epistemic standard to the effect that our beliefs are unjustified if we have left any stones unturned.

Normative Skepticism

If the program I have just described is tenable, then we may be able to argue against the most general form of normative skepticism. If there is a defensible theory of the justification conditions of some kind of standard K, then that theory argues against normative skepticism, for normative skepticism views *all* standards as quite without justification. Nevertheless, if normative skepticism were seriously on the agenda, no argument against it could be entirely satisfactory, for argument involves appeal to *some* standards, even if only the usual standards that call for coherence and consistency in argument. Hence, it is arguable that any such response to normative skepticism would be question-begging. If so, then it may not be possible to answer normative skepticism.

But this explanation of why it may not be possible to answer normative skepticism gives us no reason to accept normative skepticism. On the contrary, it suggests that an attempt to defeat normative skepticism would be an instance of the sort of enterprise Otto Neurath warned philosophers against when he urged us to remember that a sailor cannot rebuild her entire boat all at once while at sea.[8]

Furthermore, the only reason we have been given to accept normative skepticism is the basic regress argument. I have argued that the regress is not vicious. Moreover, as I shall now argue, no argument can consistently be viewed as justifying normative skepticism, if the argument is also believed to be sound. Normative skepticism is untenable.

It would be incoherent to hold that the belief in normative skepticism is justified on the basis of any argument, including the basic regress argument. For if the belief that no standard is justified is justified, then, since all justification is relative to some justified standard, it follows that the belief that no belief is justified is justified. Hence, the belief is justified that it is *not* the case that the belief in normative skepticism is justified. That is, anyone who holds that the belief in normative skepticism is justified is committed to holding that he would be justified in holding that it is not the case that the belief in normative skepticism is justified. This is a logically consistent position, but it is hardly coherent. It is akin to believing something even though one believes one would be justified in thinking it to be false. In this case, the initial belief *commits* one to believing that it *itself* is justifiably taken to be false.

Worse, it would be *inconsistent* for a normative skeptic—one who believes normative skepticism to be true—to hold that this belief is justified, for her skepticism entails that nothing is justified. There may be a valid argument from true premises that proves normative skepticism to be true. But the claim that

8. Neurath, 1959, p. 201.

such an argument would *justify belief* in normative skepticism is not one that a normative skeptic can take to be true, for it is a normative proposition which implies that some epistemic standard is justified.

This means as well that *no one* can consistently hold that the belief in normative skepticism is justified unless he avoids being committed to normative skepticism. Anyone who is committed to normative skepticism is committed to denying that the belief in normative skepticism is justified. Paradoxically, if one thinks that an argument proves normative skepticism to be true, he cannot consistently hold that the argument justifies belief in normative skepticism.

Nevertheless, it does not follow from any of this that it is incoherent for a *non-skeptic* to believe that the truth of normative skepticism is given some support by an argument. But this cannot give any comfort to the skeptic. For even if we cannot answer the skeptic without begging the question against her, we may be able to satisfy ourselves that normative skepticism can responsibly be ignored, if we can satisfy ourselves that its truth is not a serious possibility or that it is not a doctrine that can coherently be accepted.

The skeptic is in an untenable position. I have already argued that she cannot consistently accept that her skepticism has any justification. Her skepticism implies that no standard has any justification, and so it implies that no standard can underwrite the assessment of any belief as having any justification. Skepticism therefore implies that the belief in normative skepticism has no justification, and that any other position about the justification of standards would be equally justified or cogent. There is therefore no rational basis for choice between normative skepticism and its contrary. Hence, the normative skeptic cannot coherently hold that there is any reason to accept skepticism rather than its contrary.

In addition, it is inconsistent for a normative skeptic to be committed to anything, or even to have a belief in her own self-worth. A person must employ standards in deciding what to believe, what to do, and how to live. Standards of action and belief shape a person's evaluation of situations and of her available responses to them. A skeptic could consistently *make use* of standards, of course, but to be consistent, she could not believe that any of her standards have any *justification*. To be consistent, she would have to think that no belief she has, no action she performs, and nothing she values is supported by any standard with any cogency or basis and that any other belief or action or value could be equally well chosen. A skeptic could, of course, stubbornly subscribe to certain standards. But she cannot consistently be committed to anything in a sense that involves holding that the things to which one is committed have a privileged status that does not amount simply to their being stubbornly adhered to. And she cannot consistently believe that she or anyone else is worthy of respect.

Nothing I have said shows that normative skepticism is *false*. But I have argued that one cannot consistently believe it to be true while holding this belief to be justified. And one cannot consistently believe that there is an argument that both proves it to be true and justifies the belief that it is true. Nor can one consistently hold it while holding that it is supported by better reasons than its contrary. Nor can one consistently affirm it while having commitments and a belief in one's self-worth. For these reasons, although I have tried to take normative skepticism seriously, my conclusion is that it is not seriously on the agenda. It can safely be ignored in what follows.

One upshot of this reasoning is, I believe, that the rejection of normative skepticism is a precondition for any coherent thinking at all. A further upshot is that a normative skeptic cannot coherently think that the basic regress argument gives her any reason to reject the program I described in the previous section—the program for supporting a theory of the justification of moral standards. One can only think this coherently if one rejects normative skepticism. But if we reject normative skepticism, and if the philosophical standards that appear most plausible to us do in fact support a theory about the justification conditions of moral standards, then the regress can give us no reason to reject the theory. The fact that our philosophical standards have a place in an infinite hierarchy of standards is not sufficient to show that they lack justification.

Moral Skepticism

This book is about the justification conditions of moral standards. It is not concerned with explaining the justification of the most basic standards of thought and action, such as standards of consistency and coherence and non-moral standards of rational choice. A moral skeptic need not be a skeptic about the standards of epistemology, induction, logic, or rational choice. She may hold that the basic standards of thought and action are relevantly justified. She merely holds that no *moral* standard is relevantly justified.

In the remainder of this book, I shall assume that the only standards whose justification is in question are moral standards. I will feel free to rely on standards of logic, epistemology, and rational choice. And, of course, I will rely on generally accepted standards of philosophical theory and argument.

For methodological reasons, I shall proceed as though one major issue we face is whether moral skepticism is true. My reason for doing this is not that I think there is a good argument for moral skepticism, although I am convinced there are interesting arguments. Rather, we are attempting to develop a theory as to the conditions under which moral standards are justified, and one such theory is that there are *no* conditions under which any moral standard would be justified.

One might object that the project of finding an account of the justification conditions of moral standards is illicit because there is no "external standpoint" from which to evaluate moral standards. P. F. Strawson said, for example, that "the general structure or web of human attitudes and feelings" involved in our moral responses to the world of human behavior "is something we are given with the fact of human society. As a whole, it neither calls for, nor permits, an external 'rational' justification"; "questions of justification are internal to [it]."[9]

I agree, of course, that we cannot take up a standpoint that is external to *all*

---

9. Strawson, 1974a, p. 23.

of our beliefs. Yet the issue here is merely whether we can take up a standpoint that is external to our *moral* views, in the sense that we do not use any moral standards in evaluating moral standards. It seems to me that we can do this. We can evaluate legal standards without making use of any legal standards. We can evaluate the rules of baseball without arguing in terms of any of the rules of baseball. A skeptic about the existence of God can coherently demand an argument that does not rely on any theological proposition that presupposes the existence of God. A skeptic about psychic research can similarly ask for an external justification of claims about psychic phenomena. The kind of justification of moral standards that is required is not one that would be external in any extraordinary sense. It is simply a justification that is not question-begging, one that does not presuppose that any moral standards are justified.

In the next chapter, then, I discuss a variety of theories that can be construed as purporting to supply relevantly fundamental external justifications of moral standards. Each of them can be viewed as implying a theory as to the conditions under which a moral standard would be justified.

4

Theories of
Moral Justification

The standard-based theory leaves us with two central questions: First, under what conditions would a moral standard qualify as justified? And second, what is common to the content of moral propositions in virtue of which any moral proposition entails that some moral standard is justified?[1] A theory of the content and truth conditions of moral propositions should enable us to answer both questions. The philosophically interesting thing about moral propositions is that their truth depends on the existence of relevantly justified standards, and the central philosophical problem in explaining their truth conditions is to explain the conditions under which a moral standard would be justified.

We can distinguish two kinds of strategies that we could follow in attempting to answer these two questions. A *proposition-oriented* strategy would aim to provide an account of the content and truth conditions of moral propositions without invoking or using the idea of a justified standard or an account of the justification conditions of moral standards. It would aim to derive an account of the justification conditions of moral standards from the theory of moral propositions. A *standard-oriented* strategy, by contrast, would aim directly to provide an account of the conditions under which a moral standard would be justified and to use the standard-based theory to build a theory of the content and truth conditions of moral propositions out of the theory of justification conditions for moral standards. I will argue that only a standard-oriented theory would provide adequate answers to my two questions.

I will distinguish two main kinds of standard-oriented theories: reductionist theories and non-reductionist theories. I will argue that only a certain kind of reductionist theory, a practical theory, would provide adequate answers to the two questions. Yet, I will argue that the familiar practical theories are unsuccessful.

1. Recall that the entailment at issue is a *nontrivial* entailment of *paradigmatic* moral propositions. I often delete these qualifications. I use the term "entail" such that *p* "entails" *q* if it is logically or metaphysically necessary that if *p* then *q*.

50

My purpose in this chapter is not, of course, to refute every alternative to society-centered theory. It is simply to raise certain problems and to begin to motivate the society-centered approach.

Proposition-Oriented Theories

Since the standard-based theory is not widely accepted, few meta-ethical theories explicitly address the justification of standards.[2] But I am not going to classify as proposition oriented every theory that fails explicitly to propose an account of the justification of moral standards. Some such theories are more plausible or interesting if viewed as standard oriented than as proposition oriented.

One example is the divine command theory. It is best construed as standard oriented because the idea it suggests, that a moral standard is justified just in case God has commanded that humans comply with it, is of sufficient interest in its own right that it could reasonably be proposed as a theory of the justification of moral standards. My classification of the divine command theory as standard oriented illustrates my policy of classification: I will classify a theory as standard oriented if the account it implies of the justification conditions of moral standards can be independently motivated or is sufficiently interesting or plausible to be worth evaluating in its own right.

Given the standard-based theory, *any* account of the truth conditions of moral propositions implies *some* account of the justification conditions of moral standards. In a proposition-oriented (PO) theory, however, this implied account would have little or no plausibility or interest if it were not for the fact that it is implied by the theory's account of moral propositions together with the standard-based theory. This explains why theories I classify as PO cannot provide adequate answers to our two questions. A PO theory's answer to the first question is derivative from the theory's account of the content and truth conditions of moral propositions and is therefore unlikely to have any independent plausibility. Moreover, a PO theory cannot adequately answer the second question, for, in explaining the truth conditions or content of moral propositions, a PO theory makes no use of the notion of a justified standard and no use of an account of the justification conditions of moral standards. Because of this, it cannot make transparent why moral propositions entail the existence of a justified moral standard. The underlying point is that, given the standard-based theory, a moral theory cannot adequately motivate and defend its account of the truth conditions of moral propositions unless it makes clear why any such proposition entails the existence of a justified standard, and unless it also can motivate the account it implies of the conditions under which a moral standard would be justified. The PO theories do neither.

These criticisms do not turn on whether a PO theory is *naturalistic* or *nonnaturalistic*, but it may nevertheless be useful to consider theories of both kinds.

2. Exceptions include Brandt, 1979, and Gert, 1988.

I shall assume that *naturalism* is the view that moral propositions are *empirical*; that is, moral propositions are knowable (by humans) only a posteriori, or through experience.[3] It follows that moral facts are empirical, for a fact is simply a true proposition. And it follows that moral properties are empirical in the sense that propositions which entail that a moral property is instantiated are empirical.

One example of a naturalistic PO theory is a simple utilitarian theory, according to which the moral property of being right is the property of being such as to maximize overall happiness.[4] Assuming that relevant propositions regarding the maximization of happiness are empirical, the result is a naturalistic PO theory. Alternatively, a naturalist could identify moral properties with corresponding tendencies of objects to elicit appropriate moral responses from people under ideal conditions for judgment.[5] Or a naturalist could simply claim that moral properties and moral propositions are empirical, without attempting to identify the moral properties or facts in any other terms. For naturalism does not require that moral propositions be reducible in any sense to propositions of any other kind, such as propositions of the natural or social sciences.[6]

Non-naturalistic PO theories hold that moral propositions are not empirical, that they are a priori.[7] For example, G. E. Moore viewed moral judgment as involving claims about the moral property of goodness, which, he claimed, is not an empirical property.[8] Following Moore, then, one might hold that the most basic moral propositions are a priori, and that any other true moral propositions are implied by the most basic ones, given relevant empirical data.[9]

I have basically the same objections to both naturalistic and non-naturalistic PO theories: First, a PO theory does not adequately explain why a moral standard would qualify as justified in circumstances where the theory implies that it would qualify as justified. Second, a PO theory does not adequately explain the fact that any (paradigmatic) moral proposition entails that a moral stan-

---

3. Kant, 1781, Introduction, B2–3; Bradley and Swartz, 1979, p. 150.

4. See Railton, 1986a, for a theory basically of this kind.

5. Compare Brower's "dispositional ethical realism" (1993).

6. There are a variety of possible views. Moral facts and properties could be held to be identical to, to be "constituted" by, or to "supervene" on, "organized combinations of natural and social scientific facts and properties" (Brink, 1989, p. 159). Brink discusses the notions of "constitution" and "supervenience." For a discussion of reduction, see Sturgeon, 1985. Among contemporary naturalists are Nicholas Sturgeon (1985), Peter Railton (1986a), Richard N. Boyd (1988), and David Brink (1989). I have discussed some recent forms of naturalistic realism (Copp, 1990a and 1991c).

7. A theory might also be counted as non-naturalistic if it postulated special faculties of moral experience or perception, or special principles of moral justification. A view of this kind would deny that moral epistemology is continuous with the epistemology of ordinary empirical propositions.

8. Moore, 1903. Moore held that the moral content of a moral proposition is the statement it entails about what things are intrinsically good (pp. 5–6), and he held that any proposition to the effect that something is intrinsically good is self-evident, if true (p. ix; also pp. viii–ix, and 148). Our knowledge as to the things that are intrinsically good depends on the a priori "method of absolute isolation" (pp. 187–89).

9. See Moore, 1903, pp. 187–89, 21–27, especially p. 25.

dard is justified. In effect, my objection is that PO theories are unable to explain the normative nature of moral propositions because they do not explain the content of moral propositions in a way that uses the notion of a justified moral standard.

For example, the conjunction of the simple utilitarian theory and the standard-based account of normativity implies that if an action would maximize the overall happiness, then a moral standard that requires the action is justified. It is quite obscure how this could be an *entailment*, however, for the idea of a justified standard is not "contained" in the idea of maximizing happiness. The entailment needs to be explained. In general, in conjunction with the standard-based theory, naturalistic theories imply that moral propositions, which they view as straightforwardly empirical, entail nontrivially that a moral standard is justified. However, the theories do not explain the content of these propositions in a way that uses the idea of a justified moral standard. They therefore leave it quite opaque how a moral proposition could entail nontrivially anything about a moral standard. The only available explanation within a PO theory would be that the propositions in question are *moral* propositions, such as the proposition that some action is *right*. But this merely moves us back one step. The problem simply reappears as the problem of explaining how a proposition could *be* the proposition that some action is right, given that the latter entails that the action is called for by a justified moral standard, unless its content contains the idea that the action is called for by a justified moral standard. One might reply that the standard-based theory of normative judgment explains the entailment. But the standard-based theory is simply the theory that there *is* this entailment, so one cannot *explain* the entailment by citing the theory. In effect, my objection is that a naturalistic theory of this sort makes it quite opaque how it could be that the standard-based theory is true.

Nothing in what I have said argues against a naturalistic *standard-oriented* theory, according to which the obtaining of an empirical fact would imply that a given moral standard is justified and that a corresponding moral claim is true.[10] Such a theory would explain what the justification of a standard consists in, and this would enable it to explain how an empirical fact could imply that a standard is justified.[11] It would construe (paradigmatic) moral propositions as propositions partly to the effect that a relevant moral standard is justified, and it would explain in this way why a moral proposition entails that some corresponding moral standard is justified. My argument is that there is a need to defend a theory of the justification conditions of moral standards and to use it in giving an account of the truth conditions of moral propositions. I am not arguing against naturalism.

The same problems arise for non-naturalistic PO views. In Moore's account, for example, goodness is treated as metaphysically simple.[12] Given the standard-based theory, the proposition that friendship is good entails that some moral

---

10. The theory developed by Brandt in 1979 and 1985 is of this sort, for example.
11. See Brandt, 1979 and 1985. I point this out, in effect, in Copp, 1990a, pp. 257–58.
12. Moore, 1903, pp. 5–9.

standard is appropriately justified. But Moore's theory cannot explain how friendship's having the quite simple property of being good could entail (nontrivially) a proposition to the effect that there is a relevant justified moral standard.

In summary, then, the problem with PO theories is that, given the standard-based theory and given that their accounts of the justification of standards are entirely derivative, they are committed to what we might call *brute entailments*, non-logical entailments that lack any explanation.[13] They are committed either to rejecting the standard-based theory or to acknowledging that the entailment of a justified moral standard by a moral proposition is brute. It might be replied that there are other brute entailments. For example, the fact that my shirt is blue all over entails that it is not red all over, and this may seem to be a brute entailment.[14] Yet there may be some explanation for this entailment, and it surely would be desirable to have an explanation for it.

Standard-Oriented Theories

Standard-oriented (SO) theories begin with the problem of explaining the justification of moral standards and derive from their solution to this problem an account of the truth conditions or content of moral propositions. Call a theory's thesis regarding the justification of moral standards its "*J* thesis." The *J* thesis specifies a property, the "*J* property," and proposes that all and only justified moral standards have this property. It claims (1) that it is possible for a moral standard to have property *J* and (2) that property *J* is identical to, or at least necessarily coextensive with, the property of being justified, the property a moral standard must have if corresponding moral propositions are true.[15]

It is perhaps worth mentioning that there are, of course, certain principles that we take to be unquestionably justified, such as standards that prohibit the torture of children just for fun. We may even take these standards to be "necessarily" justified or "self-evidently" justified in some sense. But an SO theory must propose a *J* property for moral standards. Even if it is true that certain moral standards are self-evidently or necessarily justified, to assert this is not to specify a *J* property. It does not help us to understand what the status of being justified consists in. It does not begin to address the two central meta-ethical questions that I posed at the beginning of the chapter.

I distinguish between reductionist and non-reductionist SO theories. *Reductionist* theories attempt to account for the justification of moral standards by invoking standards of some other kind *K*, thereby reducing the problem of explaining the justification of moral standards to that of explaining the justification

---

13. They are non-logical in that they are not explained by the logical form of the propositions. For example, that the entailment between a conjunction and a conjunct is explained by the logic of conjunction.

14. I owe the example to Jeffrey C. King.

15. A proposition and a moral standard "correspond" to one another just in case the proposition entails that the standard is relevantly justified.

of standards of kind *K*. That is, they specify a *J* property that relates moral standards that have it to standards of some other kind *K*. In nearly every case, these standards are standards of rational choice or practical reason. *Non-reductionist* theories attempt to explain the justification of moral standards in some other way.

Reductionist theories do not (in their own right) explain the conditions under which the *K* standards that they invoke count as justified. Because of this, it may seem that a non-reductionist theory would be preferable to a reductionist theory. Yet this difference is only skin deep. In the first place, a reductionist theory could be *accompanied* by a non-reductionist theory of standards of the kind *K*. Second, theories of both kinds leave many things unexplained, some of which they use in explaining the justification of moral standards. Reductionist theories happen to invoke standards of some kind *K* without explaining their justification, but non-reductionist theories invoke other things without explaining them. Finally, of course, theories of both kinds would be *defended* by invoking epistemic standards or standards of theoretical virtue,[16] and neither kind of theory explains (in its own right) the justification of *these* standards. It is not the case that reductionist theories by their nature lead to a more complex, problematic, or incomplete overall philosophical position than do non-reductionist theories.

There are, of course, many different kinds of standards. One might explore the different kinds, asking in each case whether standards of that kind can be relevantly justified. In some cases, a skeptical position might seem quite plausible. For example, the rule of etiquette that an invitation expressed in the third person must be answered in the third person seems arbitrary. In the case of epistemic standards, however, skepticism seems implausible. In some cases where skepticism seems out of the question, a reductionist approach to justification may seem the more promising. For example, given the existence of conventional ways of giving offense, certain standards of etiquette may be justified by invoking moral considerations in a reductionist theory. In other cases, a non-reductionist approach may seem the more promising. For example, it may seem that standards of rational choice must be fundamental and therefore could not plausibly be viewed as resting on standards of some other kind.[17]

There are cases in which the choice between non-reductionist and reductionist strategies is problematic. For example, one might think that epistemic standards are just as fundamental as standards of rational choice. Yet some philosophers have attempted to explain the justification of epistemic standards by invoking rational choice. Keith Lehrer defines a notion of "epistemic utility" in terms of the epistemic objectives of avoiding error and reaching truth.[18] Using

16. One example is a standard according to which simplicity is to be preferred in theories.

17. There may be a way in which standards of practical reason can be used to evaluate themselves. David Gauthier (1986) argues that the theory that rationality consists in straightforwardly maximizing one's own welfare both undermines itself and supports a conception of rationality as "constrained maximization." Derek Parfit investigates how criteria of reason might be "indirectly self-defeating" (1984, part 1).

18. Lehrer attributes the idea that these are our epistemic objectives to Roderick Chisholm and William James (1977, p 20). See also Hempel, 1979, p. 58; Lehrer, 1974, p. 207; 1977, p. 22. For a similar approach, see Kitcher, 1992, esp. pp. 102–3.

Lehrer's notion, one might then propose that an epistemic standard is relevantly justified (in given conditions, for a given population) just in case compliance with it has a positive expected epistemic utility (in those conditions, for that population). The idea is that justified epistemic standards are those that it would be *rational* to comply with in seeking epistemic goals.

The choice between non-reductionist and reductionist strategies in moral theory seems equally problematic as in normative epistemology. On the one hand, moral standards may seem quite fundamental, and it may even seem misguided to attempt to reduce the authority of moral standards to that of standards of reason. On the other hand, reductionist theories are among the most familiar and venerable in that they include Kantian and Aristotelian strategies, as well as more recent strategies that invoke the widely accepted view of rational choice as a matter of maximizing individual utility. I will begin my discussion with non-reductionist theories.

Non-Reductionist Theories

As we saw, the central problem with PO theories is that they are unable to explain why moral propositions entail the existence of a justified moral standard. The central problem for non-reductionist SO theories is similar. It is to explain why a moral standard would qualify as justified if it had the property that the theory proposes as the *J* property for moral standards.

Consider the divine command theory. I do not want to discuss it at any length, for I think it is dubious that there is a God. But the theory does illustrate my worry about non-reductionist theories. It says that a moral standard is justified just in case God has commanded that humans comply with it; that is, the *J* property for moral standards is the property a standard may have of being such that God has commanded that humans comply with it. The problem is to explain why a standard with this property should be thought to qualify as justified. Perhaps it will be said that God is morally good, of necessity, and a morally good God would not command our compliance with a standard unless it were justified. But this answer simply moves the problem back one step, for God's moral goodness is a matter of God's satisfying certain justified moral standards. The theory needs to specify the *J* property for these standards and to explain why a standard with this property should be thought to qualify as justified.

For a second example, consider a version of ideal moral code utilitarianism. It says that a moral standard is justified just in case its currency in society would maximize the general happiness. The central problem again is this: Why should we suppose that the fact that a standard is such that its currency would maximize the general happiness means that the standard is justified? Why should we suppose that a necessary condition of the truth of a moral proposition is that the standard that it entails to be justified be such that its currency would maximize the general happiness?

A third example is a coherence theory of moral justification. A coherence theory of moral *truth* would assert that a moral proposition is true just in case it would be part of a "wide reflective equilibrium" (WRE).[19] This would be a PO theory. A coherence theory of the justification of moral *standards* would be a standard-oriented theory. It would assert that a moral standard qualifies as justified (in relation to a person) just in case it is a member of a coherent and mutually supporting set of beliefs and standards, all the members of which would be subscribed to (by the person) in a wide reflective equilibrium. Let me call this form of coherentism "the WRE theory."

"Wide reflective equilibrium" refers to a hypothetical state of mind in which (1) the person at issue is reflective, qualified to judge the moral standards to which he subscribes, and confident in his acceptance of them. In addition, (2) those standards form a consistent and coherent system such that less general standards can be derived from more general ones, together with empirical or other beliefs held by the person, and, more generally, the standards are mutually supporting and explanatory. Finally, (3) the social-scientific theories accepted by the person, as well as his theories concerning the metaphysics of the person and the like, are part of the system of beliefs and standards mentioned here previously, and they play a substantive role in the justification he would give of the moral standards to which he subscribes.[20]

I think the WRE theory is quite implausible. First, it is not plausible that acceptance of a standard (by a person) in WRE is necessary for it to qualify as justified (for the person). Given the standard-based theory, this would mean that the proposition expressed (relative to a person) by, say, "slavery is wrong" is true only if a corresponding prohibition on slavery would be accepted (by the person) in WRE. But whether such a prohibition would be accepted in WRE depends at least in part on contingent psychological details (about the person) that seem to have no bearing at all on whether, for example, the slavery practiced in nineteenth-century America was morally wrong. Second, it is not plausible that acceptance in WRE is sufficient to qualify a standard as justified, for whether a standard would be accepted in WRE depends again on psychological contingencies. Suppose, for example, that a Nietzschean accepts a moral standard that calls for ruthlessness of the sort exhibited by Stalin, and suppose that he would continue to accept this standard in WRE. The WRE theory implies that the standard is therefore justified relative to the Nietzschean even if widespread compliance with it would lead to social disharmony and war. It commits us to holding that the consequences of compliance with a standard are not relevant to its justification except, perhaps, relative to a person whose overall system of belief in WRE includes a belief about the relevance of conse-

---

19. Brink discusses coherence theories of moral truth (1989, p. 307).

20. For purposes of classifying the WRE theory as reductionist or non-reductionist, it matters how WRE is explained. The theory would count as reductionist if it explained WRE by invoking epistemic standards, such as standards of coherence for a system of beliefs and standards, and standards of competence in judgment. It would count as non-reductionist if, as I have been assuming, it explained the notions of coherence and competence in non-normative terms, without making reference to any standards. The notion of reflective equilibrium was introduced in Rawls, 1971. Norman Daniels discusses "wide reflective equilibrium" (1979; 1980).

quences. This is implausible. It seems obvious that consequences are relevant even if the Nietzschean is in WRE and thinks they are not.

The central problem for the WRE theory is to explain why we should think a moral standard qualifies as justified (for a person) if it has the *J* property of being such as to be accepted (by the person) in WRE. One might invoke a coherentist epistemology in an attempt to explain this, but to do so would, in effect, convert the WRE theory into a reductionist theory. The resulting theory would explain the WRE theory's proposed *J* property for moral standards in terms of epistemic standards.

Nor would the explanation be plausible. The WRE theory is not supported by—and it certainly is not a corollary of—a general coherentist epistemology. A coherentist epistemology implies, roughly, that we are justified in a belief only if we would have the belief in WRE. According to this view, therefore, we would be justified in accepting the WRE theory only if we would believe it in WRE. But whether we would believe it in WRE depends on psychological contingencies. The background coherentism gives us no reason to think we would accept the WRE theory in WRE. It may be that the beliefs we would accept in WRE would be the ones that we would then take to be best supported by arguments and evidence. But this still leaves us looking for an argument for the WRE theory. In short, even if our general epistemology is coherentist, this has no role to play in supporting the WRE theory.

In conclusion, I am not aware of a non-reductionist theory that provides an adequate explanation of the *J* property it proposes. I do not have a conclusive argument to show there is no such theory, but I am inclined nevertheless to turn to reductionist theories. In chapter 6, I will briefly discuss a non-reductionist society-centered theory.

Reductionist Theories

The reductionist theories I will discuss are among the historically most important theories of morality. I call them practical theories because they make use of a conception of "practical reason" in defining the *J* property for moral standards.[21]

The *J* thesis of a practical theory takes the following form: A moral code or standard qualifies as relevantly justified (relative to a given group of people) just in case a specified choice relating to the code or standard would be rationally made (by relevant agents, given the group at issue). Some theories of this kind are relativistic, in that the *J* property they propose is actually a relation between moral standards or codes and persons or groups of persons. Relativistic theories give rise to issues about the truth conditions of moral propositions,

---

21. Alan Gewirth's attempt to ground the existence of rights in an argument that invokes standards of consistency could perhaps be classified as an example of a non-practical reductionist theory. See Gewirth, 1978, e.g., pp. 26, 109. The WRE theory could also count as a non-practical reductionist theory, depending on how WRE is explained.

but I will set them aside until chapter 11. Kantian and Aristotelian theories are practical theories that are not relativistic.

One familiar theory of rational choice holds that rationality is a matter of maximizing one's expected "utility." There are competing theories of rational choice, however, including the needs-and-values theory that I propose in chapter 9. Each theory should be viewed as proposing a standard for choice and as claiming that the standard is relevantly justified. The expected utility theory, for example, proposes that the unique relevantly justified standard of rational choice is one that requires agents to maximize their expected utility.

A practical theory must, of course, employ a theory of rational choice that is *morally neutral* in that it does not directly entail or presuppose moral reasons. There are moral reasons only if there are justified moral standards, and our account of the justification conditions of moral standards would not be explanatory if it rested on a theory that *presupposed* that there are justified moral standards. Of course, if there are moral reasons, then any morally neutral theory of rational choice is incomplete. But this is no objection to practical theories, for an account of *nonmoral* reasons does not pretend to be comprehensive of *all* reasons. It is enough if it is correct as an account of reasons of a well-identified kind.[22] In chapter 9, I characterize the kind of reasons at issue in practical theories as "self-grounded" reasons, reasons grounded in the concerns or nature of the agent.

I will not attempt here to evaluate theories of practical reason in abstraction from the practical theories in which they are used. Rather, I will evaluate each practical theory as a whole, on the basis of its account of the justification conditions of moral standards. I will categorize practical theories as instrumental theories, Kantian theories, and Aristotelian theories. I can discuss these approaches in only a cursory manner.

Instrumental Theories

"Instrumental" moral theories are so-called because they use an instrumental theory of rational choice. They share the fundamental idea that rationality is a matter of the efficient pursuit of a good. They add two restrictions to this idea: First, reason is relative, in that the good pursued by a rational person is the good from his own standpoint. And second, reason is subjective, in that what is good from a person's standpoint is determined by facts about his own psychology, typically his desires. In short, an instrumental theory of rational choice asserts that a person's action is rational if and only if it is the best choice in the circumstances, given the presumed goal to realize the good from his standpoint. One such theory is the theory of expected utility maximization, which I mentioned previously.

An instrumental theory must specify which psychological facts about a per-

22. Similarly, a theory of epistemic reasons does not pretend to be comprehensive of all possible reasons for belief. There can be prudential and moral reasons for believing certain things as well as epistemic reasons.

son determine what counts as good for her. One option is to say that a person's good is determined by what would most contribute to her satisfying her desires; a second is to say that a person's good is a function of what would give her pleasure or happiness. It should be noted that an instrumental theory is not committed to holding that rationality consists in pursuing one's own good at the expense of other people. For example, the desire-satisfaction version can take into account desires that a person may have for the good of others.

The simplest type of instrumental moral theory is based on the conception of a moral code as a personal code to which a person would give a specific role in her life. According to one theory of this kind, for example, a moral code is justified for a person if, with complete information, she would decide to accept the way of life she would lead if she were to live in full compliance with it.[23] However, theories of this kind, *personal role theories*, blur the distinction between moral codes and merely personal codes, such as a code calling simply for daily exercise and personal hygiene. It would be more appropriate to conceive of moral codes as codes that are to play a role in a person's society as a whole. This conception lies behind *social role theories*.

Richard Brandt has proposed, for example, that a moral code is justified, in relation to a person, if and only if it is the moral code, the currency of which in his society he would tend to support in preference to all others or to none at all, if he expected to spend a lifetime in that society, and if he were "fully rational."[24] Brandt argues that no moral code would be suitable in all societies, and consequently that no code would rationally be supported for all societies.[25] As a "simplifying first approximation," he suggests that all fully rational persons would tend to support the same moral code for a given society. Yet, the underlying structure of the theory is relativistic.[26]

Social role theories face a coordination problem, for the justification of a moral code relative to a given person is assessed without taking into account the nature of the moral codes, if any, that are justified relative to other people in the society. It is possible that different moral codes would be justified relative to different fully rational persons, even in relation to one society. And it could be that one person's subscribing to her code and another person's subscribing to his would lead to conflict between them in situations where people who shared either code would be able to cooperate successfully. Each would be worse off, if each subscribed to the code that Brandt's account would imply to be justified in relation to him, than each would be if both subscribed to the same code, either to one of their codes or to some compromise code. Therefore, they will not succeed in avoiding the situation they are both rational to prefer to avoid, in which they subscribe to different codes, unless at least one of them subscribes to a code that, according to the theory, is not justified in

23. This view is suggested by remarks by R. M. Hare (1952, p. 69).
24. Brandt, 1979, pp. 182–95, esp. 185, 188, 190, 192, 194.
25. Brandt, 1979, pp. 179–82, 192.
26. Brandt, 1979, p. 188. Brandt argues that all fully rational persons would support a "happiness-maximizing moral system," but he admits "the assumptions that lead to this conclusion are not quite realistic" (1979, p. 220).

relation to him. An acceptable theory would not lead to coordination problems of this kind.

One might reply that if we made realistic assumptions about people's psychologies, such as that people share a significant set of desires and interests,[27] then it might turn out that every person in a given society would be rational to support the same moral code. Yet even if this were correct, it would not alter the logic of Brandt's theory. The objection from the coordination problem is an objection to the underlying account of justification conditions. Social role theories cannot avoid the objection, given their nature and the nature of instrumental theories of reason.[28]

People have conflicting needs and interests that would surely influence their preferences regarding morality. Other things being equal, the rich can be expected to prefer moral codes that glorify self-reliance; the poor, moralities that prescribe equality in the distribution of social benefits; men might prefer codes that provide them with a privileged place; women might prefer codes that yield them a privileged place. Given this, and given the coordination problem, it seems that each may be rational to prefer that there be a coordinated choice of some moral code for currency in society, rather than that each subscribe to the code he would be rational to support for currency. And this suggests that the relevantly justified code might plausibly be identified with a code that could be the object of a rational, coordinated choice involving everyone in the society.

Contractarian theories attempt to avoid the coordination problem essentially by arguing that *every* member of a group with the potential of beneficial cooperation would rationally agree to accept the same moral code, given the need to coordinate choice. They assume that unanimity is required to ensure that chosen standards are justified. Their fatal flaw is just below the surface. They are based on an instrumental theory of rational choice according to which the rational choice for a person is determined by the nature of his psychology. Bargaining does not change this fundamental fact, and so, unless a theory makes special assumptions about people's psychologies or about the circumstances of their hypothetical bargaining, it cannot guarantee that people who are rational by its lights would bargain to a common set of cooperative principles.

For this reason, contract theories are forced to use one or more of the following devices: First, the bargaining may be imagined to take place in an artificial circumstance, where the actual differences among people's psychologies cannot affect what they would be rational to choose; second, idealizing assumptions may be made about the psychology of the bargainers; third, special claims may be made about constraints on rational bargaining, or, fourth, the scope of the contracting group may be narrowed to exclude certain individuals from the contract. Every contractarian theory uses some such device and, because of this, they are subject to a variety of objections.

27. Recall David Hume's remarks about sympathy (1739, III-3-i, pp. 574–79).

28. Brandt might object that the moral codes I mentioned in my examples are not "causally feasible" and that this is why fully rational persons would not tend to support their currency (1979, p. 213). But the rationality of Alice's preferring a different code from Bill's code does not affect the feasibility of Bill's code. For further criticism of Brandt's theory, see Sturgeon, 1982.

Perhaps the most familiar theory to use devices of this kind is John Rawls's theory of justice, which uses the idea of bargaining in an "original position," behind a "veil of ignorance." Rawls holds that a hypothetical unanimous choice of principles of justice by rational people placed behind a "veil of ignorance" would contribute to the justification of the principles.[29] I shall generalize this approach beyond anything Rawls intended and treat the result as a comprehensive theory of moral justification.[30] According to the generalized "Rawlsian theory," a moral code is justified if and only if instrumentally rational persons in an original position behind a veil of ignorance would unanimously choose the code to serve as the public moral code in a well-ordered society.

Without the device of the veil of ignorance, different people in the original position might choose different moral principles. Rawls regards this fact as a reason for imposing the veil on the parties to the bargaining,[31] but the Rawlsian theory is only one of a family of similar theories. There is the Dictator theory, for example, which designates a dictator as the person whose choice determines which moral standards are justified. The Rawlsian theory is more plausible than the Dictator theory, but the reason why is not obvious. In the Rawlsian theory, the parties choose in ignorance both of their values and of certain empirical facts, knowledge of which would make a difference to what it would be rational for them to choose. Unanimous agreement is secured primarily because of the fact that people are deprived of relevant information. As a result, it is doubtful that the unanimity of the choice has any tendency to show that the moral standards that would be chosen behind the veil are justified.

Rawls argues that choice behind the veil is fair and that the information denied to people by the veil is morally irrelevant.[32] In the present context, however (although not perhaps in the context Rawls himself intended), it is circular to argue in this way. It is circular to argue from claims about fairness and moral irrelevance in the course of attempting to support a theory that supposedly, by specifying conditions under which a moral standard qualifies as justified, will settle issues about moral relevance and about what counts as fair.[33] Rawls also defends his approach on the grounds that it leads to principles that "characterize our considered judgements in reflective equilibrium."[34] Yet this claim leads away from the generalized Rawlsian theory to an underlying coherence theory of the

29. Rawls, 1971, e.g., pp. 11, 17, 118, 133.

30. Rawls does not himself view the argument from the original position as one that could be used to defend a "comprehensive moral position." See Rawls, 1985, pp. 245, 229–30. But I will discuss it in that guise, abstracting to begin with from Rawls's argument from reflective equilibrium. Rawls traces the device of the veil of ignorance to the Kantian idea that we are to regard "moral principles as legislation for a kingdom of ends" (1971, p. 252). I discuss it here rather than later, where I discuss Kantian theories, because Rawls builds his theory using an instrumental theory of reason.

31. Rawls, 1971, pp. 139–41.

32. Rawls, 1971, pp. 118–22, 136–45; also Rawls, 1975.

33. Rawls also links the veil to "ideals of the person," but since these are moral ideals, the same objection applies (although not perhaps in the context Rawls himself intended). See Rawls, 1993.

34. Rawls, 1971, p. 121.

justification of moral standards, and so it faces problems that I have already discussed.

Beginning with ideas of Thomas Hobbes, several philosophers have argued essentially as follows: There are limited resources in the world, relative to what people actually want. We sometimes want things that others also want, and this can lead to conflict among us. And we have insufficient sympathy for each other to eliminate all occasion for conflict. Were it not for our moral values, there would be more conflict and less mutually beneficial cooperation than there is in fact. Given these considerations, people have good reason to want a moral code to have currency in their society, a code that places restrictions on people's pursuit of their own advantage or that leads them to alter their conception of their own good, so that a greater degree of cooperation becomes possible.[35]

Bargaining theories propose that in a situation of this sort there may be a rational bargain that could be struck in principle among those who would be rational to prefer that some moral code have currency in society. Let us call these people the "bargainers" and the code that would emerge from rational bargaining in such a situation, if indeed any code would emerge, the "contractarian moral code." Each bargainer would be rational to prefer the currency of his "ideal code," the code whose currency would maximize his own good, but he may be rational to compromise. The contractarian moral code would be a rational compromise among the ideal moral codes of the different bargainers.

The contractarian code would be a code M with the following two properties: (1) Given that he cannot achieve the currency of his own ideal code in society, (a) each person (in a relevant group) would be rational to prefer a situation in which M enjoys currency in society to one in which no moral code has currency, (b) each person would be rational to agree to M's having currency, if enough other people were willing to agree to M's having currency, and (c) there is no code other than M that also has properties (a) and (b) and that each person would be rational to prefer to have currency instead of M. In addition, (2), each person would be rational to subscribe to M, provided a sufficient number of other people do likewise. A bargaining theory claims that a moral code is relevantly justified just in case it has these "contractarian properties."

David Gauthier proposes that a justified moral code must also have the property that the bargainers would be rational to comply with it.[36] But Gauthier's proposal links two skeptical challenges together: the denial that there are relevantly justified moral standards and the denial that it is (always) instrumentally rational to comply with justified moral standards. The former is moral skepticism of the kind I defined before. The latter is often expressed by the challenge, "Why be moral?" I think we do better to separate the two challenges. A theory of justification conditions would enable us to reply to the first, by showing that moral standards can be relevantly justified. We then ask whether it would be rational to comply with a relevantly justified moral standard. I think

35. Hobbes, 1651. See Kurt Baier, 1958, p. 151; J. L. Mackie, 1977, pp. 108, 111.

36. He says the contractarian code must be shown to be a set of rational constraints "on choice and action" (Gauthier, 1986, p. 17, also p. 158). Gauthier implicitly distinguishes the two contractarian properties (pp. 9, 118).

that separating the problems in this way respects the intuitions of the skeptic about compliance.[37] He can agree we have duties; he can agree there are justified standards. The issue for him is whether it is rational to comply. In short, a theory of justification conditions for moral standards is intended to answer skepticism about justified moral standards. It is not necessary that it deal with skepticism about compliance in the same breath.

Gauthier has developed a strikingly sophisticated bargaining theory. He argues that people would be rational to choose to become "constrained maximizers," which is to say, very roughly, that they would be rational to dispose themselves to comply with standards that have the two contractarian properties. Moreover, given the reasonable expectation of mutual benefit, he argues that there is a set of standards with both contractarian properties. The bargainers would be rational to dispose themselves to comply with these standards even if they had no antecedent moral preferences and no "tuistic" attachments or aversions to other people—even if they were nonmoral and "non-tuistic"—and even if they were bargaining outside society and so were not subject to the sanctions of an antecedently accepted social moral code. Gauthier claims that a moral standard is relevantly justified just in case it is defensible in this manner, as an object of hypothetical rational agreement.[38]

Instead of discussing Gauthier's theory in detail, I will develop three major objections. First is the relevance objection. Even if Gauthier is correct that there are some standards with the two contractarian properties, and even if he is correct that these standards qualify on this basis as justified, he needs to show that they qualify as relevantly justified *moral* standards. He must show that a standard has the contractarian properties just in case it is a justified moral standard.

There is some reason to think that standards with the contractarian properties may *not* be moral standards. Rational agents cooperate in order to benefit, and they are not disposed to enter schemes from which they do not expect to benefit. Given this, it can seem that a code of standards that emerged from bargaining would be, at best, a sophisticated extension to an instrumental theory of rational choice. For example, Gauthier says, the severely handicapped members of our society would be excluded from rational bargaining by the rest of us, and so would be excluded from the scope of the contractarian code.[39] But if the contractarian code is merely a code by which the strong cooperate to exploit the weak, it is irrelevant to our concerns.

In order to answer this objection, one would need a theory of the nature of moral codes, a theory of the sort I will develop in the next chapter. Gauthier does not have such a theory, but he does have a criterion that he uses in addressing the problem of relevance. He says that "our concern is to validate the conception of morality as a set of rational, *impartial* constraints on the pursuit

37. See Brink, 1989, p. 47.
38. Gauthier, 1986. I discuss Gauthier's theory in Copp, 1991a.
39. Gauthier, 1986, pp. 17, 18.

of individual interest."[40] Of course, he regards substantive moral judgments of fairness and impartiality as requiring justification. His official test of impartiality is a formal test that judges the impartiality of a principle on the basis of whether it would be an object of "Archimedean choice" behind a Rawlsian "veil of ignorance."[41] Impartiality is ensured because Archimedean choice is from behind a veil of ignorance, and Gauthier argues that a person reasoning in an ideal manner behind the veil would select exactly the contractarian code.

Unfortunately, Gauthier here faces a problem similar to the central problem faced by the generalized Rawlsian theory. He must explain why ideal reasoning behind the veil that he defines ensures the impartiality of the standards that would be chosen, given that different conceptions of the veil and of ideal reasoning are possible. Indeed, Gauthier has a different conception than Rawls does of how Archimedean choice should be understood. These different conceptions are not, presumably, equally good models of impartiality. So Gauthier needs to show that his conception of Archimedean choice is an adequate model of impartial choice and that the fact that a set of rational constraints would be an object of impartial choice, on his account of impartiality, is necessary and sufficient for the constraints to qualify as justified moral constraints.[42]

I maintain therefore that, in the absence of further argument, standards that have the contractarian properties should not be regarded as relevantly justified moral standards. It may be the case that there are standards that have the key contractarian properties and that would also be accepted from an Archimedean standpoint behind a veil of ignorance. But the standards represent a scheme that rational agents agree to for their own advantage. They seem to be standards of rational choice designed for subtle problems of strategic interaction rather than moral standards.

The second objection is that, given the instrumental view of reason on which bargaining theory is based, there may not be anything *rationally* defective in a moral code that fails to have the two contractarian properties. Bargaining theory would lose its interest and plausibility as a theory of moral justification if the bargainers could take into account their actual moral attitudes. For in an instrumental theory, one's actual attitudes affect what one is rational to choose, which means that if the bargainers could take into account their actual moral attitudes, their actual attitudes would affect their bargaining and thereby play a role in determining which standards qualify as justified. In effect, the content of the standards the bargainers actually accept would bias the result, by affecting the bargaining. To avoid this, the bargainers are assumed to be nonmoral.

40. Gauthier, 1986, p. 6, my emphasis. Gauthier recognizes that he must show the impartiality of a constraint on grounds independent of the considerations invoked in the contractarian argument about its rationality (pp. 95, 234). Gert also aims to explain morality as a system that would be "advocated by all impartial rational persons." See Gert, 1988, especially chapter 5 and p. 79.

41. Gauthier, 1986, pp. 235–36; see Rawls, 1971, pp. 17–22. Also, Gauthier, 1988, section 6.

42. The arguments he gives against the Rawlsian conception turn on substantive moral claims (Gauthier, 1986, pp. 245–54, esp. 254). They therefore cannot be used in this context.

They are also assumed to be non-tuistic in the sense explained before. The rationale for this assumption is given, in part, by the Kantian thesis "that morality makes demands on us that are and must be quite independent of any fellow-feelings we may have."[43] The contractarian strategy is to argue that the contractarian code would be agreed to by rational people even if they had no moral preferences and no tuistic attachments or aversions to other people.

Yet people do have moral attitudes and tuistic desires, and a standard instrumental theory would treat such attitudes and desires as relevant to evaluating the rationality of people's actual choices. Suppose then that a group of people accept and are deeply committed to a moral code M that does not have the two contractarian properties. Ex hypothesi, these people *would not* have been rational to dispose themselves to comply with M *if* they had not had any tuistic or moral motivations. Hence M is not justified, according to Gauthier's theory. Yet the underlying idea of bargaining theory is to evaluate moral codes from the perspective of each person on the basis of an instrumental theory of reason. And from this perspective, there is no defect in M. Certainly the people would be rational to comply with it, given their actual desires. There is no reason to think they would do as well or better, in relation to their actual preferences, if they were to be disposed to comply with the contractarian moral code instead.

Third, bargaining theory is "person-centered" in that it evaluates moral standards from the perspective of every (relevant) person in society, taken one at a time. These individuals must achieve a kind of rational unanimity in their attitude to a moral code, in order for it to qualify as justified. To put the point the other way around, anyone who would *not* be rational to choose the currency of a given code, according to an instrumental conception of reason, can veto its claim to qualify as justified. Looked at this way, bargaining theory is surely implausible. There is no reason to give the saintly, the foolish, and the evil an equal role in establishing the parameters of the moral code that is to qualify as justified in our shared society.

The three objections reveal a deep tension in the underlying strategy of bargaining theory. At root, it is the combination of a instrumental conception of reason with the person-centered demand for rational unanimity through bargaining that leads to the problems, and this combination is definitive of bargaining theories.

Kantian Theories

In the third part of the *Grounding of the Metaphysics of Morals*, Kant attempted to explain "the possibility of a categorical imperative."[44] He thought that he

---

43. Gauthier, 1986, pp. 238, 11. Gauthier has said in conversation that he would now like to avoid assuming non-tuism. This would not permit him to escape my criticism, however.

44. Kant, 1785, Ak 447. This section abbreviates Copp, 1992a. My interpretation of Kant owes a great deal to Henry Allison (1986) and Thomas E. Hill, Jr. (1985). I am indebted to Hill and Allison for helpful comments.

needed to explain this in order to show that morality is "something real, and not a chimerical idea without any truth."[45] A Kantian "imperative" is an authoritative or justified standard, one that delineates an actual requirement or prohibition.[46] As is well known, moreover, Kant held that moral imperatives are "categorical."[47] Hence Kant's problem, to explain the possibility of a categorical imperative, is to explain under what conditions a moral standard is in fact an imperative, or a justified standard.

Kant's solution to the problem is essentially that justified moral standards are standards with which anyone would comply who was *fully rational*. Kant argues that a standard that one is to do A in circumstances C is a (valid) categorical imperative just in case any person *would* (intend to) do A in C if she were fully rational and "affected" only by "purely rational incentives."[48] This thesis specifies a J property for moral standards: A justified moral standard is such that any fully rational person would comply with it if she were affected only by "purely rational incentives." The intuition underlying Kantian theories is, then, that immoral behavior is not fully rational, that the requirements of morality are requirements of reason.

This thesis can be defended as follows:[49] Let me refer to agents that are fully rational and affected only by purely rational incentives as "Kantian agents." Stipulate further that fully rational agents can distinguish justified from unjustified standards. Further, justified moral standards qualify as standards of practical reason; they govern choice. Now a "purely rational incentive" is a desire that any Kantian agent would have just in virtue of being rational.[50] It seems, then, that any *fully* rational agent who had only *purely* rational desires would intentionally conform to a standard only if it were a relevantly justified standard of practical reason. Furthermore, if a standard were a relevantly justified standard of practical reason, a Kantian agent who recognized it for what it is would intend to conform to it. It follows that a Kantian agent would intentionally comply with a moral standard only if it were a justified standard of practical reason. Such a standard would be a justified moral standard. Conversely, because a justified moral standard would be a justified standard of practical reason, a Kantian agent would intend to conform to it, to the extent possible. We can conclude that Kant's thesis is approximately correct. Any standard that qualifies as a moral standard is relevantly justified if and only if any Kantian agent would intend to conform to it (to the extent possible).

Unfortunately, this conclusion is not interesting unless we are provided with a substantive, independently plausible, and morally neutral conception of Kantian full rationality. If a Kantian fully rational agent is to be understood

45. Kant, 1785, Ak 445. See also Ak 444 and 402.
46. Kant, 1785, Ak 417.
47. They delineate requirements that are not conditional on any presupposed ends of the agent. They are not hypothetical imperatives. Kant, 1785, Ak 414–15 and 419.
48. Kant, 1785, Ak 449.
49. I did not see the possibility of defending it this way in Copp, 1992a.
50. Kant, 1785, Ak 415–16.

simply as an agent who would intend to conform to a standard (to the extent possible) if and only if it were a justified standard of practical reason, then Kant's thesis is a tautology. It is the thesis that (roughly) a moral standard is a justified standard of practical reason if and only if any agent who would intend to conform to a standard if and only if it were a justified standard of practical reason would intend to conform to it.

The central argument of the *Groundwork* is devoted, in effect, to giving content to the idea of Kantian full rationality.[51] We can think of Kant's *J* thesis as having two parts, corresponding to two questions we can ask: Which standards are moral standards? What is the *J* property, possession of which qualifies them as imperatives?[52] First, a standard qualifies as a moral standard just in case it is appropriately related to the Categorical Imperative, which says, in one formulation, "Act only according to that maxim whereby you can at the same time will that it should become a universal law."[53] Second, a moral standard is relevantly justified if and only if any fully rational agent would comply with it if she were affected only by purely rational incentives. The central argument of the *Groundwork* is devoted to showing that any standard appropriately related to the Categorical Imperative *would* be complied with by a Kantian agent. If successful, the argument would give content to the notion of a Kantian agent by showing that Kantian agents are such that, necessarily, they would comply with standards that are appropriately related to the Categorical Imperative.

There are two main steps in Kant's argument. First, if a person regards herself as rational, she must regard herself as having free will, and if she regards any other being as rational, she must also regard it as having free will; therefore, "from a practical point of view," every rational agent is free.[54] Second, a free will is necessarily "a will subject to moral laws";[55] that is, a free agent would act only on maxims that correspond to laws, in the sense that they pass the Categorical Imperative test. Our failures to act morally are due to the fact that we are "affected by sensibility, i.e., by incentives of a kind other than the fully rational." Hence, a rational agent, or at least one whose rationality is not "hindered" by the influence of "incentives that are not purely rational," would be moral. Even if we do not always act morally, we are *bound* by moral requirements, for we are—or regard ourselves as—rational.[56]

Kant's argument for the second step, the thesis that a free will is necessarily subject to moral laws, is especially difficult. I believe it depends on an equivocation. Kant's premise is that the existence of causal relations implies that there are laws that describe those relations as relations that have to be as they are by

51. Kant, 1785, Ak 446–48.

52. The distinction between these two questions corresponds to Kant's distinction between content or "purport" and "possibility" (Kant, 1785, Ak 420).

53. Kant, 1785, Ak 421.

54. Kant, 1785, Ak 448–49.

55. Kant, 1785, Ak 447.

56. Kant, 1785, Ak 449.

"necessity." Hence, he argues, since the decisions of a free will cause its actions, and since a free will is not bound by ordinary causal laws, there must be laws of some other, special kind that describe the causal relations between its decisions and its actions.[57] It does not follow, however, that these laws describe how the decisions ought to be related to these actions by moral "necessity." Kant's argument depends on an assimilation of causal necessity with the moral necessities or requirements that he hopes to show a free will is bound to respect. Moreover, the argument ignores the possibility of other kinds of normative "law." Perhaps the special "law" that describes how the decisions of a free will are related to its actions is a proposition to the effect that any free will aims to maximize the degree to which she satisfies her desires, or perhaps it is simply that any free will follows some principle or other.

Kant did not aim to *prove* that immorality is irrational, but rather to show the conceptual penalty for denying that it is. His idea is that there is a price to be paid for denying that morality is binding on all rational agents, that is, the inability to conceive of ourselves as rational agents in a sense which would imply that we are capable of performing actions for reasons that are fully our own. If I am correct, however, Kant failed to show that we must pay this price.

There are contemporary Kantian arguments which also aim to show that the price of moral skepticism is prohibitive.[58] I cannot rule out the possibility of a successful Kantian argument, but I am not aware of one. In any event, we are not looking merely for an argument that justified moral standards exist. We are looking for a theory of the justification conditions of moral standards. We need to know more than that skepticism is intellectually costly.

There remains the Kantian thesis that immoral behavior could not be fully rational, that the requirements of morality are requirements of reason. I assume that the requirements of reason are those implied by justified standards that govern choice. If this is correct, then, of course, moral requirements are requirements of reason. This means simply that requirements governing choice that are moral in nature are requirements governing choice. Nothing interesting follows. But if one begins with a substantive yet morally neutral theory of rational choice,[59] such as an instrumental theory, then it can be an interesting question whether immoral conduct could be "rational." And I see no reason to assume that the answer *must* be in the negative. It is a substantive question whether behavior that is prohibited by justified moral standards is also ruled out by the justified nonmoral standards governing choice. To answer the question, we would need a theory of justification conditions for moral standards as well as a theory of rational choice.

---

57. Kant, 1785, Ak 446, 447.

58. The best-known contemporary example of a Kantian strategy is Thomas Nagel's. See Nagel, 1970, esp. pp. 90–98, 116–24. But see Nagel, 1986, p. 159; Sturgeon, 1974.

59. A theory that does not directly entail that there are moral reasons for choosing things or that there are justified moral standards.

Aristotelian Theories

Instrumental theories assume that a rational person seeks the good from his own standpoint but treat this good as something determined by the person's own psychology. Another class of theories would hold that there are certain ends that one *must* have as a necessary condition of being rational. So, for example, a rational person seeks to satisfy his needs, to be happy, to have friends, and so on, just as a matter of being rational. I will discuss Aristotelian theories of this kind, according to which a person's good essentially involves embodying and expressing the moral virtues, including other-regarding virtues such as generosity and justice.

Aristotelian theories fall into two categories. First are instrumentalist theories according to which rationality consists in *maximizing* (or otherwise furthering) one's own good. Second is what I take to be Aristotle's own view, according to which rationality is *constitutive* of a person's good. On this view, a person's good is not something different from her exercise of reason, which she can achieve by means of the exercise of reason. Rather, a person who is doing well at exercising reason is *thereby* realizing her own good. A rational person, choosing well, thereby necessarily expresses and sustains a state of character that is good for her, and, in so doing, she also expresses and sustains human goods and virtues, including, when relevant, the moral virtues. Moral virtue is necessary to our good, which in turn is constituted by excellences of rationality.[60]

Both the constitutive and instrumentalist approaches agree that a person's good consists essentially, at least in part, in embodying and expressing the moral virtues. I will call this the "essentialist thesis." This thesis can be interpreted in different ways, depending on how essentialism is understood. On one interpretation, the thesis is that moral virtue is metaphysically necessary to the good of each of us. On weaker interpretations, it is necessary to our good as a matter of psychological law or human nature.

If the essentialist thesis is true on one of these interpretations, and if either the constitutive or instrumental view of the relation between rationality and one's own good can be defended, it follows that being morally virtuous is required by full rationality. The essentialist thesis therefore makes possible a distinctive Aristotelian account of the justification conditions of moral standards. According to this account, the moral standards of virtue qualify as relevantly justified due to the fact that conforming to them is required by full rationality because it is *essential* to the good of *any* person. Conforming to them would require having certain traits of character. If the choiceworthy states of character include certain other-regarding states, such as generosity, honesty, justice, and fairness,[61] then the standards calling on us to have them would seem to qualify as justified moral standards.

---

60. My interpretation of Aristotle has been influenced by discussions with Richard Kraut and Marcia Homiak, for which I am grateful. See Kraut, 1989; Homiak, 1985, 1990; also Irwin, 1988.

61. Aristotle, 1985, books 3–5.

The key point, then, is whether the essentialist thesis is true. It must be understood as the thesis that moral virtue is essential to being a good human in some morally neutral sense, for it is trivial that moral virtue is essential to anyone's being *morally* good. But it is quite unclear how moral virtue could be essential to being good in a morally neutral sense.

In order to understand Aristotle's argument, we need a fuller understanding of how he conceived of the best life. There is controversy about this. He does think that the best life involves reasoning, and acting for reasons, in a way that expresses the excellences of reason.[62] But we need to know what these excellences are. In book 10 of the *Nicomachean Ethics*, he claims that the best or happiest life consists in the contemplation of theoretical truths.[63] In book 1, however, he argues that the human good must be something complete, not simply one among many goods. Otherwise, it could be made more choiceworthy by the addition of any other good.[64] And he holds that the "virtues of character," including "generosity and temperance," are among the excellences of rationality in reasoning and choosing.[65] The attempt to reconcile these passages has led to two lines of interpretation. According to "dominant end" interpretations, a life of excellence in contemplation is the happiest or best life, and Aristotle is committed to the view that such a life would necessarily involve ethical virtue.[66] According to "inclusive end" interpretations,[67] Aristotle holds that a life of excellence in contemplation could be improved by the addition of moral virtue. The best life would integrate all the virtues.

The inclusive end interpretation may seem to yield the more plausible theory of the good life, yet it is worth noting the implausibility of the idea that a contemplative life would necessarily exhibit moral virtue. It may be true for the most part that the possession of other-regarding virtues would contribute to one's success in living a life of contemplation. Yet, in certain circumstances, contemplators might do better not to embody any other-regarding virtues but simply to dispose themselves to behave in ways that would best contribute to their success in living the contemplative life. They would take into account the interests of others only in ways that—and to the extent that—doing so would contribute to their success. Possession of the other-regarding virtues does not seem to be essential to success in contemplation.

Perhaps, however, moral virtue always enhances the value of a life. Terry Irwin

62. See the so-called function argument. Aristotle, 1985, 1097b17–1098a17.
63. Aristotle, 1985, 1177a11–21
64. Aristotle, 1985, 1097b17–21.
65. Aristotle, 1985, 1103a5–12.
66. For a similar interpretation, see Kraut, 1989, pp. 312–57. But according to Kraut, Aristotle allows that two kinds of life can count as devoted to reason, lives devoted to contemplation and, as second best, lives devoted to political activity (Kraut, 1989, pp. 345–53). See also Kraut, 1979, pp. 170, 181.
67. The issue of whether Aristotle has an inclusive or a dominant end conception was raised by Hardie (1965), who argued that although Aristotle wavers, he mainly has a dominant end conception. Ackrill (1974) argued that except for book 10, chapters 7 and 8, Aristotle has an inclusive end conception. These are perhaps the definitive papers in the controversy. I am indebted to Kraut for help with this bibliographical information.

holds that the fully rational and best life requires cultivating and maintaining a stable disposition to seek friendship. He argues that the reasoning that shows this can be extended to support "political friendship," or an intrinsic concern for the good of others in the wider political community. Like ordinary friendship, political friendship enables people to make plans and enter cooperative schemes that would otherwise be too risky. It therefore enables people to subject more aspects of their lives to control by reason than would otherwise be possible. Political activity would enable a person to realize the same capacities of rational agency realized in friendship, and it therefore "expresses" concerns that realize each person's capacities. This means that political friendships and political activity are "a part of each person's happiness and not simply a means to it." For these reasons, a fully rational person is "intrinsically concerned with action for the benefit of the community" and is therefore "intrinsically concerned to do just actions." In this sense, Irwin suggests, human beings are "naturally political."[68]

The problem, however, is to show that a fully rational agent would thereby take more than an instrumental interest in the existence of a political community and in the good of other members of the community. Consider a clique of robber barons who dominate and exploit an entire society, while remaining friends with each other and having an intrinsic concern for each other's good. They compartmentalize their lives. In relating to other barons, each expresses the dispositions that are essential to genuine friendship, but these dispositions do not affect their treatment of those outside the clique. For example, they share in deliberation about their exploitative policies for the society. Due to their domination of the society, they have extended the aspects of social life over which they have rational control beyond what would otherwise be possible. But they have no intrinsic concern for the good of the society or of its other members. It is conceivable that each of them has in this way realized the capacities of rational agency to a greater degree than he would if he had the concerns that would characterize the morally virtuous agent.

It might be objected that the barons would not be living happy lives. Yet, it is quite possible that in fact, and in the barons' own view of things, their "deepest desires are being satisfied" and they have "an especially affirmative attitude" toward themselves and their lives.[69] If so, then the claim that they are not happy will seem implausible, and their choice to live a life of crime will seem to have been rational.[70]

The Aristotelian strategy was to use the essentialist thesis to argue that moral virtue is a requirement of reason. I see little hope of success from an Aristotelian approach, for I think that although the thesis that one must be morally virtuous in order to achieve one's good may be true of many people in many circumstances, it is not a metaphysical truth or a matter of psychological law or human nature.

68. See Aristotle, 1985, 1097b8–11. For Irwin's interpretation, see Irwin, 1988, pp. 381, 395, 397–99, 405–6. Homiak, 1990, offers a similar interpretation.

69. This is Kraut's gloss on a conception of happiness (1979, p. 174).

70. For a somewhat different example, see Charles Dickens's portrayal of Sir John Chester in *Barnaby Rudge*.

Conclusion

This chapter began by identifying two key problems posed by the standard-based theory of normative judgment. The first is to explain the justification conditions of moral standards, and the second is to provide an account of the content and truth conditions of moral propositions. I argued that none of the familiar theories of the nature and basis of morality can provide adequate answers to these questions. The most promising are reductionist theories, including contractarian, Kantian, and Aristotelian theories, but I argued that theories of this kind are ultimately unsuccessful.

The result of the examination can only lend support to moral skepticism. To be sure, this has been a rather quick study. But if no account of the justification conditions of moral standards seems viable, this may be because the notion of a justified moral standard is empty. I do not believe this, however, and in the next chapter, I will begin to develop the society-centered theory.

5

A Conception of Morality

We are left with the two central questions I distinguished in the preceding chapter. The society-centered theory is intended to answer the first of these questions by providing an account of the conditions under which a moral standard would qualify as justified. It asserts roughly that a moral code is justified, relative to a society, if and only if the society would be rational to select it to serve as its social moral code. It is a standard-oriented reductionist theory.

I will detail my answer to the second question in chapter 11. In my view, any paradigmatic moral proposition is partly to the effect that some moral standard is justified. For instance, the claim that kindness is a virtue expresses a proposition roughly to the effect that some relevantly justified moral standard calls for people to be kind.[1] This explains why paradigmatic moral propositions entail that some moral standard is justified.

I develop the society-centered theory in the rest of the book. I will assume that the standard-based theory is the accepted account of normativity even though, as I explained in the introduction, it is independent of the society-centered theory.

The Distinction between Moral and Other Standards

In this chapter, I introduce a distinction between the *moral* standards of a person or group and the *other* kinds of standards accepted by the person or group. The society-centered theory does not depend on this distinction. The theory does not first distinguish moral standards from other standards and then look to see which of the moral standards have its *J* property. Rather, it holds that *any* standard with its *J* property qualifies as a justified moral standard. Yet, we do need the distinction in order to make sense of the thesis, which most of us accept, that some moral standards are *not* justified. Most of us would agree, for example, that moral standards that prohibit the lending of money at interest are

---

1. If the concept of kindness is a moral concept, then the standard can be expressed in terms of the concept of "quasi-kindness," as I explained in chapter 2.

not justified. To explain this fully, it is necessary to distinguish *moral* standards from standards of other kinds. This is the task for the present chapter.

In certain contexts, we would not call a standard a "moral" standard unless we believed compliance with it would be at least morally acceptable. In such a context, for example, we would not call a racist standard a "moral" standard. But in the sense of "moral standard" that I want to explain in this chapter, even a racist standard might be counted a moral standard to distinguish it from standards of etiquette and the like. In this sense, we can report that there are groups that have quite dubious moral standards.

I begin by criticizing familiar "formal" and "material" accounts of the distinction between moral and other standards. I then present my own attitudinal theory. A person's moral standards are those she "subscribes to as moral standards." In principle, any standard, regardless of its content—with an exception I will ignore until later—could be "subscribed to morally." In a sense, then, there is no distinction between moral standards per se and standards of other kinds. There is a distinction, however, among the standards accepted by people, between their moral standards and their standards of other kinds.

Formal Theories

Formal theories aim to explain the distinction between moral and other kinds of standards and judgments on the basis of logical characteristics of the moral ones, or logical characteristics of the state of accepting a moral one. Material theories allege that the distinction cannot be drawn without taking into account the content or function of moral standards or judgments.

Perhaps the best known formal theory was developed by R. M. Hare.[2] We will briefly examine his view, but it is important to see that, whereas I am attempting to explain the distinction between moral and other kinds of *standards*, Hare is aiming to distinguish between moral and other kinds of *judgments*. He argues that, with certain qualifications, there are three properties, possession of which by a judgment is necessary and sufficient for it to be a moral judgment: prescriptivity, universalizability, and overridingness.[3]

I am not going to address Hare's prescriptivism, his thesis that moral judgments are prescriptive in that they express imperatives. Prescriptivism is a noncognitivist account of the normativity of moral judgment, and I rejected noncognitivism in chapter 2.[4] Prescriptivism is also internalist, in a familiar sense

2. Hare argues that the formal properties of moral judgments "yield a system of moral reasoning whose conclusions have a content identical with that of a certain kind of utilitarianism." But he thinks that moral judgments can be identified by their formal properties (Hare, 1981, p. 4).
3. Hare, 1981, section 1.6. Hare introduced his theory in 1952, but I shall rely mainly on the later work.
4. Prescriptivism says that any "genuinely evaluative" moral judgment entails an *imperative* (Hare, 1952, section 11.2). Since imperatives express standards, prescriptivism is a precursor of the standard-based theory.

of the term, for it implies that a person sincerely believes he morally ought to do something, all things considered, only if he is motivated to do it.[5] But I rejected this form of internalism in chapter 2, where I discussed moral belief and motivation.

The thesis that moral judgments are "universalizable" can be understood in various ways. The underlying idea is that it would be inconsistent to judge a thing to fall into some moral category—to be good, or right, or just, for example—but to judge a "relevantly similar" thing not to fall into that category.[6] The key issue is what counts as a "relevant" similarity or difference. J. L. Mackie suggests that we should rule out as irrelevant "mere numerical as opposed to generic difference, the difference between one individual and another, simply as such."[7] And he takes this to rule out differences that are simply a matter of *relationships* to numerically different objects, such as the difference between Italian and German citizenship, simply as such.[8]

In a 1981 work, Hare said that universalizability "comes to this, that if we make *different* moral judgements about situations which we admit to be *identical* in their *universal descriptive properties*, we contradict ourselves."[9] Moreover, he says that spatial and temporal properties are not universal, and a difference solely as to which individuals are involved in two cases is not a difference in universal properties.[10]

Yet there have been societies that restricted moral requirements to their own members. To quote from Ruth Benedict, "All primitive tribes agree in recognizing this category of the outsiders, those who are not only outside the provisions of the moral code which holds within the limits of one's own people, but who are summarily denied a place anywhere in the human scheme."[11] Codes of this sort ought to be counted as moral codes. It is logically possible, and I suspect it is true, that at least some of the tribes mentioned by Benedict excluded outsiders from the scope of morality simply on the basis that outsiders are not of "our people," are not "one of us," or are not "from this place." Let us say that an "insider code" assigns different status to insiders and outsiders simply on the basis that outsiders are not members of the insider group. For example,

---

5. Hare, 1952, p. 20; 1981, p. 21.

6. This is basically how Hare formulates the idea in Hare, 1963, chapter 2. He gives a somewhat different formulation in Hare, 1981, pp. 114, 115. The idea has a long history. Henry Sidgwick says, "We cannot judge an action to be right for Alan and wrong for Bill, unless we can find in the natures or circumstances of the two some difference which we can regard as a reasonable ground for difference in their duties" (Sidgwick, 1907, p. 209).

7. Mackie, 1977, p. 83.

8. Mackie, 1977, pp. 85–87.

9. Hare, 1981, p. 21, my emphasis. See also p. 108.

10. Hare, 1981, pp. 114, 115; see p. 108. As Hare officially explains the notion of a "universal descriptive property," at Hare, 1981, p. 115, the universalizability thesis is a tautology. So understood, I am obviously not going to quibble with it. But I do not read it as a tautology in the text, for I take seriously Hare's specific claims about which kinds of properties are universal and descriptive.

11. Benedict, 1934, p. 7. This does not mean that outsiders are viewed as biologically nonhuman.

an insider code might forbid enslaving a person if and only if the person is a member of the insider society. An insider might judge, then, that it is permissible to enslave Alan, since he is *not* from her society, but that it would be impermissible to enslave Bill, since Bill *is* from her society.

The universalizability thesis, as interpreted by Hare, implies that either the insider's judgments about Alan and Bill are not moral judgments or her position is inconsistent. For group membership per se does not count as a "universal descriptive property."[12] The fact that Alan is *not* a member of the insider's society while Bill *is* a member is not a relevant difference between them.[13]

However, first, there is no *inconsistency* in the insider's judgment about the permissibility of enslaving Alan and the impermissibility of enslaving Bill. Her judgment may be morally appalling, but it is consistent. The insider code does not appear to be logically untenable. Moreover, second, it would be implausible to deny that the insider code is a moral code. An insider code could play the role of a moral code in an insider society. It would then be a socially enforced and culturally transmitted code that would coordinate people's activities and regulate cooperation and competition. It might be viewed by the members of the society as defining central aspects of their personalities and as prescribing considerations of the greatest importance. Moreover, insider judgments concern the very questions that we are concerned with in morality, such as how people ought to be treated. For example, the judgment that Alan may be enslaved concerns a matter that would affect the fundamental quality of his life. Since the judgment evidently conflicts with our moral view that slavery is impermissible, I see no reason to suppose that it concerns a different subject.

I cannot rule out the possibility that some versions of the universalizability doctrine are true. But I think it is false that a moral view is logically untenable if it permits mere numerical difference to count as morally relevant.

The claim that morality is "overriding" can also be understood in various ways. For Hare, it is the thesis that one's morality is something that yields prescriptions which, *as a matter of psychological fact*, one lets override all other prescriptions.[14] Hare argues that "critical moral principles," that is, judgments about what ought morally to be done, all things considered, are "overriding" in this sense.[15] There is also a thesis to the effect that moral reasons are in some sense superior to any other reasons. I will discuss this conception of overridingness in chapter 9. Here I consider Hare's psychological conception.

P. F. Strawson pointed out that the personal standards or ideals of a person may conflict with what the person acknowledges as morally obligatory. The person might choose to live by his ideal even in cases where he is convinced some other

12. Hare, 1981, pp. 114–15.

13. Of course, since Bill is a member of the insider society and Alan is not, there are differences between them that are differences in their universal descriptive properties. But this is irrelevant to the issue of whether the insider's judgments violate the universalizability constraint, unless no judgments ever violate the constraint.

14. Hare, 1981, pp. 56, 24.

15. Hare, 1981, pp. 55–62.

specific thing ought morally to be done, all things considered.[16] Bernard Williams discussed the example of Gauguin, who took up the life of a creative artist.[17] Suppose Gauguin made this way of life his *ideal*, viewing it as best for him and striving to live up to it. He might well agree, of course, that this uncompromising way of life leads him sometimes to neglect what he ought morally to do, all things considered. Yet he lets his ideal override what he takes to be his duties.

Hare has two available replies. First, he might contend that a person in such a situation has no moral beliefs. For example, Gauguin's judgment that he ought to lead an artistic life is not a moral judgment, since Gauguin does not treat it as universalizable. And since his judgment that he ought to take care of his family rather than paint is not overriding, it, too, is not a moral judgment. Perhaps, then, Gauguin has *no* moral views. This reply seems quite implausible. Gauguin might agree with us that he is violating a moral duty in pursuing his painting at the expense of his family. It would be obtuse to insist that he *cannot* really think this. Second, Hare might argue that personal ideals, such as Gauguin's, are actually moral ideals. Hare thinks that "people *mean* by the moral words something to do with *commitments* to ways of life."[18] If a person is committed to an ideal, and if it concerns what he *ought* to do, then the standards he commits himself to on its basis are his *moral* standards. This reply also seems implausible, however. Gauguin might agree with us that his ideal life is not morally ideal, in that it sometimes leads him to violate his moral duties.

In Hare's theory, the work of distinguishing between a person's moral judgments and her judgments of other kinds is done by the idea of an overriding disposition to comply with a universalizable imperative. But a person may let other normative considerations override what she acknowledges to be moral considerations. Hare's view fails to allow for the person who believes he morally ought to do something, all things considered, yet is not motivated to do it, and it treats the moral failing of a person whose moral convictions are not universalizable as if it were a logical failure.

Material Accounts

It may seem that these flaws in Hare's theory could be corrected only by a material theory that identified moral standards on the basis of their content, rationale, or function. It may seem that only a material theory could distinguish between moral standards and personal ideals and distinguish morality from prudence and etiquette.[19] A material conception of morality may also be presupposed by the common idea that we should tolerate moral views that differ from our own. Many who accept this idea would not think it applied to racist views or to views that are bizarre or without any intelligible rationale.

16. Then again, he points out, one might make it one's ideal that moral considerations override all others (Strawson, 1974b, p. 41).
17. Williams, 1981b, esp. p. 24.
18. Hare, 1981, pp. 81, 85.
19. W. K. Frankena, 1970, p. 158.

I will consider two families of material theories. The first proposes that moral standards must have a content or function that connects them appropriately to human good and harm or to human welfare, broadly conceived. The second thinks it is characteristic that moral standards are enforced by internal psychological sanctions and that it is the business of a person's moral view to regiment those sanctions in appropriate ways.

Social Content and Function

Philippa Foot discusses a person who claims that "clasping the hands three times in an hour [is] a good action." She argues that, in order to make this claim intelligible, we would have to imagine a "special background" that would give a "point" to the action. We would have to imagine that the person believes there is some "connection" between the action of clasping the hands three times in an hour and "human good and harm."[20] W. K. Frankena proposes that morality has the function of making possible "some kind of cooperation or social activity between human beings" and that a moral view must include principles concerned with interpersonal relations and the effects of actions on others.[21]

In order to consider a family of views of this kind, let me generalize by speaking of the alleged "social content" of moral standards and of their alleged "social function." According to social content theories, a standard accepted by a person qualifies as a moral standard only if it has a relevant social content or it is derived within the person's view from more basic standards that have a relevant social content. Moral standards govern interpersonal relations or call for a concern with others' welfare or a concern with human good and harm.[22] According to social function theories, a standard accepted by a person qualifies as a moral standard only if it has a relevant social function or is derived within the person's view from more basic standards that have a relevant social function. Relevant functions include making cooperation and social life run more smoothly, maximizing human good, and minimizing harm to humans.[23] A theory could combine these concerns, for social content could be held to explain in part the social function, or vice versa.

Let us begin by assessing Foot's example about the person who believes it is morally good to clasp one's hands three times in an hour. Foot may be correct that we would not find it intelligible that the person believes this unless we were given an explanation that showed how he connected hand clasping with human good and harm. But it does not follow that his view would not otherwise count as a moral view. Foot's argument trades on a confusion between the "intelligibility" of a belief that p and the logical possibility of believing that p. It is the latter that is relevant here. We may not find it "intelligible" that someone believes his dog is God, for example, even though we know he believes it and therefore know it is logically possible for him to believe it. And I say it is logi-

20. Foot, 1978a, p. 119–20.
21. Frankena, 1970, pp. 158, 156. For a similar view, see Strawson, 1974b, p. 36.
22. See Steven Smith, 1974, pp. 95, 126.
23. See Smith, 1974, p. 120. For a view of this sort, see Warnock, 1971, p. 26.

cally possible that someone believe both that hand clasping is morally good and that this has nothing to do with human good and harm. The view is bizarre and implausible, but it is nevertheless possible for a person to believe it.

There have been (or may well have been) groups that accepted a variety of bizarre moral standards: Some groups thought it morally wrong to worship statues; some prohibited the use of the color green in carpets; some thought slavery to be permissible; some prohibited the lending of money at interest; some regarded treachery as a virtue; and some prohibited sex between people of the same sex and between people of different races. There are explanations for all of these views, of course. Perhaps in most of these cases the people who accepted the bizarre standard did so because they believed it could be derived from a background moral code with an appropriate social content. Yet many people in these groups, including children and the less intelligent members, would not have understood the rationale for the standard, and many may not have believed there *is* a rationale. Bizarre standards about sexual conduct are often accepted by people in a "visceral" way, with no justification in the offing. Moreover, a group's moral code can change. A group that begins by accepting a bizarre standard that is derived from more basic standards with an appropriate social content might change to the point that, although the bizarre standard continues to be accepted, the standards from which it was derived are no longer accepted. The standard might still count as among the group's moral standards.

It may now be suggested that if a moral code does not contain basic standards with an explicit social content, social considerations must enter into its basic rationale. Yet people can agree in their moral standards without agreeing about a rationale, and some might even think that no rationale is needed. Furthermore, as Steven Smith suggests, the rationale that members of a society would tend to give for their moral view might change with time. If a set of views is counted as a moral code at one time, it might well continue to be counted as a moral code even if the social justification people initially accepted is displaced by, for instance, a merely visceral conviction.[24]

Let me turn now to social function theories. It seems that the actual function of a code may be independent of whether it is accepted as a moral code. We do not need to ascertain the actual function of a standard or code in order to determine whether it is a moral standard. Moreover, there appear to be moral codes that tend to increase social disharmony, such as cults of racial purity. Also, there appear to be codes, such as sexual moral codes, that once had a given social function but have lost it because of changed circumstances. They should still be counted as moral codes.[25]

There are, however, two quite different interpretations of the thesis that the function of morality is to serve a social role. It may be interpreted as the claim that any moral code actually does serve the role. But a more interesting interpretation takes it as a claim about the *evaluation* of moral codes. The function

24. Smith, 1974, pp. 128, 134–35, 132. The idea of a "visceral" moral code comes from Smith.
25. These arguments are from Smith, 1974, pp. 147, 149, 150.

of the heart is to pump blood, but not every heart actually accomplishes this task. To attribute a function to some kind of thing, in this sense, is to provide a basis for evaluating its operation. Consequently, on this reading, the claim that moral codes have a social function can be interpreted as a thesis about the conditions under which moral codes are *justified*. I am inclined to agree that a justified moral code would be one that made cooperative activity possible. If this is correct, then the intuitions behind social function theories can be preserved in a theory of moral justification.

The error of functional accounts, then, is to treat as definitive of morality something that should be regarded instead as a condition of a moral code's being justified.[26] Indeed, there is a tendency to confuse the distinction between a person's moral standards and other standards with the quite different distinction between standards that qualify as justified moral standards and standards that do not. The bizarre standard of Foot's example presumably is not justified, for instance. The intuitions behind a variety of formal and material accounts may in fact be correct, if they are taken to be intuitions about which standards qualify as justified, rather than as intuitions about which standards are moral standards at all.

Moral Attitudes and Emotions

Some theorists have invoked moral attitudes and emotions, such as disapproval and guilt, to explain the distinction between a person's moral convictions and her other convictions.[27] Allan Gibbard claims, for example, that morality consists of norms governing when it makes sense to feel guilt or resentment. He offers this as an account of morality in the "narrow sense," which he distinguishes from practical reason "in the fullest sense."[28]

Theories of this kind risk a charge of circularity. It may be that a person's attitudes of guilt and resentment cannot be distinguished from similar nonmoral attitudes without invoking the person's moral convictions. But it is not even clear that guilt is a distinctive *moral* emotion. We can feel guilty for a variety of reasons, of which moral reasons are only one instance. For example, we often feel guilty when we fail to live up to our own personal standards and ideals, even if we think that no moral failing is involved.

Theories of this kind also risk a charge that they are too narrow. Feelings of resentment and guilt may be characteristic of certain cultures without being involved in every moral view. It may be that every moral view includes norms regarding the appropriateness of negative responses in cases where moral standards are violated. But it is not clear that every moral view involves guilt and resentment. Gibbard discusses moralities of shame and fear, for example, and positive feelings of moral approbation.

26. Compare Smith, 1974, p. 116.
27. For example, "emotivism" uses the idea that there are distinctive "moral attitudes." See Stevenson, 1944.
28. Gibbard, 1990, pp. 40–41, 47–49.

Gibbard holds that the issue as to which standards are moral standards is "one of stipulation," for, he says, the term "moral" is used in many different ways.[29] He is likely correct that any theoretical line we draw between moral standards and other kinds of standard will be somewhat stipulative. Yet, there is a territory we want to describe, and we do not want to distort its shape or location.

The Attitudinal Conception

The theory I shall now propose holds that a person's moral standards are the standards, if any, to which she takes a certain characteristic complex of attitudes. I shall say that a person's moral standards are those that she *subscribes to as moral standards* or that she accepts in some closely related way. Moral subscription to a standard consists, at least in part, in making conformity with the standard a policy, and wanting conformity to be a policy for others in one's society. The standards one subscribes to as moral standards play a central and characteristic role in one's life. As we shall see, moral subscription and the related attitudes differ in subtle ways from the attitudes we take to standards that play other roles in our lives.

The notion I aim to capture may not be familiar. We are used to thinking of a person's moral view as captured by her moral beliefs. If we give any thought to a person's moral standards, we are likely to think her standards are simply the standards that correspond to her beliefs. Yet the notion I will try to capture makes room for divergence between a person's moral standards and her moral beliefs.

The idea should not be entirely unfamiliar. On the one hand, we do sometimes take a kind of moralizing attitude toward certain standards, such as rules concerning personal hygiene or logical rules, even though we do not believe that the standards are morally binding.[30] The prohibition against eating with one's elbows on the table is merely a rule of etiquette, yet some people take an attitude toward violations of it that would be appropriate only if it were a moral prohibition. They presumably do not think that having elbows on the table is morally wrong. But if they have the relevant attitude to the standard and to violations of it, then, regardless of their beliefs, I would count it as among their moral standards. On the other hand, there could be people whose tolerant attitude toward violations of a moral standard, such as the prohibition on torture, is as if the standard were merely a standard of etiquette. They might insist that torture is morally wrong. Yet, if they do not take the relevant attitude toward the standard and toward violations of it, then I would say that it is *not* among their moral standards.

People normally subscribe morally to the standards that correspond to their moral beliefs, but they are not guaranteed to do so. A person might believe

29. Gibbard, 1990, pp. 51–52.
30. I owe the examples to Walter Sinnott-Armstrong (personal correspondence).

torture is morally wrong, for instance, yet fail to subscribe morally to a corresponding standard. Or a person might subscribe morally to a prohibition on eating with one's elbows on the table, yet believe that having one's elbows on the table is not morally wrong. In the sense I have in mind, then, a person's moral standards are the standards she subscribes to morally, and these are not necessarily the standards that correspond to the moral propositions that she believes.

I introduced these ideas in a preliminary way in chapter 2. I argued there that believing a moral proposition commits one to the belief that a corresponding standard is relevantly justified. But one can subscribe morally to a standard without believing it is justified.[31] One can also subscribe morally to a standard without believing it is a moral standard.

To forestall misunderstanding, I should say that a standard that is not subscribed to as a moral standard by anyone at all may nevertheless qualify as justified. It may have the relevant *J* property. We may therefore speak of it as a "moral standard" in the sense that it meets relevant criteria of justification. In this chapter, however, I am attempting to explain what makes a standard among a person's moral standards.

I begin with a series of "definitions" that characterize the various complex attitudes one takes toward one's standards. Only later do I offer arguments to support my claims about these attitudes. There is a unity to the complexes of attitudes that I define, due to the role moral standards play in our lives and in our relations to others, as well as in the larger society in which we live. They are syndromes, characteristic combinations of attitudes toward standards. Yet it is true that the syndromes can come apart in certain borderline cases.

A person can have various affirmative attitudes to a standard without meeting all of the conditions for subscribing to it as a moral standard. There is the attitude of "endorsing" a rule, where, as Wayne Sumner proposes, endorsing is a matter of using conformity to the rule "as a standard for judging or evaluating the conduct of those to whom the rule applies."[32] *Endorsement* could be defined as follows:

> (*DI*) One endorses a standard relative to a group just in case
> (1) one tends to have a favorable attitude toward those in the group who comply with it, and toward their compliance, and to support conformity with it;
> (2) other things being equal, one tends to have a negative response toward anyone in the group who (intentionally) fails to conform, or toward failures to conform; and
> (3) one regards such failures as creating a presumption of liability to a negative response.

31. Compare R. B. Brandt's remark that an individual must believe his moral code to be "justified—not arbitrary but in some sense proper" (1979, p. 169). Note that a moral skeptic may subscribe to a moral standard even though he thinks no moral standard is justified.
32. Sumner, 1987, p. 64.

If you subscribe morally to a standard, you endorse it relative to your society. But endorsement of a standard does not imply that you subscribe to it morally, for it does not imply that you have any intention to comply with it yourself or that you care about its currency in society. For example, as an informed citizen, you would presumably endorse a variety of rules of judicial procedure (for the judiciary), but they would not be among your moral standards.

It will be useful to have a more general notion of subscription than *moral* subscription. Accordingly, I will define *subscription to a standard* as follows:

> (D2)   One subscribes to a standard just in case
> (1) one intends to conform to it and is disposed to conform to it;
> (2) one tends to have a favorable attitude toward oneself for complying with it, and toward one's compliance;
> (3) other things being equal, one tends to have a negative response toward oneself, or one's failure, if one (intentionally) fails to conform; and
> (4) one regards such failures as creating a presumption of liability to a negative response.

Members of the judiciary typically would both endorse the rules of due process and subscribe to them. But they might not subscribe to them as *moral* standards, for they might not care about their currency in the larger society.

Here, then, is the definition of *subscription to a standard as a moral standard*:

> (D3)   One subscribes to a standard as a moral standard just in case
> (1) if it is a standard to which one can conform, one intends to conform to it and one is disposed to conform to it;
> (2) one intends to support conformity to it within one's society, and one is disposed to support conformity;
> (3) if one is a member of a society, then one desires that the standard have currency in one's society;
> (4) one tends to have a favorable attitude toward those in one's society who comply with it, and toward oneself for complying with it, or toward conformity with it; and
> (5) other things being equal, one tends to have a negative response toward oneself, or one's failure, if one (intentionally) fails to conform, and to have a negative response toward anyone else in one's society who (intentionally) fails to conform, or toward failures to conform, and
> (6) one regards such failures as creating a presumption of liability to a negative response.

For simplicity, I will often speak of "subscribing morally" or of "moral subscription" to a standard.

When I speak of "negative responses," I have in mind negative conative and emotional responses, such as disapproval, reproach, blame, indignation, anger, resentment, shame, regret, the desire of punishment, and so on. For these purposes, I do not count a normative *belief*, such as the belief that a standard has been violated or that something wrong has been done by someone, as a "negative response." Of course, such beliefs are typically accompanied by conative and emotional responses, and one can express a negative response by making a normative claim. But in these cases, the conative or emotional response itself is the negative response. In the same way, favorable attitudes are also conative or emotional responses. For simplicity, I will often use the terms "blame" and "approval" rather than "negative response" and "favorable attitude."

In brief, with exceptions I will introduce, I hold that a standard is someone's moral standard only if the person subscribes to it as a moral standard. A person may, for example, endorse the standards of the legal system and subscribe to various standards of etiquette as well as to standards calling on her to exercise vigorously and regularly. She may have similar attitudes toward rules of hygiene and logical rules. But to be part of a person's moral code, a standard must be subscribed to morally. We do not ordinarily care whether people in distant parts of our society follow rules of hygiene or think that people who make logical mistakes deserve the negative responses that their mistakes often elicit in us. But let me now proceed to explain the details.

The Psychology of Subscription to a Standard

Moral subscription is a complex group of attitudes toward a standard that is reflected in a person's motivations to conform and in his attitudes toward others' conformity. It is important to see that this complex set of attitudes is not merely a disunified cluster. I said before that moral subscription is a syndrome that is unified by the role moral standards play in our lives, and I will have more to say about this in the concluding section of this chapter.

The central point is that there are certain standards that define a person's policies both with respect to his own behavior and character and with respect to the behavior and character of others and the behavior and character of groups and institutions of the larger society. These policies are intentions to conform to the standard and to support conformity in the society, and they are characteristically accompanied by desires that others in the society have similar policies and by tendencies to have favorable and unfavorable responses toward, respectively, compliance and failures to comply.

In typical cases, people come to subscribe morally to standards as a result of their upbringing. A process akin to religious conversion may be needed, if an adult is to come to have moral values who lacked them ahead of time.[33] Moral argument can extend a person's moral values. It can lead a person to subscribe morally to a standard about the treatment of animals, for example, if she already subscribes morally to a standard about the treatment of persons and if argument leads her to see an important analogy between the two cases. But a person who begins by lacking any moral values would not come to have such values as a result of accepting the conclusion of an argument. He would not decide, as

33. I follow suggestions of John McDowell (forthcoming).

a result of rational argumentation, to assemble this syndrome of attitudes toward a standard in a deliberate manner, piece by piece. Nothing rules this out except human psychology, but, certainly, typical cases of significant change in moral values would involve holistic changes in attitude, with the result that the syndrome I have described comes to be in place. Such changes could be brought about only by complex psychological processes.

The psychology of all of this is quite difficult.[34] I will discuss two problems. First, a person may have moral standards even if he is not able to formulate them in any way that he finds satisfactory, and even if he would not be satisfied with anyone else's formulation. This needs to be explained, for it may seem that a person could not intend to conform to a standard or desire that it have currency in society if he were uncertain about what would count as conforming to it. Second, if subscribing morally to a standard entails the intention to conform, it may seem that moral weakness is not possible.

Regarding the first point, I believe it is possible to intend to conform to a rule, or to desire its currency, even if one does not know how to formulate it. One must be *aware* of the rule, but this does not require knowing its formulation. For example, I may subscribe to my parents' standards without knowing the most accurate way to state their standards. In order to intend to conform, I must intend to act in a way that counts as conforming or to bring about what counts as conforming. Similarly, in order to approve of compliance, I must approve of behavior that I believe counts as being in conformity, when the behavior is intended to be in conformity. And in order to desire that certain standards have currency, I must be capable of forming a desire that refers to the standards. But none of this means that I must be able to state, or be readily able to recognize, necessary and sufficient conditions of conformity.

However, there must be some level of awareness of the conditions for conforming to a rule to which one subscribes. I could hardly be said to subscribe to the rules of English grammar if I could not even recognize a grammatical sentence. Yet there are many rules of grammar that I cannot state, and there likely are rules about which I am quite mistaken. Similarly, if a person subscribes to a moral standard, she must be able to recognize conformity with the standard in a wide range of circumstances and be able to see what would count as conformity. I do not mean that her recognition must be infallible and without difficulty or doubt; I mean only that she can recognize what counts as conformity with rough accuracy.

A person who subscribes morally to a standard intends to conform to it; that is, there is a description of the standard under which she intends to conform to it, and she is capable of recognizing conformity to a good approximation. She is disposed to conform to the standard; that is, she has a tendency to form the intention to do what she believes is necessary for her to conform. She desires that

---

34. Gibbard discusses the notion of accepting a norm, at Gibbard, 1990, pp. 55–82. He explains the existence of a "normative control system" in humans by claiming that it evolved "because of the advantages of coordination and planning through language" (p. 57). I am not competent to evaluate this suggestion, but I do recommend Gibbard's discussion. It seems to me that I could accept most of the things Gibbard says about the psychology of norm acceptance.

the standard have currency in her society; that is, she has appropriate attitudes toward social change. If a certain change in the attitudes of people in society would give greater currency to the standard, then she desires that change, or would desire it if she realized that the change would give greater currency to the standard.

Turn now to the problem of moral weakness. It will be useful to distinguish, among a person's moral standards, between those with which she can conform and those with which she cannot conform. Call the former "action standards." Examples are standards calling on people not to lie and to be kind. Examples of the latter are standards calling for legal institutions to provide for due process of law. A person can, of course, *support* conformity with a standard of both kinds, in the sense of favoring conformity and compliance, encouraging it, and the like, but it makes no sense to think of an ordinary person conforming with a standard calling for legal institutions to provide for due process of law.

A second useful distinction is between relatively specific action standards, each of which calls for a particular thing on a particular occasion from a specific agent, and relatively general action standards, standards that are general in the sense that they call for things of a certain kind on occasions of a certain kind from agents of a certain kind. An example of a specific standard is the standard calling on me not to lie at dinner tonight in reporting my day's activities. An example of a general standard is the standard calling on people not to lie. Of course, there are differences in degrees of specificity and generality, but this does not affect the point I want to make.

A person's *moral* action standards are not fully specific. Specific action standards are not subscribed to as moral standards, as a quick inspection of *D3* will reveal. I have no desire that the standard calling on me not to lie at dinner tonight while reporting my day's activities have currency in my society. Indeed, the idea of its having currency in society makes very little sense.[35]

For our purposes, moral weakness consists in knowingly and intentionally failing to conform to a standard to which one subscribes morally. The issue is whether it is possible to subscribe morally to a general action standard while intentionally failing to conform to it, given that subscribing morally entails intending to conform. How can one intend to conform to a standard while intentionally failing to conform?[36]

An intention to comply with a specific standard is a future-directed intention, akin to more familiar future-directed intentions, such as my intention to eat dinner tonight. However, an intention to comply with a general standard is a "personal policy," as is, for example, my intention to wear my seat belt while driving.[37] Moral subscription to a general standard involves a personal policy

35. Compare Dancy, 1993, pp. 60–72. Expressed in my framework, Dancy's idea seems to be that there are no general moral standards regarding action. If this is his idea, I mean to imply that it is incorrect, but not that it is nonsense. *D3* is what rules out the idea, and I do not claim that it would be nonsensical to deny *D3*.

36. I am grateful to Rachel Cohen for raising this question, in discussion.

37. Michael Bratman describes such policies as intentions that are "general with respect to their occasions of execution" (1989, p. 444). In the discussion that follows, I am indebted to Bratman's work.

of complying with the standard. It also involves, of course, the policy of supporting conformity on the part of others and various other psychological components.

The important point is that one can intentionally fail to conform to a policy. In an emergency, I can intentionally fail to wear my seat belt, even though I have a policy of wearing my seat belt. I may view my policy as suspended because of the emergency. On a short trip, I might intentionally fail to wear my seat belt because of laziness, which is a weakness of will similar to moral weakness. In both types of case, I still have the policy. I fail to wear my seat belt, but this does not mean I have abandoned, reconsidered, or qualified my policy. There is, however, a kind of inconsistency between my policy and my specific intentions on the occasions when I fail to wear the seat belt.[38]

Matters are no different when moral policies are involved. Moral policies are intentions to conform to general action standards to which one subscribes morally. It is possible for me intentionally to tell a lie at dinner even though I have a policy of conforming to a standard that prohibits lying. This is possible for me despite a kind of inconsistency between this policy and my intentions, when I intentionally lie. But, because inconsistencies of intention are possible, weakness of will is also possible.

The Desire of Currency in One's Society

Moral subscription to a standard involves the desire that it have "currency" in one's society. Of course, one *might* desire that everyone else, without restriction, subscribe to one's moral standards. But anyone who subscribes morally to a standard must desire *at least* that it have currency in his society. This desire can be specified as follows:[39]

> (*D4*) One desires the currency of a moral standard in a society if and only if
>   (1) one desires that it be generally so, in the society, that people (a) conform to the standard and (b) subscribe to the standard, if it is a standard to which they can conform, and (c) support conformity with it, and (d) endorse the standard relative to the society; and
>   (2) one would prefer a situation in which more people in the society had these properties to a situation in which fewer people had them, other things being equal.

Notice that one need not care whether others in the society desire that the standard have currency.

I will explain the notion of a society in the next chapter. As I will argue, societies can be nested within larger societies and can overlap, so that most people actually belong to several societies. This raises the question: Which of the societies to which a person belongs is to be viewed as *her* society, for present

---

38. Bratman, 1989, contains a thorough discussion of these issues.
39. I borrow the term "currency" from Brandt, 1979.

purposes? A minimal proposal is that a person who subscribes morally to a standard must desire that it have currency in at least *some* society to which she belongs. But this seems too weak, for a person who recognizes that she belongs to more than one society, and for whom this fact is salient, would surely desire that her moral standards have currency in every society to which she belongs.

I therefore suggest the following more complex condition: A person who subscribes morally to a standard desires it to have currency in some society to which she belongs, and she desires it to have currency in every society to which she sees herself as belonging and which is salient to her. All that I need, in order to develop the kind of view I want, is the minimal condition. Yet I believe the more complex condition is more plausible. I will say more about this in the section on society as the scope of morality later in this chapter. In what follows, I will speak vaguely of a person's desire that her moral standards have currency in "her" society.

Suppose you belong to no society. If so, then it must be that if you *were* a member of a society, you *would* desire the currency of your moral standards in your society. Definition *D3* is worded in a way that is meant to take account of such cases. I will ignore this qualification in the future.

The desire that one's moral standards have currency in one's society is a desire only to some degree, and other things being equal. It does not involve a desire to proselytize. We may desire that people have a certain attitude without desiring to influence their attitudes. Also, the desire that our standards have currency does not imply an intolerance of moral differences, for we may tolerate differences that we desire not to exist.[40] Finally, the desire that one's standards have currency may be outweighed by other desires. For instance, we may know that an evil neighboring society would destroy our society if our moral standards were to gain currency. Then we would *not* desire that our standards have currency, all things considered, but we would still have a desire that they have currency.

Liability to Negative Responses

Moral subscription to a standard implies a tendency to have a favorable attitude toward compliance with it and an unfavorable attitude toward non-compliance. It also implies a tendency to respond negatively to anyone in one's society who fails to conform to the standard, and to regard such failures as creating a presumption of liability to a negative response.

One might object that the notion of *liability* is both a moral notion and a notion peculiar to certain moral outlooks. Although I agree that the concept is *normative*, it is not a *moral* concept. Neither, incidentally, are the concepts of blame and blameworthiness moral concepts.[41]

---

40. We may also tolerate differences that elicit negative responses in us and that we regard as "liable to" negative responses. Toleration is not indifference. We may have the negative responses without expressing them overtly, and we may view them as appropriate without viewing the intolerant expression of them as appropriate.

41. My thinking here has been influenced by the work of Joel Feinberg (see his 1970). See also H. L. A. Hart, 1968, pp. 211–30.

The concept of liability is used in law as well as in morality. Legal criteria of liability are different, of course, from the familiar criteria of moral liability, and there are different legal criteria in different areas of law and in different jurisdictions. However, the concept is the same. It is, roughly, that a person is liable to a response R just in case the person's being subjected to R would be in conformity with a relevant standard (given the person's relationship to some performance that conformed or failed to conform to a standard).[42] If I am liable to be fined for a parking violation, then I have violated the parking statutes; given this, it would be in conformity with these statutes for me to be assessed a fine.

In order, then, for a person to be liable to a negative response, she must have failed to meet some relevant standard, and, as a result, some relevant standard must deem a negative response to be appropriate. I suggest, then, that a person subscribes to a standard A as a moral standard only if she accepts a standard B that governs negative responses to people who fail to conform to A. It is not necessary that she subscribe morally to B. Otherwise, she would have to subscribe to a standard C that governed negative responses to people who fail to conform to B, but this is not necessary. For example, I subscribe morally to a standard prohibiting theft, and this means that I accept a standard that calls for blaming people who steal, other things being equal. Yet it is not required that I also regard people who do not blame people who steal as themselves liable to blame for failing to blame the thieves.

I can now explain clause 6 of $D3$. A person who subscribes morally to a standard must accept in some appropriate sense a standard _governing negative responses_:

> (D5)   One subscribes to a standard A as a moral standard only if
> (6) there is a standard B such that (a) B calls on one to respond negatively, in certain ways and in certain circumstances, to (intentional) failures to conform to A on the part either of oneself or of anyone else in one's society, and (b) one is disposed to conform to B, and (c) if one is a member of a society, then one desires that it be generally so in one's society that people conform to B, and are disposed to conform to it, and one would prefer a situation in which more people in the society had these properties to a situation in which fewer people did, other things being equal.

This illustrates one way in which a person's moral standards form a system or code. Moral codes include pairs of A and B standards. For simplicity, I will describe a pair consisting of an A and a B standard as "a standard" subscribed to as a moral standard. (Clauses 3 of $D1$ and 4 of $D2$ need to be explained in similar ways, although with obvious amendments that I will not pause to detail.)

---

42. The concept of liability makes room for _vicarious_ liability, which is liability on the basis of something done by someone else, provided that the other person stood in some appropriate relationship to oneself.

I have specified that people who subscribe to a moral standard *tend* to regard deviants as liable to negative responses and *tend* to have such responses, *other things being equal*. This language is to allow for excusing conditions, such as we find in our own moral view. We will excuse a person if his action was unintentional, for instance. Other moralities may have different excusing conditions,[43] but a person's code of standards would not count as a moral code if it provided that no one could ever be deemed liable to any kind of negative response.

Ideals of supererogation do require an amendment to my view, for we do not view failures to live up to a supererogatory ideal as warranting a negative response. On the contrary, compliance with a supererogatory ideal warrants a positive response. A person who views helping the needy as supererogatory would view helping the needy as warranting praise. She would not view failures to help as warranting blame.

I will not attempt to give truth conditions for propositions about supererogatory actions. Instead, since supererogatory actions are regarded as morally good, I propose the following as an account of *accepting a standard as a standard regarding the good*:

> (*D6*) One accepts a standard *A* as a standard regarding the good just in case
>
> (1) one tends to have a favorable attitude toward those in one's society who comply with *A*, and toward oneself for complying with it, and toward compliance with it; and
>
> (2) if one is a member of a society, then, other things being equal, one would prefer a situation in which more people in the society intended to conform to *A* and were disposed to conform to it to a situation in which fewer people had this intention and disposition; and
>
> (3) there is a standard *B* such that (a) *B* calls on one to respond positively, in prescribed ways and circumstances, to instances of compliance with *A* on the part either of oneself or of anyone else in one's society, and (b) one is disposed to conform to *B*, and (c) if one is a member of a society, then one desires that it be generally so in one's society that people conform to *B*, and are disposed to conform to it, and one would prefer a situation in which more people in the society had these properties to a situation in which fewer people did, other things being equal.

For simplicity, I will describe such a pair of standards as "a standard" regarding the good. One might accept standards regarding the good that call for certain actions, certain attitudes, and so on. For example, a standard that calls on people to choose to seek or maintain friendships might be accepted as a standard regarding the good.

Since standards regarding the good are moral standards, I should not say that

---

43. A moral code might even allow for no excuses from blame. There would then be a kind of *absolute* moral liability. But compare Hart, 1961, pp. 168–69, 173–75.

every moral standard is morally subscribed to in the sense given in *D3*. Yet I do think that a *moral code* must include *some* standards that are subscribed to as moral standards, for it must include some that are paired with standards governing negative responses. A moral code could not consist entirely of standards regarding the good.

I will soon attempt to defend this claim. To forestall misunderstanding, however, I want to say right away that I am not saying that every moral code must include standards that purport to create *duties*. For all that I have said, a person's moral code could be a code of virtues, consisting entirely of standards concerned with states of character. If so, however, the person would have to subscribe morally to the standards, which means that he would have to subscribe to standards calling for a negative response to failures of virtue.

Moral Codes

Most of us accept a plurality of moral standards, a plurality that cannot be regimented as a deductive system with a single moral principle as logically basic. One's moral code is a system of all of these standards, and technically it is a standard itself. I shall say that a person's moral code is a standard to which the person subscribes as a moral code:

> (D7)   One subscribes to a standard as a moral code just in case
> (1) one subscribes to it as a moral standard in the sense given in *D3*,
> (2) it includes some and excludes no standards to which one subscribes morally,
> (3) it includes any standards one accepts in the sense given in *D5*, standards that govern negative responses to failures to comply with the standards to which one subscribes morally,
> (4) it includes all standards one accepts in the sense given in *D6*, standards regarding the good,
> (5) it includes no other standards, and
> (6) it applies non-vacuously to every member of one's society.

This implies that every moral code must incorporate standards that govern the expression of negative responses.

This does not rule out the possibility of a "quietistic" moral code, which requires that everyone "mind his own business."[44] A quietistic moral code might prohibit the overt *expression* of negative responses, but it would still call for negative responses in cases where the code is not complied with. A code that prohibited *all* negative responses, whether covert or not, would amount to a code regarding the good. I will argue that a code of this kind should not be counted as a moral code.

The possibility of conflict among different standards to which one subscribes

---

44. I owe this example to D. G. Brown (in conversation).

morally means that conformity to one's *code* does not imply conformity to *each* of the standards to which one subscribes morally, considered one at a time. A person can do what we think is right, all things considered, even though he fails to comply with one or more of our moral standards. For example, we may think that a person could have sufficient moral justification for telling a lie even if we accept a standard that prohibits lying. Hence, conforming to one's code means conforming to the system of standards subscribed to morally, considered as a whole.

Clause 6 of the definition says that one's moral code "applies non-vacuously to every member of one's society." This means it is not the case that there are people in one's society who would conform to one's moral code no matter what they did. A moral code does not treat the behavior of certain people in society as morally indifferent in this way. We do sometimes endorse standards targeted to subgroups of society, such as standards for doctors, the judiciary, or parents. For instance, the rule that doctors are to secure informed consent says, in effect, that if one is a doctor, then one is to secure informed consent. People who are not doctors conform to it vacuously. They do not satisfy its antecedent, and so nothing they do can count as a failure to conform to it. One's moral code cannot be such that, in a similar way, certain people in one's society would conform to it no matter what they did.

Conclusion

The details of my account of moral subscription are less important than its overall structure, and the more specific details and structural features are less important than the more general features. Most central is my underlying idea that a standard of behavior is constituted a person's moral standard by being the object of an appropriate attitude.[45] This idea could be accepted by someone who rejected some details of my account. The overall shape of my account is also important. It is crucial that moral subscription to a standard involves the intention and the disposition to conform, the desire that the standard have currency in one's society, and acceptance of a standard governing negative responses to (intentional) failures to conform.

It is now time to provide some arguments in favor of my conception and to reply to objections. I shall concentrate on the attitudes toward others implied by moral subscription, such as the tendency to respond negatively to others in one's society who fail to conform, and the desire that one's moral standards have currency in one's society. I will conclude by explaining how the attitudi-

---

45. This idea would be left intact if I accepted Sinnott-Armstrong's suggestion (in correspondence) that it matters why one subscribes to a standard. If one subscribes to it for self-serving reasons, it is not among one's moral standards. I disagree, however. It matters that a person forms the syndrome of attitudes defined by *D3*, but I do not think it matters *why* she does. Notice that if I accepted the suggestion, my theory would rule out theories such as Gauthier's (1986).

nal conception accounts for the distinction between moral standards and standards of etiquette.

Negative Responses: Norms and Tendencies

Moral subscription to a standard implies a tendency to respond negatively to people who fail to conform to the standard, and it implies that one subscribes to a norm governing negative responses to failures to conform. I will attempt to support these claims in this section. For the moment, we need to ignore standards regarding the good.

We would reject a person's claim to accept sincerely a standard calling for truth-telling if we found that she has no intention at all to conform to it. Similarly, we would reject her claim if we found that she has no tendency at all to view herself negatively if she fails to conform to it, and we would reject her claim if we found that she has no tendency at all to respond negatively to other people who fail to conform to it. We would also reject it if she did not view her negative responses as *appropriate*. The account of moral subscription can explain the basis of these intuitively plausible lines of thought.

One can take many different attitudes toward a standard. Someone might simply use a set of standards as an abstract body of rules to categorize the behavior of others, without having any tendency to disapprove of failures to conform or to regard such failures as indicating a liability to a negative response: "Oh, Smith tells lies, I see, and constantly violates the rule against lying." This alienated attitude or lack of conative response toward others' noncompliance with a standard is not compatible with subscribing to it as a moral standard. Neither would a similar unresponsiveness toward one's own non-compliance be compatible with this. A person whose moral view includes a prohibition of lying would at least *tend* to blame himself, if he were to lie, other things being equal, just as he would tend to respond negatively to the liar Smith or to his lies.

It may be objected that moral weakness can involve a kind of conative unresponsiveness. One can subscribe to a standard and yet intentionally fail to conform, and one might not even feel guilty. Intentions and dispositions are only so effective. Competing motivations can gain the upper hand and result in cases of moral weakness and alienation. I am claiming merely that a lack of *any* intention to conform to a given standard, lack of a *policy* of conforming, is not compatible with subscribing to it as a moral standard. Similarly, a lack of any tendency to blame those who fail to conform to a standard is not compatible with subscribing to it as a moral standard.

I have claimed that a person's moral code could not consist entirely of standards accepted as standards regarding the good. It seems to me that the concept of morality is the concept of standards that are of sufficient importance that some negative reaction is warranted for failures to comply. This idea, which is derived from John Stuart Mill,[46] is not, as I have conceded, accurate to all

---

46. Mill, 1863, chapter 5.

moral standards. Standards regarding the good are standards that warrant a *positive* reaction in case of compliance rather than a *negative* reaction in case of non-compliance. Yet the Millean idea survives to this extent: A moral code must include standards subscribed to as moral standards, and standards of this kind are paired with standards that call for negative reactions in case of failures to comply.

An example suggested by Michael Bratman may cast doubt on this idea.[47] Suppose cosmic rays destroy our ability to have negative emotional reactions, but leave us exactly as we are in all other respects. Suppose that, as a result, we eventually cease to accept standards that call for negative reactions. It seems that we might still have a moral code, and, if so, then a moral code need not include standards that call for negative reactions. To my mind, however, we would *not* continue to have a moral code in this case. We would no longer view torture as morally wrong if we did not accept a standard that called for some negative response to torture. Even in the cosmic ray world, we *could* accept standards that call for negative responses. For example, we could accept norms according to which it is appropriate to desire that the unkind suffer and that torturers be punished. This would give a sufficient foothold for attributing moral attitudes to us.

Walter Sinnott-Armstrong has suggested a slightly different example.[48] Suppose that cosmic rays change our psychology so that it becomes counterproductive to have negative responses. Because of this, we come to accept standards that call on us to use praise and rewards to encourage people and that do not call for any negative responses. We might still have a moral code, for we might still accept standards that, for example, forbid torture and call for kindness to strangers. To my mind, however, we would not still have a moral code. We would no longer view torture as morally wrong or kindness as morally virtuous if we felt that acts of torture or acts of unkindness did not merit any kind of negative response.

The kind and degree of negative reaction that are viewed as appropriate can vary from culture to culture; within one culture, different moral requirements may be treated differently. As H. L. A. Hart points out,

> deviations from the moral code meet with many different forms of hostile social reaction, ranging from relatively informal expressions of contempt to severance of social relations or ostracism. But emphatic reminders of what the rules demand, appeals to conscience, and reliance on the operation of guilt and remorse, are the characteristic and most prominent forms of pressure used for the support of social morality.[49]

By comparison with our own society, of course, other societies might be more or less aggressive in the typical case of violation of the shared morality.[50]

47. In discussing Gibbard's views.
48. In personal correspondence.
49. Hart, 1961, pp. 175–76.
50. Smith, 1974, p. 76.

One's Society as the Scope of Morality

A person who subscribes morally to a standard must desire that it have currency at least in his own society. He must also accept a standard that treats anyone in his society who fails to conform to it as liable to blame. It is time to discuss these claims.

It is important to emphasize that a person who subscribes morally to a standard *may* have a tendency to blame anyone at all who fails to conform, other things being equal, and *may* desire that the standard have currency in every society. My claim is about what is *required* as a matter of subscribing morally.

Some will object to my claim by insisting that one need not desire that one's morality have currency in *any* society. Others will object that one must desire that one's morality have currency in *every* society. Some will object that one need not tend to blame others in one's society who fail to conform. Others will object that one must tend to blame anyone who fails to conform, without restriction. Consequently, my argument needs to resist both a narrowing tendency and a widening tendency. The former would allow standards subscribed to merely as personal standards or ideals to count as moral. The latter would refuse to count insider codes as moral codes.

I have already argued both that insider codes ought to be counted as moral codes and that merely personal standards and ideals are not moral standards.[51] Let me say more about personal standards, however, for we do sometimes speak of our personal standards or ideals as "moral ideals." Even if they are merely standards of hygiene or exercise, we can feel guilty for failing to live up to them, and we may feel that we "must" live up to them. We may even believe we have a "duty" to comply with them. If the standards in question are justified in a relevant way, then, according to the standard-based theory, it might even be true that we have such a duty. Yet it would not be a *moral* duty unless the standard were justified in a morally relevant way. And the complex of attitudes we take toward personal standards still falls short of moral subscription.

I do not know whether personal standards can be relevantly justified. It may be that they are best regarded as optional commitments, in the way the moral skeptic regards moral commitments, for we choose them simply as standards for our own lives. Of course, since we choose them for our own lives, our subscription to them can be evaluated from our own standpoint, on the basis of our own goals and needs. Yet it is not clear whether, for example, the proposition that I ought to have daily outdoor exercise is true if it is merely that my subscription to a standard that calls for such exercise qualifies as rational.

Vegetarianism is simply a personal standard for some people, although it is a moral standard for others. According to the attitudinal conception, the difference between subscribing morally to a standard and accepting it merely as a personal standard is that, in the former case but not the latter, one tends to blame at least some others who fail to conform to it, and one desires that it

---

51. The distinction between moral standards and merely personal standards was noticed by P. F. Strawson (1974b, pp. 27–28).

have currency in one's society. I think this is the correct account of the difference. For example, a moral vegetarian would regard as blameworthy anyone in his society who willingly eats meat, without an excuse, and he must surely desire that vegetarianism gain currency at least in his society. But a personal vegetarian would not regard the eating of meat by others as blameworthy.[52] She likely would *prefer* that more rather than fewer people be vegetarians, but she would have no desire that a standard prohibiting the eating of meat gain currency in society, for she does not desire that people tend to regard the eating of meat as creating a presumption of liability to blame. In short, the distinction between our personal ideals and standards and our moral standards turns on the attitudes we take toward compliance with the standards on the part of other people in our society.

There is, however, an obvious objection to my position, which begins by pointing out that a person's desire that people have the intention to conform to a standard can differ in comprehensiveness, from cases where he desires merely that he intend to conform, to cases where he desires that every person without exception have the intention to conform. The case where he desires the currency of a standard exactly in his own society is only one case in a range of possible cases. I therefore need to explain why I take this case to be definitive.

Four lines of thought support my view: One is based on the nature of moral skepticism, a second is based on the centrality of society and culture in our lives, the third involves a renewed appeal to our intuitions about conative unresponsiveness, and the final argument is from conceptual simplicity.

As I defined "skepticism" in chapter 3, the moral skeptic denies that anything that could serve as a social moral code is relevantly justified. To be sure, she would deny that any code has a relevant justification with a truly universal scope, applying to humanity as a whole, and she would likely also deny that any more specialized code, such as a code of professional ethics, has a relevant justification. But it would not be adequate to defeat her view if we could only justify codes intended for specialized groups of less than societal scale, such as associations of lawyers or doctors or gangs of criminals. Groups of these sorts have common objectives and closely related interests that may well provide a basis at least for an interesting kind of intersubjective justification. Yet societies are comprehensive enough to include people with quite disparate interests and objectives in life, and with conflicting needs and values. It would be quite significant—and I think it would be sufficient to defeat moral skepticism—if we could establish a basis for relevantly justifying social moral codes. We would then have a powerful result, especially if, as I argue in chapter 7, humanity as a whole may well constitute a society.

In directing our attention to codes that are subscribed to in the sense defined by *D3*, we do not limit our attention to codes that already have currency in a society. Instead, we regard the skeptical challenge as a challenge to justify codes

---

52. Of course, she may respond negatively to non-vegetarians, in the way that anyone may respond negatively to something disliked, but she would not view the eating of meat as creating a *liability* to a negative response.

that we view as candidates for the status of social moral code, in that we desire them to have currency in our society. This is why codes that people desire to have currency in their society are of central interest. It does not really matter whether codes of other sorts, to which we have different attitudes, might also be called "moral codes" in ordinary language.

Given that societies are characterized by shared standards of interaction that are part of the culture, as I shall explain in chapter 7, it is no surprise that we desire the fellow members of our society to share the standards to which we morally subscribe. Our society is a network of our more important interpersonal relationships, such as our friendships and our families, and it links us with others in cooperative relationships that give structure and sustenance to our lives. We are united in our society both by its network of personal relationships and by the standards of interaction that govern it. The culture of every society includes a system of behavioral standards, for a society is characterized by interaction governed by standards that are widely subscribed to by its members. And it is at least typical for a society's culture to include a social moral code. If a person's moral code deviated from his society's social moral code, he surely would tend to view his own code as a competitor of society's code, and he would prefer that his code replace it.

It may be objected that some people might be so alienated that they have no desire that a code they subscribe to have currency in their society, or they might be so alienated from certain members of the society that they do not care whether these people conform to their code. Yet could this be so, if the code at issue is their moral code? There is a kind of not caring that results from a loss of hope, but it does not necessarily imply a loss of desire. For example, a teacher might "stop caring" whether his students are doing well because he has given up, yet in a typical case he would still desire that they do well. This kind of detachment is no problem for my view.

In order to undermine my view, it would have to be shown that a person could entirely lack the desire that her moral code have currency in any society to which she belongs. For instance, suppose she knows that many people in her society eat their unwanted children, charcoal-broiled. She recognizes that these people are failing to conform to her standards for the treatment of children, but she has no desire at all that they conform and no tendency at all to blame them for failing to conform. This attitude would reflect a moral alienation or a conative unresponsiveness of a kind and degree that would surely indicate that the standard is not part of her moral code. It is not something she subscribes to as a moral standard.

The intuition I am relying on does not extend beyond the scope of a society. The relationships or potential for relationships with members of other societies may be much less salient to a person than the relationships to members of his own society. Moreover, a person may have no desire that those from outside his society conform to his moral code: He simply may not care whether they conform. He may not view them as persons, or, although he views them as persons, he may regard their departures from his morality as alien, rather than as creating a presumption of blameworthiness. Or he may think that they are in such different circumstances that his own moral standards are not appropriate. In the latter case, society-centered theory allows that he may be correct. His standards may not be appropriate in the sense that they may not be justified relative to the other societies.

The final argument is from conceptual simplicity. We use the term "morality" to refer to the socially enforced and culturally transmitted codes of behavior that are a feature of the culture of every society. We also use it to refer to certain codes subscribed to by individual persons, even if they deviate from the codes generally subscribed to in their societies. My account of the concepts of a moral standard and moral code finds a unity in these two cases. In essence, I say that a moral code is either a society's code of behavior or a competitor of such, in that those who subscribe to it want it to become current in their society.

The concept of a society is vague in the ways I will explain in chapter 7. Therefore, there is an unavoidable vagueness in the claim that a person desires his moral code to have currency in his *society*. For this reason, there can be cases at the margin, where a standard seems to qualify as among a person's moral standards even though the person has no evident desire for the conformity of certain people who seem to be members of his society.

Morality and Etiquette

A typical code of etiquette is found where there are conventional ways of behaving—conventions of etiquette—and it consists of requirements to conform to the conventions.[53] It is a set of standards as to how things "are to be done" in certain contexts, where complying with the standards consists in conforming to a convention. In the code of etiquette I am familiar with, for example, one sets a dinner table with each person's table knife to the right of the dinner plate. This is the way things "are to be done." Corresponding to this standard is a convention of setting the table with the knife to the right.

Nothing prevents a person from subscribing morally to standards about setting the table and the like, but people usually are more clear-headed than this and take a different attitude toward standards corresponding to conventions of etiquette than they take toward their moral standards. They neither desire that the standards have currency in society nor tend to blame those who fail to conform to the way things "are done." Of course, if a person deliberately flouts a convention in order to give insult, then he may be regarded as liable to blame. However, a person who sets the table "incorrectly" is more typically viewed with some amusement, as ignorant or uncultured. Moreover, in my experience, people do not care whether the conventions that they accept are observed throughout society. It is enough if etiquette is observed in their presence, by their dinner companions, for instance. Subscribing to a standard as a conventional rule of etiquette is therefore quite different from subscribing to a standard as a moral standard.

53. For the notion of a convention, see Lewis, 1969.

Some requirements that are sometimes described as matters of etiquette are not conventional in the way that the rules of table-setting are conventional because alternatives would not suit just as well. For instance, one is to keep quiet during a concert. Not to do so is inconsiderate or impolite. Alternatives would hardly be as acceptable to a group interested in the concert. I will call requirements of this sort "standards of consideration." People typically subscribe to these standards as moral standards, for it is typical to hold that one morally ought to be considerate of other people. The impoliteness or inconsiderateness of a person who makes noise in a concert hall is described as "rude," but it is typically regarded as blameworthy and as the sort of behavior one does not want to become current in society. Strictly speaking, I want to say, standards toward which a person takes this attitude are part of her moral view, even though they are sometimes described as matters of etiquette.

Some standards of consideration are dependent on the existence of conventions. For instance, certain hand signals are conventional ways of giving insult, and using them is a way of being inconsiderate. But they can be used to give insult only because of the existence of background conventions about their meaning, so the prohibition on their use makes sense only because of the existence of these conventions. Given an appropriate background, any convention of etiquette can give rise to a standard of consideration in a similar way, for the flouting of a convention can be a way of giving insult or indicating disrespect.

In the typical case, people who subscribe to a standard of consideration do desire that it have currency in their society and do tend to blame those who fail to conform. But their desire of currency and tendency to blame are conditional on the existence of the corresponding conventions regarding insults or inconsiderateness. If we subscribe morally to the prohibition on insulting signals, for instance, our subscription is conditional on the existence of the corresponding convention.

The interplay between morality and etiquette is complex. There is a distinction to be drawn, however, and the key to it is a difference between the attitudes definitive of moral subscription and the attitudes we take toward standards we treat as a matter of etiquette.

Moralities as Social Moral Codes

The attitudinal conception classifies as moral codes the social codes that are elements of the cultures of societies or of large-scale social groups. Examples are the morality of the Dobu and contemporary bourgeois North American morality. It classifies insider codes as moral codes, as well as codes with what seem to us to be bizarre features.[54] It also classifies as moral codes the objects

---

54. Among the Dobu of northwestern Melanesia, Ruth Benedict found "a premium upon ill-will and treachery," which were "the recognized virtues of their society" (1934, p. 131). She says, "We might suppose that in the matter of taking life all peoples would agree in condemnation. On the contrary, in a matter of homicide, it may be held that ... one kills by custom his first two children, or that a husband has right of life and death over his wife, or that is the duty of the child to kill his parents before they are old" (p. 45).

of smaller groups' or of individuals' attitudes of moral subscription. Examples here are the moral codes of certain fringe groups in our own society with unconventional views about, say, sex, drugs, work, and political violence.

Social moral codes are socially enforced and culturally transmitted codes that are generally subscribed to as moral codes by the members of a society. An individual who is *realistic* in subscribing morally to a standard would also desire that it be socially enforced, culturally transmitted, and generally subscribed to in her society. That is, we could say, the moral code of an individual is a *model* for a social moral code. Let me explain.

A person who subscribes morally to a code desires that others in her society generally conform to it, intend to conform to it, and so on. Now, given human psychology as we know it, a widespread intentional conformity to a standard in a society is likely only if the standard is widely subscribed to and socially enforced in the society. Blame is a kind of informal social sanction, and a widespread tendency of people to blame themselves and others for failures to conform to a code would be a mechanism of social enforcement. Without some such mechanism, widespread compliance with the code would not be likely. Moreover, given human psychology, a code is unlikely to be socially enforced and widely subscribed to in a society unless it is or becomes part of the culture. Therefore, to be *realistic* in subscribing morally to a standard, one must desire that it be socially enforced, culturally transmitted, and generally subscribed to morally in one's society. This is a sense in which one's morality is a *model* for a social moral code.

Unrealistic, utopian, and esoteric codes may still be moral codes.[55] For instance, a person might subscribe to a moral code according to which no one is ever to be coerced or pressured to conform to the code and according to which children are never to be punished in the course of teaching them to comply with the code. As a matter of subscribing to this code, we may assume the person desires that the code not be socially enforced and not be culturally transmitted in the usual ways. But she is being unrealistic, for subscribing to the code entails desiring that it have currency in society, and this desire is not likely to be satisfied unless the morality is socially enforced and culturally transmitted.[56]

---

55. I owe the examples in this paragraph to D. G. Brown (in conversation).

56. Henry Sidgwick argued that utilitarian morality is likely to lead to bad results in the hands of the "vulgar," given the "inevitable indefiniteness and complexity of [the] calculations" that are involved in applying it. And so, he concluded, "in the actual condition of civilized communities," it may be best from a utilitarian point of view that utilitarian morality be esoteric (Sidgwick, 1907, p. 490.) If Sidgwick is correct, then we should not want the utilitarian principle to serve in our society as the social moral code. Also, we should not subscribe morally to the principle, for to subscribe morally to it would be to desire it to have currency in our society, and Sidgwick thinks it would be best that it not have currency. Sidgwick himself presumably does not subscribe morally to the principle. Of course, he may still subscribe to it as a personal standard and endorse it relative to some supposed elite, and he may still think that it is justified. He presumably believes that utilitarian moral propositions are true. But if so, then his moral standards, if any, do not correspond in the natural way to his moral beliefs. Parfit discusses the idea that consequentialism is "self-effacing" (1984, pp. 40–43). Williams discusses "esoteric morality" (1985, pp. 108–9; 1973, pp. 134–35).

There are mechanisms that tend to destabilize morality, for a moral code may call on a person to act to his disadvantage. However, the social enforcement and cultural transmission of a moral code and the general subscription to it contribute to its stability by attaching psychological and social sanctions to it and thereby making deviations from it less eligible. The social enforcement and cultural transmission of a moral code go together, for teaching and reinforcement are part of cultural transmission and also part of what is meant by social enforcement. The process of moral training and education tends to preserve a social moral code from generation to generation, as does the social enforcement of the code, which contributes both to the moral training of children and to the reinforcement of moral attitudes among adults. It is for these reasons, among others, that social moral codes are socially enforced and culturally transmitted. And it is for these reasons that to subscribe realistically to a moral code one must in effect view it as a model for a social moral code.

6

Society-Centered Moral Theory

We have seen that any paradigmatic moral proposition entails, nontrivially, that some relevant moral standard has a specific authoritative status. Under what conditions would a standard have that status? I speak of this status as that of being "justified." What is the nature of this status?

According to the attitudinal theory, a moral code either is, or is a "model" for, a social moral code. Call this the "model principle." Given this principle, I will suggest, it is natural to evaluate moral codes on the basis of *how well* they would serve as the social moral code in a given society. A moral code is justified, for a given society, if it is the code that would serve *best* as its social moral code.

An obvious difficulty with this proposal is that there appear to be many different criteria that could be used to rank moral codes with respect to "how well" they would serve as a social moral code. Any given putative code may be ranked best by *some* standard of evaluation. Hence the question becomes, Which standard of evaluation for moral codes is the relevant one? According to society-centered theory, the relevant standard is given by standards of rational choice, and the relevant standpoint of appraisal is that of the society in question.

This chapter presents arguments for the society-centered view and explains some of its features. Subsequent chapters fill in the details. What is a society? Chapter 7 answers this question in detail. Are societies capable of rational choice? Chapter 8 argues that, surprisingly, this question can plausibly be answered in the affirmative. What are the standards of rational choice? Chapter 9 develops a theory I call "needs-and-values" rationality. This theory is used in chapter 10 to explore features of the "needs-based" version of society-centered theory that I favor. Other theories of rational choice would, of course, yield different versions of the theory. Chapter 11 deals with various metaphysical, epistemological, semantic, and other meta-ethical issues raised by the society-centered view.

The Justification Thesis of Society-Centered Theory

The central idea of society-centered theory can be expressed by the following characteristic justification thesis, or "*J* thesis":

A code is justified as a moral code in relation to a society just in case the society would be rationally required to select the code to serve in it as the social moral code, in preference to any alternative.

I will often use the term "rational" to abbreviate "rationally required."

A code is the social moral code in a society if it is the public moral code that is socially enforced, culturally transmitted, and generally subscribed to by the members of the society as a moral code. One alternative for a society may be to have *no* social moral code. If a society would be rational to choose to have *no* social moral code, then there is no *justified* moral code, in relation to the society. This means that society-centered theory is compatible with the skeptical thesis that no moral standard is justified.

A moral code is justified, according to the *J* thesis, only if a society would be rational to choose it. Of course, it may well be that no society has ever *actually* chosen a moral code to serve as its social moral code, but the theory requires of a justified moral code only that a relevant society *would* be rational to choose it.

This initial formulation of the *J* thesis will need to be amended as we proceed. For example, it ignores the possibility of moral codes that are tied as best. In chapter 10, I will propose a minor amendment to allow for ties and introduce three additional amendments, including one designed to deal with the fact that some societies have members in common. Later in this chapter, I will introduce an amendment to deal with "state of nature" situations.

As stated, the *J* thesis of society-centered theory is independent of the standard-based theory of normative judgment. But I want to defend a claim that links the two theories. According to society-centered theory, the *J* property for moral standards is a *relation* between standards and societies. For a given society, it is a *relational property*, the property of being included in the code that the society would be rationally required to select, in preference to any other code, to serve as its social moral code. I will defend the claim that standards and codes with this property are justified in the sense that is necessary for the truth of corresponding paradigmatic moral propositions. According to the standard-based theory, a moral proposition entails, nontrivially, that a standard is relevantly justified. I claim that a standard is relevantly justified just in case it has this *J* property. In general, paradigmatic moral propositions are true only if some standards have the *J* property. I will treat this claim as part of the overall society-centered theory.

Because the *J* property is relational, this doctrine implies that moral propositions are relational in a corresponding sense. I will address the relativistic implications of this idea in chapter 11.

Moral Skepticism and Societal Needs

Given the discouraging results of chapter 4, we need to take seriously the skeptical view that there are no relevantly justified moral standards. Given the standard-based theory of normativity, moreover, this skeptical view entails that there are no true paradigmatic moral propositions. Hence, we need to take seriously this doctrine as well.

It is difficult to take these views seriously from an intuitive point of view, however, especially from the viewpoint of someone engaged in moral thought, for the "natural participant attitude" is to take one's moral claims to be true. Indeed, certain moral propositions seem true beyond any reasonable doubt, such as, for instance, the propositions that slavery was unjust and that it is wrong to torture people just for fun.[1] It is therefore difficult to take seriously the idea that these claims are simply *false*. The skeptic thinks they are false, not because of some hitherto unnoticed features of slavery or torture, but because of a quite general problem, the non-existence of any justified moral standards. Yet it is difficult for a participant in moral thought to take seriously the idea that there are no justified moral standards. It seems beyond reasonable doubt that the standards that prohibit torturing just for fun are justified. These standards seem as credible and warranted as the epistemological and logical standards that one would typically employ in assessing skeptical arguments.

Yet the skeptic denies that moral standards have a credibility of the kind enjoyed by the best standards of epistemology and logic. Rather, moral standards can be compared to standards of an outmoded and rejected code of etiquette, such as courtly love. Neither kind of standard has any justification or relevant standing. Claims in courtly love, as to how men ought to behave in relation to women, for example, seem at best to be quaint and curious. Given that the standards of courtly love have no currency in our society, and given that they lack an appropriate or relevant justification, the paradigmatic claims of courtly love, such as the claim that men must treat women as objects of worship, are just false. The skeptic views moral claims as on a par with claims in courtly love. They too are false.

These consequences of skepticism are difficult to accept, but there are even worse consequences. If skepticism is true, it would seem, then enlightened good sense would require purging oneself of moral beliefs and ceasing to subscribe morally to any standards.[2] One might subscribe to them as personal standards, but if no moral standards have any relevant justification, then subscription to the moral standards one was taught would appear to involve an irrational "rule worship." It would involve pursuing policies required by the moral rules, even though the moral rules have no relevant standing at all.[3] An enlightened man no longer subscribes to the standards of courtly love and no longer has courtly beliefs. Similarly, an enlightened person would not subscribe to moral standards

---

1. For the view that such claims express necessary truths, see Judith Jarvis Thomson, 1989.

2. Recall that I am using "moral skepticism" to name the doctrine that there are no justified moral standards. This implies in turn that none of our (paradigmatic) moral beliefs is true. As I use the term in this context, moral skepticism is not simply the thesis that our moral beliefs are epistemically unjustified.

3. J. J. C. Smart criticized rule utilitarianism for "rule worship." But there is a deeper and more troubling kind of irrational rule worship involved in following moral rules, if skepticism is correct, than there would be, according to Smart, under the rule utilitarian approach. See Smart, 1973, p. 10.

or have moral beliefs. If a person did subscribe morally to certain standards, he would have no basis for thinking himself as on any firmer ground in subscribing morally to them than would be the case if, in the late twentieth century, he were to subscribe morally to the standards of courtly love. Similarly, it would seem, if no moral standards are justified, then an enlightened society would purge its culture of moral rules, except perhaps in the guise of rules of etiquette. It would not train its children to have beliefs about moral right and wrong, any more than it would train them to have beliefs about ghosts. Its culture would view moral standards as merely conventional standards of propriety, much as we view our own standards of etiquette.

To be sure, these are not consequences merely of skepticism. They follow from skepticism combined with assumptions about what enlightenment and rationality require of people and societies. But the additional assumptions seem plausible. For it seems plausible to hold that an enlightened society is a society of enlightened people and that rational, enlightened people aim to have true beliefs and to subscribe to rules that have some relevant warrant.

Common sense suggests that, if skepticism has these consequences, then it must be false. For we *need* morality in order to get along together in our social life; that is, *societies* need morality; a society needs to have a social moral code. And the societal need for a moral code would better be served by the currency of some moral codes than it would be by the currency of certain other moral codes. Some moral codes are better than others, from the point of view of their impact on the ability of a society to meet its needs.

The idea is that unless a moral code has currency in a society, the members of the society will tend to suit their actions to their personal desires and needs, aiming to achieve advantages for themselves. The things people want are in limited supply, and people sometimes desire the same things. Moreover, although people's natural attachments of affection and caring, combined with their need for companionship, do lead them to see a personal advantage in some other people achieving what they want and need, these attachments and needs are limited in their effect. We care about some others who are close to us, not about all others with whom we compete for the things we desire. So there is a tendency for conflict to emerge among the people in a society.[4] To flourish in a society, however, people need to avoid harmful conflict. They need to cooperate in joint activities and to coordinate expectations, and in order to achieve these ends, they need to be able to expect each other to keep agreements and to comply with social conventions around which they can coordinate their behavior. The currency of a moral code is, I think, the most efficient way to reduce the harmfulness of conflict and to give people the assurance they need in order to be able to trust each other to cooperate and coordinate successfully.

One might think a society could get by without a shared *moral* code as long as its members endorse *some* standards of behavior, even if merely the rules of the legal system. But a legal system cannot exist unless at least some people view

4. See Hobbes, 1651, chapter 13.

themselves as under a duty—an extra-legal duty—to conform to the rules.[5] If legal rules exist, then it is trivial that people are under legal duties to do as the rules require. But, I am claiming, if a legal system is to exist, at least some people must think there is more to it than that. They must think they are under a duty to comply with law that is not merely a matter of the fact that the rules call for them to comply with the rules. Of course, coercion can go some way toward enforcing compliance with law. Yet coercion is costly and, other things being equal, a legal system can be less coercive to the degree that more people view themselves as under an extra-legal duty to conform to the law. Other things being equal, we do better, as a society, to have law accompanied by the view that there is a background moral obligation to comply with the law. So it remains that, as a society, we need some social moral code.

Etiquette will not do the job that morality can do. Failures to comply with a code of etiquette are viewed as much less serious than failures to comply with a code that is subscribed to morally. People tend to blame each other and to feel guilty for failures to conform to a code they subscribe to morally, and they desire that the code have currency throughout the society. They give it a kind of preferred status. But if they subscribe to a code merely as a matter of etiquette, then they view it as merely a convention, with reasonable alternatives. They think of it as merely a code conventionally selected from a set of codes, any one of which would have served just as well as it does. For these reasons, it would contribute more to reducing harmful conflict if people subscribed to the code as a moral code. They would then view deviation from the code as a more serious matter.

The upshot of this reasoning is to cast new light on the implication of skepticism that an enlightened society would purge itself of morality. Common sense says that a society needs to have a social moral code. Therefore, if this implication of skepticism is correct, common sense implies that societies need to avoid being enlightened and need to avoid having many of their members become enlightened. Societies need to avoid having the skeptical thesis be widely understood and accepted.

A further and more telling upshot of the commonsense position is to cast doubt on skepticism itself. The following seems entirely reasonable: If every society needs to have a social moral code in order to reduce the incidence of harmful conflict in the most efficient way, and if there is some moral code whose currency would better contribute to a society's achieving this goal than any other, then that code is justified in a fully relevant and adequate way. The requirements of that code are simply requirements. If the code requires that we not torture each other for fun, as it surely does, then we would be wrong to torture for fun. This claim is simply true, and moral skepticism is simply false.

To be sure, this is a view of matters that needs some philosophical backfilling. It is, however, a view that is licensed by the theory I will be developing in the rest of the book. It might be objected that this anti-skeptical argument

5. This is, I think, the implication of H. L. A. Hart's views regarding the minimum necessary and sufficient conditions for the existence of a legal system (1961, p. 113).

amounts simply to claiming that moral beliefs are useful fictions.[6] But according to the view I am attempting to develop, the utility of moral standards to the flourishing of societies is precisely what makes moral beliefs not be fictions. To be sure, this is not something I can prove. Rather, it is a view that I hope to make plausible on the basis of its explanatory virtues.

In this section, I have attempted to connect a commonsense response to moral skepticism with the central thesis of society-centered moral theory. The commonsense response is that skepticism must surely be false, given that any society needs to have a social moral code. The needs-and-values theory of rational choice, which I develop in chapter 9, takes it to follow that any society would be rational to select some moral code to serve in it as the social moral code. Given the needs-and-values theory, then, society-centered moral theory agrees with common sense. Society-centered theory connects the societal need for the currency of a moral code with the falsity of skepticism by making two connections. It connects the societal need for the currency of a code to the justification of the code, on the basis of the needs-and-values theory. And it connects the justification of the code to the truth conditions of moral propositions, on the basis of the standard-based theory of normative judgment.

Social Viability of Justified Moral Codes

Consider a code that contains a number of eccentric prohibitions and requirements. I will refer to it as the *Eccentric Code*. It forbids anyone to cooperate with anyone else. I will call this the *Non-cooperation Rule*. It forbids heterosexual intercourse. This is the *No-Heterosex Rule*. It requires everyone to commit suicide at the next full solar eclipse: the *Suicide Rule*. I will not concern myself with its remaining rules, for it should already be clear that it is not *socially viable*. Its currency in a society, in any society, would cause that society to cease to exist, other things being equal.

I think it is plain common sense that the Eccentric Code is not justified. A moral code is not justified, other things being equal, unless it is socially viable. More fully, a moral code is relevantly justified only if it is possible that it be universally followed in a society without that society's existence thereby being fatally undermined, other things being equal, and given the way human beings and human societies work. I shall refer to this thesis as the "social viability requirement." I want to show both that this thesis is intuitively quite plausible and that it can be explained by the society-centered theory.

We sometimes wish to argue for a moral principle, or even for the importance of morality itself, without presupposing agreement on any moral issues. In contexts of this sort, a principle very much like the social viability constraint often plays a role. Peter Mullen is a Yorkshire vicar who published a plea that morality be taken seriously in public debate.[7] He claims that "no society could

---

6. I owe this objection to Walter Sinnott-Armstrong (in correspondence).
7. Mullen, 1983.

survive for five minutes on the maxim that it is right to break one's word." He continues,

> [Consider] all the old moral universals. Stealing is wrong. Why? Well, what could its opposite possibly mean? Human society would not be a possibility if it were ever built on the maxim that "stealing is right." Even the most progressive disciple of Jeremy Bentham will agree that this holds in the case of murder. . . . Liberal societies, just as much as repressive societies, depend for their existence on being able to distinguish between right and wrong.

Mullen's argument rests on premises about traditional morality as well as dubious assumptions about the conditions under which a society would be destroyed. But one premise it rests on is very much like the social viability requirement, and I think it has intuitive appeal. To my way of thinking, the idea of a social viability requirement, which underlies the vicar's argument, is nothing but solid common sense.[8]

To be clear about this, we need to be clear about the idea of social viability. Any moral code would be causally incompatible with the continuing existence of some society under some imaginable circumstance. Suppose that the Evil Genius would destroy us unless we changed our moral commitments. In these circumstances, there is a clear sense in which our moral code is non-viable. But this sort of case is irrelevant. A moral code lacks social viability in the sense I am defining only if *no* society could survive its being universally followed, other things being equal. The virtue of the hypothetical Eccentric Code as an example is that it illustrates the relevant sort of non-viability.

In extreme circumstances, even an apparently reasonable moral code could imply a socially non-viable injunction. For instance, suppose we learn that every member of the next generation will die a horribly painful death due to a plague. In this circumstance, we may well be obligated to refrain from having any children in order to avoid causing unnecessary pain.[9] The injunction to refrain from having any children is socially non-viable in the relevant sense.[10] Yet this does not mean that our own moral code is socially non-viable, for there are many circumstances in which it does not support an obligation not to have any children.

Very few, if any, moral codes that are actually subscribed to lack social viability in the relevant sense. It is true that socially non-viable codes have gained currency in certain groups, such as among the Shakers, who had a rule of celibacy. However, this fact should not undermine the appeal of the social viability requirement. First, as we will see in the next chapter, the Shakers did not

---

8. There is a superficial similarity between Mullen's argument and the much-criticized argument of Lord Patrick Devlin in favor of the legal enforcement of morals (Devlin, 1965). But Mullen is not saying anything about the legal enforcement of morals, and he is appealing to an intuitive form of the social viability requirement, not to Devlin's hypercautious principle for invoking the law to buttress conventional morality.

9. The example is due to Richmond Campbell, 1984.

10. Aberle and colleagues remark, "A cult of sexual abstinence, if universalized, would terminate [a] society" (1950, pp. 103–4). Advances in non-sexual human reproductive technology might alter the situation. See the discussion in the next chapter.

constitute a society. Second, we do not think that the Shakers actually were morally required to be celibate. Third, it is likely that the Shakers were much more interested in spiritual matters than in the benefits of society. We should take this to mean "other things" were not "equal" in this case.[11]

Because subscribing morally to a code involves desiring that it have currency in one's society, a person would not subscribe morally to a socially non-viable code unless she either did not realize that universal compliance with the code would cause the demise of her society or she did not care very much about the survival of her society. This fact surely explains, in part, the appeal of the social viability constraint. Everyone has an interest in the existence of society, for everyone needs things that could not be attained—or attained as fully or as well—in the absence of a society. This is true even of the Shakers. For this reason, it is hard to see how any rational person could fail to care about the survival of her society. To point out the social non-viability of a code is therefore to argue that it would not be rational to desire the code to have currency in society. And to argue this is to argue that it would not be rational to subscribe morally to the code.

There is no difficulty seeing how society-centered theory would explain the social viability requirement, for society-centered theory implies that a code is justified as a moral code relative to a society only if the society would be rational to choose the code to serve as its social moral code. Other things being equal, it would not be rational for a society to favor a social moral code, universal compliance with which would cause its own demise. Hence, other things being equal, a moral code is justified only if it is socially viable.

Functionalism

There is a common intuition that the function of morality is to make society possible. This intuition seems to lie behind the "social function theories" discussed in the preceding chapter. I argued that the major error of these theories is that they treat a necessary condition of a moral code's counting as justified as if it were a necessary condition of a code's counting as a moral code at all. I now want to develop this idea more fully and show how the intuition about the function of morality can be explicated by society-centered theory.

I need to make a few remarks about the notion of a function, but this is not the place for a detailed or sophisticated discussion. My goal is simply to understand a common intuition. Consider, then, the notion that the function of the eye is to enable us to see. There are, I think, three ideas bound up with this. First, the eye *enables* us to see; it is partly *causally responsible* for the fact that we see. Second, the eye is there *in order to* enable us to see. Finally, a person's eye is *failing* if it does not enable him to see. I will call these the "causal,"

11. On the Shakers, see Kern, 1981, and the *Encyclopedia Britannica* (15th edition), which reports that Shaker membership declined from about six thousand in 1840, grouped in about twenty communities, to approximately a thousand in 1905. The first U.S. community was established in 1777.

"genetic," and "evaluative" ideas, respectively. There presumably are cases in which each of these ideas dominates our thinking about a function, but the evaluative idea is often the most important.

Begin with the causal idea. Something that fails to fulfill the function of things of kind *F* may still be an *F*. Indeed, the *majority* of members of a functional kind may fail to fulfill the function, for dysfunctions are very common in some cases. Hence, an epidemic could lead to a situation in which the vast majority of people are blind. The genetic idea assumes that the fact that the eye is responsible for our ability to see has a certain kind of explanation. It might be explained, for example, by the hypothesis that the eye was designed—by God—to enable us to see, or it could be explained by the hypothesis in evolutionary biology that the eye's being responsible for vision is a result of the fact that the species evolved in conditions in which the eye's contribution to vision was fitness-enhancing.[12] Yet there may be no God, and the biological function of the eye may actually be to enable us to avoid predators and find food, rather than to enable us to see more generally. Even if so, and even if most humans were blind, we might still think that the *function* of the eye is to enable us to see. For we might still think that eyes that are not sighted are *failing* or *misperforming*.

The evaluative idea, then, is that things with functions are failing or misperforming if they do not perform the function well. Understood in this way, to attribute a function to something is to provide a basis for attributing malfunctions, errors, successes, and failures.[13] Something that fails to fulfill the function of things of kind *F* may still be an *F*, but it would not then be a *good F*.

Let me turn now to the intuition that the function of morality is to make society possible. First, given the causal idea, it can be interpreted as the view that any moral code actually would contribute to sustaining a society, if it became the society's social moral code. Yet this is not true of the Eccentric Code, although it could be someone's moral code. Moreover, even if all social moral codes were dysfunctional, we might still think that morality has the *function* of sustaining society. Or second, given the genetic idea, the intuition can be read as the view that there is a true functional explanation of the origin of moral codes which shows that they exist in order to sustain societies.[14] Yet this is speculative sociobiology, and the functionalist intuition is not restricted to those who speculate about such things. For these reasons, I think there is more to the intuition than can be captured by either the causal or the genetic idea of a function, or by both in combination.

I think that the intuition is best understood in terms of the evaluative idea. The idea is that a moral code is unsuccessful in some relevant way if it does not or would not contribute to sustaining a society in which it was the social moral code. More fully, one moral code is "better" than another, in relation to a society, if its currency in the society would contribute better to the society's ability to meet its needs and to flourish.

---

12. These ideas are presented clearly and concisely by Gibbard (1990, pp. 62–63).
13. Matthen and Levy, 1984.
14. Gibbard explores ideas of this kind (1990, pp. 61–68).

This idea can be explained as an intuition about the justification of moral codes. It is concerned with functions and malfunctions of moral codes, and there is a sense in which codes that are not justified are malfunctional and codes that are justified are functional, relative to the role moral codes are "meant for," the role of social moral code. I propose, then, that the functionalist intuition can be captured or explicated in a systematic way by the society-centered theory.[15]

According to society-centered theory, a moral code is justified relative to a society just in case the society would be rational to choose it as its social moral code. I think this is one way to interpret the idea that moral codes are to be evaluated on the basis of their contribution to societies. Given the needs-and-values theory of rational choice, society-centered theory offers an even better explication of this idea. It offers an explication of the intuition that the better moral codes are the ones whose currency in a society would contribute better to the society's ability to meet its needs and to flourish, and that codes that are not well suited to sustaining societies are malfunctional.

The Model Principle and Society-Centered Theory

According to the "model principle," a moral code is either a social moral code or a "model" for a social moral code in the sense that, to subscribe to it realistically, one must *desire* that it be the social moral code. That is, one must desire it to be socially enforced, culturally transmitted, and generally subscribed to as a moral code in one's society.

Society-centered theory holds that it is appropriate to evaluate a would-be social moral code from the perspective of the society as a whole. The underlying intuition is that any society needs to have a social moral code if it is to continue to exist and to flourish. It is for this reason that any society would be rational to choose a code to serve in it as the social code. And it is for this reason that moral skepticism must be rejected. Morality is not merely optional, and this is shown by the societal need for a social moral code. Society-centered theory aims to develop this basic idea into an anti-skeptical moral theory.

Consider an analogy: A code of parliamentary debate is a code of standards. It is not a theory or anything that we would attempt to evaluate as true or false. Moreover, it seems sensible to say, if a proposed code of parliamentary debate can be justified, it can be justified on the basis of its ability to serve the needs and purposes of the relevant parliament. If it serves these needs and purposes well, then it has a rationale or a justification that is appropriate and relevant. But how is the idea to be explained in detail? It would be a mistake to suppose that a code of parliamentary debate is not adequately justified unless every member would be rational to accede to it as the code to govern debate. It would be a mistake, that is, to demand unanimity. If some members can achieve what

---

15. The idea that socially non-viable moral codes are not justified does offer a partial explication of the intuition. But the society-centered theory captures it more fully.

they want only through extensive filibustering, they might be rational to hold out for rules that permit filibustering, rules that it would not be rational for the parliament as a whole to select. On the view that demands rational unanimity, these members would have a veto, in that their disagreement would undermine the justification of the rules. This is hardly sensible. Instead, we should say, if a code of debating rules serves the needs and purposes of the relevant parliament *as a whole*, it is justified.

The analogy has its drawbacks, of course. Claims about what is permissible in parliamentary debate, if relativized to the rules that are actually in force in a given parliament, would be type-one normative. Moral claims are type-two normative. My point is merely that if a body of rules is intended for a particular parliament, and offered to that parliament as rules that could be used to govern its debates, then it is sensible to evaluate the rules from the point of view of the parliament as a whole.

Now, according to the model principle, there is a sense in which any given moral code is intended to serve as a social code in a given society. Similarly, then, it is sensible to evaluate it from the point of view of the society as a whole. It is not plausible, I think, to suppose that a moral code is justified only if every member of society would be rational to accede to its selection as the social code. This would mean that each individual member has a veto in that her rational disagreement would undermine the justification of a code, even if the society as a whole would be rational to select it. This would not be a sensible position. The model principle makes it natural to think instead that the justification of a moral code would be a matter of showing its suitability to serve as the social moral code. This conception suggests that if a moral code is justified at all, it is justified on the basis that it would be rationally chosen by a relevant society as a whole.

Recommending Social Change

A person who subscribes to a code as a moral code in relation to her society is implicitly *recommending* the code to her society as a social moral code. Moral subscription to a code involves the desire that the code have currency in one's society. But, as we saw in the preceding chapter, basic facts about human behavior and society imply that, in order for a code to have currency, it must be socially enforced, culturally transmitted, and generally subscribed to as a moral code. Unless it is a social moral code in this way, one could not reasonably expect that the code would be complied with by the members of the society. Hence, as we have seen, a person's subscription to a moral code is realistic only if she also desires that the code be the social moral code in her society. This is the model principle.

The import of this is that the realistic subscription to a moral code is the implicit recommendation of the code to some society; it is a recommendation to that society of a certain state of affairs involving the currency in it of a social moral code. If that code is not already the social moral code, then to make the code become the social code, the society must undergo a process of large-scale social change. Society-centered theory implies that such a recommendation would be justified only if the society as a whole would be rational to choose the recommended state of affairs.

We can, of course, evaluate a recommendation as an act performed by an agent that will have a certain impact on the welfare of that agent. We can evaluate the act from the perspective of the agent making the recommendation. But we can also evaluate the substance of the recommendation. If the recommendation is directed to another agent, we can evaluate it from the standpoint of that agent, the agent to whom the recommendation is made. For example, if one person recommends that someone else read a given book, we can evaluate the recommendation from the standpoint of either of the two persons. The second standpoint, that of the agent to whom the recommendation is made, is the appropriate one for the evaluation of a recommendation as such. I say this because a recommendation purports to present the thing recommended as worthy of choice by the agent to whom it is recommended. Hence, the recommendation of a book to someone is justified or warranted only if the book is worthy of being chosen by the person to whom it is recommended. In general, then, a recommendation can be evaluated as such on the basis of the characteristics of the thing recommended and from the standpoint of the agent to whom it is recommended.

We are now in a position to construct a second argument from the model principle to a society-centered theory of moral justification. The model principle shows a sense in which subscribing to a code as a moral code is implicitly recommending the code to a society. Given the preceding considerations about evaluating recommendations, we may conclude that the recommendation of a moral code to a society can be evaluated as such (1) from the standpoint of the society and (2) on the basis of the characteristics of the moral code. Is the code worthy of choice by the society? According to society-centered theory, this is exactly the question to ask. If a code is rationally worthy of choice by the society, it is justified. Society-centered theory asserts, in effect, that the recommendation of a moral code to a society as the social moral code is justified only if the society would be rational to select it as the social moral code.

Justification of Moral Codes and Subscription to Moral Codes

Let me offer one final argument in favor of the society-centered view. This will be a more abstract argument, based in the attitudinal conception of morality.

Begin with an analogy. No code of rules and principles counts as a legal code just as such. Rather, a code is constituted as a legal code by being institutionalized in the appropriate way. For this reason, the justification of a legal code could not be simply the justification of a code of rules as such; it must be the justification of a code qua legal code, and this would be the justification of its being institutionalized as a legal code.

A person who subscribes morally to a moral code or standard desires that it have currency in her society; that is, roughly, she desires that others in her society generally conform to it, intend to conform to it, and tend to blame themselves when they fail to conform. The attitudinal conception implies that a code is constituted as a moral code by being subscribed to as a moral code. This means that no code is a moral code just as such; no code is essentially a moral code.

Given this, the justification of a moral code cannot be simply a matter of the justification of a code of standards as such. It must be a matter of the justification of a code qua moral code. And since a code is constituted a moral code by being morally subscribed to, it would seem that the justification of a moral code must be a matter of justifying moral subscription to it.

To explain this, it will be useful to consider an analogy with justified belief. Belief is an attitude toward a proposition, whereas moral subscription is an attitude toward a standard, and this is an important weakness in the analogy. But the analogy may still be instructive.

The issue of whether a person is epistemically justified in believing something is, roughly, the issue of whether the person met relevant standards of epistemic responsibility in coming to believe it. Epistemic standards are not well understood, but in most instances they presumably call on us to believe something if we have adequate evidence or reason to believe that it is true. We can distinguish the issue of whether a person is epistemically justified in believing something from the issue of whether she has reasons of some other kind for believing it.

There is a similar issue of whether a person is "epistemically" justified in subscribing to a given moral code.[16] A moral code is a standard, and so it is not something that could be true. The standards of "epistemic" responsibility that govern subscription to a moral code do not, therefore, call on us to subscribe to a code if we have reason to believe the code is *true*. But moral codes and standards can have a status that is relevantly analogous to the status a proposition can have of being true. This is the status of being justified as a moral standard. The status of being justified plays a role in explaining the idea of "epistemically" responsible subscription to a moral standard that is analogous to the role played by truth in explaining the idea of epistemically responsible belief in a proposition. Hence, I think, a person is "epistemically" justified in subscribing morally to a standard if she has adequate evidence that the standard is justified as a moral standard.

The conclusion we reached before was that the justification of a moral code must be a matter of justifying moral subscription to it. We can now state this conclusion more accurately: The status a code can have of being justified as a moral code is a status that explains our epistemic justification in subscribing to it as a moral code. It is a status such that if people have adequate evidence that

16. I have put scare quotes around "epistemically" because, as the term is standardly used, "epistemic" justification is a kind of justification of *belief*, the kind that is required for *knowledge*. I use the term here for want of a better one. I explain what is meant in the text. As I explain matters, we can distinguish the issue of whether a person is "epistemically" justified in subscribing morally to a standard from the issue of whether she has reasons of some other kind for subscribing morally to it, such as prudential reasons. I return to this distinction in chapter 11.

a moral code has the status, then they are epistemically justified in subscribing to it as a moral code.

The next step: Moral subscription relates a person to his society; a person who subscribes to a code as a moral code desires that it have currency in his society. Combining this point with the last, the upshot is as follows: The issue of whether a code has the status of being justified as a moral code is the issue of whether the code has a status such that people would be epistemically justified in morally subscribing to it in relation to a given society, if they had adequate evidence of its status. The characteristics of particular individuals that might explain their accepting a given code or that might give them non-epistemic reasons for subscribing to it would not be relevant to determining whether that code is justified. Instead, the relevant factors would be the characteristics of the code, of the society, and of the attitude of subscribing morally to a code.

Given these considerations, society-centered theory is surely a reasonable proposal. On the one hand, suppose a society would be rational to select a code to serve in it as the social moral code. The code then has a status with the following characteristics: The status depends on the characteristics of the code and of the society, for it is the society's choice of the code to serve as the social moral code that is judged rational. The status also depends on the nature of the attitude of subscribing to a code as a moral code, for a code's being a social moral code implies that it is generally morally subscribed to by the members of the society. Further, a moral code's having this status does not turn on the idiosyncratic or specific characteristics of any given person in the society, such as her objectives or goals or whether she is herself committed to a given moral view. Hence, a code that would be rationally selected by a society to serve as the social moral code has a status that is a function of the characteristics of the society, of the moral code in question, and of the attitude of moral subscription. Moreover, the fact that something would be rationally chosen by a given chooser for a given purpose indicates a sense in which the thing is justified for that purpose, relative to the chooser. Therefore, the status of a code that would be rationally chosen by a society to serve as the social code is a normative status, appropriately viewed as a variety of justification or warrant for the code.

On the other hand, suppose that a given moral code is relevantly justified. Our reasoning in this section indicates that it must then have a status such that people would be epistemically justified in subscribing to it in relation to a given society, if they had adequate evidence of its status. It must then suit the society in some especially relevant way. The society as a whole would find it especially suitable that the members subscribe morally to it. Hence the proposal of society-centered theory: The society would be rational to select the code to serve in it as the social moral code, such that it is generally subscribed to morally by the members of the society.

I do not present society-centered theory as a discovery of what it is to justify a moral code. I do not believe that we begin moral theorizing with a conception of the justification of moral codes, a conception that only needs to be uncovered. Rather, society-centered theory is a proposal that should now appear to be reasonable.

Rational Societal Choice

Until this point, I have been attempting to motivate society-centered theory by linking it to some commonsense ideas about morality as well as to the attitudinal conception of morality. However, I have not yet addressed two central questions: (1) Is it in fact possible for a society to make a choice? If so, (2) can the choices of a society be assessed for their rationality? These and related questions will occupy chapter 8, but I need to say something right away in order to quiet worries.

One could compare a parliament's need for a code of debating rules with a society's need for a moral code. Just as we can evaluate a code of debating rules from the perspective of the parliament, we can evaluate a moral code from the perspective of a society, asking in each case whether the relevant body would be rational to choose the code to govern what takes place within it. One important way in which the comparison may seem misleading, however, is that whereas parliaments have authoritative decision-making procedures, societies may not. For this reason, the idea that a parliament can make a choice is much less troubling than the idea that a society can make a choice.

Some preliminary points may help to clarify matters. Society-centered theory does not assert or imply that moral codes owe their existence to choices by societies to incorporate them into their cultures. That this is no part of the idea should be clear, given the conception of a moral code developed in the last chapter. In fact, society-centered theory does not imply that any society has ever made any choice at all. It merely asserts that the question of whether a moral code enjoys the status of being justified turns on whether a relevant society *would* be rational to choose it to serve in it as the social moral code. Assessing this requires assessing a counterfactual: Regarding a given moral code and a given society, if the society *were* to choose the code as the social moral code, *would* it be rational to do so?

If society-centered theory is coherent, it must be coherent to suppose that a society could choose a moral code to serve as the social moral code. And it must be coherent to evaluate the choice for its rationality. Are these ideas coherent?

Let us first be clear that these ideas are needed. One might think that the intuitions I have been developing could be worked into a theory of moral justification without invoking the idea of societal choice. The commonsense ideas I have discussed may have suggested this, in fact. They may have suggested, that is, that a moral code is justified in relation to a society just in case it would serve the society's needs and contribute to the society's flourishing better than any other. This proposal makes no mention of rational societal choice. It is a society-centered theory, yet it does not require the problematic idea of rational societal choice.[17]

To see the problem here, recall that the guiding idea of reductionist standard-oriented theories is to explain the justification of moral standards on the basis that a relevant choice of them is called for by standards of some *other* kind. Reductionist theories set aside questions about the justification of these other standards for another occasion. Typically, standards of rational choice are

17. Patricia Greenspan proposes a theory of this kind (1994).

invoked in this way; the familiar reductionist theories are "practical" theories. Society-centered theory is a practical reductionist theory in this sense.

The alternative proposal that is under consideration is a non-reductionist society-centered theory. The justification of moral standards would be explained directly in terms of societal needs and societal flourishing. No connection would be drawn between societal needs and flourishing and standards of rational choice, or standards of any other kind.

The central problem with this approach is that it would leave unanswered the crucial question: Even if the currency of a given standard would contribute to meeting the needs of a society or to its flourishing, why should this secure for the standard the normative status of being *justified*? Why should this make it the case that corresponding moral propositions—propositions that entail that the standard is justified—have secured a necessary condition of their *truth*?

Consider, for instance, a moral standard that requires people to meet the needs of wild animals and to see to it that wild animals thrive. Its currency in a society would contribute to the meeting of the needs and the thriving of wild animals. This would not show that we are required to ensure that wild animals thrive, for it would not show that the standard in question is justified. But then, why should the fact that the currency of a given standard would contribute to the meeting of the needs of *society* show that the standard is justified?

It might be replied that there is a special connection between societies and morality, a connection that is expressed by the idea that the function of morality is to make society possible. But as I argued, this functionalist idea is best understood as a way of expressing an idea about the justification of moral codes. It cannot explain why making society possible serves to justify moral codes because it seems a way of expressing the idea that making society possible serves to justify moral codes.

The problem is to explain the connection between the *justification* of a standard and the *contribution* that the currency of the standard would make to a society's meeting its needs and flourishing. The society-centered theory that I am proposing would explain this by invoking the *rationality* of a society's *choosing* to meet its needs and to serve its values.

Returning, then, to the main issue, let us ask whether these ideas are coherent. For the moment, let me ignore any differences there might be between preferring and choosing.

The idea that a society can make choices is neither unintuitive nor unprecedented. For example, from the point of view of common sense, it seems quite clear that no society would be rational to choose the Eccentric Code as its social moral code. But given that any society needs the currency of some moral code, any society would be rational to select some code to serve as the social moral code. These ideas seem unremarkable and intuitively acceptable. Peter Railton writes, for example, that moral norms reflect a conception of rationality from "a social point of view." He contends that the "criterion of moral rightness" is what would be rationally approved of from this social point of view.[18] This idea

18. Railton, 1986a, pp. 190–91.

is clearly a cousin of my own idea of society-centered moral theory. But my point here is simply to weaken the impression some readers may have that my idea is a pitch from the bleachers.

Begin with the choices of small groups. You and I can choose, together, to be bound by a given set of rules in a joint project. We can agree to share our work according to the rules. If the group of the two of us can choose that a given set of rules should have currency among us, then so too can a group of three. There does not appear to be any upper limit to this, at least not in principle. Difficulties of communication and shortages of time, as well as other costs of making a choice and reaching agreement, would of course preclude terribly large groups from choosing much at all. But the issue is merely whether it is possible in principle for a society to choose the currency of a moral code. There does not appear to be a theoretical barrier to a society's making such a choice. In short, there is no difficulty understanding how it can be that small groups choose things. And there appears to be no discontinuity between the case of small groups and the case of societies of a kind that would support the idea that, although small groups can choose things, societies cannot.

Families choose many things, such as where to go for the weekend picnic and which television programs to watch. We know that there is a difference between cases where the choice is in fact the choice of a parent and cases where the choice is made by the family, and we know that choices can be made by families under favorable circumstances.

If it were unanimous among the members of a society that *A* is preferable to *B* for the society, then *A* would be the preference *of* the society. Let us distinguish between cases where everyone in society happens to choose the same thing for himself, such as a case where everyone chooses to buy a lottery ticket, and cases where everyone chooses the same thing for society, such as a case where everyone prefers democracy. I am claiming that a sufficient condition for attributing a choice to a society is that its members have a unanimous preference of something for the society. Similarly, a mob with the common purpose of storming the Bastille could literally be said to choose to storm the Bastille.[19] If these claims are correct, then it is possible for a society to make a choice.

I do not think it is always possible for a society to make a choice, no matter what may be the situation and no matter what may be its members' preferences. Some societies may be too divided to choose anything or for any preferences to be attributed plausibly to them. Other societies may never have the opportunity to choose, for their members may never have a set of social alternatives formulated for them, and so they may never form preferences regarding the available social options.

If societies can make choices, their choices can be assessed for rationality. There may be cases where we lack the information to appraise a given choice, and there may be cases where we lack a clear enough conception of rationality to know what conclusion to draw about the rationality of a choice. But societal choices and other cases of collective choice are not alone in these respects.

19. See Copp, 1980 and 1979a.

We may not know enough about Jim Jones to evaluate his choices, and we may be puzzled in other cases where we need greater clarity about what rationality is. So, too, we may not be able to decide whether it would be rational for our society to choose to replace the present smorgasbord of moral views with a social moral code containing a permission for abortions "on demand." Our indecisiveness regarding the rationality of this hypothetical choice may be due to lack of information about society or it may be due to lack of clarity about rationality. But the choice can be evaluated in principle.

I conclude, therefore, that it is possible in principle for a society to choose a social moral code and that the choices of a society can be evaluated for their rationality. Hence, we can make sense of the question whether it would be rational for a society to choose a given code to serve as its social moral code. In the rest of this chapter, I shall simply assume that this is agreed. I return to societal choice in chapter 8.

Alternative Approaches

The theories I canvassed in chapter 4 do not provide as rich or satisfactory an explanation of the justification of moral standards—and of the truth conditions of moral propositions—as does society-centered theory. Proposition-oriented theories simply do not provide interesting accounts of the justification conditions of moral standards. In fact, I do not count a theory as proposition oriented if its account of the justification conditions of moral standards has any independent plausibility. Standard-oriented theories can be reductionist or non-reductionist. Non-reductionist theories are not sufficiently explanatory. In the preceding section, I discussed a non-reductionist society-centered theory, according to which a moral code is relevantly justified in relation to a society when its currency in the society would best enable the society to meet its needs and to flourish. A theory of this kind would leave unanswered the question of why a code should count as justified if its currency would best enable a society to meet its needs and to flourish. Reductionist theories do at least attempt to explain why certain considerations count toward the justification of moral standards. Hence, to find competition for the society-centered conception I am proposing, we must look among other reductionist standard-oriented theories.

Typical reductionist theories are person centered in the sense that they demand rational unanimity as a condition of counting a moral code as justified; they demand unanimity among the members of the group, all the members of which are held to be bound by the code. According to theories of this kind, if a moral code is to count as justified in relation to a society, then every person in the society would have to be rational to accept it, subscribe to it, or accede to its becoming the social moral code. In effect, this means that each member of a society has a veto. Yet there are fanatics and ordinary self-interested people whose desires are such that, according to standard instrumental theories of rational choice, they would be rational to veto any code that the rest of us would find rational to accept, and to veto it for reasons independent of the code's suitability to serve as the social moral code. An antisocial fanatic could, in effect, veto any moral code, in a sense that would mean it is unjustified relative to our society, even if it best served the needs of society.

To be sure, a person-centered theory would view a person's veto as relevant only if it would be rational. And given a suitable theory of rational choice, it could turn out that the veto could be exercised rationally by someone only if it would be exercised rationally by everyone in society. On a theory of this kind, the demand of rational unanimity might seem unobjectionable, for the absence of rational unanimity would imply the existence of unanimous rational dissent. This would make for a more plausible person-centered theory, but it would depend on an implausible theory of rational choice. At least, the needs-and-values theory of rational choice, which I defend in chapter 9, does not have this universalistic implication.

The idea of rational choice by a society is different from the person-centered idea of rational unanimity among all the members of society. For, as I shall explain in chapter 10, the rationality of every member of society's choosing something is not necessary for the rationality of the society's choosing it. Suppose, for example, that we assume a conception of rationality as utility maximization. It is possible that a given societal option would maximize the social utility even though it would not maximize the utility of every member of society; it is therefore possible that the society would be rational to choose something even though some member would not be rational to choose it. Think of the analogy with a code of rules for parliamentary debate. The filibustering malcontent presumably would not be rational to approve a code that places time limits on speeches, but the parliament as a whole might well be rational to approve such a code. Similarly, an antisocial fanatic might be rational to veto a code even though the society as a whole would be rational to select it as the social moral code. Yet the fact that the fanatic's veto might be rational seems irrelevant to the question of whether moral skepticism is true. Society-centered theory can explain why it is irrelevant.

Amendment to the Theory: The State of Nature

It may seem that the arguments of this chapter make too much of the intuition that societies need morality. People may find themselves outside societies and nevertheless have moral duties, such as duties not to kill one another. Society-centered theory seems to imply, however, that no moral standard is justified unless there is some society that would be rational to select a social moral code. Given the standard-based theory of normative judgment, it seems to follow in turn that people do not in fact have moral duties unless some society exists. Therefore, because people could exist in a state of nature in which there are no societies, and because they would nevertheless have duties, society-centered theory must be incorrect.

There are two cases to consider. In the first, exactly one person exists. He is Adam, the sole survivor of a nuclear holocaust, let us say. I think that a solitary person would not have any moral duties, so I do not think that this case constitutes an objection to society-centered theory. It is, of course, a substantive moral question as to whether my hypothetical Adam would have any duties, but my overall theory does not imply otherwise. It does not imply that the belief that the solitary Adam would have duties is incoherent, for example. It simply implies that Adam would not have duties.

In the second state-of-nature case, more than one person exists, but no society exists. Perhaps, for example, Adam and Eve are the only people to survive the nuclear holocaust. If the radiation destroyed their ability to reproduce, and if they have no inclination to cooperate with each other, then, as I will explain in the next chapter, the group of Adam and Eve would not count as a society. Yet even though no society would exist in this case, I agree that Adam and Eve would have moral duties with respect to each other.

This example does, then, indicate a problem in society-centered theory. But the problem can be dealt with by means of a minor amendment to the *J* thesis, and the amendment is within the spirit of the theory. For suppose that the group of Adam and Eve were a society. Then it might well be rational for them to choose a given moral code to have currency in the group, and if so, then it would be within the spirit of society-centered theory to count the code as justified. Hence, to account for state-of-nature examples, the *J* thesis should be taken to have the following clause:

> If a group is neither a society nor a part of a society, then a code is justified as a moral code in relation to it just in case, if the group were a society, the group would be rationally required to select the code to serve in it as the social moral code, in preference to any alternative.

This amendment will not be important in what follows.

There is a further problem of a related kind, however. For we do not restrict attention to our *own* societies. We evaluate situations in other societies, using our own moral values. We have no real alternative but to evaluate things by our own lights. Yet even if our values are justified relative to our own society, this does not ensure they are justified relative to any other society. It seems, therefore, that society-centered theory will judge as unwarranted our natural inclination to judge other societies by our own values, even if, by the lights of the theory, our values are fully justified.

This objection goes to the issue of moral relativism. Society-centered theory relativizes morality to societies in a way that raises a variety of problems. I will address these problems in the concluding chapter.

Conclusion

Many additional questions need to be answered about the society-centered theory. Some of the questions concern details that I will work out in the next few chapters, questions about the nature of a society and about societal choice and rationality. Other questions concern the substantive moral implications of the theory, and still others concern technical meta-ethical issues, including issues in metaphysics, epistemology, and semantics.

As these questions arise, it will become clear that the theory I have introduced in this chapter needs additional amendments. It will be easier to explain them, however, if I wait until later. It will be clear, once the need for the amendments is explained, that they are not ad hoc. They have a natural motivation in the arguments given in this chapter.

In chapter 10, I will distinguish between the *ideal* code for a society and the *justified* code for the society. For all I have said, the code that is "justified" relative to a society, in the sense explained so far, may be quite radically different from the moral code that is actually embedded in the society's culture. Indeed, in some cases the "justified" code may be poorly suited to the society as it is, and for this reason, it may seem implausible to view it as justified for the society as it is. I will propose a minor amendment to deal with this issue.

The relativism that is implicit in the society-centered view is mitigated by two factors that I will discuss in chapter 10. First, I will argue that societies are sufficiently alike that, at a general level, they have the same needs. What a society needs is largely what determines the content of the moral code the society would be rational to choose as its social moral code. Because of this, it is reasonable to expect, given certain simplifying assumptions, that the moral code justified relative to one society has pretty much the same content as the moral code justified relative to any other society. Second, societies can overlap and be nested within one another. When there is an overlap of societies, a moral code that one of the overlapping societies would be rational to choose, *if* it were isolated from all other societies, may not, in fact, be justified. For, as I will argue, a moral code is not justified relative to a society unless it satisfies a coherence constraint. Here again, I will want to amend the basic society-centered theory I have introduced in this chapter.

I have so far ignored the possibility of ties, of situations in which several moral codes would be equally rational for the society to choose. I will introduce a minor amendment to the theory to deal with this possibility.

Since the justification of moral codes is to be understood as relativized to relevant societies, the standard-based theory of normative propositions implies that moral propositions must be understood as relational. This gives rise to technical issues in the semantics of moral sentences and propositions as well as to familiar moral and meta-ethical issues. I will discuss these issues in chapter 11. But society-centered moral theory is not only a version of relativism. The fully developed version I favor is also a version of naturalism and of realism. It allows for divergence between belief and truth, and between subscription to a standard and the standard's being justified, divergence of the sort that is characteristic of areas of knowledge that we construe realistically.

7

The Concept of a Society

The concept of a society is central to the project of this book. It enters into the conception of a moral code, and it is obviously pivotal in society-centered moral theory.

This chapter aims to distinguish societies from collective entities of other kinds, such as nations, states, organizations, and families. A satisfactory ontology of societies must obviously mesh with a general ontology of collectives. Such things are not sets or any other kind of abstract entity. A society typically occupies a territory, for example, but an abstract entity, such as a set, necessarily has no spatial location at all.[1] I have argued elsewhere that a society is a "mereological sum" of its members during those periods of their lives when they are members.[2] But I shall not concern myself with ontological issues here, for society-centered moral theory does not require agreement on ontology beyond acknowledgment that societies exist.

My project is partly one of conceptual analysis, for I aim to provide an account that is sensitive to our intuitive understanding of a society as a "comprehensive social community."[3] I also want my account to fit with sociological theories of society. Yet the final test of the concept of society that I propose is its utility in the overall theory I am developing. Our intuitive concept may need to be refined in order to achieve explanatory or other theoretical gains.

What Is a Society?

Lack of attention to the concept of a society can hamper assessment of any theory in which the concept is pivotal, and it is pivotal in many theories in moral and political philosophy, including John Rawls's theory of justice and Richard

---

1. Yet Talcott Parsons is committed to the view that a society is a set of rules (1966, p. 9). Mario Bunge says a society is a "self-supporting" ordered triple (1979, pp. 21, 23; also 1974). He also asserts that a society is "a concrete totality" (Bunge, 1979, p. 19; also 1974, p. 183).
2. See Copp, 1984. For the notion of a mereological sum, see Leonard and Goodman, 1940.
3. *The Concise Oxford Dictionary of Current English* (4th edition).

Brandt's meta-ethics.[4] Rawls intends his principles of justice to govern the distribution of the results of cooperation in society, not to govern every situation in which some have more and others have less.[5]

Rawls distinguishes societies from private associations and other "less comprehensive social groups,"[6] and he assumes that a society is "a more or less self-sufficient association of persons who in their relations to one another recognize certain rules of conduct as binding and who for the most part act in accordance with them." He also supposes that these rules "specify a system of cooperation."[7] This account is reasonable, as far as it goes, yet it implies incorrectly that an isolated agricultural commune is a society in the relevant sense. Rawls makes the idealizing assumptions that "the boundaries of [a] society are given by the notion of a self-contained national community" and that a society is "a closed system."[8] But societies are not "closed" or "self-contained," and they are not paired one to one with nations or with states. For instance, there is a North American society that contains at least two other societies as parts, and these societies are obviously interdependent.[9]

The sociological literature does not provide a definitive account of the notion of a society. Leon Mayhew summarized the situation as follows: "Analytical definitions usually treat a society as a relatively independent or self-sufficient population characterized by internal organization, territoriality, cultural distinctiveness and sexual recruitment. Specific definitions vary considerably in regard to which of these elements is emphasized."[10] As far as I can tell, however, there has not even been agreement on the points Mayhew mentioned.

For instance, D. F. Aberle and colleagues argue that cultural distinctiveness is not required. They say, "Two or more *societies* may have the same *culture*, or similar cultures." Hence, they contend, the Greek city-states were separate societies even though their cultures were quite similar. Moreover, they say, "One society may be composed of groups with some marked differences in culture."[11]

Talcott Parsons suggests three different definitions in three different works. In one book he says, "A society is a type of social system, in any universe of social systems, which attains the highest level of self-sufficiency as a system in relation to its environment."[12] And he explains that a self-sufficient group that is a society must contain cultural materials and "role opportunities" that are "sufficient for individuals to meet their fundamental personal exigencies at all stages of the life cycle without going outside the society, and for the society to

4. Rawls, 1971; Brandt, 1979.

5. Rawls 1971, pp. 60–65.

6. Rawls, 1971, p. 8.

7. Rawls, 1971, p. 4.

8. Rawls, 1971, pp. 457, 8, respectively.

9. Rawls also remarks that "a society is a co-operative venture for mutual advantage." This is an ideal, however, rather than a description of societies, for, as Rawls points out, societies are marked by conflict as well as by shared interests (1971, pp. 4, 520; see p. 84).

10. Mayhew, 1968, p. 577.

11. Aberle and colleagues, 1950, p. 102.

12. Parsons, 1966, p. 9.

meet its own exigencies."[13] Unfortunately, Parsons's claim is too strong. It would rule out as societies all groups with a shortage of men, or with a shortage of food, because some members would then have to look outside in order to find a mate or to find food.

In an earlier book, Parsons suggested a somewhat weaker requirement: "A social system . . . which meets all the essential functional prerequisites of long term persistence from within its own resources will be called a society."[14] This definition allows a group facing a famine to count as a society, as long as the group has enough food to survive, but it incorrectly implies that there could not be a society that had to import all of its food. And it wrongly implies that a man and a woman living alone on a subsistence farm would constitute a society.

In a third work, Parsons suggested that a society is "a collectivity. . . which is the primary bearer of a distinctive institutionalized culture and which cannot be said to be a differentiated subsystem of a higher-order collectivity oriented to most of the functional exigencies of a social system."[15] He explained that a society's "distinctive institutionalized culture" would be a system of norms governing coordination and cooperation and embedded in the society's culture or its institutions. I agree that societies are characterized by such norms, but the second part of his account is incorrect, for it seems to imply that a society cannot be contained within a larger society. Yet we know that French society is contained in European society.

Mayhew explained the difficulties quite well.

> The search for a universally valid definition of the nature and boundaries of a society as a self-contained unit may obscure the complexity of social life. . . . Economic, religious, political, educational and other types of activity come to cohere into partially independent systems with unity, boundaries and mechanisms of their own. These systems overlap; and when a relatively broad range of such systems cohere around a common population, we may speak of a society. There is no reason to suppose, however, that this society will be self-contained, that it will not overlap with other societies, or that its boundaries will be uniform across its constituent systems.[16]

The Concept of a Society

A satisfactory account must distinguish societies from states and from nations while also explaining that the population of any state or nation will typically comprise a society. Collectives such as families, business organizations and monasteries are not societies,[17] and neither are typical North American towns.[18]

13. Parsons, 1966, p. 17.
14. Parsons, 1951, p. 19.
15. Parsons, 1961, p. 44. Quoted in Stanley Benn, 1967, p. 473.
16. Mayhew, 1968, p. 583.
17. Parsons, 1966, p. 17.
18. Aberle and colleagues, 1950, p. 102.

Then again, ancient Athens and Sparta, the United States, Europe, the early Mormon settlement in Utah, and many of the small-scale social groups discussed by social anthropologists are societies, or, at least, their populations comprise societies.[19]

The following seem to be key characteristics of societies: First, they are multigenerational and extended through time. Second, membership is not a matter of choice, at least not initially, for one's society is inherited at the beginning of one's life, along with one's family. Third, the members of a society interact among themselves in activities directed to securing the material necessities and priorities of life, or to securing priorities identified in their culture. Fourth, their interaction is governed by a system of rules that is at least implicitly accepted in the group as defining the norm for interaction, and perhaps incorporated into the group's culture. Finally, a society provides the framework for its members' lives, embracing the bulk of their friends and socially most important acquaintances.

The concept of a society is vague along at least two dimensions. First, the factors that enter into determining whether a given collective is a society can vary in degree, and the concept of society does not establish a determinate threshold regarding these factors. For instance, a society must be socially closed to some degree, but we cannot say precisely to what degree. Second, the boundaries of a society are permeable. People can sometimes leave and join other societies. Because there are no formal membership criteria, we will often be unable to determine whether some given person is a member of a society.

I propose a two-stage account, according to which a society is a kind of societal population.[20] I shall simply state my proposal and then proceed to explain the terminology and the details. First is the account of a societal population:

> (*S1*) *P* is a *societal population* if and only if *P* is a group of people characterized by a quasi-closed, multigenerational, temporally extended network of social relationships, including relationships of friendship, affection, and kinship (as appropriate), and relationships productive of new generations of members.

Second is the account of a society:

> (S2) *P* is a *society* if and only if
> (1) *P* is a societal population within which there is interaction in behavior directed to securing the material necessities or priorities of life, or to securing priorities identified by a culture characterizing *P*, where this interaction is governed by a set of behavioral standards that is generally followed and shared by the members of *P* and used by them as a standard for criticizing behavior, and

19. Johnson, 1960, pp. 11–12; Benedict, 1968; Aberle and colleagues, 1950, p. 102.
20. I am following suggestions of Mayhew (1968) and of Aberle and colleagues, (1950).

(2) there is no P^* such that

(a) P is a proper part of P^*, and

(b) P^* is a societal population that satisfies clause (1), and

(c) the kinds of interaction in P, in virtue of which P satisfies clause (1) also occur with roughly comparable frequency within P^*-P and between the members of P^*-P and the members of P, and

(d) from the point of view of the members of P, there are no alienating differences between (i) the most salient behavioral standards governing such interaction in P, (ii) the most salient standards governing such interaction between the members of P^*-P and the members of P, and (iii) the most salient of the standards believed by the members of P to govern such interaction in P^*-P, salience in each case being assessed relative to the members of P.

Roughly, a society is a multigenerational, temporally extended population of persons, embracing a relatively closed network of relationships of friendship, affection, kinship, and cooperation in reproduction, and limited by the widest boundary of a distinctive system of instrumental interaction. Simplifying greatly, a society's borders are to be found where the borders of a social network coincide with the borders of a system of interaction that appears salient to the people embraced by the network.

Societal Populations

In defining a society as a kind of societal population, I am following Mayhew.[21] But Mayhew's definition of a societal population has several shortcomings. For him, a societal population consists of the inhabitants of a "maximal" territorial area within which mating is common and residence is relatively permanent, where membership is conferred by birth, and where it is relatively rare that territorial boundaries are crossed for purposes of mating or to establish a new residence.[22]

The first problem is that his account requires a societal population to consist of the inhabitants of a *maximal* territorial area with certain characteristics. Because of this, it does not permit one societal population to be a proper part of another, in the way that French society is a part of the larger European society. Second, Mayhew requires that a society be territorial, and I assume that he has in mind *continuous* geographical territories, but Jewish society did not occupy a continuous territory during the diaspora, and a society may continue to exist even if its territory is conquered and occupied by foreigners. In both of these cases, the group's "territory" would be scattered and broken up by areas

21. He thinks that a society is not to be identified with a societal population; rather, a society is a "system of action," a kind of abstract entity in which a societal population may participate (Mayhew, 1968, p. 585). Common sense suggests, on the contrary, that a society *is* a population of people.

22. Mayhew, 1968, p. 585.

where outsiders reside. Third, it need not be rare for members of a societal population to cross hitherto established societal boundaries in order to find new residences. An example is American society during the eighteenth and early nineteenth centuries. Finally, although this is a conceptual point with, perhaps, little practical significance, I shall argue that it is not logically necessary that a society produce new generations of members by ordinary sexual mating.

A society is a group that provides a framework for its members' more important interpersonal relationships and transactions. People tend to find or to seek their friends and other objects of affection and association, including their mates and their kin, among fellow members of their society. As a result of this, a society exhibits a network of social relationships whereby members are bound to other members of the same generation, and to members of earlier and later generations. In the simplest case, a societal population would be closed under the relations *ancestor of*, *descendant of*, *friend of*, and *mate of*. Every friend, mate, ancestor, and descendant of any member would also be a member, and this characteristic would distinguish societal populations from families, corporations, mobs, and so on. Unfortunately, societies are not closed in this way, and there are cultural differences in the nature of social relationships. Therefore, we need a more sophisticated understanding of the kind of social network that unifies societal populations. It will be useful to begin by discussing certain out-of-the-way examples.

An exogamous society would illustrate both that a society can admit members from outside and that culture can affect the nature of social relationships.[23] Just as there are taboos against incest, there could be a society with a taboo against sex between people who are both born into the group. We can imagine a pair of exogamous societies living in a kind of symbiosis in which each takes mates for its boys (or girls) from the other, and sends mates to the other group for that group's boys (or girls). In an exogamous society, one supposes, if a child were born to a couple, both of whom were born into the society, the child might not be recognized as a member of the society at all. At a minimum, the child's social status, or that of its parents, would be tarnished. An exogamous society would include both "hereditary members," who inherited membership by birth to a pair of members, and "non-hereditary members," who gained membership by way of the custom that accords membership status to people recruited or acquired as sexual partners from the outside.

Sociological accounts naturally assume that societies maintain themselves by sexual reproduction, yet, while this may be true in fact, it does not seem to be logically necessary. A society could exist that lacked the capacity for sexual reproduction. A large group of homosexuals could isolate itself and develop the characteristics of a society, or a society could lose the capacity for sexual reproduction—perhaps sterility is caused by a local aberration in the earth's magnetic field.[24] A society without the capacity for sexual reproduction would obviously have to perpetuate itself in some other way, such as by kidnapping

---

23. John Baker reminded me of exogamous groups.
24. These possibilities were suggested by Walter Edelberg.

or ideological recruitment or by means of an exotic new reproductive technology. All the new members of such a society would be non-hereditary members; that is, they would not inherit membership by birth to a pair of members.

Ideological recruitment into a society is not impossible. However, a *complete* reliance on ideological recruitment would typically involve a great deal of interaction between members of the group and potential recruits in the outside world, and it would typically mean that a large proportion of the group's members would be new members with continuing ties of affection to people outside the group. For these reasons, groups that recruit entirely by ideological means—such as monasteries and sects with a rule of celibacy, like the Shakers—often do not have a sufficiently independent social network to count as societies.[25] Sufficient independence for such a group to qualify as a society could only be gained, I would think, by the members' physical removal or emotional alienation from the outside. This may have been achieved by certain sects or cults of recent history.

Similar factors would tend to undermine the social independence of exogamous groups that exchange mates. Families are exogamous because of incest taboos, and this is one reason why families and kinship lineages come to be grouped together into larger societal populations. Ties of affection and kinship link families. In the same way, the exogamous clans of the Baringo and Nuer are unified into larger societal populations by the social relationships that follow both logically and naturally from the linkages between exogamous groups that trade in mates for their children.[26] In order to realize my fantasy of a pair of symbiotic exogamous societies, the groups' social independence would have to be established by a sufficient physical or cultural alienation or separation to counteract the unifying links of marriage.

Any society will lose some members. A member may leave it to join another society, be ostracized, or be traded as a mate into another society. Almost any society will have some non-hereditary members who have joined the society voluntarily, as a result of being traded as a mate, or what have you. There must be some characteristics which mark the fact that an erstwhile member has left the society, and some which mark the fact that a former non-member has become a member. The relevant characteristic often will be culturally defined. For instance, a former member may have been ostracized, or a non-hereditary member may have been selected in a culturally sanctioned way as a mate for a member. On other occasions, the characteristic may be external to the culture. A non-hereditary member, like a hereditary member, will typically be disposed, to some significant degree and in a non-temporary way, to choose friends and companions from within the group and to choose mates either from within the group or from within groups sanctioned by the culture of the group. A person's joining a society will typically be marked by his acquiring such a disposition, and a person's leaving will typically be marked by his acquiring a non-

25. On the Shakers, see Kern 1981, and the *Encyclopedia Britannica* (15th edition).
26. I am indebted to Alison Wylie for references to the anthropological literature: On the Baringo, see Hodder, 1982, pp. 16–35, especially p. 16; on the Nuer, see Evans-Pritchard 1940a and 1940b, especially 1940b, p. 284.

temporary disposition to choose friends or mates from outside. Members of a society are connected with other members by the friendship, kinship, and sexual relationships characterizing the societal population. Hereditary members are linked to other members of the social network both in the past and in the future, non-hereditary members are linked to other members only or mainly at times after their times of joining, and erstwhile members are linked to members in the past, but to relatively few members in the future.

In the early period of the North American settlements, aboriginal societies shared a single land mass with segments of several European and African societies. American society developed gradually, and it has always included a high proportion of new members, especially during its formation and the periods of heavy immigration. The mark of a new member was the disposition to seek any new friends and mates from within the group. This explains the respect in which many of the Irish immigrants to America effectively ceased to be members of Irish society. They identified with their adoptive communities in that they would have preferred to find new friends and mates from this new larger community. Other immigrants effectively remained members of Irish society, despite their physical separation from the bulk of the society. They continued to identify themselves as Irish, and they lived in Irish communities where possible. These cases are clear enough. However, the many immigrants who were ambivalent would be borderline cases who would neither have abandoned Irish society nor have joined the adoptive society.

A person's disposition to seek any new friends and mates within a certain group may reflect his preferences, but it may also reflect geographical, social, cultural, and political factors. "Identification" with a group is one thing, but the availability or non-availability of people as potential friends and mates is also a factor, for there may be political borders or social or geographical barriers to meeting people from outside. The result may be that one comes to be disposed to seek any new friends or mates from inside the group. So, one can acquire this disposition just as a result of coming to live in the territory occupied by a societal population, if the move makes it difficult to meet anyone from outside. Then again, cultural and social barriers can make it very difficult for one to meet anyone who *is* a member of a group, even if one lives in the group's territory. One can be ostracized from a society, and, if the ostracism is effective, one may lose membership or fail to gain it, despite a desire to belong.

The idea, then, is that a societal population is characterized by a quasi-closed, multigenerational, temporally extended network of social relationships, including, as appropriate, relationships of friendship, affection, and kinship, as well as relationships concerned with the production of new generations of members. I need to explain this idea systematically.

First, the network of social relationships must be multigenerational, in the sense that it contains members who are or could be ancestors or descendants of one another, and it must have a substantial extension through time and exist over several generations. Of course, in most cases, a society's generations are biologically related. The social network includes relationships "productive of new generations of members." For the most part, these will be sexual relationships, of course, but there remains the logical possibility of a non-sexually reproducing society.

Second, a network of social relationships, in the sense I have in mind, would typically include a network of biological kinship relationships and of natural affective relationships, such as relationships of mate-of and offspring-of. It need not include a culturally defined kinship *system*, by which I mean a network of relationships governed by a shared set of cultural standards regulating such things as responsibility for parenting. Societal populations are not necessarily organized by a culture, so they are not necessarily characterized by *systems* of kinship relationships.

Third, there are temporal limits to the persistence of societal populations. For example, English society today may be a different society from medieval English society, and not merely a later part of the very same society, even though there were medieval ancestors of present-day English people.[27] There are two kinds of cases in which a crude temporal limit can be identified. First, as in the English example, there may be sufficient change in the interactive standards characterizing a societal population at different times that we would not regard temporally distant parts of the population as parts of the same society. Second, there may be discontinuities in networks of social relationships, and they may indicate the temporal limits of societal populations. For example, the emergence of an American society was marked by discontinuities between the previously existing European and African social networks and the later American social network, which developed a significant degree of independence from later stages of the former networks. The result was the emergence of a North American societal population.

27. This example was suggested by Paul Teller. G. W. Fitch pointed out that if there is one female who is the ultimate ancestor of every human, then my account implies that there is only one societal population. In order to deal with this objection and with certain other technical problems, I shall introduce two notions. First is the notion of a *minimal* societal population. I shall say that a minimal societal population is a societal population that extends into the future and the past, from a given time, to include only those generations that people of the time generally take into account in thinking about their ancestors and descendants, and about which they have specific knowledge or expectations. For example, few English people today are likely to know anything specific about their medieval ancestors, as opposed to medieval English people in general, or to think of any specific medieval English people as their ancestors. In our culture, the minimal societal population to which a person belongs likely extends at most three generations into the past and one or two into the future. Second is the notion of a mereological sum of a "temporally dense overlapping sequence" of minimal societal populations. A "temporally dense overlapping sequence" is a temporally ordered sequence of minimal societal populations such that (1) every minimal population that could be ordered in time between any two members of the sequence is also a member of the sequence, except that (2) if there is a time at which two groups in the sequence both have members, then each of them has exactly the same members at every such time. The existence of temporal limits on the persistence of societal populations means that not every such mereological sum is a societal population. I will not invoke the notion of a minimal societal population in the text, and I will ordinarily have in mind "maximal" societal populations: A maximal societal population is a mereological sum of a temporally dense overlapping sequence of minimal societal populations that extends to temporal limits of the kinds explained in the text; that is, either it is bounded by a relevant discontinuity in a social network, or it is bounded by significant change of a relevant kind in interactive standards. These notions were explained previously.

For the rest, the basic idea is that a multigenerational group that is a societal population is closed by and large under the key social relationships. If we were to trace relationships of friendship, affection, companionship, and mating, beginning with any member, we would find that we remained among the group's members, on the whole. The exceptions would be rare. We can also trace relationships of kinship, if they are defined by the culture of the group. By and large, within the temporal limits mentioned here and at least in established endogamous societies, the ancestors, descendants, and other kin of a member are also members, as are the ancestors, descendants, and kin of a member's friends and mates, the ancestors, descendants, and kin of those people, and so on. The exceptions will be frequent in exogamous or non-sexually reproducing societies, in formative societies, or, more generally, in societies that contain a large proportion of non-hereditary members, or where relatively large numbers of former members are now members of other societies.

If we could ignore the exceptions and the temporal limits, we could say that a societal population is closed under kinship relations and under relationships of friendship, affection, and mating. However, we can only say that societal populations are "quasi-closed" under these relations. By and large, the social relations link members of a societal population to other members.[28]

This account allows societal populations to be nested, one within another, and it allows them to overlap, having members in common. For example, French society constitutes a societal population by my account, and European society also constitutes a societal population. Jewish society during the diaspora was also a societal population, even though its members were often also members of the national societies they lived in, such as French society.

I do not believe that the vagueness in this account can be avoided. There cannot be a non-arbitrary and precise conceptual boundary in a situation where the underlying realities are matters of degree, and the realities underlying the coalescence of people into societal populations are matters of degree: the degree to which members of a group are disposed to choose friends and companions from within the group, for instance. The greater the degree in which these things are so, or the greater the relevant proportions, the greater the degree to which a group should qualify as a societal population.

---

28. A societal population cannot be artificially constructed simply by adding a randomly chosen alien to the population of some genuine society; that is, one cannot be constructed simply by taking the mereological sum of a societal population and a randomly chosen alien. The alien would be neither a new member nor a hereditary member: Her ancestors and descendants would not be part of the group, nor would her friends, nor would it be true that she is disposed to find new friends or mates from within the group. The situation would not be fundamentally different if we augmented the group by adding our alien's ancestors, descendants, mate, and mate's ancestors. The resulting subgroup still would not be part of the network of social relationships characteristic of the group as a whole. It is true, however, that the mereological sum of two randomly selected societal populations is a societal population. But this is not an embarrassment, for the notion of a societal population is an artificial one anyway. Moreover, it does not follow that the mereological sum of two randomly selected societal populations is itself a *society*.

Societies and Societal Populations

A society is a societal population with two additional characteristics. Let me begin with the first clause of *S2*: The members of a society interact among themselves in instrumental activities and share a set of behavioral standards that govern their interaction.

A societal population can be socially fragmented to the degree that it is not a society. For instance, the small family groups living on a tropical island might be so widely scattered, and so well supplied with food, that the members of different groups see no need of cooperation and hardly ever meet except to fight for sexual partners. The population as a whole would not be a society even though it would be a societal population. It would not become a society unless a pattern of interaction developed in the entire population in a way that could give rise to mutual coordinating expectations about their interaction. For example, a set of trading rules might come to be accepted on the island, with the result that the different families could meet at accepted times and places to trade their products and could reasonably expect to be able to continue to do so. If this set of rules became part of the culture, it would sustain patterns of cooperation that would contribute to tying the population together and to making it more akin to a society. Of course, the population could also be tied together by a pattern of exploitation, for a system of slavery could develop. Yet the examples illustrate why I suggest that a society is a group whose members interact in a way that is governed by a set of behavioral standards that they generally follow and share.

The standards must have currency in the society. It must be generally so, in the society, that people conform to the standards, subscribe to the standards, support conformity with them, and endorse the standards relative to the society. And their currency must be common knowledge. Hence, there must be certain regular patterns of interaction in the group, such as patterns of cooperation and coordination. Behavior conforming to these patterns must be commonly expected and commonly known to be expected. Behavior that does not conform must be expected to be criticized or sanctioned as a result and known to be likely in this way to attract criticism. It must be true and common knowledge in the group that the regularities are widely conformed to in the group, almost everyone expects widespread conformity, and, at least among the expected beneficiaries of the patterns of interaction, almost everyone desires that everyone else in the group conform, given that almost everyone conforms.[29] In typical cases, it would be a consequence of the culture of the group that all of this is the case. The widespread conformity—and the knowledge of the widespread conformity and of the fact that it is expected and desired—would encourage and enable coordination of future plans for interaction.

It is important what *kinds* of behavior are governed by the normative standards of a group. Suppose, for example, that a societal population shares a language. This means that verbal interaction among its members is rule governed,

29. Compare David Lewis on conventions (1969, pp. 78–79).

but it does not follow that the group is a society, for it does not follow that the relevant kinds of instrumental behavior are rule governed. In a society, there are cultural standards or characteristic norms that govern interaction among the members that is directed toward securing the material necessities and priorities of life, such as food and shelter, or to securing priorities specified in the culture, such as religious salvation. There must be rule-governed economic relationships or kinship relationships or religious rites, and so forth. The following examples illustrate this point.

Aberle and colleagues suggested that a group of people in "the [Hobbesian] war of all against all" would not be a society.[30] The Hobbesian war of all against all is an imaginary situation in which there is a scarcity of needed and desired things, in which people are of roughly equal strength and power, in which there is no organized government, and in which people pay attention only to instrumental efficiency in selecting means to their ends. There are no effective cultural or moral restraints on a person's choice of the means he will use to achieve his ends. No behavioral standards governing instrumental interaction have currency in the group.

Aberle and colleagues also suggested that a society would be destroyed by the dispersion or "apathy" of its members.[31] But there have been societies of hunters and gatherers that scattered for long periods of time over large territories. The dispersion of a group is important only to the degree that it interferes with the members' ability to sustain rule-governed instrumental interaction, by interfering with their ability to sustain a culture, communicate, find mates within the group, or otherwise cooperate or interact among themselves. Similarly, indolent people living in a condition of abundance on a tropical island might never become a society. The critical factor in these cases would be the lack of sufficient rule-governed interaction in instrumental behavior.

The *degree* to which there is rule-governed instrumental interaction among the members of a societal population is also important to determining the degree to which the group merits being regarded as a society. The Ik is a tribal group in Uganda that was described by the anthropologist Colin Turnbull.[32] Turnbull denied that the Ik cooperated among themselves and that they had any social system or social organization. He said, the "disturbing thing was the loss of sociality, the reduction of systematized human relationships to the bare minimum where the expediency of the moment was the only system there was."[33] On this basis, Turnbull seemed to want to deny that the Ik constituted a *society*, and, in my view, he would have been correct in this, if his description of the Ik as lacking relevant rule-governed interactive social relationships had been correct. Turnbull's claims were controversial among anthropologists. There was no question that the Ik constituted a societal population, for they were united by social relationships such as kinship, friendship, affection, an emotional attach-

30. Aberle and colleagues, 1950, pp. 103–4.
31. Aberle and colleagues, 1950, pp. 103–4.
32. This example was brought to my attention by Alison Wylie. See Turnbull, 1972; Wilson and colleagues, 1975.
33. In Wilson and colleagues, 1975, p. 356.

ment to the group, and a desire to live together.[34] The disagreement concerned whether the rule-governed relationships implicit in this degree of social unity, especially in kinship arrangements and friendships, were sufficient and of the right kind for the Ik to constitute a society. The Ik did seem to regard their patterns of cooperative behavior as important to preserve, and they engaged in group social activities.[35] In any event, the example of the Ik shows the importance of rule-governed interaction as a factor in our conception of a society.

The second characteristic that distinguishes a society from a mere societal population is captured by the second clause of S2. Intuitively, the idea is that instrumental interaction in a society is governed by standards of behavior that seem relevantly different to its members from the standards governing interaction of the same kinds in larger societal populations of which it is a part. This characteristic distinguishes societies from societal populations that are merely subsocietal parts of larger societies.

The population of a typical town in France, for example, does not constitute a society in its own right. The most salient standards governing interaction among the town's population are the same as the most salient standards governing interaction in French society as a whole, and they are also the same as those governing interaction between the rest of the French and the townspeople, that is, most likely, the French legal system. However, from the point of view of the French, the most salient standards governing interaction in France are French rather than European, and the most salient standards that govern interaction in the rest of Europe are not the same as those that govern interaction in France. So, the French population is a society in its own right, even though it is a part of the larger European society, but the population of the town is not a society because of the way in which it is a part of the larger French society. Clause 2 merely generalizes these ideas.

A societal population P is a society only if it is not a proper part of a larger societal population P^* that has both of the following characteristics: First, the relevant kinds of instrumental interaction that occur in P also occur with roughly comparable frequency within the rest of P^*, namely, P^*-P, and between the members of P^*-P and the members of P. For example, a Mormon community within a larger secular society might count as a distinct society, assuming it had the other characteristics of a society, for it would not be part of a larger group within which Mormon religious interaction took place with the same frequency as in the Mormon community itself.

Second, from the point of view of the members of P, there are no alienating differences between (1) the most salient behavioral standards governing relevant instrumental interaction in P, (2) the most salient standards governing such interaction between the members of P^*-P and the members of P, and (3) the most salient of the standards believed by the members of P to govern such interaction in P^*-P. Salience in each case is assessed relative to the members of P.

---

34. See remarks by McCall and Geddes (Wilson and colleagues, 1975); Turnbull does not deny their claims (Wilson and colleagues, 1975).

35. See Wilson and colleagues, 1975, p. 348.

Hence, for example, a Mormon community within a larger Mormon society presumably would not count as a distinct society. If one religious community is part of a larger religious community, then it counts as a society in its own right only if the more prominent behavioral standards with currency in the remainder of the larger group seem to the members of the smaller group to be alien or different from their own standards.

There is unavoidable vagueness in the idea of a "kind of interaction" as well as in the idea of an "alienating difference" between "salient" behavioral standards. I have in mind fairly abstract kinds of interaction, such as worship or trading in general, rather than, for example, trading in a specific commodity. The relevant standards of behavior are those that by and large govern interaction in the relevant groups (or are believed by the members of P to govern interaction by and large). By "alienating differences" between standards, I mean differences between the standards, or other factors, that would lead the members of P to view the more salient standards of the other groups as not "their own"—those are not "our" standards, we might say, if we were members of P. Finally, "salient" standards are standards that seem especially prominent or conspicuous to the members of P. Legal rules are typically the most salient rules governing social interaction in a group. If so, this proposal would imply that a state with a unified legal system typically is one society, and that two states with distinct legal systems typically are each a single society.

It is therefore possible for a conquered society to remain distinct from the empire that conquered it, despite the ruthless imposition of an alien legal system. Its members may continue to be motivated by an indigenous system of behavioral standards, even if none of them dares to violate the imposed laws of the empire. They likely would continue to regard the indigenous system as their own, and they likely would tend to or want to conform to it partly in order to conform, and they likely would regard it as the more important to preserve. If so, it would be the more salient system from their point of view. In addition, they likely would continue to view the laws of the empire as "alien," and not "their own." According to my account, then, the conquered society would continue to be a society in its own right as long as the more salient standards in the rest of the empire continued to seem alien and different from the most salient standards in the conquered society.

Implications and Examples

Collectives such as families, business organizations, monasteries, and the United Nations are not societal populations, and so they are not societies. For instance, the members of a monastery would retain many ties of friendship and affection with non-members, and they would typically not be disposed to select friends specifically from within the monastery, as opposed to selection from the rest of the church or outside society. However, the early Mormon community in Utah was a society, if, as seems likely, it was characterized by a quasi-closed network of social relationships of the required sort and if, as seems likely, its religious code of behavior was the salient code from the point of view of its members. This code differed from the standards of behavior that were current and most prominent within the larger American society of which it was a part. Similarly, the populations of ancient Athens and Sparta and of the United States constituted societies. These implications seem appropriate.

Societies exist where the boundaries of quasi-closed, temporally extended networks of relevant social relationships coincide with the boundaries of salient rule-governed patterns of instrumental behavior. These boundaries do not always coincide. Some societal populations are not themselves societies because of the way in which they share a pattern of interaction with a larger group; the French town illustrates this phenomenon. Also, some groups that have distinctive patterns of rule-governed interactive behavior are not societal populations. This phenomenon is illustrated by tribal groups within the Nuer and the Baringo in Africa.[36] Among the Nuer, for instance, the tribe is a quasi-legal and political unit. Evans-Pritchard describes it as the largest group that combines for offense and defense and whose members think that disputes among members should be settled by arbitration rather than fighting.[37] A tribe shares a system of cooperation that does not govern interaction between members of the tribe and members of different Nuer tribes. However, a tribe is not a societal population, for the different tribes are unified by a lineage system in which the same clans and kinship lineages exist in different tribes, and there is marriage and trade across tribal lines. The Nuer as a whole constitute a society.[38] The situation seems to be similar among the Baringo, where ties of kinship are spread across tribal borders, and there is intermarriage and migration between tribes.[39] Hodder refers to the Baringo tribes as "ethnic groups" and to the entire Baringo as a "society."[40]

A group may *become* a society as, to a greater *degree*, it comes to be characterized by a network of social relationships, as the members tend more and more to look inside it for friends or mates, as it comes to be governed by more salient and distinctive standards of instrumental interaction, and so on. *Societyhood* is a matter of degree. It is associated with a set of "society-making properties" such that a group is a society to a greater degree as it possesses more of the relevant properties to a greater degree. But we do not need to abandon the intuitive and convenient practice of speaking as if certain groups simply *are* societies. We should think of societyhood as being associated with a set of society-making properties and a threshold for each, such that groups which possess the relevant properties to greater degrees than those established by the corresponding thresholds count as societies, while those which do not, do not count as societies. Unfortunately, the thresholds cannot be specified in any very useful way.

I said earlier that societies may be *nested*. For instance, the French and the Germans constitute societies, and they are parts of a larger European society

36. I owe these references to Alison Wylie.
37. Evans-Pritchard, 1940b, pp. 278–79.
38. Evans-Pritchard, 1940b, p. 279.
39. Hodder, 1982, pp. 16–35.
40. Hodder, 1982, pp. 35, 85, respectively.

that embraces them both. The standards of interaction that are most salient from the point of view of the French are different from the standards that are most salient from the point of view of the citizens of any other European country. Hence, the French and the Germans constitute distinct societies. Nevertheless, the population of the European Community also constitutes a society, for it is an interacting societal population governed by a set of behavioral standards. Hence, the definition permits the nesting of societies.

The definition also permits the partial overlap of societies. The Jews during the diaspora constituted a society and, so did the population of France. The two overlapped, but were nevertheless distinct societies.

Global Society and Apartheid Society

Societies are not generally characterized by a sense of unity and solidarity, an "identification" with a common history or tradition, or an absence of social conflict. Societies are typically rife with social, economic, and political conflict that undermines psychological unity. Societies are not ideal communities; they are not necessarily united by a common aim, interest, or moral ideal.

According to my account, societies are unified, not by means of a sense of commonality or an absence of conflict, but by a unity forged from an overlapping network of social relationships, including instrumental interaction governed by salient standards.

A society with an apartheid system seeks to keep certain of its people apart in a legal economic and social ghetto where they are deprived by law of the human rights, civil liberties, and economic opportunities enjoyed by the rest of the population. However, the society as a whole includes the exploited class as well as the advantaged class. Consider South Africa during the 1970s. The whites constituted "the society" in one sense, perhaps, for they were the ruling class, and the socially and economically most advantaged class in the country. However, they were only a portion of the comprehensive social community that was South African society in the sense of the term we have been concerned to understand. Each racial community in South Africa was perhaps a societal population, for as a result of the rigid enforcement of the laws governing interracial relationships, each community was likely characterized by a separate network of social relationships. In addition, some tribes and communities may have been societies in their own right. Yet there was a salient set of behavioral standards governing instrumental interaction throughout the country as a whole, namely, the set of legal and conventional restrictions that institutionalized apartheid. The system defined the privileges of the white community as it defined the disadvantages of the black community. This means, in effect, that as matters stood at the time, despite the conflicts and inequities, the South African communities and societies were part of the larger society of South Africa.

Humanity constitutes a societal population. Whether this societal population is a society depends on whether there is within it instrumental interaction governed by standards of behavior; it depends on whether there are regularities of interaction that are known to be widely conformed to and that are widely expected and desired to be conformed to in the ways sketched here. Of course, there is instrumental interaction within each of the societies that coexist in the global population. But, we are concerned with the nature of the interaction among these societies and among the members of different societies. If these societies were isolated and closed, or if all of the interaction between societies were unrestricted warlike behavior, then there would be no global society because there would be insufficient intersocietal rule-governed instrumental interaction. The societies of the globe would be like the individuals on the imaginary tropical island we discussed earlier, and there would be no society embracing them all.

There certainly has not always been a global society, for there have been isolated and closed societies within the larger human population. Even now, there may be tribes that are fully isolated from the outside. I nevertheless do think that there is a global society or, if there is not yet a global society, there soon will be. For there are patterns of interaction among the societies and people of the globe, patterns that exhibit widely accepted standards of interaction and that exhibit regularities of behavior that are widely known, expected, and desired to exist. There is an international economic system. There are patterns—and expectations regarding the patterns—of trading relationships. There is an intersocietal system for communication. The United Nations is a forum for intersocietal cooperation. International law, weak as it is, is a set of intersocietal cooperative standards. Tourism and business bring people to corners of the globe where they and those they visit can witness not only the diversities but also the possibilities of communication and cooperation. Educational and cultural exchanges and visits bring a few people each year from the less-well-off societies to the better-off societies and vice versa. There is an intersocietal scientific and intellectual community. And I think that the cooperation and instrumental interaction among the peoples and societies of the world is sufficiently pervasive for it to be true that there is a global society embracing all of humanity.

Identity and Change

Societies change as time passes. Some changes would destroy a society, and some would result in the replacement of one society by a distinct society. Consequently, it can seem pressing to ask how much and what sorts of change can be tolerated and what characteristics must be preserved over time if a society is to survive change.

For instance, one might think that societies are essentially characterized by their moral standards and conclude on this basis that any change in the moral code that has currency in a society would result in the replacement of one society by another. This would be a very extreme and implausible view. Lord Patrick Devlin once said, "There is disintegration [of a society] when no common morality is observed and history shows that the loosening of moral bonds is often the first stage of disintegration, so that society is justified in taking the same steps to preserve its moral code as it does to preserve its government and other essential institutions."[41] Devlin does not think that _any_ change in a society's moral code would mean that one society "has disappeared and another has taken its place."[42] Nevertheless, he seems to think that the wholesale _replacement_ of one moral code by quite a different one would entail the replacement of one society by another.

It is clear, however, that the members of a society could in principle choose to adopt a new moral code. The society that would exist after the change would have the same membership as the society before the change. There would be historical continuity in the membership of the society before and after the change, and we could presumably explain the characteristics of the new morality in terms of the characteristics that the society had before the change. The society before the change would, or surely at least could, be identical to the society after the change.

Harry Johnson suggests that some continuity of social structure is necessary to the continuing existence of a society.[43] To be sure, he says that any given social "mechanism" could in principle disappear and be replaced with another mechanism that had the same or a very similar function. But there are limits to this, in Johnson's view, for "every social structure imposes some limitations on the structural innovations that would be compatible with it."[44] He says, "It would, for instance, be absurd to speak of the effects of introducing polygamy into a model of the English marriage system unless one included among the 'effects' all the changes in attitude and behavior that must occur before the introduction of polygamy would be possible. And these changes would produce a new society requiring a new model."[45] If Johnson means by "a new society," a "numerically distinct society," then I disagree with him.

It is important to distinguish clearly between, on the one hand, changes in the properties of a society that are drastic enough to require a new account of how the society functions and, on the other hand, changes that destroy a society and replace it with another society. Changes of the latter sort produce a society that is not merely different in its properties but is a different society, in the sense of a distinct or a new society. The introduction of polygamy into an erstwhile monogamous society is logically possible and is compatible in principle with the society's survival, but it would obviously be a nontrivial change. There is no reason to believe that the introduction of polygamy would entail the destruction of one society and its replacement with another.

Earlier, I said that modern English society and medieval English society may be stages of distinct societies and not merely different stages of one and the same society. Following Paul Teller, I suggested that the explanation for this is the degree to which the interactive standards that characterized the medieval society are different from those that characterize the modern society. It may seem

41. Devlin, 1965, p. 13.
42. Devlin, 1965, p. 13, n. 1.
43. Johnson, 1960, pp. 68–69.
44. Johnson, 1960, p. 69.
45. Johnson, 1960, p. 69, quoting Marshall, 1956, p. 64.

crucial, as Teller proposed to me, that an English person of today could fit into 1920 English society without major "retooling" of his behavioral standards, but "if transported to 1300" he might have to start from scratch.[46] That is, although no given change in interactive standards, such as a change from monogamy to polygamy, would inevitably spell the end of one society and the beginning of another, a global change of sufficient psychological importance can do so. Perhaps, then, two temporal stages of a temporally extended population linked by the social relations are parts of the same society only if a member of one would have been able to fit into the other without serious psychological disorientation.

The position I have reached is vague, but it can be compared to the vague identity conditions of families. A family is constituted by its membership and distinguished from other families by differences in membership. I do not count every indefinitely distant biological ancestor as a member of my family. Yet if we are given the membership of my family at one time, then we can find its past and future membership by tracing the relations *descendant of* and *ancestor of*. Similarly, the network of social relationships that characterizes a societal population traces out the past and future membership of that population. We continue to deal with numerically the same society only if there is the right kind of historical continuity in the membership. But, as I explained earlier, there are temporal limits marked either by discontinuities in the social network, as in the American example, or by significant change in the nature of the interactive standards characterizing the group, as in the English example.

The behavioral standards accepted in a society, and indeed the social moral code of a society, need not remain unchanged. A society must be characterized at every time by the acceptance of a set of behavioral standards, but this does not mean that the set accepted at one time must be identical to, or even similar to, the set accepted at any other time. Yet the English example suggests that sufficient change in the interactive standards accepted can lead to a "hiving off" of one society from an ancestor society.

Conclusion

To summarize: A society is, roughly speaking, a multigenerational, temporally extended population of persons, embracing a relatively closed network of relationships of friendship, affection, kinship, and cooperation in reproduction, and limited by the widest boundary of a distinctive system of instrumental interaction.

46. Teller suggested, in personal correspondence, that "the problems here have much in common with the problems with identity over time of species. How much does a species have to evolve before we say 'new species'?" He said, "One approach to this problem in biology is to say that two temporal segments of an evolving interbreeding population are (parts of) different species if a member of one would not have been able to interbreed with a member of the other if the two organisms had coexisted. You might be able to do something crudely similar, with [interactive] standards playing the role of interbreeding."

This account aims to "construct" societies out of persons and their social relationships. Accounts of this sort are sometimes criticized on the ground that the characteristics of a person depend as much on those of the society of which he is a member as the characteristics of that society depend on the characteristics of its members. Rawls asserts that "membership in our society is given, . . . we cannot know what we would have been like had we not belonged to it (perhaps the thought itself lacks a sense)."[47] I think that this is an overstatement. But it would be a misunderstanding of my account to suppose it to narrow our options in explaining human psychology. It seems obviously to be true that the nature of one's society and one's position in it have profound effects on one's psychology. My account has no implications to the contrary.

From the point of view of society-centered moral theory, there are two significant features of my account. First, it implies that a society exists only where there is instrumental interaction directed to securing the material necessities and priorities of life or the local cultural priorities, and governed by standards of behavior that are shared in a group. It follows that the concept of a society is to be understood in terms of the concepts of standards of interactive behavior and of needs and cultural values. Nothing of great interest follows directly from this. But, as we have seen, a moral code is one kind of standard of behavior. A societal population is a society if it shares a moral code having appropriate properties.

Second, societies can be nested and can overlap. Because of this, most of us are members of more than one society. If our duties are given by the moral code justified relative to "our" society, and if different moral codes can be justified relative to different societies, then in principle we can face different moral demands relative to the different societies to which we belong. Call this the "overlap problem." To avoid the problem, a society-centered theory must impose a coherence constraint on its account of justification, as I shall explain. I will return to the overlap problem in chapter 10.

The effect of the coherence constraint is to dampen the influence on morality of differences between societies. This dampening effect is especially strong if, as I have argued, there is a global society. For if there is a global society, then there is a harmony among all the codes justified relative to all of the smaller societies that are nested within it.

---

47. Rawls, 1977, p. 162.

8

Can Societies Be Choosers?

Society-centered theory commits me to the thesis that societies can be choosers, that societies are capable in principle of making choices that can be assessed for rationality. Many will see this idea as the height of philosophical folly. They will charge it with various sins, including holism, anthropomorphism, and the fallacy of composition. Yet, as I will argue, the idea that a society can make a choice does not have any worrisome metaphysical commitments.

I divide the issue in two. First, is it possible in principle for a society to make a choice? Second, can societal choices be assessed for rationality? I begin with a preliminary discussion of societal preferences and choices. I propose a theory about the conditions under which a society would actually make a choice or have a preference. I argue that the metaphysical implications of these notions are very modest. I then discuss certain typical objections and argue that the notion of societal choice can escape them. I also claim that it can escape any skepticism that might be engendered by Kenneth Arrow's famous impossibility argument. Near the end of the chapter, I discuss the rational assessment of societal choices.

Group Preference and Consensus

For the moment, let me set aside metaphysical concerns and simplify by ignoring any difference there may be between preference and choice. I begin by discussing small groups.

Small groups often engage in joint activities, and in order to do so, they need to make choices and to act in order to implement their plans. For example, if you and I choose to move the piano from the kitchen to the study, we will need to plan how to move it. We may choose to move it through the eating area rather than to move it outside and then try to push it into the study through the window. Joint activities of this kind can involve joint intentions of a surprising complexity. *We* intend to move the piano. But this intention we have involves each of us in having complex and interlocking intentions and beliefs, including intentions as to the effectiveness of both of our intentions in bringing us to move the piano.[1]

1. See Bratman, 1993 and 1992; also Tuomela and Miller, 1988; Tuomela, 1990, 1991; Gilbert, 1990; Searle, 1990.

I am here interested in the much simpler phenomenon of group choice and preference. Before we undertake to move the piano, you and I must presumably decide to move it, and our decision will rest on our desire that the piano be moved. If *each* of us desires that *we* move the piano, then the *group* of us wants to move the piano. It seems sufficient that each of us have this desire. It does not seem, for example, that we must each know that both of us want us to move the piano. This kind of mutual knowledge does not seem to be required. It also seems *necessary* that each of us desire that we move the piano in order for the group of us to want to move the piano. If each of us merely desired that the piano *be moved*, for example, our desires would be satisfied if some other person moved it. Our desires would not be about *our* moving it. It would be implausible to describe this situation as one in which the *group* of us wants to move the piano.

This is, of course, a very simple case. And it may seem unnecessary to speak of it as one in which "the group of us prefers to move the piano," if this is meant to express a different proposition from the proposition that *we* prefer to move the piano. Yet that is just as it should be, for a preference or choice of a group must surely consist in a complex of preferences and choices of the members of the group. In any event, this is the hypothesis I am working with here.

If the group of the two of us can choose to move the piano, then so too can a group of three. As I said in chapter 6, there does not appear to be an upper limit to this, at least not in principle. Of course, very large groups, such as societies, unless they are well organized and unless the members are similar in their values, may not be able to make choices. For they may not come to know the options that are available to the group, and they may not know the relative desirability of the options. Even if they know about the options, they may fail to agree in their rankings of the alternatives. Yet there does not appear to be a theoretical barrier to a society's having a preference, for there is no discontinuity between the case of the pair of us and a society. Hence it seems that if the pair of us can desire to move the piano, then, in principle, societies can desire or prefer things.

Let me now turn to a more complex case. If all the members of a family prefer that the family picnic at Alice Lake rather than at Lighthouse Park, then the family prefers to picnic at Alice Lake. But even if the family is not unanimous, it still prefers Alice Lake if it is nearly unanimous. One of six children may be in a contrary mood and therefore prefer Lighthouse Park, but if the other five and the parents prefer Alice Lake, then the family does. It certainly does not prefer Lighthouse Park, and it is hardly indifferent. Is it undecided? Is its preference indeterminate? I claim not. The parents would be speaking accurately if they said to their disagreeing child, "We are going to Alice Lake, because that is what the family wants." The example illustrates that unanimity is not required, among the members of a group, in order for the group to prefer something.

The existence of a consensus is sufficient. A consensus need not be a unanimous view, except in a small group, such as the pair consisting of you and me. In a larger group, such as a family, a consensus exists if a proposition is accepted with near unanimity by those who have a view about it, or if something is desired with near unanimity. In my example, the family has a consensus in favor of Alice Lake, and so the family prefers Alice Lake.

In the contexts I am interested in, the term "the family" serves as a definite description that picks out the family as such, the collective entity. But it can also be used to abbreviate phrases such as "each member of the family" or, perhaps, "most members of the family," which express "restricted quantifiers" over persons.[2] For example, in "the family has eight members," the subject term, "the family," picks out the family as such. But in "the family eats chili" and "the family falls asleep before nine o'clock," the term "the family" is doing duty for "each member of the family." In general, then, collective terms, such as "the family" and "the society," can function either as definite descriptions, which pick out the collective entities, or as restricted quantifiers over persons. These two uses are sometimes called the "collective" and "distributive" uses, respectively. I am interested in the collective uses.

Now, on the one hand, if the family were nearly unanimous in preferring to eat chocolate chip cookies rather than red licorice, we would not want to say that the family as such prefers to eat the cookies. Eating a cookie is not an option for a family. Families as such do not eat things; the individual members of families eat things.[3] We might say, "the family prefers the cookies," but this would be interpreted as a claim about most members' preferences rather than about the preferences of the family as a whole. On the other hand, if the family were nearly unanimous in preferring to picnic at Alice Lake, then the family as such would prefer to picnic there. Picnicking is a possible family activity. In the picnicking example, then, the preferences of the family members are over options for the family, whereas in the cookie case, their preferences are not over options for the family. A group as such prefers something only if that thing is, in principle, an option for the group.

The point can be expressed as follows: Where a group as such has a preference, there is a property the group could have in principle, and each member of the group who is party to the relevant consensus prefers that the group have that property. In the picnicking case, most members of the family prefer that the family have this property: that it picnic at Alice Lake. In the cookie case, although most members prefer to eat cookies rather than licorice, their preference is not that the family have a given property. It is that their diet have a given property.[4]

<hr>

2. See Barwise and Cooper, 1981. I owe this reference to Jeffrey C. King. Of course, definite descriptions may also be construed as disguised quantifiers (see Russell, 1905). This does not affect the distinction I am drawing.

3. Walter Sinnott-Armstrong pointed out (in correspondence) that a family can split a cookie. But it is still the members that eat it.

4. A situation in which I have cookies rather than licorice is a situation in which my family has the property of being such that the member identical to me has cookies rather than licorice. Hence, if I prefer cookies to licorice, then my preference will be satisfied if my family has this property. But it does not follow that my preference is a preference that my family have this property. My desire to have a swim is not a desire that my house have the property that the person who owns it have a swim.

I do not have a general account of the kinds of properties groups of different kinds are capable of having. But the idea here is not mysterious. We do not have a general account of the kinds of properties individual persons can have, but this does not prevent us from deciding whether a given property is an option for a person.

I conclude that a sufficient condition of a group as such having a preference for something is that there be a property the group could have which is such that the members of the group have formed a consensus, or are nearly unanimous, in being in favor of the group's having that property.[5] I will speak of a "group option." A group prefers an option if the members are nearly unanimous in preferring that option for the group.[6] I maintain that this is also a necessary condition of a group's having a preference.

It is worth mentioning that our preferences are always held in relation to given data and considerations. For example, the family may be nearly unanimous in preferring Alice Lake, taking into account only the merits of the picnic grounds. If so, the family prefers Alice Lake "on the merits," but it might prefer Lighthouse Park on a more restricted or more extended view of the choice. I shall therefore relativize the account to sets of considerations: A group prefers x over y, in relation to a set of considerations, just in case x and y are group options and the members are nearly unanimous in preferring x over y in relation to that set of considerations.

Societal Preference and Consensus

I have claimed that the existence of a consensus over group options is both necessary and sufficient for a group to have a preference. Societies are but large-scale groups. Hence, the existence of a consensus among the members of a society over a set of societal options should be necessary and sufficient for the society's having a preference among the options. Let us consider an example.

American society prefers democracy to any other kind of governmental system and prefers the U.S. constitutional system to any other democratic system.

5. Propositions to the effect that the members of a group are nearly unanimous are vague. We might say this means there are situations in which they are indeterminate. Propositions about group preferences are indeterminate when the corresponding propositions about the near unanimity of the members are indeterminate. On vagueness and indeterminacy, see Stalnaker, 1984, p. 166.

6. Larry May does not explicitly discuss group preference, but I think he would object that group preferences require solidarity. There is a group preference only if the members of the group are related to each other in solidarity, and only if each member has the same preference for a group option. See May, 1987, pp. 33–40, 59–65, 113–18. I have already explained why I think unanimity is not required. Nor is solidarity required (at least, not beyond the attenuated form of solidarity that is entailed by a consensus over options for a group). Solidarity exists in a group when there is an interest that each of the members has, and when each takes an interest in the realization of that interest by the others in the group. The requirement of solidarity is therefore quite strong. For example, even if the members of a family unanimously prefer to picnic at Alice Lake, so that they share an interest in the family's picnicking there, they may not each take an interest in the realization of that interest by the others, for the family may be riven by conflicts. Yet if the conflicts do not prevent a consensus, then the family may still prefer to picnic at Alice Lake.

But it is not the case that American society prefers to abolish capital punishment rather than maintain it. How would we support these claims? Few of us have seen reliable opinion surveys on the point, but we are quite confident on the one hand that if Americans were asked their preference, they would almost unanimously opt for a democratic system as opposed to any other, and they would almost unanimously opt to continue with the existing constitution.[7] On the other hand, Americans are not anywhere near unanimous in their views about capital punishment. These remarks indicate the kind of evidence that would be relevant to evaluating these two claims about the preferences of American society. If we did not have in mind the philosophical objections I shall discuss, I submit that there would in fact be no controversy as to whether American society prefers democracy to dictatorship.

These examples are, of course, in line with the consensus theory. There is a consensus about democracy at least among the members of the society who have a view about government. (The fact that a large number of children have no view about government does not mean there is not a consensus.) And the consensus is about a societal option, for a society may, of course, have a governmental structure. The existence of the consensus implies that the society as a whole prefers democracy. The example about capital punishment suggests that, in the absence of consensus, there is not a societal preference. Taken together, the examples argue that the existence of a consensus over a societal option is both necessary and sufficient for societal preference.

I conclude, therefore, that a society prefers an option just in case the option is a societal option and the members of the society who have an attitude toward it are nearly unanimously in favor of the society's taking the option. A society can in principle be characterized by a given social moral code, and it is possible for the members of a society to be in consensus about a social moral code. Hence, it is possible in principle for a society to *prefer* a given social moral code.

My overall position requires that I show it is possible in principle for a society to *choose* a moral code to serve in it as the societal moral code. But choice appears to be a different phenomenon from mere preference. A person can prefer something without choosing it. The phenomenon of societal choice therefore needs separate attention from societal preference. I will return to this issue in the section on societal choice and society-centerd theory, but I think it will be useful at this point to consider a cluster of objections to what I have argued so far.

The Ontology of Societal Preference

James Buchanan said that every philosopher must make an "either-or" choice. Either "individualism" is correct, in which case individual persons are the only entities with preferences, or "organicism" is correct, in which case "the collec-

---

7. Russell Hardin reminded me that there likely are many people who would opt for the constitution, but who do not know what it says. They might not opt for it if they did understand it.

tivity is an independent entity possessing its own value ordering" or its own preferences. If individualism is correct, then there are no societal preferences, and no question of societal rationality "may be raised." If organicism is correct, then the rationality of a society can be tested only against its own preferences.[8] My own view is that there is a sensible middle position. *Individualism* is not correct, for collectives can and do have preferences, and *organicism* is not correct, for collectives are not "independent" entities with their own preferences "independent" of the preferences of their members.

I have already argued that societies exist and have properties. A society is a kind of collective entity; it is roughly a mereological sum of its members during those periods of their lives when they are members.[9] One might object that groups are not "single entities." But there are as many different ways to count things as there are kinds of things. The philosophy department is one department, although it consists of several persons. Similarly, if we are counting societies, American society is one.

The interesting question is what kinds of property a society can have. Societies do have properties. Consider, for example, the proposition that American society is populous and violent. Here, the term "American society" picks out the society as such, and the proposition attributes the properties of being populous and being violent to the society.

I assume that flesh-and-blood persons have preferences only if they have physical properties that underwrite the existence of, and are otherwise appropriately related to, their preferences. It is common for materialists to say that the psychological properties of a person "supervene" on her physical properties, where her physical properties may include relations between her and certain states of the "external" world. Of course, it is controversial both whether this supervenience thesis is true and how it should be understood. The intuitive notion is that if two people are indiscernible with respect to all of their physical properties, then they are indiscernible with respect to their psychological properties.[10] The idea can be expressed more precisely as follows: Necessarily, for any person and psychological property (such as a preference), if the person has the psychological property, then there are physical properties of a relevant kind such that the person has those properties and, necessarily, if any person has those physical properties, she has that psychological property.[11] This is only one of a family of supervenience notions, but I will use it in what follows.

My view is that a society can have the properties of preferring and choosing; that is, a society can have the very same properties that persons have when they have preferences or make choices.[12] Yet this is not to say that the preferences and choices of societies supervene on the same sorts of properties of societies as

8. Buchanan, 1954, p. 116.

9. Copp, 1984. See Leonard and Goodman, 1940.

10. See Stalnaker, 1984, p. 154. Stalnaker discusses claims about collectives on pp. 161–62.

11. This is Kim's notion of strong supervenience. See Kim, 1987, p. 316; Teller, 1983, p. 144.

12. That is, for example, I do not believe that "prefers" is ambiguous in the sentence "Albert prefers democracy to dictatorship" and cannot be disambiguated until it is determined whether "Albert" refers to a flesh-and-blood person or to a society.

underwrite the preferences and choices of flesh-and-blood persons. Perhaps the preferences and choices of persons supervene on their neurophysiological properties. Yet it is quite clear that the preferences and choices of societies do not supervene on *their* neurophysiological properties, for, of course, societies do not have brains of their own. The account of societal preference that I sketched in the last section implies that the preferences and choices of societies supervene on relevant preferences of their members, together with any other relevant properties of the environment that are necessary to make it the case that the society has options.[13]

For convenience, I will say that every way of distributing preferences over a societal option, among the members of a society, corresponds to an "individual preference property" of the society. Given this way of speaking, if there is near unanimity among the members of a society in favor of an option, then the society has the individual preference property of being such that there is a member who prefers the option, another member who prefers the option, another who does not prefer it, and so on. It is necessarily the case that, if a society has a given preference, then there is an individual preference property possessed by the society and, necessarily, if any society has that property, it has the relevant preference; that is, societal preference supervenes on the preferences of individuals, given that there are relevant societal options.

The account I proposed in the last section could be taken to establish, not only that societal preferences supervene on the preferences of their members, but also, more significantly, that societal preferences are reducible to the preferences of their members. It is easy to be misled by the terminology, however, so I want to insist on four caveats: First, the equivalence between truths about societal preference and truths about individual preference shows what societal preference consists in. It would be a mistake to conclude that the notion of societal preference is theoretically redundant, as I will explain in the next section. Second, the "reducing" propositions about the preferences of persons are not purely individualistic, for they contain terms that pick out the relevant society. Third, there are equivalences between propositions about societal preference and the corresponding propositions about nearly unanimous individual preferences. Hence, the existence of a societal preference is entailed by relevant propositions about nearly unanimous individual preferences. And finally, obviously, a "reduction" of societal preference to individual preference does not support the idea that every societal property P is such that instances where a society has P can be "reduced" to instances of the having of P by the members of the society. Societies can be populous, but no person is populous.

When a society has a given preference for a societal option, the world is no different from the way it is when there is a corresponding pattern of nearly unanimous preferences among its members. A society's making a choice or having a preference is not some mysterious "further fact"; it is a fact that con-

---

13. If the preferences of persons supervene on their neurophysiological properties, it may follow that the preferences of societies supervene on the neurophysiological properties of their members.

sists in the existence of an appropriate pattern of preferences among its members.

Nevertheless, a society's preferring a given societal option cannot be identified with any one pattern of nearly unanimous preference in favor of that option among the members of the society. Although *some* such pattern must exist if the society has the preference, and although the existence of such a pattern entails the existence of the societal preference, *any* such pattern would have been sufficient for the existence of the societal preference. In fact, in a realistic case, a societal preference may persist over time, in the way the preference of American society for democracy over dictatorship has persisted, even while the membership of the society changes and the membership of the consensus group changes within the society.

Society-Centered Moral Theory

A brief digression may be useful at this point, for it may appear that my account of societal preference entails that there can be nothing of interest in society-centered theory. If the preferences of a society are reducible to patterns of preferences among its members, it may seem to follow that every society-centered moral theory is logically equivalent to some corresponding person-centered theory.

This is not obvious. If I am correct, a society prefers a given social moral code just in case there is a relevant pattern of facts about preferences among its members. Yet it does not follow that the *J* thesis of any society-centered theory is logically equivalent to the *J* thesis of some person-centered theory. For the *J* theses speak to the *rationality* of various choices and preferences, and nothing has yet been said about the relation between the rationality of societal preferences and the rationality of individual preferences.

A society-centered theory says that a society's moral code is justified if and only if the society would be rational to choose that code as its social moral code. One type of person-centered theory, a "unanimity" theory, says that a society's moral code is justified if and only if *every member* of the society would be rational to choose that code as the society's social moral code. To show that every theory of the former sort is logically equivalent to some theory of the latter sort, one would have to show that a society is rational to choose something if and only if every member of the society is rational to choose that thing. This thesis is quite clearly false, as I will show in chapter 10. Unanimous rational choice of something by the members of a society is neither necessary nor sufficient for rational choice of that thing by the society. Hence, a moral code or standard could have the *J* property specified by a society-centered theory without having the *J* property specified by the corresponding unanimity theory.

Yet there is another issue. A society-centered theory will not be shown to be redundant unless the logically equivalent person centered theory, if there is one, has an independent plausibility. If it is merely a jerry-built theory that would have no plausibility in its own right, independent of whatever plausibility attaches to its twin society-centered theory, then the theoretical work is being done by the society-centered theory. No theoretical gain would be achieved by dispensing with it in favor of its person-centered twin.

An interesting reduction of society-centered to person-centered theory would have to meet the two conditions of logical equivalence and plausibility. My accounts of societal choices and preferences simply have no bearing on whether either of these conditions can be met.

A Series of Objections

Why would a philosopher object to claims such as the claim that American society prefers democracy or that the family prefers to picnic at Alice Lake? Is there anything mysterious or queer about these claims? I shall consider a series of epistemological and metaphysical objections before turning to concerns derived from Arrow's theorem about social choice.

A Societal Mind?

First, it may seem that having a preference entails having a mind. Then, if a collective entity were capable of having a preference, it would follow that it has a mind, or at least that it is capable of being in a mental state. But it is not credible that a society might have a mind or be in a mental state. Therefore, the notion that societies could have preferences simply is not credible.

I agree entirely that societies do not have minds or "mental states." I say this, but I cannot say in any other terms precisely what this means. It does seem clear, however, that American society prefers a democratic form of government and that it would choose such a form of government if it were given the opportunity to choose. Yet, it also seems obvious that American society does not have a mind and never has been in a mental state. It is also clear that, in my example, the family prefers to picnic at Alice Lake. Yet the family certainly does not have a mind and is not in any mental state. Families and societies are not capable of having minds or of being in mental states.

The criteria for possession of a mind and for being in a mental state are poorly understood. I do not claim that only humans can have minds. Perhaps a mind could come into existence as a result of high-technology linkages among human brains, each of which, when independent, supports its own mind. Yet an ordinary collective entity is not a sort of thing that could itself have a mind. The explanation is, perhaps, that its members are not in fact linked by the kind of communication network that would be required. Not even a very tightly organized collective entity, such as the American military, is sufficiently tightly structured to have a mind. And if having a mind is necessary for having a mental state, then collective entities also cannot have mental states.

Yet it is possible for a collective entity to have a preference or make a choice. I might add that certain collective entities, such as military organizations, can acquire information, process information, have beliefs, and have intentions. For example, the Allied army intended to storm the beaches of Normandy. At least, this is a historical thesis about what happened, and historians would know how to dispute it. The claim is not logically false.

It follows from my position that it is possible to prefer something without having a mind and without being in a mental state. I do not see any contradiction in this position. It is not mysterious that a society may prefer a democratic form of government, and it would be a mistake to make this seem mysterious by supposing that having such a preference necessarily involves having a mind or a mental state.

Notwithstanding all of this, I am willing to make a terminological retreat. If it is insisted that having a mental state is *entailed* by preferring, then I would permit it to be said that collective entities can have mental states. I would simply insist that it would then be no more mysterious that a society can have a mental state than it is that a society can have a preference.

A Collective Decision Procedure?

It seems clear that certain collective entities can make choices. Parliament makes a choice when a majority of its members vote in favor of a piece of legislation. A state makes a choice when its constitutional procedures are followed as required. Hardly anyone would deny that, for example, many states have chosen on many different occasions to wage war.

The second objection concedes that it is possible for collectives of these kinds to make choices, but it alleges that it is not possible for a society to have a preference or make a choice. It claims that only a collective with a collective decision procedure can choose, and a society necessarily lacks a collective decision procedure.[14]

It is true that a society need not have a decision procedure, yet it could have the use of one. If a society or its people were to constitute a state, then certain choices made in accord with the constitution would at least plausibly be viewed as choices of the society. I will explain this later. And a society need not have achieved statehood in order to have access to a decision procedure. For instance, if the United Nations sponsored a referendum among the Palestinian people, and if there were a consensus in favor of a Palestinian state, then it would be correct to say that the Palestinian society favored statehood.

I see no good reason, moreover, to believe that a decision procedure is a necessary condition for a collective entity to have a preference. For example, if the members of a family unanimously prefer to picnic at Lighthouse Park, then I see no point in denying that the family prefers to picnic there. One might insist that, in this context, "the family" is an abbreviation for "every member of the family." But it is not clear why the absence of a decision procedure should preclude the family as such from having a preference. If we are agreed that a fam-

---

14. See Peter French, 1979 and 1984. He argues that only collectives with collective decision procedures can perform actions, and his arguments would also imply that only such collectives can have preferences. For some criticisms, see Copp, 1986.

ily *could* have preferences if it did have a decision procedure, it is unclear why it cannot have a preference if it lacks a decision procedure.

Misleading Language?

The third objection points out that we can be misled by the devices we have for speaking concisely of situations in which many individuals in a collective have a property in common. For example, when enough Americans are acquisitive, we may say, "American society is acquisitive." But although this sentence is true if "American society" is taken to abbreviate the restricted quantifier "almost every member of American society," it should not be taken to attribute a property to the society as such. Similarly, the objection continues, if a sentence that seems to attribute a preference to a society appears to be true, the underlying fact is simply a fact about the preferences of members of the society. Because of this, sentences of this sort should be construed as simply attributing preferences to the bulk of the members of the societies. They should not be taken to attribute preferences to the societies as such.

The objection is not the flat denial that societies have properties. Rather, it is the denial that a society as such prefers a societal option when nearly every member prefers the option. But this is question-begging in the absence of an argument. The fact that we *can* be misled by disguised restricted quantifiers does not show that it is not possible for a society as such to have a preference.

It does follow from my position that we could replace all sentences that overtly attribute preferences to societies with sentences about the patterns of preferences among the members. My position allows the possibility of replacing one way of picking out facts about societal preferences with another way of picking out those facts. It does not follow, however, that societies as such do not literally have preferences.

Evidence of Societal Preferences

Even if the notions of societal preference and choice are tenable as such, the fourth objection alleges, there is no reason to believe that societies make choices or have preferences. For the notion of societal preference plays no essential explanatory role in social theory. Anything we could explain by means of hypotheses about societal preferences could be explained equally well or better, and explained more simply, by citing relevant preferences of the members of the society. And we would have to suppose that these persons had exactly these preferences in any event.

Yet I believe hypotheses about societal preferences and choices can have explanatory utility. For example, we are able to explain the fact that democracy has thrived in the United States and the stability of the constitutional system partly by means of the hypothesis that American society continues to prefer democracy. Also, we are able to explain why federal enforcement was needed in several southern states in order to bring about the end of Jim Crow by means of the hypothesis that the corresponding societies did not choose or desire to abolish the laws. These explanations are not the most detailed and nuanced explanations available, but they are at least part of the truth.

It may seem that these explanations add complexity to our ontology. But our ontology already includes societies, choices, and preferences, so this is not the case. It may seem that the explanations do no explanatory work, but this, too, is not the case. American society has a property that explains why democracy has thrived in the United States, the property of preferring democracy to dictatorship. It may be possible, of course, to give a more complete and nuanced explanation of the flourishing of democracy. But to explain it in terms of the existence of a consensus in favor of democracy over dictatorship is not to give a genuine alternative to the explanation in terms of the society's preference, for the society's preference is entailed by and entails the consensus. Moreover, the explanation is at the appropriate level of generality. It is the existence of the societal preference that explains the thriving of democracy, not the precise nature of the panoply of facts about individual Americans in virtue of which the societal preference exists.

The role of society-centered moral theory in explaining the nature and justification of morality is, I submit, an additional reason for supposing that societies are capable of having preferences and making choices.

Arrow and the Possibility of Societal Choice

From an abstract point of view, my proposal about societal preference can be viewed as specifying a *function* from preferences of members of societies into preferences of societies, a "consensus function." Functions of this kind are studied in social choice theory, and a number of important theorems have been proven about them. Most important is the disturbing result that is due to Kenneth Arrow.[15] Arrow argued that it is logically impossible for a "social choice function" to meet all of the conditions that would be necessary for it to be both plausible and non-arbitrary.

Charles Plott argued that the theorem shows that no society could have a preference.

> [T]he concept of a social preference itself must go.... [T]he concept of social preference involves an illegitimate transfer of the properties of an individual to the properties of a collection of individuals.... [T]he Arrow theorem demonstrates that the concept of social preference involves the classic fallacy of composition, and it is shocking only because the thoughts of social philosophers from which we have developed our intuitions about such matters are subject to the same fallacy.[16]

I shall argue, however, that Arrow's theorem demonstrates no such thing.

Arrow proposed that a defensible social decision procedure would base social preferences in an aggregation of the rational preferences of individuals and would

15. Arrow, 1963.
16. Plott, 1976, p. 525.

guarantee that social preferences are rationally consistent. He defined two sets of conditions on such procedures: conditions on the aggregation of individual preferences and conditions to assure the rationality of the derived social ordering. His theorem asserts that there is no social choice function that meets all of these conditions.[17]

Arrow was thinking of *methods* or *procedures* of social choice.[18] His goal was to state conditions that would be met by an ideal method for translating the preferences of the members of a society over social options into a decision or choice that depends on these preferences in a fair way, given reasonable and plausible political norms. This decision or choice is the so-called "social choice," and Arrow's conditions are intended to capture intuitions about fairness and rationality.[19] In these terms, Arrow's theorem is that no method of social choice can be ideal.

It follows from the theorem, then, that the consensus function is not ideal, assuming it is a "social choice function."[20] It fails to meet at least one of the conditions Arrow specified. The function is "gappy." It does not determine—for *every* society and *every* possible pattern of preferences of individual members of the society over societal options—a corresponding preference of the society. Depending on how it is formalized, its gappiness can be described technically as its failure to satisfy one of the following conditions specified by Arrow: "universal domain," the requirement that the social preference ordering be "connected," or the "Pareto condition."

This gappiness is not a cause for concern. As I said, Arrow was concerned with conditions on ideal political institutions that are both rational and politically defensible. My problem, however, is a metaphysical one. If I were proposing the consensus function as a political procedure for deciding among social options, its gappiness might be a problem, but I am not. I am proposing it as an account of the conditions under which a society actually has a preference. Let me discuss the three conditions that the consensus function can be construed as violating.

First, the condition of universal domain can be taken to say that an ideal method for deciding among societal options must yield a decision in every case

17. The original proof was given in the first edition (1951) of Arrow, 1963, in chapters 3 and 5. Arrow provided an improved proof in the second edition, pp. 96–103. A more recent formulation is found in Wilson, 1972, and textbook explications are in Moulin, 1983, and Schwartz, 1986. The proofs are discussed in Plott, 1976. The standard account is Sen, 1970.

18. His book begins with a discussion of "methods by which social choices can be made" in a capitalist democracy, such as voting and market mechanisms (Arrow, 1963, p. 1). Much of the discussion of Arrow's argument has focused on voting procedures. See Plott, 1976, pp. 554–87.

19. James Buchanan argues that they do not capture such intuitions (Buchanan, 1954). Aanund Hylland claims that social choice theory is intended to facilitate the evaluation of social systems (Hylland, 1986).

20. As it is defined, it is not a social choice function. For it takes a consensus about any societal option into a societal preference. But social choice functions are defined as functions from individual preferences over completely specified states of the society as a whole into social preferences. Russell Hardin pointed this out in conversation. See Arrow, 1963, p. 17. We can, however, define a restricted consensus function that takes near unanimity over complete social states into a societal preference. This restricted function qualifies as a social choice function.

where individuals have preferences over the options, regardless of the nature of their preferences.[21] The requirement of connectedness can be taken to say that an ideal procedure must rank every pair of social options in its purview by deeming one preferred to the other or by deeming them to be indifferent.[22] Taken together, these requirements express an ideal of effectiveness; a political system ought to be effective without restriction in reaching social decisions among competing societal options, as long as the options are genuine and people have preferences among them.

There can be a need for a political decision even in cases where there is not a consensus. This is why societies use voting procedures. But it is not plausible to suppose that the society has a preference in every situation, regardless of how much conflict there is among the preferences of individual people. There may in fact be very few cases where a society has a preference in its own right. There is often too much conflict among the preferences of individual persons to generate a societal preference, and so a theory of societal preference cannot be expected to satisfy the condition of universal domain.

For similar reasons, a plausible theory cannot be expected to satisfy the requirement that the societal preference ordering be connected. When the members of a society are in conflict over two societal options, there obviously will be no consensus in favor of one of them. If the conflict is deep enough, there will not be a consensus that the choice between the options is a matter of indifference. In such a case, it would be implausible to say that the society prefers one of the options to the other, and it would also be implausible to say that the society is indifferent between them. This means that a societal preference ordering may not be connected.

Similar considerations show that a plausible theory of societal choice would not satisfy the "Pareto condition." The Pareto condition requires that if at least one member of the society prefers x to y and no member prefers y to x, then a social choice function must assign to the society a preference for x over y.[23] Suppose, however, that one member of society prefers that a highway be built by a northerly route around a mountain, but that every other member is indifferent between the northerly route and a southerly route. In this case, it is not even clear that an ideal political system would select the northerly route. But it certainly would not be plausible to say that the society as such prefers the northerly route, for there is a consensus that the choice is a matter of indifference. This means that the Pareto condition would not be met by a plausible theory of societal choice.

21. That is, the social choice function must determine a social ranking of the social options for every combination of rankings by the members of society. For Arrow's formulation, see Arrow, 1963, p. 24. See Plott, 1976, p. 518.

22. That is, the social choice function must be such that, for any set of social options, it yields a social ordering which is "connected" in that, for any pair of options in the set, either one is preferred to the other by the society, or the society is indifferent between them.

23. In the first edition, Arrow used several conditions in place of a Pareto Principle, and he introduced a Pareto Principle only in the second edition (Arrow, 1963, p. 96). My formulation is based on James Buchanan's (1954, p. 115). Arrow's version is stronger than Buchanan's, and the consensus function does not violate it.

Nothing I have said is in conflict with Arrow's theorem or any other theorem of social choice theory. I am simply claiming that a plausible account of the conditions under which a society would itself have a preference would not meet all of the conditions Arrow proposes for a social choice function. Social choice theory is concerned with a political issue while "societal choice theory" is concerned with a metaphysical issue.

The conditions imposed on the social preference ordering in Arrow's argument are not in fact generally met by preferences. For example, the universal domain and connectedness requirements entail that every pair of societal options is ordered by the social preference ordering. But the actual preferences of individual people obviously are not connected over the universal domain of the options facing them, for people can be undecided among options. Since persons can have preferences that are not connected and that do not satisfy universal domain, there is no reason to think that the preferences of a society would have to be connected and satisfy universal domain. Arrow does not suppose otherwise, of course, for he proposes his conditions as requirements a social preference ordering must meet to qualify as "rational," not as conditions on the very existence of a social preference ordering.

Once we fix clearly in mind that Arrow's conditions reflect ideals of rationality as well as political norms, it should be obvious that Plott's argument is confused. Arrow's argument is compatible with the existence of social preference orderings that fail to meet one of his conditions. The failure to meet certain of the conditions might mean that a preference ordering is not rational, but it would not mean that it does not exist. In short, Arrow's argument is compatible with my thesis that it is possible for a society to have a preference, and it does not undermine the consensus theory.[24]

It may seem, nevertheless, that Arrow's theorem creates problems of a different sort for my overall view, since it shows that there cannot be a *rational* social preference ordering. Arrow's theorem shows nothing of the kind, however. Although some of Arrow's conditions are intended as requirements on a rational social ordering, others are intended to express political ideals. So Arrow's proof is compatible with the existence of a rational social preference ordering. What it shows, at most, is the non-existence of a rational social preference ordering that also meets certain political ideals. Moreover, Arrow's rationality conditions are controversial. For example, it is doubtful that a rational person's preferences must be connected. For there can be incommensurable factors relevant to the ranking of options, and this may prevent a rational person from ranking them, even from ranking them as equal. Consider a choice between two cities as places to live. One may reach no preference for one city

---

24. Economists ought to reject Plott's argument, for, as Arrow points out, classical demand theory assumes that households have preferences (Arrow, 1963, p. 9, n. 1). As Arrow points out, the preferences of a household depend on the preferences of members of the household, and the derivation of household preferences from the preferences of members is a special case of the derivation of social preferences from the preferences of individuals. Hence, if Arrow's theorem shows that societal preference does not exist, it also shows that household preference does not exist.

over the other, and yet, if one's feelings are in conflict, one certainly would not be indifferent between them.[25] Should one then judge one's preferences as irrational? Well, a rational agent would perhaps *aim* to reach a ranking. Connectedness of preference may be a desirable *ideal*, at least over options among which one must choose, but a failure to realize this ideal is not sufficient to show that one's preferences are irrational.

Arrow's result is profound and important, and it must be taken seriously. However, the non-existence of an Arrow function from individual preferences into social preferences does not imply that the consensus theory is incorrect.

Group Choice and Decision Procedures

I have argued that a society as such prefers an option just in case the option is a societal option and the members of the society are nearly unanimous in favor of it. This idea is, I think, shared by Arrow and Buchanan.[26]

It is rare to find near unanimity among the members of a society. Yet a society or other group can select an option by means of a voting procedure or some other form of group decision procedure, in cases where the procedure is accepted with near unanimity. It can do this in the absence of near unanimity about the option. Agreement on decision procedures explains how groups can make choices in many cases where they are very sorely divided on the merits of the options they face. For there may be a consensus on *how* to decide, even if there is not a consensus on *what* to decide. When this is so, a group can reach a choice via a mechanism I shall call "conversion to near unanimity."[27]

Nothing prevents a group from accepting a decision procedure that violates

25. This example can be interpreted as either an objection to the axiom that rational preference is connected or an objection to universal domain, reformulated to apply to individual persons' preferences. The example suggests that it is not the case that, for any pair of options he faces, a rational individual always will either prefer one to the other or be indifferent between them, regardless of the conflict there might be among his preferences for the options with respect to dimensions on which they differ. Of course, if "x is indifferent to y" means "neither x nor y is preferred to the other," then the connectedness axiom becomes a tautology. However, we now can easily find counterexamples to the axiom that rational preference is transitive. For I may strictly prefer x to z but be indifferent between x and y and between y and z. Failures of transitivity of this kind are unremarkable. For the lack of a valued difference between neighbors in a ranking is compatible with the existence of valued differences between items at the extreme ends of the ranking. If I am deciding among options that form such a ranking, I would be irrational not to form my preferences accordingly: to be indifferent between close neighbors, but to prefer the item at one end of the ranking over the item at the other end. This violates, strictly, Arrow's Lemma I (Arrow, 1963, pp. 14–15). On related issues, see the discussion in Schwartz, 1986, chapter 5.

26. Arrow says that "like attitudes toward social alternatives . . . are needed for the formation of social judgements" (Arrow, 1963, p. 74). Buchanan suggests that "a genuine social choice" requires a consensus (Buchanan, 1954, p. 119). He says, "In a very real sense collective choice cannot be considered as being reached by voting until relatively unanimous agreement is achieved" (p. 121).

27. Buchanan discusses the importance of a consensus on procedure (1954, p. 121). I first used the notion of "conversion to near unanimity" in Copp, 1979c.

one or more of Arrow's conditions. If the most charismatic person in a society manages to attract a nearly universal loyalty, she might become a dictator with the ability to speak for the society. Her choices of social options would become the society's, by a process of conversion to near unanimity.

Suppose, for example, that a family were to adopt a decision procedure for its weekly picnics: The members take turns deciding between Alice Lake and Lighthouse Park. Unanimity or near unanimity would be sufficient for the family to prefer this procedure. Now suppose that the difficult child always chooses contrary to the known preferences of the others. When it is his turn, he decides that the family will picnic at Lighthouse Park. Suppose the members remain nearly unanimous in their preference that the family choose by this new decision procedure. Once the contrary child selects Lighthouse Park, the seven other members' preference for the decision rule commits each of them to preferring, given the child's choice, that the family picnic at Lighthouse Park. Solely on the merits of the respective picnic grounds, the family is nearly unanimous in opposing Lighthouse Park, but their continuing preference for the procedure commits them to near unanimity in favor of Lighthouse Park. In this situation, it seems correct to say, the family chooses to picnic at Lighthouse Park.

Recall that preference is to be relativized to a set of considerations. The members of a group may be nearly unanimously committed to preferring option x over option y, given that x has been selected by a decision procedure that they prefer with near unanimity. This is possible even if they are not anywhere near to being unanimous in preferring x over y relative only to the merits of the options. In this case, I shall say, the group prefers the implementation of x over y relative to the verdict of the group's decision procedure. There is room for a set of group preferences to be in conflict. Suppose, for example, that a group prefers to let a dictator decide between options x and y, and suppose the dictator chooses x. The members are then committed with near unanimity to preferring the implementation of x, and I shall say that the group prefers the implementation of x, given the choice of the dictator. Yet the members might still be nearly unanimous in preferring y and in preferring that y be implemented, given the relative merits of x and y.

My proposal is as follows: For any group options x and y, first, a group prefers x over y, given certain beliefs about x and y, if and only if its members are (at least) nearly unanimous in preferring x over y given those beliefs. Second, however, a group prefers that x rather than y be implemented, given the group's decision procedure D, if and only if the group's members are (at least) nearly unanimous in preferring that procedure D be used to decide which group options to implement, and D yields the decision to implement x rather than y. Since societies are but large groups, this account implies an account of societal preference.

The ability of a society to form a preference among social options depends on the situation and on the nature and profile of its members' preferences. Many societies are organized into states and their members are sometimes in near unanimity regarding the constitutionally prescribed decision procedures. Societies that are so organized, and whose members nearly unanimously support the constitution, may be able to make a wide variety of choices regarding societal options and their implementation. They may be in a position to make choices even if they are quite divided on the merits of the options.

Societal Choice and Society-Centered Theory

So far I have not drawn a distinction between choices and preferences, but there is a distinction to be drawn. One need not choose what one prefers on the merits or prefer on the merits what one chooses. Alan may choose vanilla even though he prefers chocolate. He may want to prove he can resist temptation.

If preference is a matter of *ranking* one's options, choice has to do with the *taking* of an option. A person who chooses something prefers to take it, rather than to take an alternative, but it does not follow that he prefers it on the merits. For the taking or implementing of an option may involve costs of a sort that lead a person to choose a different option from the one he prefers on the merits.

Even though choosing an option requires preferring to take it or implement it,[28] this is not sufficient. Alan could prefer to take the vanilla but not actually choose it. A person who chooses an option is led by his preference to (try to) take what he prefers. Hence, a person who chooses the vanilla does actually take the vanilla, and he takes it as a result of his preference for taking it. These reflections suggest the following general account: To choose something is to (attempt to) take or implement it (or to bring about its implementation) because one prefers to take or implement it (or to bring about its implementation).

In this sense, I believe (or hope), American society has chosen to pursue greater equality among the races, and this indicates in part that the society has decided that a new moral consensus must replace the old consensus that tolerated the discriminatory Jim Crow laws. Of course, some of the original choices were made by courts and the Congress. But given the consensus among individual Americans regarding the Constitution, and given that constitutional procedures led to the implementation of certain strategies designed to further equality, it follows, according to my account, that American society chose to pursue greater equality. A policy of greater equality has been implemented in accord with constitutional procedures. Because of this and because there is a consensus that the Constitution is to be respected, the policy can be attributed to the society, and the preference to implement the policy can be attributed to the society. Had there not been the consensus about the Constitution, the policy likely could not have been implemented. Hence, the implementation of the policy depends on the consensus in a way that supports the claim that the society has chosen the policy.

28. To be sure, a person who suffers from a kind of weakness of will or who simply is not paying attention might "choose" an option different from the option that he prefers to take. I will not count cases of this sort as cases of choosing in the strictest sense. I will say that in such cases the person takes or accepts the option, but does not genuinely choose it because he does not *prefer* to take it.

The *J* property of society-centered theory is the property a moral code can have of being rationally "chosen" by a society to serve as its social moral code. Yet the costs of actually attempting to bring it about that a code is the social moral code are not relevant. Attempting to bring this about could be extraordinarily costly for reasons that have nothing to do with whether the code is justified. Hence, even if a society would not be rational to attempt to bring it about that a code is the social code, it may be that it would be rational to prefer to have the code *be* the social moral code. I will continue to speak of the rationality of "choosing" a code. But let me be clear that the issue in society-centered theory is whether a society would be rational to prefer that a given moral code be its social moral code.

Given this, the distinction between choosing and preferring is not important in society-centered theory.

Rational Societal Choice: The Extension Thesis

Choices are a kind of thing that can in principle be assessed for rationality. It follows immediately that the choices of a society can be assessed for rationality. If societies can choose in principle, then their choices are subject in principle to evaluation by reason.

Now there would be a pleasing unity in an account of rational choice if the theory of rational *collective* choice were simply an extension to the case of collectives of the theory of rational *individual* choice. This aesthetic consideration is one motivation for attempting to make the extension. A more important consideration is that it is unclear that there is any sensible alternative. A theory of rational choice for persons and one for collective entities are both theories of rational choice, even though they apply to agents of different types. If collective entities are capable of making choices, then these choices ought to be within the scope of a general theory of rational choice. There is no reason to think that the concept of rationality does not apply to collective choice or that there is a different concept for collective choice from the concept that applies to individual choice.[29] Hence, if a theory of rational individual choice does not directly apply to the case of choice by collectives, it ought to be possible to generalize the theory so that it does apply. There ought to be a more general version of the theory that applies to agents of all types. If there is not, then there is reason to think that the theory is incorrect.

For example, one theory asserts that the rational choice for a person in a situation is the choice that will maximize his expected utility or welfare. This suggests an analogous account of collective rationality, according to which the rational choice for a collective entity in a situation is the choice that will maxi-

---

29. Climates, diets, and organisms can all be described as "healthy," but the property in virtue of which a climate is healthy is different from the property in virtue of which an organism is healthy. "Rational" could be similar, as an anonymous referee pointed out to me: The property in virtue of which an individual's choice is rational could be different from that in virtue of which a collective's choice is rational. I claim, however, that there is no reason to think this is so.

mize its expected utility or welfare. If the utility maximization theory is plausible for the case of individual persons, then the analogous account would be reasonable, as a first hypothesis, for the case of collectives. It might be defeated if utility cannot be aggregated among the persons in a collective, for then there would presumably be no such thing as a collective's utility. But then, according to the extension thesis I wish to defend, the theory of individual utility maximization would be thrown into doubt unless it could be viewed as a special case of a more general theory that applied to collectives as well as to individuals.

The extension thesis asserts basically that if there is an adequate principle of rational choice for persons taken one at a time, then it is possible to "extend" the principle by analogy to societies taken one at a time. Of course, I do not mean that a suitable extension must be mechanical and obvious.

John Rawls and David Gauthier have discussed and rejected doctrines similar to the extension thesis in the course of criticizing utilitarian theories of justice. They each accept a version of individual expected utility maximization as a theory of individual rational choice and mistakenly think they need to reject a version of the extension thesis in order to avoid being committed to a utilitarian theory of justice. It will be useful to examine their arguments. I do not want to defend a social utility maximization theory in any guise, so arguments against this particular type of theory do not greatly concern me; but I do want to defend the parallel between rational societal choice and rational individual choice. Rawls and Gauthier both intend to reject this parallel.

Rawls discusses "a way of thinking about society which makes it easy to suppose that the most rational conception of justice is utilitarian."[30] He describes it as follows:

> Just as the well-being of a person is constructed from the series of satisfactions which are experienced at different moments in time and which constitute the life of the individual, so the well-being of society is to be constructed from the fulfillment of the systems of desires of the many individuals who belong to it. Since the principle for an individual is to advance as far as possible his own welfare, his own system of desires, the principle for society is to advance as far as possible the welfare of the group, to realize to the greatest extent the comprehensive system of desire arrived at from the desires of its members. The principle of choice for an association of men is interpreted as an extension of the principle of choice for one man.[31]

Rawls says this position involves "conflating all persons into one." It "does not take seriously the distinction between persons."[32]

Rawls intends this objection to apply to uses of an extension strategy in arguing for a utilitarian theory of justice. But it seems that it would also apply to uses of the extension thesis in arguments for a social utility maximization theory of rational societal choice on the basis of the familiar expected utility theory of rational individual choice. When Rawls says that the extension strat-

---

30. Rawls, 1971, p. 23.
31. Rawls, 1971, pp. 23–24.
32. Rawls, 1971, pp. 27, 29.

egy does not take seriously "the distinction between persons," he presumably means that it does not give this distinction the significance it must be given in a satisfactory theory of justice. But one might also think that "the distinction between persons" is not given proper significance by the theory that rationality for a group consists in maximizing the aggregate group utility.

To defend the claim that a social utility maximization theory does not give proper significance to "the distinction between persons," however, one would need an independently supported theory of rational societal choice. Otherwise, the claim would simply beg the question. As an analogy, consider the dispute between present-time and lifetime theories of rational individual choice.[33] A theory of the former sort may say that rationality for an individual at a time consists in maximizing the satisfaction of the desires she has at that time. A theory of the latter sort may say that rationality for an individual at a time consists in maximizing the realization of the system of her desires over the course of her entire life. It would beg the question to claim that lifetime theories do not take seriously enough "the distinction between times" unless one had an independent argument in favor of a present-time theory.

Rawls attempts to shift the burden of proof to extension strategies.

> There is no reason to suppose that the principles which should regulate an association of men is simply an extension of the principle of choice for one man. On the contrary: if we assume that the correct regulative principle for anything depends on the nature of that thing, and that the plurality of distinct persons with separate systems of ends is an essential feature of human societies, we should not expect the principles of social choice to be utilitarian.[34]

But, of course, utility maximization theories of societal rationality *are* relevantly different from individual utility-maximizing accounts of rational individual choice. In particular, the former involve aggregating the systems of desire of all the people who are members of a society, while the latter do not.[35]

Of course, I agree that the correct principle of rational choice for a thing depends both on general facts about rational choice and on specific facts about the nature of the thing. Hence the fact that collective entities have persons as proper parts of them, although persons do not, does indeed suggest that a plausible account of rational collective choice would differ in some ways from a plausible account of rational individual choice, even if both are special cases of the same general theory. But the extension thesis does not say otherwise.

Gauthier claims that there is an asymmetry between rational individual and rational social choice: "The rational individual pursues his or her good; the rational society pursues (its) justice."[36] Principles of justice, he says, "are not principles for rational choice by an individual seeking his or her good, but principles for rational choice by a society—a group of individuals—seeking justice,

33. See Parfit, 1984, part 2.
34. Rawls, 1971, pp. 28–29.
35. Rawls's arguments are discussed in McKerlie, 1988.
36. Gauthier, 1984, p. 251.

and so derivatively principles for choice by each person as a justice-seeking member of the society."[37] This supposed asymmetry undermines the extension thesis, for it implies that, while the theory of rational individual choice is logically independent of moral theory, the theory of rational societal choice is a part of moral theory.[38]

Gauthier's identification of the principles of rational societal choice with the principles of justice depends on conceiving of society as "a cooperative venture for mutual advantage." He argues that the conception of society as a cooperative and mutual venture implies that a rational society would aim above all to ensure cooperation and mutuality.[39] Yet even if a society that aimed at cooperation and mutual benefit would pursue justice, it does not follow that a *rational* society would pursue justice, simply in virtue of being rational. The conception of society as a cooperative venture for mutual advantage is a conception of an ideal society. It may be correct to say that a morally *ideal* society would pursue justice, but rational societies are not necessarily morally ideal ones. I conclude, therefore, that Gauthier has not shown an asymmetry between individual and societal reason.

Of course, society-centered moral theory does maintain that there is a connection between what a rational society would choose and what justice requires. But the connection is not as close as Gauthier's argument requires. Gauthier needs to show that a rational society is, ipso facto, a society that pursues justice. Society-centered theory depends on the weaker and quite different claim that, roughly, if a rational society were to choose a social moral code, that code would, ipso facto, be justified.

I used a very simple argument for the extension thesis. An account of rational collective choice and an account of rational individual choice are both accounts of rational choice. Hence, it is reasonable to expect each of them to be a consequence of the same fully general theory of rational choice. In this sense, a theory of rational collective choice ought to be an extension to the case of collective entities of a theory of rational individual choice. We have seen no reason to reject this conclusion.

Ideal Moral Code Utilitarianism

In general terms, "ideal moral code utilitarianism" asserts that a moral code is justified for a society just when its currency in the society would maximize expected social utility. Of course, there can be different accounts of the notion of social utility. Rawls suggests that maximizing social utility is a matter of realizing "to the greatest extent the comprehensive system of desire arrived at

37. Gauthier, 1984, p. 252.
38. On Gauthier's view, a social welfare maximization theory of rational societal choice implies a utilitarian theory of justice, and Gauthier argues that the implausibility of the latter implies the implausibility of the former. Compare Gauthier, 1984, p. 253.
39. Gauthier, 1984, p. 255.

from the desires of its members."[40] Different theories of social utility give different versions of ideal moral code utilitarianism.

A utilitarian theory of this kind can be derived from the *J* thesis of society-centered theory. According to a "utilitarian" theory of rational societal choice, a society's choice is rational if and only if it maximizes the society's expected utility. If a version of this view of societal rationality is combined with the *J* thesis, the result is a corresponding version of ideal moral code utilitarianism. In this way, society-centered theory can provide conceptual underpinning for ideal moral code utilitarianism. Yet the support that this way of looking at things can give to ideal moral code utilitarianism depends on the plausibility of the utilitarian theory of societal rationality. And I shall argue that no utilitarian theory of societal rationality is correct.

Given the extension thesis, one way to argue this would be to argue against analogous views of individual rationality, such as the view that the rational choice for an individual is the choice that would maximize his expected utility. In the next chapter, I will argue that theories of this kind are implausible, if maximizing utility is construed as maximizing the realization of the individual's overall system of desire. If I am correct, then the extension thesis gives us reason to doubt analogous utilitarian theories of societal rationality.[41]

The fact that ideal moral code utilitarianism can be viewed as a version of society-centered theory links my approach with the developed literature in utilitarian moral theory. This is a mixed blessing, of course, yet my point here is simply to illustrate certain ideas. Theories of this kind are familiar, so it is useful to take them as a point of departure. In order to discover a plausible society-centered theory, I have been arguing, it is necessary to discover a plausible theory of societal rationality, and the extension thesis suggests that we begin by investigating the theory of individual rational choice. This is the task I undertake in the next chapter.

40. Rawls, 1971, pp. 23–24.

41. Here is a complication: If maximizing an agent's utility is understood to consist in maximizing the satisfaction of its preferences, then we need to invoke the theory of societal preference in order to devise a societal analogue of individual preference satisfaction. There is a societal preference just in case there is a consensus in a society regarding a societal option. Given this, the theory that a rational society chooses options that maximize its preference satisfaction amounts to the theory that a rational society chooses options, the implementation of which would lead to results about which there is or would be a consensus among its members. The resulting society-centered theory would say that a justified moral code is one whose currency would tend to lead to results about which there is or would be a consensus. This is not a typical ideal moral code utilitarianism.

9

Needs, Values, and Reason

I have argued that the choices and preferences of societies can be evaluated on the basis of principles of rational choice. In this chapter, I propose a theory of "self-grounded" rational choice, called the "needs-and-values" theory. I suggest that it is the appropriate theory to use in developing the society-centered theory.

A theory of rational choice specifies a standard for choice and implies that the standard is appropriately justified. But there may be different kinds of justified standards for choice, and, if so, there are different kinds of reason. There may be moral reasons and epistemic reasons as well as the self-grounded reasons studied in the theory of rational choice. In order for a theory of reasons to suit our purposes in developing the society-centered theory, it must postulate reasons of a relevant kind.

There are two constraints. First, society-centered theory is a reductionist theory; it aims to explain the justification of moral standards and so the existence of moral reasons by invoking an idea of what it would be rational for a society to choose. Hence, the theory of reasons it uses must be morally neutral. The theory can presuppose neither that there are moral reasons nor that there are justified moral standards. Second, society-centered theory is an expression of the intuition that societies need morality because of something about their nature. We therefore require a theory of reasons that would assess the rationality of a society's hypothetical choice of a moral code on a basis grounded in the society's nature. In a more general form, it would assess an agent's choices on a basis grounded in the agent's nature. As I shall say, the theory must be a theory of "self-grounded" reasons. The "needs-and-values" theory meets both of these constraints.

I first explain the notion of a reason and discuss the justification of standards of reason. I then explain the idea of self-grounded rationality and go on to explain and defend the needs-and-values theory. I propose the theory initially as a theory of individual rationality. But the extension thesis, which I defended in the last chapter, implies that if the theory specifies the standard of self-grounded rational choice for individual persons, then a generalization of it will specify the standard of "socially grounded" rational choice for societies as well.

Reasons and Justified Standards

There are reasons of a given kind only if there are standards of that kind with an appropriate standing. For example, as I proposed in chapter 2, the proposition that there is a moral reason to choose *A* is true just in case there is a justified moral standard that calls for *A* to be chosen. In general, there is a *K* reason to choose *A* just in case (1) there is a *K* standard that calls for *A* to be chosen and (2) the standard has the relevant *K* standing.[1] And a fact is a *K* reason to choose *A* only if, given that fact, a *K* standard calls for the choice of *A*.[2] This is the natural position to take, in light of the standard-based theory of normative propositions. It follows, then, that each kind of justified standard we can use in evaluating our actions and choices underwrites the existence of a kind of reason.

A standard must be justified or have some appropriate standing in order to ground the existence of reasons. In this chapter, as I will explain, I am interested in standards of "self-grounded reason." However, this is not the place to attempt to develop a general theory regarding the conditions under which a standard of self-grounded reason would be justified. We need to take *something* as a given in any project. In a reductionist moral theory, such as society-centered theory, the justification of moral standards is explained by invoking standards of some other kind. The project of explaining the justification of those standards is a separate matter. Hence, although I will defend the needs-and-values theory, I will do so on the assumption that some standards of self-grounded reason are justified. I will not propose a general account of the justification of such standards.

It seems to me that standards of self-grounded reason have a special status in our lives. In order to cope with things, we need to think that some choices are better than others and that some choices are rationally defensible, from our own standpoint. This idea does not help us to know *which* standards of rational choice are justified or what it is in *virtue* of which they are justified. But, if I am correct, we must act on the assumption that some standards of self-grounded reason are justified.

In any event, I take myself to be entitled to ignore problems about the justification of standards of rational choice while dealing with problems about moral standards. This entitlement is presupposed by the reductionist strategy.

Self-Grounded Rationality

The needs-and-values principle that I shall propose evaluates an agent's choices on a basis grounded in her nature. The reasons it postulates are facts having to do with the nature *of the agent*. In this sense, they are "agent-relative" or "self-grounded." They are facts about the agent's needs, values, and desires.

---

1. As I said in a note to chapter 2, if a *K* standard "calls for" something, it "calls for" things that are means to, or "necessary enablers" of, that thing. For the idea of a "necessary enabler," see Sinnott-Armstrong, 1992, p. 400.

2. To a first approximation, the fact that agent *S* is *R*-related to *A* is a *K*-reason for *S* to choose *A* just in case a *K* standard with the relevant *K* standing calls for agents to choose things that are *R*-related to them.

There are, however, competing theories of self-grounded reason, the most familiar of which are instrumental theories of rational choice, some of which were mentioned in chapter 4. According to instrumental theories, the rational choice for an agent is the option that will best promote *the agent's* (expected) good, or the (expected) good *from the agent's standpoint*. Of the different interpretations of this idea, consider two. A "welfare theory" holds that the rational option is the one that will best contribute to the agent's *welfare*. A "desire theory" (or utility theory, as I have called it before) holds that the rational option is the one that will best satisfy the agent's *desires* or, perhaps, his *rational* desires. Because an agent may desire to contribute to the welfare of *other* people, and because the desire view would take this desire into account along with the agent's other desires, the welfare theory and the desire theory are not equivalent. Because of this, moreover, it would be misleading to describe self-grounded reasons as reasons of *self-interest*.

The view I will defend is different in fundamental ways from both the desire theory and the welfare theory. As against the welfare theory, I think that an agent who values the welfare of others may be rational to sacrifice her own welfare, if doing so will better enable her to promote the welfare of others. In this, I am in agreement with the desire theory. But I also disagree with the desire theory. First, I think there is an important difference between one's preferences and one's values. A rational person gives priority to her values over her mere preferences. Yet, second, I think an agent may be rational to forgo satisfying her values if doing so is necessary to protect her ability to meet her own needs. And I shall defend a conception of "objective" needs. This means I disagree with the idea that underlies the desire theory, the idea that self-grounded rationality consists in promoting a good that is a function of one's subjective psychology.

I also disagree, however, with the idea that underlies "perfectionist theories," the idea that rationality consists in the efficient pursuit of one's own "objective" good, a good that consists in such things as the development of one's talents. It seems to me that views of this kind confuse rationality with wisdom or, in more typical cases, with common sense. Wisdom and common sense help us distinguish things of genuine value from the mere pretenders. But self-grounded rationality is a more instrumental virtue, which is concerned with our ability to live a life directed by our own values. We do, of course, want our children to have wisdom and common sense, as well as moral virtue, for then their values will be warranted. But we also want them to be self-groundedly rational; we want them to direct their lives by their own values.

According to the needs-and-values principle, then, mere rationality does not guarantee that one's values are justified. Self-grounded rationality consists, basically, in directing one's life by one's own values and, at the same time, in sustaining one's ability to meet one's basic needs.

The Case of the Powerful Urge

Suppose I am at the edge of a platform at the top of a very tall tower, which I have climbed in order to inspect the view. I am suddenly assailed by a very powerful urge to jump. The case I have in mind is not one in which the urge is grounded in values, such as a valuing of danger or excitement, nor is it grounded in an unhappiness with life. I am living a generally happy life, and I can reasonably expect to continue to do so. It is simply that I am assailed by a very powerful urge. In the case I have in mind, it seems to me, I have no reason whatsoever to jump, despite the fact that I have this powerful urge to jump. Indeed, my urge gives me a reason to back away from the edge, rather than a reason to jump. Moreover, the more powerful we imagine the urge to be, the stronger the reason it gives me to back away from the edge. The urge is simply an unfortunate psychological force, which I must resist.[3]

It is not, I submit, that the urge gives me *some* reason to jump, a very weak reason, and that the reason is outweighed by reasons against jumping.[4] Nor do we think that the more powerful the urge, the stronger the reason it gives me to jump. The normative significance of the urge is opposite to what desire theories imply, for it gives me a reason to back away from the edge, not a reason to jump.

This simple example undermines desire theories, which explain rational choice as a matter of choosing in a way that contributes to the satisfaction of one's desires. To be sure, a plausible theory of this kind would restrict the desires that qualify as rational considerations to those that would survive an ideal process of reflection and deliberation. According to such "rational desire theories," any desire that would survive the specified process counts as giving the person who has it a reason to bring about what will satisfy it. And the weight of the reason would depend on the weight the desire would have in the agent's overall psychology at the end of the specified process. Yet the tendency to have urges to jump may be deeply ingrained in me. Indeed, given the nature of such urges, it is unlikely that I could eliminate it or eliminate my tendency to have similar urges by means of a process of deliberation and reflection. The urge might even persist if I were fully and vividly informed of the horrors of plunging to one's death. If so, then according to a rational desire theory, my urge to jump gives me a reason to jump, and the stronger the urge, the stronger the reason it gives me. I find this quite implausible.

To be sure, the details matter, and there are different rational desire theories.[5]

---

3. For a similar view, see Gert, 1988, chapter 2, esp. p. 29. I owe this reference to Walter Sinnott-Armstrong.

4. It would not be plausible to say, for example, that the urge gives me some reason to jump because it may cause me to feel frustrated or uncomfortable if I do not jump. On this proposal, I would always have some reason to kill myself, for there are always sources of frustration and discomfort.

5. Peter Railton says that "an individual's good consists in what he would want himself to want . . . were he to contemplate his present situation from a standpoint fully and vividly informed about himself and his circumstances, and entirely free of cognitive error or lapses of instrumental rationality" (1986b, p. 16). But consider the case of the powerful urge. Let us suppose that I am not only afflicted with the urge, but with a desire to have it. Moreover, when I become afflicted with the urge, the nature of my life and my circumstances on top of the tower become suddenly quite vividly clear to me. I am not making any cognitive error or suffering from a lapse in choosing means to satisfy my desires. The urge overwhelms my other desires, and the step I must take to realize my desire to jump is entirely clear to me. Hence, it may well be that Railton's conditions are satisfied in the case. Yet I say that, even if so, my good does not consist in jumping.

David Gauthier holds, for example, that the desires that give us reasons at a given time are restricted to desires held at that time that are both "considered" and "coherent."[6] But this does not prevent my urge from counting as a reason to jump. It may be that no information, experience, or amount of consideration would make a difference to how I feel. If so, then, even on the theory of considered and coherent desires, my urge gives me a reason to jump. In a similar way, an urge to eat ice cream would give me a reason to eat ice cream, if no information, experience, or amount of consideration would make a difference to how I feel about it. Indeed, on Gauthier's account, it seems, I may have every reason to jump and no reason not to jump, if my urge causes all my other desires to disappear at the moment in question.[7]

One might think that the mistake here is to restrict attention to desires the agent has at the time of choice. A more complex theory might claim that rationality consists in maximizing the satisfaction of a coherent system of preferences that would somehow incorporate the desires and interests one will or would have over one's entire lifetime, provided that these desires and interests would survive deliberation and reflection. Ignoring uncertainty and risk, the lifetime theory says that rationality consists in choosing and executing the plan for one's life that offers the most in the way of satisfied qualifying desires. Of course, in the example, if I jump I will not be able to satisfy the desires I would otherwise have had in the future. Unfortunately, however, even a lifetime theory of this sort will count my urge to jump as giving me a reason to jump, if it would survive deliberation and reflection.[8]

Such a theory may even tell me that the urge brings it about that I am rationally required to jump. Let us change the example and suppose that my future is hardly worth living, by the standards of the lifetime theory. No matter what

6. Gauthier, 1986, pp. 23–24, 29–32, 37–38.

7. It might seem that other desires would still be relevant, for they would still exist, even if they were not "occurrent." Even if they were submerged by the urge, they would still exist. Yet we can imagine that they do go away, even if only temporarily. "At that moment, I didn't care about anything else." See Gauthier's discussion of "rejected interests" (1986, pp. 33–35).

8. Michael Bratman has developed a complex position about the rationality of plans and intentions that, it may seem, can blunt the problem of the powerful urge (1987). Bratman argues, in effect, that once an agent makes a plan, rationality may require that the plan remain stable (pp. 60–106). In the case at hand, I would not be rational to reconsider my life plan in the face of a sudden urge to jump (p. 66). Moreover, intentions provide "framework reasons," which constrain the admissibility of options (pp. 32–35). In the case of the powerful urge, the framework reasons provided by a rational life plan would exclude the option of jumping. In this sense, my urge would provide me with no reason to jump. However, Bratman's theory does not deal fully with my worry. First, his theory is not a (standard) rational desire theory, for Bratman argues that intentions are different in kind from ordinary pro-attitudes (pp. 10, 15–18). Moreover, second, Bratman allows for what he calls the "external" evaluation of actions, which abstracts from the framework reasons provided by the agent's prior plans (pp. 42–49). My argument in the text takes up this external point of view, so framework reasons do not directly address the problem raised by the sudden urge. Finally, Bratman simply assumes that some form of desire theory accounts for the rationality of choices when they are evaluated from the external point of view (pp. 20–23).

I do, many of my more important and deeply felt desires will not be satisfied, for many of them are desires to achieve things that I cannot achieve. Moreover, these desires would survive the ideal process of deliberation and reflection specified in the theory. Hence, the overall balance between the satisfaction and frustration of qualifying desires will be pretty much evenly balanced in my future, so that I would be hardly more fortunate to live than I would be to die right now, if I could die painlessly. From this point of view, I may be lucky to be assailed by the urge to jump off the tower for it tips the balance in favor of killing myself, making that path offer me more in the way of net desire satisfaction than the path I will follow if I step back from the edge.

Even in this case, however, assuming I have the ability to carry on and at least to meet my basic needs, I want to say that *the urge* gives me no reason to jump. I may have reasons to jump, but the urge does not add another one. Moreover, I want to say, I am not rationally *required* to jump. I would not be making a mistake of any kind if I were to step back from the edge and climb back down the tower.

Yet urges and whims do sometimes give us reasons. This is true even of urges that are orthogonal to the ordinary direction of our desires. For example, even if one normally has no desire to smell the flowers, an urge to smell a rose is ordinarily a reason to smell a rose. Even the urge to jump off a tower would give me a reason to jump if I were attached to the tower by a bungee cord. This must be explained, but it means that a desire theory cannot simply stipulate that whims and urges are not sources of reasons.[9]

Desire satisfaction theories share the core idea that a rational person aims at a good the nature of which is determined by facts about the person's own psychology. The two cases I have discussed undermine this idea. In the case of the powerful urge, for example, I have needs that will be frustrated if I jump, and this is true no matter what the state of my psychology. This is why I have a reason not to jump. The case of the powerful urge suggests, then, that the reasons an agent has are not straightforwardly a function of her psychology and do not depend simply on what she happens to be motivated to pursue.

Reason and Needs

In this section, I introduce the concept of a basic need and explain its role in an account of self-grounded reasons. I will defend three doctrines about basic needs. First, people have certain basic needs, and what a person basically needs is not determined by her desires or other psychological states. I shall call this the "objectivity of needs thesis." Second, if a person has a basic need for something, then she has a reason to secure it for herself or to keep it if she already has it. I shall call this the "weak reason and needs thesis." Third, if doing a certain thing would

---

9. Ruling them out by fiat would be ad hoc, and it would put at risk the core idea of desire theories.

prevent a person from meeting her basic needs, then she is not rationally required to do it. This is the "strong reason and needs thesis."

The weak thesis implies that, in the case of the powerful urge, I have a self-grounded reason *not* to jump. Given the objectivity of needs thesis, I have this reason regardless of any facts about my psychology. I have this reason even if my urge is overpowering enough to cause me to lose temporarily all the desires I would otherwise have. The strong thesis implies that I am not rationally required to jump off the tower, since doing so would prevent me from meeting my basic needs.

Basic needs must be distinguished from things we need only in light of other things we desire or value. For example, if I want to be studying, I need quiet. Here the status of quiet as something I need depends on the fact that I want to study. Needs of this sort may be called "occasional needs." Basic needs are more fundamental. For example, I need food and water, shelter, the ability to move safely in my environment, health, and a sense of self-respect, among other things. These are needs I have in common with every other person. They are needs for things that are ordinarily essential to every person's good. I call needs of this sort "basic needs."[10] It is basic needs that enter my account of self-grounded reasons.

The *concept* of a basic need may be controversial, but, as David Braybrooke has claimed, anyone with the concept would agree that the things I listed are matters of need.[11] Of course, he points out, a need can be met in different ways, by different "forms of provision," and it can be met to different degrees, even though there may be a "minimum standard of provision" appropriate to each person under each heading of need. For example, we believe there is a need for sleep, but we are not committed to thinking that everyone needs the same amount of sleep and in the same kind of bed and so on. The minimum amount that would meet one person's need for sleep might be different from the minimum amount that would meet another's need.[12]

A basic need gives rise to derivative needs for the things required in order to meet it. For example, if the ability to move safely is a basic need, and if I am trapped down a mine, then I need a flashlight and a hardhat. Because there is no presumption that everyone in the human population needs a source of artificial light, we do not classify it as a matter of basic need. But a source of artificial light is a "form of provision" that may be required in certain circumstances in order to meet a need. In some cases, cultural or social factors give a person certain derivative needs. For example, I need self-respect, but social acceptance is needed for a person to have a sense of self-respect, and in different cultures, different things contribute to social acceptance. Things that are required for meeting a basic need may be called "required forms of provision." The distinction between such things and matters of basic need is dependent on background

10. For the distinction between occasional and basic needs, see, for example, James Griffin (1986, p. 41). David Braybrooke calls basic needs "course-of-life needs" (1987, p. 29).
11. Braybrooke, 1987, p. 36.
12. Braybrooke, 1987, pp. 38–47.

circumstances; if everyone were trapped in a mine, we might come to classify having a hardhat as a matter of basic need. But this does not undermine the usefulness of the distinction.

When it is claimed that a person needs something, it is always appropriate to ask what she needs it *for*.[13] A matter of occasional need, for example, is needed in order to achieve something that is desired or valued. I shall speak of the "ground" of a need, in referring to the thing a matter of need is needed for. I confess that I am not certain exactly what relation obtains between a matter of need and its ground. It would be too strong to say that matters of need are, strictly speaking, *required* for their ground. For example, I need quiet in order to study, but quiet is not strictly *indispensable* to my studying. Rather, my studying will suffer substantially if I do not have quiet. This seems enough to justify saying I need quiet, even if there is some chance that I could manage to study without quiet, as long as (it is highly likely that) my studying will be impaired without quiet. I therefore suggest, as an approximation, that N is needed in order to achieve G just in case (it is highly likely that) N is necessary to prevent impairment in achieving G.[14]

In order to understand basic needs, we need to identify the ground of the basic matters of need. If G is a ground of the basic needs, then N is a basic need just in case it is highly likely that N is necessary to prevent anyone's being impaired in achieving G. There may be more than one such ground. But to suit my purposes, a ground must help to explain the connection between reasons and needs. The weak reasons and needs thesis, for example, is a substantive thesis about self-grounded reasons. The very idea that something has a need does not entail that it has a reason. Plants have needs without having reasons, for example. I must therefore discover a ground of the basic needs that will explain why we have a self-grounded reason to try to secure for ourselves a minimum standard of provision of matters of basic need. This means that the ground I propose should be something that we have a self-grounded reason to try to achieve or keep, independently of our desires, preferences, or values.

It is plausible to think that survival and biological flourishing are a ground of the basic needs. For example, the needs of a plant are the things it most likely requires to avoid biological impairment. However, it is not the case that everyone has a reason to secure the things needed to avoid biological impairment. Suppose, for example, that mechanical hearts became very much more reliable and that their installation became quite routine. Life with a mechanical heart would still have to be counted as *biologically* impaired, yet we might have no *reason* to prefer life with a biological heart to life with a mechanical heart. We are not entitled to presume that every person has a reason to prefer a life that is not biologically impaired. This means that even if survival and biological flour-

13. This has been said by many writers on needs. David Wiggins seems to deny it, in the case of basic needs (1987, p. 9).

14. I do not know precisely how to explain the kind of necessity involved. Perhaps the laws of nature are such that (it is highly likely that) my studying will be impaired if I do not have quiet. Wiggins speaks of the needs as "required," given the "laws of nature, unalterable and invariable environmental facts, or facts about human constitution" (1987, p. 15).

ishing do *ground* the basic needs, I must look elsewhere to ground them in a way that will explain the doctrines about reasons and needs.

One might propose that the matters of basic need are grounded in the fact that they are means to our ends, whatever our ends may be; they are all-purpose means. An occasional need is something required by a given agent in order to achieve some *given* thing that she desires or values; a basic need is something required by *any* agent in order to achieve *anything* that she desires or values. But this connects needs to *reasons* only on the hypothesis that reasons are ultimately derived from our desires or values, and this hypothesis is undermined by the case of the powerful urge. In this case, I have a reason not to jump that is grounded in my needs, and yet, given how my ends have been shaped by the urge, jumping may be the only available means to the satisfaction of my ends. One therefore cannot explain the doctrines about reason and needs on the hypothesis that the basic needs are all-purpose means.

Two ideas seem central to the idea of a basic need. First, a person must meet her basic needs in order to avoid harm. Garrett Thomson suggests that if a person has a basic need for something, then her life would be "blighted or seriously harmed without it."[15] This suggestion connects meeting basic needs with acting rationally, for there is a presumption that every person has a reason to avoid a blighted or harmed life. Yet in what respect would a person's life be harmed if she were deprived of a matter of basic need?

The second central idea is that basic needs are the requirements of a "normal" life. Hence, Braybrooke says that basic needs are the things that are "essential to living or to functioning normally."[16] This idea is slippery, of course, for people in different circumstances have different ideas about what is to be expected in human life. But in the present context, a viable conception of normal life would have to be connected with the idea that the basic needs are required to avoid a blighted and harmed life. What the theory counts as normal life in this context must be such that a person who is deprived of (the ability to live) a normal life is ipso facto leading a blighted and harmed life.[17] A statistical conception of normality is therefore not to the point. In certain historical contexts, for example, a statistically normal life would be a life of illiteracy, and yet a person who is "deprived" of the "opportunity" to be illiterate, by being taught to read, is not thereby harmed.

What I require, then, is a conception of a form of life, deprivation of which would constitute a harm, such that anyone can be presumed to have a reason to want such a life. That is, the ground of the basic needs is a kind of life that (1) is "normal" for persons and (2) is such that if a person's life failed to be of this kind, it would count as "harmed" or "blighted." Moreover, given the doc-

15. Thomson, 1987, p. 8. See also Wiggins, 1987, pp. 10, 15; Feinberg, 1973, p. 111; Stampe, 1988, p. 135.

16. See Braybrooke, 1987, p. 31. See also Griffin, 1986, p. 42.

17. Braybrooke explains that "normal life" is as a certain kind of life in a society, involving "a combination of basic social roles, namely, the roles of parent, householder, worker and citizen" (1987, p. 48). But a person who has freely chosen a non-standard life may nevertheless be leading a non-blighted life even if he is not serving in some of these roles.

trines about needs and reasons, this kind of life is such that (3) every person can be presumed to have a reason to try to secure it for himself and to keep it. The matters of basic need are the things that, it is highly likely, are necessary to prevent anyone's being impaired in achieving such a life.

My proposal is that the kind of life at issue is one that would be *normal* for a *rational agent*. My proposal has two parts: (1) The basic needs are the things that, most likely, are necessary to prevent anyone from being impaired in living a minimally rational life, and (2) a person is living a minimally rational life just in case she subscribes to standards for her life, is capable of deciding for herself which standards to accept, and is able to choose how to live her life on the basis of such standards.[18] I think that every person can be presumed to have a *reason* to seek the things that are necessary to prevent impairment in achieving such a life, since it is a minimally *rational* life. Moreover, loss of such a life would be a harm.

Rationality is a matter of being responsive to reasons. Being responsive to reasons is being responsive to justified standards, as I explained. Hence, responsiveness to justified standards is characteristic of rationality, and so is subscribing to justified standards. For subscribing to a standard is simply a matter of making one's responsiveness to the standard firmly entrenched in one's character. There is then a link between being rational and subscribing to standards.

It would not be plausible, however, to say that a rational person subscribes only to standards that are justified. For, first, this again would be to confuse rationality with wisdom and common sense. It takes more than mere rationality to know exactly which standards are justified, and a person who fails of wisdom or common sense is not thereby condemned to a life that is "blighted" from the point of view of its rationality. Second, I am attempting to elucidate a threshold of normalcy, such that one's life is blighted if one falls short of it. I am not trying to elucidate an ideal kind of life. Third, there are certain standards that could be accepted even by a fully rational and wise person, although they are not susceptible to any relevant kind of justification. For example, I may set myself an exercise routine and subscribe to a standard that calls on me to follow it, even if my routine has no special justification by comparison with other routines I could follow instead. Finally, I am attempting to elucidate self-grounded rationality. The justification of a standard may depend on properties of entities other than the agent; because of this it would be a mistake to insist that a person has failed with respect to self-grounded reason if some of her standards are not justified.

For these reasons, then, we may think of a minimally rational agent as one who subscribes to standards for his life, is able to choose how to live on the basis of these standards, and is capable of choosing which standards to accept. The life of a minimally rational person is autonomous, in an important sense, and the basic needs are, approximately, requirements of that kind of autonomy.[19]

---

18. Notice that I have not said that the ability to get what one values is necessary for a minimally rational life. Rather, I have said that the ability to choose how to live on the basis of one's values is necessary.

19. In Copp, 1992c and 1993, I took a kind of autonomy to be the ground of the basic needs.

The basic needs are, then, the things that (at some time in the course of life) are most likely required to avoid impairment of minimal rationality; that is, they are required to avoid impairment of the capability of having standards, choosing how to live one's life according to one's standards, or deciding which standards to accept. To suffer impairment of these capabilities, as I shall explain in the next section, is to suffer a significant loss. Matters of basic need are the means to avoiding this loss.

Most of the things standardly taken to be basic needs can be accounted for on this basis. A person requires bodily and psychological integrity in order to have standards and the capability of pursuing their satisfaction. Survival and the requirements of survival, such as food and water, are requirements of bodily integrity. Physical survival is a basic need because survival is essential if one is to choose how to live one's life. In ordinary circumstances, development of the capacity to live by one's standards would be impaired unless one were nurtured and loved in childhood and unless one were given an education, at least of a basic sort. Freedom from constant extreme fear is something we need, for extreme fear would impair one's ability to live by one's own standards. Friendships give a person the psychological security and the help that are means for most people to pursue a life according to their standards. And, for a final example, humans ordinarily require sleep in order to preserve their psychological integrity.

Some things that are needed at one stage of life are not needed at another. A person who is living a minimally rational life may be deprived of friends at a later stage in life and find that he does not need to have friends, even though he once did need to have friends. The forms of provision for the basic needs and the way in which one needs these things will vary with one's nature and one's circumstances, including the culture of one's society. Some people need less sleep than others do, and some need much less companionship than others need. There are many complications, but I think they can be dealt with.[20]

I believe that my account of the ground of the basic needs explains why every agent has reason to satisfy her basic needs. But to understand this fully, we must be clear why a person would be harmed if she suffered impairment of her ability to have standards and to pursue their satisfaction.

Reason and Values

To live a minimally rational life, in the sense I have explained, a person must subscribe to standards that pertain to choices central to her life. I want to claim, more exactly, that a person must have "values."

A person's values are her stable and endorsed standards about the course of her life:

> To have values at time t is to subscribe at t to standards about the course of one's life such that (1) one's subscription to them is stable over a period

---

20. Richard Kraut helped me to see some of these complications (in correspondence).

in one's life which includes t, (2) one is at t content to subscribe to them, and (3) one would not be content at t to anticipate ceasing to subscribe to them, where (4) the attitudes mentioned in (2) and (3) are themselves stable.

This may be a somewhat stipulative use of the term "values."[21] But let me explain what I mean and explain why it is important to have values in this sense.

It is not necessary to have a precise definition of what is meant by standards regarding one's life or the course of one's life. The standards I have in mind are standards to which a person gives central importance in deciding how to live, such as the various personal ideals or standards people sometimes adopt for their own lives. A person may value the life of a businessman, for example. A person's moral standards are normally among her values, provided her subscription to them is stable and endorsed in the way I will explain. The idea is that a person's life is blighted if she lacks any values, for these would be standards that give direction to her life.[22]

To have values requires more than simply subscribing to some standards at some time. It requires also a degree of stability to one's subscription. A person who subscribes to the standards in one set at one time, to the standards in an entirely disjoint set shortly thereafter, and so on, does not have the sort of commitment to the standards that is characteristic of one's values. To have values is also to "endorse" one's subscription to the standards that give direction to one's life.[23] Without such endorsement, even if a person's life has a stable direction given by his standards, he would still lack the sort of acceptance of his standards that is characteristic of one's values. Such lack of acceptance would mark an important failure in the way his life is given direction by the standards. I am not claiming that a rational person must *explicitly* endorse her subscription to her standards, for she may not have given them much thought. But she must endorse them in that she is content to subscribe to them, she would not be content to anticipate ceasing to do so, and she would continue to feel this way if she considered them explicitly. For example, she does not explicitly regret them, and this lack of regret must itself be stable.

It may be objected that a person may have values even if he is content to realize he will one day subscribe to quite different standards. For example, a person who values excitement could be quite content to realize that he will eventually prefer comfort.[24] But such a person would ordinarily subscribe to some standards for his life in a stable and endorsed way, even if not to a standard that

---

21. In Copp, 1992c and 1993, I explained values as, roughly, stable and endorsed *preferences* about the course of one's life. Here I am able to bring to bear my theory of standards in a better explanation of the notion of a value. There are more subtle ways in which my position here differs from my position in those papers.

22. This helps to explain why the standards that I am interested in here, which I call "values," are standards about "the course of one's life."

23. Here I do not use the term "endorse" in the sense I introduced in chapter 5. In that sense, endorsement is an attitude toward a standard. Here the issue is one's endorsement of one's *subscription* to a standard.

24. This example is due to Garrett Thomson (in correspondence). For similar examples, see Parfit, 1984.

calls for a life of excitement. He may, for example, value living in accord with relatively stable course-of-life preferences. Now he has a stable desire for excitement, but he realizes he will eventually instead desire comfort in a stable way. In this case, he does not value excitement per se, but he does value living in accord with his desire for excitement.

In the last section, I explained the minimally rational life as requiring that one subscribe to standards regarding one's life. I now want to say that, in order to be living a minimally rational life, a person must have values, be able to choose how to live on the basis of her values, and be capable of deciding for herself which values to accept. But a person's standards for her life normally qualify as values because one's standards are normally stable and endorsed. I therefore think that the amendment I am introducing makes little practical difference.

This is not an overly intellectualized conception of the minimally rational life, and it does not, I think, presuppose the values of our own culture in an objectionable way. Consider the following examples.

To begin, imagine a painter who is deeply content to be an artist. He subscribes in a stable and endorsed way to a standard that calls for him to live this life. Yet suppose that he has been so influenced by the prevailing ideology of his society that he believes, for the conventional reasons, that life as a businessman would be intrinsically best for him. According to my account, what he values is the artistic life he is living rather than the life of a businessman, even though he would deny that the artistic life is intrinsically good. For to have values is to subscribe to standards that shape one's fundamental attitudes toward one's life and one's choices of how to live. This example shows that a person may value his life on my account even if, at a more superficial psychological level, he believes a different kind of life would be intrinsically best.

For a second example, imagine an unsophisticated potter in a primitive society, and suppose that she lacks the concept of the intrinsically good. Let us suppose she is deeply content with her life and is conforming to her standards for her life. I would say she values the life she is living even though, because she lacks the concept of the intrinsically good, she is not in a position to form the belief that her way of life is intrinsically valuable. This example shows that the attitudes that are required of a person, according to my account of a minimally rational life, are not overly sophisticated or difficult to acquire.

Now I want to argue that a person's life would be harmed or blighted if he lacked values and the capacities to choose his values and to live according to his values. This argument will complete my case that the ground of the basic needs, life as a minimally rational agent, is a kind of life that we have reason to want and deprivation of which would constitute a harm.

A person without values might still subscribe to standards for her life, but there may be little stability to this. Or, if she does subscribe to certain standards in a stable way, she is not content to subscribe to them, or she would be content to anticipate their loss. In this case, her life lacks any substantive and lasting direction with which she identifies. One's values determine what we may think of as the *direction* of one's good; a person without values is without an "orientation" in life. There is not a good that she can discern, for she does not even value satisfying her needs or her preferences. Hence, a person without values has no compelling reason to pursue anything except things that are the means to acquiring a sense of direction or of value in life. These are the things for which she has a basic need. Fundamentally, a person without values needs to acquire values, and she has reason to seek to have values. The satisfaction of her less fundamental basic needs would still leave her without direction, even though it would provide her with the resources to proceed in some direction or other. Hence, our fundamental need is to possess a set of values, and I think it fair to presume of every agent that she has a reason to seek to have values.

In the a life of a person with values, a whim to have an ice cream cone would offer a preferred and happy diversion from the direction given by her values. But in the life of a person without values, a mere preference or desire would not be a reliable indicator of the direction of her good. To be sure, the pursuit of value in one's life may involve exploring one's preferences, for values can develop out of our mere preferences through experience. Hence, one's need to find value would ground a reason to satisfy one's preferences. However, mere preferences by themselves cannot provide one with direction, for preferences without values would be like the shifting wind, where one must settle on a destination in order to give direction to one's life.

Of course, even though the unsophisticated potter has values, her life may still seem blighted if she lacks the capacity to appraise reflectively her values, or if she lacks the capacity to pursue any values different from her actual ones.[25] Having values provides one with something to choose. It provides direction. But it is equally important to have the capacity to choose one's direction, and, having chosen, it is important that one have the capability of moving in that direction.

The basic needs are things that are (most likely) required to avoid impairment of one's capacity to live a minimally rational life, a life directed by values that one can choose and appraise. This is a kind of life that we have reason to want, for deprivation of it would be a harm. We therefore have reason to satisfy our basic needs. Furthermore, the reasons given us by our basic needs deserve a place in a complete account of self-grounded rational choice. Although a deeply self-destructive person may not want to meet her needs, the things she needs are the means to having and pursuing values, and having and pursuing values are essential to the life of a rational agent. Hence, the reason we have to meet our needs is grounded in something fundamental to our lives as rational agents.

Competition among Values, Preferences, and Needs

I have claimed that if a person has a basic need for something, she has a self-grounded reason to secure it for herself. Yet I also want to argue that we have

---

25. I am not arguing that a person's life would be blighted if she did not actually reflectively appraise her own values. I am merely arguing for the importance of having the capacity to appraise one's values.

self-grounded reasons to pursue satisfaction of our values. It is natural to say this, given what I said about the importance of values in giving direction to one's life. We need to have values for this reason, as I argued. But if we have values, we have self-grounded reasons to pursue their satisfaction.

Recall, for example, the case of the contented painter. He subscribes in a stable and endorsed way to a standard that calls for him to paint. Subscription involves the intention to comply with the standard; it involves a kind of personal policy or commitment. A stable and endorsed policy of this kind is precisely the sort of thing we look to in our lives when we want to decide how to go on. The painter's belief that life as a businessman would be intrinsically best for him does not give him a similar kind of reason to go to business school, for it does not involve a policy or commitment of this kind. Indeed, in the example, the painter has no commitment to go to business school; instead, he has the stable and endorsed policy to carry on with his life as an artist. We take it that we have reason to follow through with such policies.[26]

It is possible, however, for there to be conflict between achieving what one values and satisfying one's basic needs. I shall argue, in effect, that there are three sources of self-grounded reasons: basic needs, values, and mere preferences. Needs and values are equally important, and they have strict priority over preferences in a sense I shall explain. Needs and values can conflict, however, and because of this, something must be said about what rationality requires when they do conflict.

Let me begin with some examples. The firefighters and other cleanup workers who entered the area of the stricken nuclear power plant at Chernobyl faced obvious health risks, but if they were volunteers, they may have faced the risk in order to contribute to the safety of the population at large, something they must have valued. Surely, it will be said, someone can rationally choose to pursue something of immense value to her, even if the cost is a substantial risk or even a loss of a matter of basic need. Surely the firefighters were rational to do what they did. A mountain climber puts at risk her ability to satisfy her needs, and she need not be irrational in doing so. A person working among the victims of an epidemic may put his ability to satisfy his needs at risk, and have good reason to do so, given what he values. A person's values may give him reason to put his needs at risk in order to further the needs of others. In general, a person may rationally pursue the course of life that he values while neglecting or putting at risk his ability to satisfy his needs.

It remains true, of course, that the firefighters had a reason to avoid risks to their health. I constructed the examples to show that it could be rational to risk a matter of basic need in order to further the agent's values. But the same examples can be used to show that it could be rational to forgo something the agent values in order to protect a matter of basic need. A firefighter would have been rational to decide not to enter the area of Chernobyl. Perhaps it will be said that in so choosing, the firefighter would reveal that she values less contribut-

---

26. Of course, if our endorsement falters and we begin to reconsider, then we may question whether we have a reason to follow through. But then, too, the policy is no longer a value.

ing to the safety of the population at large than she would have revealed, had she chosen to participate in the attempt to extinguish the fire. Yet this is not clear. She may have been torn by the decision, worrying about her health on the one hand, but feeling the push of her moral values on the other. It seems clear that, on the one hand, it would not be irrational to refuse to fight the fire, for the firefighter would thereby be securing a matter of basic need, and on the other hand, it would not be irrational to fight the fire, even at risk to her health, for the firefighter would thereby be pursuing something of great value to her. From the perspective of her values, it would be best for her to fight the fire, but from the perspective of her needs, it would be best for her to refuse. Either choice would be rationally permitted.

Let me now state the position I wish to propose. A rational person tries to achieve the satisfaction of her needs over the long run, at least to an appropriate minimum standard of provision, and she seeks to promote her values when she can. Conflict between these objectives can be resolved either way; that is, if each of her options is in conflict either with serving her needs on balance or with serving her values on balance, then it is indeterminate how best to serve her good. Reason does not determine which way she ought to choose. If there is not a conflict between a person's needs and her values, then she is required to choose the option that would best serve both her needs overall and her values overall, to a sufficiently good approximation. If several options are essentially indistinguishable with respect to how well they would serve her values and needs, as in choosing a flavor of ice cream, she is required to choose the one that she prefers.

These reflections suggest the following principle of choice, which I call the principle of needs-and-values rationality:

> An agent is rationally required to do A, rather than any other action among a set of relevant options, if and only if, either (1) doing A is the option that would best serve on balance both his basic needs and his living in accord with his values, or (2) his intrinsic preferences at the time would best be served by his doing A, and no other option would better serve either his basic needs or his living in accord with his values.[27]

The principle supports the strong reason and needs thesis, according to which a person is never rationally required to do something that would prevent her from meeting her basic needs. It implies that a person is never rationally re-

27. I assume that "rationally forbidden" and "rationally optional" can be defined in terms of "rationally required" in the obvious ways. It is not always "irrational" to refrain from actions that are rationally required. I may be rationally required to smell a rose, if I have an urge to do so, and if abstaining would not better serve my needs or my values. But if I abstain from smelling, my action is not *irrational*. It would not be a sufficiently serious infraction to be called "irrational." Kraut and Sinnott-Armstrong made objections (in correspondence) that helped me to see this. I believe we are rationally required to do what would be *best*, by the lights of our needs and values. A "satisficing" approach would say otherwise, but I think my theory can explain the intuitions behind satisficing theories by reference to the values of the person for whom actions that appear to be merely satisficing are rationally required. But see Slote, 1989.

quired to do otherwise than best serve her basic needs. And a person is never rationally required to do otherwise than best serve her values.

To take account of uncertainty and risk, the principle ought ideally to speak of the "expected contribution" of actions to the agent's meeting her needs and serving her values. In the case of the mountain climber, climbing has the highest expected contribution to her values, but refraining from climbing has the highest expected contribution to her ability to meet her needs. Neither option is rationally required.[28] By contrast, a person who considers jumping off a tower on a whim, and who does not value excitement or anything else that would be relevant, is rationally required to refrain from jumping. For refraining has the highest expected contribution to her ability to meet both her needs and her values.

One might object that the values of a person should not be taken to qualify as sources of reasons unless they are properly informed.[29] Yet, as I explained before, if a person has values at all, then she subscribes to relevant standards in a stable and endorsed way, and she would continue to endorse these standards if she considered them explicitly. This surely is sufficient for her to have a self-grounded reason to pursue what she values, even though it does not guarantee that her values are wise or justified, or that they would not change in light of further information. Suppose, for example, that Alice now values her mountain climbing, yet suppose she would cease to value it if she knew more about, say, the amount of money made by equipment manufacturers. I think she has good *self-grounded* reason to continue with her climbing as long as she does, in fact, value it.

The idea that preferences must be properly informed, if they are to be a source of reasons, is due, I think, to the realization that many of our preferences are self-destructive or harmful to us. But information does not necessarily eliminate harmful desires. The case of the powerful urge is a vivid example. The reason the desire to jump off the tower does not give me any reason to jump is that jumping would prevent me from meeting my basic needs, not that my desire is not fully informed. In general, according to the needs-and-values principle, our desires are sources of reasons unless there is conflict between serving our desires and serving either our basic needs or our values. When there is no such conflict, our desires and even our whims are sources of reasons, even if they would disappear with fuller information. Allan Gibbard imagines that my desire for ice cream would disappear if I brought to mind all that is known about digestion.[30] But this does not mean that I have no self-grounded reason to eat ice cream.

The needs-and-values principle is an idealization or model that may not be adequate to certain examples. In the rest of this section I shall clarify it and test it against objections. There are complexities that the theory ignores.

---

28. But if she is going to climb and her relevant options are different ways of climbing, she may be rationally required to climb with "protection" rather than to climb without protection.

29. In this paragraph, I argue for a position different from the position I took in Copp, 1993.

30. Gibbard, 1990, pp. 18–22, esp. p. 20.

In complex situations, different needs might be in conflict with one another, and so might different values be in conflict with one another. In such cases, there may not be an ordering of one's options on the basis of how well they serve one's needs overall or on the basis of how well they serve one's values overall. It may be, then, that there is no option that *best* serves *both* one's needs and one's values, and it may be that the option that best serves one's preferences is worse than other options, with respect to both one's needs and one's values. In such cases, no action qualifies as required, yet it may be objected that the options need not all be equally eligible.

It may also be objected that the choice between serving one's needs and serving one's values is not always rationally indifferent. Certain of a person's values are relatively trivial and certain needs are extremely important, and vice versa. The choice between a trivial value and a pressing need—or that between a pressing value and a trivial need—is not rationally arbitrary in the way the theory seems to imply. For example, a person may be rationally required to put his life work ahead of the need for just the right amount of iron in his diet.

In reply to these objections, I should stress that the needs-and-values principle is meant to make reference to what will best contribute on balance and on the whole to one's living in accord with one's values, and to what will best contribute on balance and on the whole to one's meeting one's needs to a relevant minimum level of provision. One's basic needs are things that are required to avoid impairment of one's ability to have values and pursue valued things over the course of one's lifetime. These ideas are unfortunately vague. But while forgoing just the right amount of iron may be compatible with serving one's needs on the whole, depending, of course, on medical details, mountain climbing puts at risk a person's ability to meet her needs on the whole and over her lifetime. It is in cases like that of the mountain climber, where there is conflict between a person's valued activity and her ability to pursue valued activities over the long run, that the choice of whether to pursue the activity is indifferent.

The needs-and-values principle gives quite different treatment to values and to desires, yet it may be objected that certain desires regarding our lives are stable and endorsed in a way that ought to mean they are as important as our values. Consider, for example, that a typical hobbyist may have a strong, stable, and endorsed desire to paint, which gives his painting a significance in his life comparable to the significance it would have if, instead, he subscribed to a standard that called on him to paint. Yet there are important differences between the syndrome of attitudes characteristic of subscription to a standard and a mere desire. The hobbyist likely *would* subscribe to a standard that calls on him to pursue a hobby—the hobby he prefers. He would likely be content to think of himself in five years with a new hobby, but not content to think of himself without any hobby at all. In this case, he values having a hobby, even if not his painting per se. Hence, there likely is a value in the background that endorses the hobbyist's desire to paint. This may explain why his desire seems as important as a value.

I am proposing a standard of reason that endorses our values in two ways. It endorses the standards we subscribe to as a matter of having values, for it implies that each person has a self-grounded reason to conform to them, regardless of whether they are themselves justified.[31] It also implies that a person has a self-grounded reason to pursue the things that he needs in order to have values, and the capacity to choose values and to satisfy them.

In Defense of External Reasons

Bernard Williams has argued that so-called "external reason statements" are false, incoherent, or, at best, misleading.[32] He seems to think it follows from his position that the fact that a person needs something is no reason by itself for her to pursue it.[33]

"Reason statements" are statements to the effect that something is a reason for someone to do something. A reason statement is "internal" just in case it would be "falsified by the absence of some appropriate element from" the agent's set of motivations.[34] An external reason statement, by contrast, "can be true independently of [the specifics of] the agent's motivations."[35] For simplicity, I will assume that Williams wants to claim that there are no *true* external reason statements. He thinks something is a reason only if an appropriate statement regarding the agent's motivations is true. More exactly, he thinks, if an agent is not motivated to do *A*, if this lack of motivation is not due to factual ignorance or mistake, and if he could not acquire a motive to do *A* "from motives he has" and acquire it by means of deliberation alone, then he has no reason to do *A*.[36]

Recall the case of the powerful urge. In that case, as I now stipulate, my urge overwhelms me to the extent that I am not motivated at all to step back from the edge, and my urge is so powerful that it makes it impossible for me to deliberate. I therefore cannot acquire a motive to step back from the edge by *deliberation*.[37] Yet my lack of motivation is not due to factual ignorance or mistake. Williams must therefore deny that I have any reason not to jump off the tower. More specifically, he must argue that the fact that jumping will kill me is no reason at all for me not to jump.

Williams's argument for this position depends on the quite intuitive idea that, as he says, "If something can be a reason for action, then it could be someone's

---

31. My value is a standard I subscribe to. This standard may not be justified, but the standard that calls on me to promote my values is justified. It is a justified standard of self-grounded rational choice. This explains why I have a reason to promote my value.

32. Williams, 1981a, p. 111.

33. Williams, 1981a, pp. 105–6.

34. Williams, 1981a, p. 102.

35. Williams, 1981a, p. 107.

36. See Williams, 1981a, pp. 105–9.

37. In discussing such cases, Williams says we will seldom *know* that a person who seems uninterested in pursuing his needs is genuinely someone who could not become motivated to pursue them by means of deliberation (1981a, pp. 105–6). But I *stipulate* that, in this case, my urge prevents me from deliberating. Perhaps I *could* acquire a motivation not to jump by a process of deliberation, if I *could* deliberate. But that is a different matter from what I can actually do, given my urge.

reason for acting on a particular occasion, and it would then figure in an explanation of that action."[38] This principle connects normative "reasons," or considerations that *justify* choice, with an agent's "reasons," or considerations that *explain* an agent's choice, whether or not they also justify.[39] I will call it "the explanation principle." I take it to mean that if R is a (normative) reason for S to do A, then R could be S's reason for doing A.[40] Here then is Williams's argument.

An external reason statement entails nothing about the specifics of the agent's motivations. Hence, the mere truth of such a statement could not by itself explain anyone's intentional action. If an external reason is to be someone's reason, the agent must believe that the reason obtains;[41] that is, if R is an external reason for S to do A, it must be possible for S's doing A to be explained by his believing truly that R is a reason for him to do A. And for this to be possible, it must be possible for S to be motivated to do A simply as a result of believing that R is a reason for him to do A. It is irrelevant that people can acquire beliefs by means of processes that alter their motivations, for the issue raised by the explanation principle is whether an external reason, or simply the belief that it obtains, can motivate a person. Hence, given the explanation principle, if R is an external reason for S to do A, and if S comes to believe that R is a reason for him to do A, he must thereby acquire a new motivation to do A, even if he acquires the belief in a dispassionate manner, through deliberation. Williams sees "no reason to suppose" that this "could possibly" happen.[42] For, "ex hypothesi," S may have no existing motivation, the nature of which could explain the fact that his deliberation results in a motivation to do A. If deliberation leads to a certain motivation, the explanation of this must surely depend, at least in part, on the nature of the agent's prior motivations.

This last point expresses a very weak version of "Humeanism." Of course, if deliberation leads to a certain motivation, there must be an explanation of this. The Humean point merely adds that the explanation must depend on some fact about the motivational states of the agent. This could be simply the fact that the agent has a tendency to acquire motivations under certain conditions, such as, perhaps, to acquire motivations to do what he believes he has a reason to do.[43]

Even if the Humean point is correct, however, it does not imply that there are no external reasons. Williams's argument depends on an implausible understanding of relevant counterfactual situations. The explanation principle says that if R is a reason for S to do A, then R could be S's reason for doing A. To

38. Williams, 1981a, p. 106.

39. Something may be an *agent's* reason for doing something even if the agent has no *self-grounded* reason to do it. Recall again the case of the sudden urge. If I were to jump off the tower, my reason would be to satisfy my urge. But my urge is not a self-grounded reason for me to jump. It is important not to be confused by this. To describe something as "an agent's reason" for acting is not to make a normative claim. It is simply to *explain* the agent's action.

40. This is compatible with the idea that S may need additional information, or may need to deliberate, in order to be motivated to do A. Williams, 1981a, pp. 103–5.

41. Williams, 1981a, pp. 106–7.

42. Williams, 1981a, pp. 108–9.

43. Williams, 1981a, p. 105. See Wong, 1994.

determine what *could* be an agent's reasons, we need to consider counterfactual situations. For example, in describing the case of the powerful urge, I stipulated that I lack any motivation not to jump. Yet I could refrain from jumping. Consider, then, the counterfactual situation in which I do not jump. It is otherwise very much like the situation we have imagined, but since it is a situation in which I do not jump, it is obviously one in which I am not overcome by my urge. I do not jump, and it is quite possible that my reason is that jumping would kill me. The fact that we have a reason to satisfy our needs entails nothing about the specifics of our actual motivations. Yet a person may be able to be motivated by his needs even if he is not actually motivated by them and cannot actually be motivated by deliberation about them. For if he has the option to do what is necessary to satisfy his needs, it could be that if he did so, his reason would be that doing so will satisfy his needs.

Williams reads the explanation principle in a different way. He takes the principle to mean that if R is a reason for an agent to do A, then, given the agent's actual motivations, or motivations the agent can actually acquire by deliberation, R could be the agent's reason for doing A. Yet I do not see why we should accept the principle on this interpretation of it. On this interpretation, a person who cares not a bit about the consequences of her actions, and who is impervious to deliberation about them, is thereby exempted from any reason to care. People who are intuitively the least rational turn out instead not to have the reasons we intuitively thought they had. In the case of the powerful urge, because I cannot acquire a motivation not to jump by deliberating, given my actual motivations, I have no reason not to jump. I see no reason to accept this.

Underlying Williams's view is the concern to understand the truth conditions or "force" of reason statements.[44] I sympathize with this concern, yet the standard-based theory implies an account of the truth conditions of propositions about reasons. According to the account, the truth of a proposition to the effect that something is a self-grounded reason for an agent depends on the existence of a relevant justified standard. "External reason statements" are no more problematic than "internal reason statements." The problem with both is to explain the circumstances under which a standard of self-grounded choice would be justified. This problem seems no easier if we restrict attention to standards that connect reasons to desires.

Williams does not provide an argument for the explanation principle, but, in light of the standard-based theory of reasons, a close relative of it seems virtually a truism. Suppose there is a K reason R for S to do A. Then there is a K-standard with a relevant status, and it calls on S to do A because of R. And suppose ignorance is not a factor and there are no extraordinary factors interfering with S's autonomy. Then S at least could understand and subscribe to the standard and realize that it calls on her to do A because of R. If she did subscribe to it, and if she did A in order to comply with it, then R would be her reason for doing A. Hence, if something is a reason for an agent to do A, then,

44. Williams, 1981a, p. 109.

ignorance and extraordinary factors aside, it could be the agent's reason for doing *A*.

Moral Reasons and Self-Grounded Reasons

Given that there are different kinds of reasons, we need to distinguish between the existence of a reason of a kind *K* and the existence of a *self-grounded* reason to act on that *K* reason. This is quite obvious in the case of reasons of etiquette, for there may be reasons of etiquette to place cutlery in a certain pattern even if some given person lacks any self-grounded reason to do so. The existence of reasons of etiquette seems less important, from this point of view, than the existence of a self-grounded reason to act on reasons of etiquette.

The analogous facts about moral reasons may be more disturbing. For the existence of a moral reason also does not entail that any person is motivated to comply with it, or that any person has a self-grounded reason to comply with it. There are moral reasons just in case there are moral standards with the relevant justification. And it does not follow from the existence of a justified moral standard that any person subscribes to it or is motivated to comply with it.[45]

If a person subscribes to a moral standard in a stable and endorsed way, then he has a self-grounded reason to comply with it. Some of our values are moral values, and our values give us self-grounded reasons. But our moral values need not be *justified* moral standards, nor is it necessarily the case that justified moral standards are among anyone's values. A morally *virtuous* person subscribes to justified moral standards and does so in a way that makes them among his values. But if an agent is amoral, if he does not subscribe to any moral standards, or if the standards he subscribes to are not justified, then moral reasons are not self-grounded reasons from his standpoint. Of course, he may still have self-grounded reasons to comply with moral reasons. But a person can acknowledge the *existence* of moral reasons without having any moral standards among his values, and so without the moral reasons being self-grounded reasons for *him* to act morally.[46]

The self-grounded reasons a person has in virtue of her moral values are, of course, connected to her motivations. In general, to the extent that our self-grounded reasons are grounded in our values and desires, they are connected to our motivations. But it does not follow that a person will always be motivated to do *A* if his values or desires give him a self-grounded reason to do *A*. The person might not see that he must do *A* in order to realize his values or desires, and even if this is brought to his attention, he might feel a lack of drive to do *A*. He might be suffering from weakness of will, or he might be depressed and temporarily uninterested in his values.

---

45. This might follow, given certain theories of the justification of moral standards. It does not follow in society-centered theory.

46. As I explained in chapter 2, a person can have a moral belief without subscribing to any corresponding moral standard.

Given the theory of reasons I have developed, there is no obvious basis for the idea that moral reasons are "overriding," in the sense that they must always rationally prevail if there is a conflict between a moral reason and another kind of reason.[47] Indeed, the idea that morality is overriding in this sense suggests there is some overarching justified standard that demands our compliance with moral reasons in preference to reasons of any other kind. One might think that the justified moral standards themselves would be the overarching ones, but I do not see how to make this idea intelligible except by supposing it is made relative to some other putatively justified standard that calls on us to give priority to moral reasons. This standard would itself give rise to reasons, and if it determined the relative priority of moral and other reasons, then the reasons it gave rise to would be the dominant or prevailing ones, even if they always called on us to comply with moral reasons. This does not rule out the possibility that there is a justified standard of this kind, of course. Yet it is quite unclear what would give it its status as justified.

From the standpoint of society as a whole, moral reasons do in a sense have priority over the merely self-grounded reasons of individuals. Indeed, according to society-centered theory, moral reasons exist in virtue of the fact that relevant societies have "socially grounded" reasons to prefer that some moral code have currency in them. They have reasons to prefer that this be so and that people give the standards of the social moral code priority over whatever self-grounded reasons they otherwise would have.[48]

In a well-ordered society, the extant moral culture would involve the currency of justified moral standards. People would come to subscribe morally to these standards in the ordinary course of events. These standards would be among people's more important values; people would give them a central role in their lives. Hence, in a well-ordered society, people typically would have self-grounded reasons to be moral. Then, too, in ordinary situations we obviously are motivated to meet our needs. A well-ordered society would strive to bring about conditions in which there are few significant conflicts between our needs and our moral values. Our moral values would motivate us, we would be self-groundedly rational to be so motivated, and our needs would not generally be a barrier to our acting morally. I will explain these ideas in the remaining chapters.

47. Compare Foot, 1978c, pp. 183–88, 157–73.
48. Compare Baier, 1981, p. 337.

10

Morality and Society

In order to yield substantive moral implications, the characteristic *J* thesis of society-centered theory must be combined with a specific theory of societal rationality. In this chapter, I develop the societal analogue of the needs-and-values theory and combine it with the *J* thesis. I call the result the "needs-based society-centered theory."

In the course of the chapter, I will propose various minor amendments to the *J* thesis. I will postpone addressing technical meta-ethical issues until the concluding chapter.

Societal Rationality: Needs-and-Values Theory

According to the extension thesis, which I defended in chapter 8, if the needs-and-values theory offers an adequate standard of self-grounded rational choice for persons, then it is possible to extend the theory by analogy to the choices of societies. The result should be a satisfactory account of "socially-grounded" rationality. In order to flesh out the analogy, we need to view socially grounded rationality as a function of the society's needs, values, and preferences.

Begin with societal preferences, which I discussed in chapter 8. According to the consensus theory, the preferences of a society are patterns of nearly unanimous preferences of its members over societal options.

Turn now to societal values. Values are standards that are subscribed to in a stable and stably endorsed way. And, just as the preferences of a society are patterns of preferences of the members over societal options, so the values of a society are concerned with societal options. For example, a standard of personal hygiene would not count as a value of the society itself, even if it is subscribed to with near unanimity, for societies as such do not have bodies to keep clean. A society's values are strategies for coping with its life. So, I propose, a society has a value just in case a standard regarding societal options is the object of a stable consensus among the members of the society, where there is a consensus in endorsing the stable consensus. A standard is a value of a society just in case it is a standard regarding societal options, the members of the society are nearly unanimous in subscribing to it, and their near unanimity is stable and endorsed by them with near unanimity.

The notion of a societal need is not problematic, but we need to investigate whether the grounding of societal needs is analogous to the grounding of individual needs. I proposed that the ground of the basic needs of persons is a minimally rational life: A person is living a minimally rational life just in case she has values for her life, has the ability to choose how to live her life on the basis of such values, and has the ability to decide for herself which values to accept. The following proposal is a close analogue of this: The ground of the basic societal needs is a state of society in which the society is able to cope in a minimally rational way with societal problems as they arise over time.[1] A society is in such a state only if it has values, the ability to choose its values, and the ability to order its life in accord with its values.

Societal problems do arise, of course, and if a society has no values, it may lack any sense of a unified direction it can take in dealing with them. Then, too, if it cannot choose solutions to its problems on the basis of its values, it may be unable to cope with its problems in a rational way. And if its values are ossified or if it cannot choose its values or exercise any control over them, then it may not be able to cope with novel problems, and it cannot cope with problems that may be caused by its having the values it has.

However, problems that afflict a society as a whole and call for societal action to deal with them may arise only infrequently. We individuals act on a daily basis to deal with our own problems, and we need values to direct our coping actions. But societies may be able to cope even if they do not have values in the sense I have explained. It may be enough if they enjoy a consensus in their members' preferences regarding societal options, provided that the consensus is stable and endorsed with near unanimity in a stable way. For these reasons, although I do hold that the ground of the basic societal needs is the ability to cope in a minimally rational way with societal problems, I do not want to explain this in terms of the society's having values in the strict sense I explained. For a society would be able to cope if it had stable and stably endorsed preferences over societal options, the ability to alter such preferences, and the ability to order its life in accord with such preferences.

I therefore propose that the basic needs of a society are the things that are required in all likelihood by any society in order to avoid impairment of the capacity to have a system of values or stable and endorsed preferences over societal options, as well as the capacity to pursue and to alter these values or preferences. For simplicity, when the context does not make the distinction important, I will not distinguish between societal values and stable, endorsed societal preferences.

In a society without any stable and endorsed preferences or values, a preference of the society would be a relatively short-lived coalescence of individual preferences regarding a societal option. If longer-lived, it would be a coalescence

---

1. Patricia Greenspan suggested that I express my idea in terms of what is required in order to cope.

that is not endorsed with near unanimity, and so on. Such a temporary agreement in preference regarding a societal option or an agreement that is not endorsed is, I suggest, no reason for the society to implement the option. Societal
options are social arrangements that can be implemented only over significant
stretches of time and for significant stretches of time. Examples are alterations
in the constitution of the nation-state that embraces the society, public works,
and alterations in the culture, including the putting in place of a social moral
code. A merely temporary coalescence of individual preference regarding such
an option does not, I believe, give a society any reason to implement it.

Of course, if there is a need for a decision, and a stable, endorsed consensus
that, say, majority rule be used as the social decision procedure, then matters
are different. But then the society would not be entirely without stable and
endorsed preferences or values.

If I am correct that a society's mere preferences over societal options are not
a source of reasons for it, we can simplify the needs-and-values principle: A
society is rationally required to choose societal option x rather than y if, and
only if, option x would best serve on balance both its values or stably endorsed
preferences and its basic needs.

Let me take this opportunity to explain, as I promised I would, that a society
may be rationally required to choose something even if some members would
not be rationally required to choose it. For example, suppose a society must
decide between a parliamentary system of government and a presidential system, and suppose that there is a stable and endorsed consensus in favor of the
parliamentary system. If the parliamentary and the presidential systems would
have served the needs of the society equally well, and if no other societal values
are relevant, then the society is rationally required to choose the parliamentary
system. However, despite this, there obviously could be a member of the society whose needs would be equally well served by either system but who so values a presidential system that he would be rationally required to choose that
system, if he could implement it himself. Accordingly, a society may be rationally required to choose in ways that differ from the ways some of its members
would be rationally required to choose. This means that there is no prospect
for a simpleminded reduction of a society-centered moral theory to a theory
that explains the justification of moral standards in terms of the rational choices
of persons. The rationality of a society's choice of a given moral code to serve
in it as the social moral code does not entail that every member would be rational to choose it for that purpose.

Societal Needs

I think that societies have few values of any kind and few preferences over societal options.[2] If I am correct, we can approximate the results of society-centered

2. As I explained in chapter 7, any society is characterized by the existence of cooperative
interaction governed by a distinctive set of behavioral standards. But this does not mean that a
society must have values, for these shared standards are concerned with interaction among the

theory by initially restricting attention to societal needs in attempting to determine the nature of the moral code that a society would be rational to select. Societal needs will do most of the work.

The needs of persons can be classified as needs for bodily integrity, needs for psychological integrity, and needs for supportive relationships with others. These classifications may overlap, but no matter. Food and water are things we need for bodily integrity, while freedom from constant fear is a requirement of psychological integrity. Friendships and security from aggression are things we need under the last heading, and we need education under all three headings.

The needs of societies fall under analogous headings, but they obviously differ from the needs of persons because societies are different in nature from persons. As I explained in chapter 7, a society is a multigenerational population of persons embracing a relatively closed social network, and limited by the widest boundary of a distinctive and salient system of cooperation.

A society normally does not need to continue to be a society, nor does it need to avoid being absorbed by another society. It might become a proper part of some successor society or be absorbed by another society without impairment of its capacity to have and pursue values. Yet a society does need to ensure the continued existence of the population that it is. A society depends on the existence of this population just as a person depends on the existence of his body. Analogous to a person's need for bodily integrity, then, is a society's need for physical integrity, which requires that it ensure that the population that it is continues to exist. In order for a societal population to continue to exist, it is not enough that its members have descendants. There must be the right kind of historical continuity of membership. The social network established by relationships of kinship, friendship, and so on must encompass the population at different times.

A society also has a need for cooperative integrity, which is analogous to a person's need for psychological integrity. On this basis, a society needs to ensure that its population continues to be characterized by a system of cooperation that is salient for its members. This requires that its population continue to constitute a society or at least be part of a society. Meeting this need will contribute to internal social harmony.

Analogous to a person's need for supportive relationships is a society's need for peaceful and cooperative relationships with neighboring societies. I think, in fact, that this need is best met in the modern world of rapid communication and travel—and of astonishingly destructive weapons—if the international situation is such that the global population is a global society that is able to meet its needs for physical and cooperative integrity.

The most important consequence of these ideas is that a society needs to ensure that at least a sufficient number of its members are able to meet their basic needs. A basic need of a society is to ensure the survival of the multigenerational population that the society is. And this requires ensuring satisfaction of at least the

members of the society, not necessarily with societal options, and they may not be endorsed or subscribed to with near unanimity.

basic bodily needs of the members of that population, so this too is a basic need of the society. Moreover, to meet its need for cooperative integrity, a society must ensure that a sufficient number of its members live in a context in which they can satisfy their psychological and social needs, as well as their bodily needs. It must ensure that a sufficient number of its members enter into cooperative social and economic relationships with other members of the population. It will do better at this if it can assure that its members see these relationships as rational for them from their own standpoints. Therefore, the basic physical, psychological, and social needs of a sufficient number of the members of a population must be reasonably well served if the society is to do well at meeting its needs.

A corollary is that a society needs to ensure that its members will continue to have the capacity to have and to pursue satisfaction of values. This follows from the ground of societal needs, for if the members' capacity to have values is impaired, a society's capacity to have values is also impaired. It also follows from the society's need to ensure satisfaction of the basic needs of its members. The members of a population need the things required in order to avoid impairment of their capacity to have and to pursue satisfaction of values.

Further, if a society is to serve the basic needs of its members, it must ensure that it continues to be—or continues to be a part of—a society. For people need to live in a society, or at least to grow up in one. Perhaps we would develop some values outside society in a "state of nature" and be able to pursue certain values. However, in order to avoid the likely impairment of one's ability to develop an articulated set of values and to pursue their satisfaction, one must grow up in a society with a relatively stable culture and widely accepted standards of cooperation. And having grown up in a society, we are unlikely to be able to do well at meeting our needs outside a society.

These are among the considerations that determine the substantive moral implications of society-centered theory. And given that societies have the same fundamental needs, we can expect similar results in every society. Given the societal needs I have been discussing, we can expect that a justified moral code would require that people's basic needs be well served and that it would promote the capacity of people to choose and sustain their values and to pursue them. I will return to these points later.

The most important remaining basic societal need is to have a social moral code. I discuss this in the next section.

The Societal Need for a Moral Code

In chapter 6, I discussed the intuitive idea that societies *need* morality. I argued that this idea provides support for the society-centered theory. I now want to give an argument for a close relative of this intuition, the proposition that any society is better able to meet its needs with a social moral code than without one. If the argument is successful, its conclusion meshes nicely with the needs-based society-centered theory, for given the theory, it follows that, most likely, any society is such that some moral code is *justified* relative to it.[3]

Any society is characterized by a shared system of cooperation, and I have argued that any society has socially grounded reasons to choose to continue to be characterized by such a system. First, a society needs internal harmony. Second, a society needs to ensure the continued existence of its population in a state in which the members can expect beneficial economic and social interaction with their fellows. This means the members must widely subscribe to standards governing their interaction. Third, a society needs to serve the basic needs of its members, who need to develop their values and to have the capacity to pursue their values. To meet this need, they need to live in a stable social context where interaction is governed by generally accepted standards of cooperation.

As background to the argument, I assume that if there were not a shared system of cooperation in a population, its members would act by and large on their self-grounded reasons, given whatever values they were able to develop and given their basic needs. I do not think that the result need be a Hobbesian war of all against all.[4] People would develop ties of affection with certain other people, and their basic needs would lead them to form groups and to cooperate in certain contexts. Gradually, they would come to accept systems of cooperation, and societies would emerge. Meanwhile, however, people would generally do worse at meeting their needs and serving their values than they would if they lived in a society, and the population as a whole would do worse than it would if it were characterized by a shared system of cooperation.

It does not follow, however, that a society needs to have a social moral code. The shared standards of cooperation in a society would be subscribed to, socially enforced, and culturally transmitted, but it does not follow that they would be subscribed to as moral standards. Subscribing to them would involve intending to conform to them and being disposed to conform to them. Subscription to them as *moral* standards, however, would involve, in addition, the desire that the standards have currency in one's society. And it would involve tending to blame oneself if one failed to conform to them, and tending to blame anyone else who failed to conform.

Yet if the members of a society did generally have these attitudes toward the standards they share, they would be more likely than otherwise to choose to comply with the standards, to teach them, and to enforce them informally among their fellows. They would have self-grounded reasons to do these things. And under these conditions, the society would be more likely than otherwise to be able to meet its needs for internal harmony and for physical and cooperative

3. This does not follow strictly. To show that any society is such that some moral code is *justified* relative to it, it would have to be shown, not only that each society would do better with some social moral code rather than none, but also that each society would do best with some given code serving as its social moral code. But I think exact ties are quite unlikely, and I soon will introduce an amendment about ties.

4. Hobbes, 1651, chapter 13.

integrity. For these reasons, I believe that any society is better able to meet its needs if it has a social moral code than would otherwise be the case.

It may be objected that these arguments rely on empirical premises. Because the conclusion is merely contingent, it cannot be used to show that *any* society in *any* circumstance needs a social moral code. It may also be objected that the argument does not show that a social moral code is, strictly speaking, needed. Indeed, some morally pluralistic societies seem quite successful. Perhaps, moreover, it would be enough if a society were characterized by a shared system of rules that are simply subscribed to, without being morally subscribed to, or perhaps a society could meet its needs by means of a coercive legal system, even if it did not have a shared moral culture. I discussed some of these ideas in chapter 6, but I will add a few remarks here.

First, I agree it may not be strictly true that a society *requires* the currency of a moral code in order to meet its needs. But the currency of an appropriate social moral code would better enable a society to meet its needs than would any alternative arrangement. And if so, then leaving aside societal values, the society is rationally required to choose to have a social moral code.

I also agree that it is a contingent matter whether any given society needs a social moral code. It is possible that morality will be superseded by some alternative means by which societies can meet their needs. I believe, nevertheless, that it is a deep feature of the nature of societies and persons, and a deep feature of what is required for cooperation, that the currency of a moral code is the best way for a society to meet its needs. But whether deep or shallow, this is not a necessary truth.

A more serious objection is that a society could do as well by means of a coercive legal system. Yet the success of a legal system depends on widespread subscription to certain basic standards in a society, standards that prohibit such things as murder, assault, and theft. For the success of law depends on the voluntary compliance of most of the members of society. Not even modern technologies of enforcement can successfully force people to comply if they genuinely resist. And a culture in which people subscribe to these core prohibitions will be more efficient than a culture that relies on other means of securing conformity to the criminal standards. If people subscribe to the standards, they will tend and intend to conform to them and to enforce their own conformity, and they will be self-groundedly rational to do so, for doing so will contribute to realizing their values. The more a legal system is assisted by widespread, self-enforced conformity to the core standards, the more efficient it is, and so the more likely it is that the society will meet its needs.

Moreover, other things equal, it will better serve the needs of society if people subscribe morally to the core prohibitions. The alternative would be that people merely subscribe in the basic sense. Both forms of subscription are self-enforcing, but moral subscription also leads people to tend to enforce other people's compliance with the standards because people who subscribe morally to standards tend to view those who fail to comply as liable to blame. This can motivate an informal sanctioning of those who fail to comply with the standards.

And people who morally subscribe to standards tend to want to pass on their attitude toward the standards to other people, including their children, because they *want* the standards to have currency in the society as a whole. The standards are therefore self-transmitting from generation to generation, simply as a matter of people pursuing their own values and teaching their values to their offspring. In short, if standards are subscribed to as moral standards, then people have corresponding values, and they have self-grounded reasons to enforce the standards, to spread them through the society, and to pass them on to subsequent generations.[5]

Finally, let me address the objection from moral pluralism. The issue is not whether morally pluralistic societies can survive. It is whether they could better meet their needs if they were not morally pluralistic. I think it is quite likely that they could. Moreover, the morally pluralistic societies with which we are familiar are not deeply and pervasively pluralistic. Their members tend to share moral attitudes toward the central features of the criminal law, for example, and they share moral attitudes toward the central political features of their society, such as its democratic constitution. The existence of societies in which people disagree about a number of moral issues is no evidence against the proposition that societies are better able to meet their needs if they are characterized by a social moral code. Indeed, as I explain later, a certain amount of disagreement is to be expected, for a variety of reasons.

Amendment to the Theory: Societal Moral Values

Before I investigate some substantive moral implications of the needs-based theory, it will be useful to introduce some amendments to the theory's *J* thesis. I will introduce four.[6]

The point of society-centered theory is to *evaluate* moral standards, including social moral codes. We therefore need to ignore a society's *moral* values when we ask how well a society's needs and values would be served by the currency of a given moral code. A society's existing moral values must not be among the values taken into account when we use the needs-and-values theory to assess the rationality of a society's selecting a social code. I therefore propose the following amendment:

> A code is justified as a moral code in relation to a society just in case (were the society to lack any moral values) it would be rationally required to select the code to serve in it as the social moral code, in preference to any alternative.

5. To make my case fully, I would need to show that societies benefit from all of the components of the complex syndrome of attitudes characteristic of subscribing morally to a standard. I have not done this, but I have discussed the most important components.

6. Recall the amendment I introduced in chapter 6 to deal with groups that are not societies. For simplicity, I ignore it in what follows.

A society's *moral* values are its values that are *morally* subscribed to with near unanimity by the members of the society.[7]

This amendment must surely seem quite natural, for, without it, any moral values of a society would automatically have an advantage over the alternatives, simply because they are values of the society. Given the point of developing the society-centered theory, however, the moral values of a society, like the other standards in the social moral code, should be evaluated on a morally neutral basis that gives them no initial advantage over alternatives to them.

It is rare, however, that a moral standard is shared with near unanimity by the members of a society. And most of the standards in a social moral code pertain to its members' lives and choices, rather than to choices among *societal* options. Because of this, societies have few moral values, and the amendment is of little practical importance.

Amendment to the Theory: Ties

According to the position we have reached, a society is rationally required to choose a given social moral code just in case the currency of the code would best serve on balance both the nonmoral values and the basic needs of the society. There may be situations, however, in which several moral codes are equally eligible to serve as a society's social moral code, given the society's needs and nonmoral values. Such situations are at least theoretically possible. For example, several codes may be equally well suited to enabling a society to meet its needs, or it may be that one code would be best from the point of view of the society's needs and a different code would be best from the point of view of its nonmoral values. In such cases, the society may be rationally required to choose among the codes, but the question is which of them, if any, qualifies as justified.

I am not entirely clear what to say about such cases. One proposal would be to say that the society would be *rational* to choose *any* of the codes among which it is rationally required to choose. On this proposal, the *J* thesis implies that *each* of the codes is justified. Given the standard-based theory and proposals I made about the truth conditions of propositions about moral requirements, it would follow in such cases that the requirements of each of the codes correspond to actual moral requirements. Unfortunately, the requirements of the codes could be in conflict. A person could be required to do some action, given the content of one of the justified codes, and yet be permitted not to do the action, given the content of another justified code. This is the stuff of contradiction.

It seems better to say, in cases of this kind, that the society would be rationally *permitted* to choose any one of the codes among which it is rationally required to choose, yet none of the codes is *justified*. This proposal seems more in line than the first proposal with the intuitions underlying society-centered theory and the

---

7. For simplicity, I do not mention standards that can be derived from a society's moral values. But they also are among a society's moral values.

needs-and-values principle. For none of the codes that are tied actually does *best* serve the society's needs and values. Yet if the codes have some standards in common, it is natural to say that these standards are justified.

In a case where several codes are tied as best, the arguments I gave about the societal need for a moral code imply that the society is rationally required to choose among the best codes. The society therefore is rationally required to choose one of the codes. Perhaps none of them is justified, but if one of them did have currency in the society, as the social moral code (or if a standard included in one of them did), then it would be justified. It would be included in the moral values of the bulk of the people in the society, values of central importance in their lives and in their sense of themselves. I therefore propose that "choice breaks ties." This proposal does give a preference to the moral status quo, but not in the way I objected to in the preceding section. It gives preference to the social moral code only in cases where there is no alternative that the society is rationally required to choose, given its needs and nonmoral values.

The proposal is of minor importance, for it is unlikely that any society's culture does actually incorporate a moral code that is tied for best with respect to the society's needs and nonmoral values. Yet the proposal does suggest an inelegant amendment:

> A code is justified as a moral code in relation to a society just in case either (1) (were the society to lack any moral values) the society would be rationally required to select the code to serve in it as the social moral code, in preference to any alternative, or (2) the code is the society's social moral code and (were the society to lack any moral values) the society would be rationally permitted to select it to continue as the social moral code.

Also, a moral standard is justified relative to a society just in case either (1) it is a part of, or derivable from, the moral code that is justified relative to the society, or (2) it is a part of, or derivable from, every moral code that the society is rationally permitted to select as its social moral code.

Amendment to the Theory: Ideal Codes and Actual Codes

According to the position I am developing, our actual moral duties are generated by the code that is justified relative to our society, not by the code that is actually embedded in its culture. The actual social moral code of a society is not necessarily justified. And the justified code might prohibit actions that are required by the actual code, or vice versa.

Yet, of course, we act in situations where most people's actions and expectations, and the sanctions we may face, are based to some extent on the actual social code. Most other people may expect or demand that we behave in ways that are called for by the actual social moral code. Because of this, there may be unfortunate consequences if we act as the ideal code would require. There could be coordination problems, with the result that all of us are worse off than we would be if all of us complied with the actual code. Or some of us may be punished or morally blamed for actions that were, in fact, morally required by the justified code. Yet it may be that we would be deemed blameworthy by the justified code if we attempted to avoid such consequences by coordinating or cooperating with those who are following the actual social code, by following that code ourselves. And it may seem that it would be quite mistaken to judge someone as acting immorally who is merely trying to avoid conflict, coordination problems, or undeserved punishment by adjusting his behavior to social reality. For these reasons, a theory of moral justification needs to take into account in some way the actual moral culture.

The natural solution to this problem is to distinguish between the *ideal* code, relative to a given society, and the *justified* code. The ideal code is the code that the society would be rational to choose to serve as its social code, ignoring the fact that a moral code may actually be embedded in its culture. But the ideal code is not necessarily the justified code, for justification requires taking into account the full context of choice. The justified code for a society is the code the society would be rational to choose to serve in it as the social moral code given the actual context of the choice at the time in question.

As we have seen, the rationality of a society's choice of moral code is to be evaluated on the basis of its needs and nonmoral values. Yet the existence of societal moral values and of a social moral code may affect the *means* by which the society might best realize the societal needs and nonmoral values that, if it is rational, it would seek to satisfy in choosing a moral code. The society's moral values and its social moral code are taken into account in this way, as aspects of the situation in which the societal choice is evaluated. The society's moral values are not among the values that the society's choice is to serve, but they are relevant data to take into account, along with the society's actual social moral code, in assessing the alternatives.

We can think of the *justified* code as the code justified for the time being, given the cultural context. We can think of it as the rational next step for the society. The *ideal* code specifies a goal to be striven for in the long run, by means of such steps. The ideal code is the one that would best serve societal needs and nonmoral values, in abstraction from the actual moral values of the society, if it were the society's social moral code. Yet no culture can be transformed at a stroke. People must change their values little by little over time until the society is gradually transformed. At each step, some code will be justified, pending the cultural consolidation that would prepare the society for the next step. One would hope that the ideal code will eventually become culturally entrenched. Yet at any given time, our actual duties are specified by the code that is justified for our time and place, not ignoring facts about the culture. If we comply with our actual duties, we will contribute to the moral progress that, ideally, will culminate with the ideal code becoming the culturally entrenched moral code, or so one would hope.[8]

8. An analogous issue arises in utilitarian theory. L. W. Sumner proposes a similar solution to it (1987, section 5.1, esp. pp. 146–48).

The Substance of the Needs-Based Society-Centered Theory

In this section, I will investigate certain substantive moral implications of the theory. My goal is not to derive specific moral standards or a specific moral code. This degree of precision is not to be expected here. But I think we can expect to discover boundaries within which a justified moral code would be found.

The arguments I present are not decisive and are not intended to be. They do indicate, however, the kinds of considerations that are relevant in society-centered theory. I will be engaging in some armchair sociology and psychology, but there is no avoiding sociological and psychological issues if I am to say anything substantive about the moral implications of society-centered theory.

For simplicity I assume, to begin with, that we are dealing with a society that is sealed off from any other societies, and I also assume that the society has no relevant values and no social moral code. The latter assumption represents a twofold simplification. First, because "choice breaks ties," the existence of a social moral code in a society can create a determinate result in a situation where otherwise the society-centered theory would have to say there are two or more equally acceptable possibilities. And second, an existing social moral code needs to be taken into account "as data," and this may affect the rationality of various options that a society might be in a position to choose.

After discussing this simple case, I will consider some of the complications that result if these assumptions are relaxed. I will postpone addressing general theoretical issues until later.

Needs and Equality

The ground of the basic needs of societies is the society's capacity to have values or stable and endorsed preferences, and to choose and to realize its values. The matters of basic need for a society are the things required in all likelihood to avoid impairment of this capacity.

Certain propositions that follow from this enable us to draw conclusions about justified moral codes. First, a society needs to promote conditions of social harmony and stability. In these conditions its members can be nearly unanimous in having stable and endorsed preferences or values regarding societal options, and so they are conditions under which a society can have values. If we restrict attention to societal needs and to what societies would be rational to choose in light of the needs they share, it follows that a moral code is justified only if its currency would promote societal stability. Second, in light of a society's need for peaceful and cooperative relationships with neighboring societies, a justified moral code would call for attitudes among the members of the society that would enhance the likelihood of their supporting a global system of cooperation, an intersocietal law of nations and persons.

Third, a society needs it to be the case that the population that it is persists and is stable. This means a society will have to ensure that the basic needs of the bulk of its members are met to some decent minimal level. People must have their basic needs met to some minimal level merely to survive. Moreover, they must normally have their needs met to rather a more generous level in order to subscribe to standards regarding options for their society—to perceive certain problems as having a common societal basis and to have preferences regarding options for solving them. In short, any society has reason to ensure that the needs of the bulk of its members are met to a decent level. I argued for these claims earlier in this chapter.

There is at least a prima facie argument here for equality in providing for basic needs. For, assuming that the physical circumstances of a society would permit all of its members to meet their basic needs over a normal lifetime with rough equality, a society would normally have no reason grounded in its needs not to ensure that its members are able to do so. It has no reason based in its needs for favoring the needs of one group over the needs of another. And it has the following reasons for ensuring that its members are able to meet their needs with rough equality. The persistence and stability of the society's population are more likely, other things being equal, if all its members are roughly equally able to meet their needs. And the members of a society are more likely to be nearly unanimous in their attitudes toward societal options, other things being equal, if their needs are provided for with rough equality. I assume that if there is not a rough equality in people's ability to meet their needs over their life-times, then people will tend to perceive this inequality and to perceive conflicts of interest regarding societal options. And this will prevent their achieving near unanimity in their preferences over the options, and it will increase the likeli-hood of social conflict. Conflicts of interest and inequalities of welfare are, I think, more likely to threaten societal consensus and stability when the inequality is noticed and resented. And I believe that inequality is most likely to be re-sented when some people whose needs would not be extraordinarily expensive to meet still do not have the wherewithal to meet them. Therefore, when the physical circumstances of a society permit, it has reason grounded in its basic needs to ensure that its members are able to meet their basic needs with rough equality over a normal lifetime.

This argument says nothing about the distribution of any surplus of resources that may exist after people's needs have been provided for. It is not designed to support equality of welfare or equality in the distribution of resources as such. It supports "roughly equal provision" for people's basic needs, but I need to explain what this amounts to.

I am not arguing that societies have reason to ensure that every member is able to meet her needs in every stage of her life and in every circumstance. Some people may have needs that are extremely expensive to meet. Extreme medical needs, combined with recent developments in exotic and expensive medical technologies, create the worry that the need for health care might become a "bottomless pit."[9] Yet my argument does not support the proposition that a society has reason to provide unlimited resources to extend the normal life span of its members or to prolong the life or improve the health of its elderly and

9. Braybrooke, 1987, p. 301.

infirm members. What the argument does support, I think, is the claim that a society has reason to ensure that its members are roughly equally able to meet their basic needs to a decent minimal level over a normal lifetime. Even if a society does ensure this, however, people whose needs would be extraordinarily costly to meet may be unable to meet them.

There is, of course, vagueness in the idea of "rough equality" in meeting needs, as well as in the idea of meeting needs to a "decent level" over a "normal lifetime." I do not see how to eliminate the vagueness. But a society may be doing all that it has reason to do if it enables every member of society to have access to resources that would enable almost everyone in the society to meet his basic needs over a normal lifetime to a level that enables him to avoid impairment in his ability to develop values over societal options.

If I am correct, a society would best serve its needs by choosing a social moral code that calls for the individual members of the society to be enabled to meet their needs with rough equality over a normal lifetime.[10]

This result is not written in stone. The argument is empirical. Moreover, first, there may be circumstances in which a society would best meet its own needs if it permitted substantial inequality in its members' ability to meet their needs; an example might be a situation in which there is a shortage of food. The conclusion that is warranted is that equality is called for in circumstances that are sufficiently benign that equality is compatible with society's meeting its needs. Modern Western societies are in circumstances of this kind. Second, I have been ignoring societal values, but there may be meritocratic societies that value inegalitarian institutions of various kinds. It seems likely, however, that such values would be moral values, in which case they would be irrelevant. It is possible to have nonmoral meritocratic values, but I think it is unlikely that the members of a society would be nearly unanimous in a stable way in preferring institutions that are known to lead to inequality in providing for basic human needs. It is even less likely that they would be nearly unanimous regarding which group is to be given the less favorable treatment. In any event, I will soon discuss cases where societal nonmoral values run counter to societal needs.

Needs and Liberty

A person's basic needs are the things required to avoid impairment of the ability to have values for one's life, to choose how to live one's life on the basis of such values, and to decide for oneself which values to accept. They are requirements of a life that is autonomous in a recognizable sense. Among the requirements of such a life are the civil and social liberties. To have the ability to decide for oneself which values to accept, a person needs to be free from certain kinds

---

10. For related arguments, see Copp, 1992c. I am indebted to Harry Brighouse and Marc Fleurbaey for helping me to see the need to introduce the qualification about a "normal lifetime." The idea that a justified moral code would promote equality in meeting basic needs implies that a justified moral code would promote the ability of people to meet their basic needs regardless of their race and their sex. More generally, there is the basis here for an argument that a justified moral code would be neither racist nor sexist.

of interference, interference on the part of the state as well as on the part of individuals in the society. Roughly speaking, people need to have freedom of conscience and freedom of speech, and they need to be left free from manipulative and coercive interference with their values.

I have argued that a society has reason to ensure a "roughly equal provision" for meeting needs. Because each person needs to be left free from certain kinds of interference, a society has reason to leave each person free from these kinds of interference. Given the *J* thesis, and ignoring complications due to societal values, we can conclude that a moral code is justified relative to a society only if its currency as the social moral code would promote a state of affairs in which people were left free from the forms of interference that would prevent or inhibit them from deciding for themselves which values to accept. It would promote the civil and social liberties.

There can be circumstances, however, in which a society very much needs to achieve consensus. It may face a pressing problem that calls for societal decision and action. In such circumstances, it might need to be active in promoting certain values among its members, so that they come to be in consensus about the society's options, and so it might rationally choose to suspend the civil liberties. This is to say that a justified code should allow for circumstances in which the civil liberties would permissibly be suspended.

Compassion and Psychological Boundaries

So far I have restricted myself to the fundamental societal needs. I have been assuming, in line with the arguments I have given, that all societies have the same needs at the most fundamental level. Their circumstances do differ, of course, and because of this, they may provide for their needs in different ways. This does allow for some moral variation among societies. But societal nonmoral values can introduce additional variation. For example, differences between societies' nonmoral values regarding the treatment of human corpses can make for different moral requirements regarding the treatment of corpses. Values concerning the treatment of (nonhuman) animals provide a more interesting example. Before I discuss the example, however, I want to sketch a theory about the treatment of animals that does not turn on the existence of any relevant societal values.

We saw that a society needs to promote conditions of social harmony and stability. This need is better served if its members show compassion and kindness in their dealings with one another than if they do not. Because of this, and because the nature of the social moral code can affect our sense of compassion, the needs of a society are better served if the social moral code calls for kindness and compassion than if it does not.

We tend, I think, to respond with compassion and kindness toward those in need whom we see as relevantly similar to us. It is not easy for us to see the boundaries of our society and our species as boundaries beyond which beings are not relevantly similar. True, our tendency to respond to others with kindness and compassion is acquired or shaped in childhood. It is shaped by the culture and by the expectations of our society's moral code. But compassion and kindness are emotions or attitudes that are elicited by certain needs in others, and once we have the tendency to have these emotions, we tend to have them with respect to any beings that have the relevant needs, once the needs are noticed and made salient to us. Our psychology cannot easily be tuned so that we respond with compassion and kindness only to members of our own society or only to humans. If we lose our tendency to respond to those outside with compassion and kindness, even if they are in need and this is salient to us, this weakens our tendency to respond to those inside our society with kindness and compassion. Kant claimed that "he who is cruel to animals becomes hard also in his dealings with men."[11] I would add that he who is cruel to people outside his society becomes hard in his dealings with members of his society. Schopenhauer claimed that "boundless compassion for all living beings is the firmest and surest guarantee of pure moral conduct."[12] I would say it supports our compassion for members of our own society. These remarks imply a number of generalizations about "psychological boundaries."

Kindness and compassion tend to be elicited by certain needs, I have said. Humans outside our society can have these needs, as can (nonhuman) animals, if they are sentient and can experience pain and suffer. And so beings of these kinds tend to elicit compassion and kindness, if we see them as sentient and as capable of pain and suffering. A newborn infant can have these needs, and I think that most people who considered the matter would tend to view a fetus at eight months as relevantly similar to a newborn infant in this respect. This is partly why late-term abortions tend to disturb even people who are liberal about abortion.

Now, a society needs its members to show compassion and kindness in their dealings with one another, but it would normally have no need to have its members show no compassion and kindness, or to show less, in their dealings with non-members. In fact, given the generalizations about psychological boundaries, it seems a society is likely to do better at meeting its needs if the societal code calls for compassion and kindness toward animals and toward humans generally than if the code explicitly limits its call for compassion to members of the society.[13] If this is correct, there is reason to think that a justified moral code would call on people to show compassion and kindness to humans in general and also to sentient beings that can suffer and experience pain.

11. Kant, 1930, p. 230.
12. Schopenhauer, 1965, section 19. I owe this reference, and the reference in the preceding note, to Midgley, 1983, pp. 51–52.
13. There are exceptions to the generalizations, for there are cases where people who, although compassionate toward members of one group, lack compassion toward members of other groups that are different in some salient way. Some racists may illustrate this. But it is enough if the generalizations are true as such, for a society is to choose a moral code for all of its members. The issue is whether a society would be rationally required to choose a code that called on us, or permitted us, to treat non-members (including nonhuman animals) differently from members. Such a code would call on us, or permit us, to tailor the boundaries of our sentiments of compassion and kindness so they coincide with the boundaries of our society (or of the species). I say a society ordinarily has no reason to choose a code of this kind, and because the currency of such a code might weaken our tendency to feel these sentiments toward fellow members of the society, a society ordinarily has a reason to avoid such a code.

Matters would be otherwise if a society needed to restrict its members' sense of compassion in some way. But a society would have to be in especially difficult circumstances, it seems to me, for its ability to meet its needs to be hurt by its members' compassion toward animals. There is, then, an argument for a moral duty or virtue of compassion toward animals that relies only on considerations about societal needs.

I should note that a similar line of argument about psychological boundaries would show that a justified prohibition on killing would normally extend to non-members as well as to members of the society. In general, we should expect a justified moral code to give non-members the same moral status as members to the extent that this is without cost to the society. A society may need to restrict possession of some of the rights that it recognizes, so that only its members have rights against its resources.[14] But there is no similar need for a society to choose a moral code according to which its members have no duties to non-members, and I have been arguing that considerations about psychological boundaries provide a reason for it not to choose such a code.

Societal Values and Animal Welfare

Let me now turn to societal values and preferences. For reasons I explained at the beginning of this chapter, we can ignore societal preferences that are not stable and preferred, as well as preferences that are not preferences over societal options, and we can ignore a society's moral values. Given these points, I believe that there are very few instances in which a society has values or stable and endorsed preferences that would affect the nature of the moral code justified in relation to it. But there may be some instances, and I therefore need to consider societal values.

There are two types of cases. In the first, there is no conflict between societal needs and nonmoral values. Perhaps codes M and M' would be expected to serve the society's needs equally well, if either were the social moral code, but code M' would better serve the society's values. In such a case, the society would be rationally required to choose code M'. We can think of M and M' as having a core in common, but M' would have additional normative characteristics to reflect the society's values.

For example, suppose the society values the welfare of animals in that, although its members give priority to satisfying basic human needs to a decent minimal level with rough equality, they nearly unanimously want to use societal resources to promote the welfare of animals as well. This desire is stable and endorsed with near unanimity. Of course, if the nearly unanimous valuing of animal welfare were unstable, or if it were a *moral* value, it would not be relevant. Yet otherwise, the society would be rationally required to choose a code the currency of which would further animal welfare. The code would, however, favor human welfare in cases of conflict between animal welfare and basic human needs.

14. I have in mind the right that the resources of society be used to enable each person to meet her basic needs. This right is presumably restricted to members of the society. For, unless it were extraordinarily rich, a society could not reasonably choose a moral code including a standard that called for its resources to be used to enable *every human without restriction* to meet her basic needs.

In the second type of case, there *is* a conflict between societal needs and non-moral values. Perhaps code *M* would be expected to best serve the society's needs, if it were the social moral code, but code *M'* would better serve the society's values. In such a case, the choice between the codes would be optional. *M* and *M'* might have a core in common, and if so, the society would be rationally required to choose the standards in the core. These standards would then be justified. But presumably *M* and *M'* would each include additional standards, beyond the core, and these standards would *not* be justified.

Suppose, for example, that a society values animal welfare *more* than human welfare, and that this value is stable and endorsed with near unanimity. And suppose it is not a moral value. It is simply the case that people would prefer—with near unanimity and in a stable and endorsed way—that, in cases of conflict, societal resources be used to further the welfare of an animal rather than the welfare of a human. We can still say that, except for cases where there is conflict between the welfare of animals and the needs of humans, the story is just as I have been telling it so far. The society would be rationally required to choose a moral code whose currency would lead to the maximal overall realization of both its needs and its nonmoral values, leaving aside circumstance where there is conflict between human and animal welfare. This code would be justified, leaving aside the principles it contains for resolving cases of conflict between humans and animals.

However, principles governing the distribution of societal resources in cases where there is conflict between human needs and animal welfare would *not* be justified. For in cases of conflict between needs and values, a society is not rationally required to choose one way rather than the other. If a society would be rationally permitted to choose either a standard that favors human needs, in cases of conflict with animal welfare, or a standard that favors animal welfare in such cases, then neither standard is justified relative to the society; that is, neither is justified unless one of them is part of the society's actual social moral code.[15]

Restricting attention, then, to standards that are not included in the actual social moral code, it appears that no such standard is justified if it calls for behavior that would undermine societal stability or the realization of basic human needs to a decent minimal level and with rough equality. Even in societies with relevant nonmoral values that conflict with these needs, there is no *justified* standard that would call for people to undermine stability or the meeting of basic needs to a decent level with rough equality.

Moral "Personhood"

The members of a society are "subject" to the moral code justified for their society in the sense that they have the duties specified in the code or that they are expected to exhibit the states of character that the code specifies to be virtues. They are also subjects of moral concern. For as we saw, the currency of a

---

15. Recall my discussion of "ties." If one of these standards is part of the actual social moral code, then because, ex hypothesi, the society would be permitted to choose it, it would qualify as justified.

justified moral code would normally promote the ability of people to meet their basic needs to a decent minimal level over the course of their lives and with rough equality. This implies that there is normally a duty not to deprive people of resources they require in order to meet their basic needs or that there is a corresponding virtue of character. And it implies that equality of provision for the meeting of needs is normally a requirement of social justice.

There may be other agents subject to morality. In a modern complex society, many powerful institutions are capable of affecting people's ability to meet their needs. Moral individualism denies, while moral collectivism affirms, that collective entities can be subject to moral duties. Society-centered theory can underwrite moral collectivism. Corporations, organizations, and various other kinds of collective entity can be subject to moral requirements similar to those that are incumbent upon the individual members of society. They are subject to moral requirements just when the justified moral code posits such requirements.

Collective entities may also be subjects of moral concern. Some institutional structures may facilitate the development and realization of societal values. For example, a society that is organized into a state is presumably in a better position to meet its needs and its societal values than a society that is not organized in this way. This offers a way to justify the state.

We saw in the last section that animals may be of moral concern to a society. Societal needs would normally underwrite standards calling for compassion toward animals. Societal nonmoral values may mean that certain standards are justified that require furthering the welfare of animals. In a similar way, various elements of the environment may justifiably be of moral concern to certain societies.

Given the current interest in the morality and politics of abortion, it would be agreeable if society-centered theory entailed a position on the moral status of the fetus. Let us therefore compare a standard that permits abortion without restriction, a standard that prohibits abortion without exception, and a standard that permits abortion in the early stages of pregnancy but prohibits it otherwise, except where an abortion is required by the needs of the mother.

A variety of considerations suggest that the permissive standard is not justified. If I am correct, fetuses in the late stages of pregnancy seem to most people who have considered the matter to be relevantly similar to infants because of the physiological similarities between late-term fetuses and newborns. Because of this, the currency of the permissive standard would tend to undermine the currency of a prohibition on infanticide, and vice versa. Other things being equal, societies have reason to avoid choosing codes that contain standards that conflict psychologically in this way. And societies normally have no need to permit late-term fetuses to be aborted without restriction. Hence, it is reasonable to expect that a justified moral code would not include the permissive standard.

The argument depends on the idea that there is a justified prohibition of infanticide. This idea is supported by the fact that any society needs to protect the welfare of infants because it needs to produce new generations of members. Moreover, there is generally a shared valuing of the welfare of infants. Hence, a prohibition of infanticide is almost certainly justified both on the basis of societal values and on the basis of societal needs. Of course, it is possible to imagine a society that would need to permit infanticide in certain circumstances. But this is just to say that the reasoning depends on empirical claims.

This reasoning cannot be used to show that there is a blanket prohibition of abortion. To be sure, a society does need to protect the welfare of late-term fetuses for the same reason that it needs to protect the welfare of infants. And it is possible to imagine circumstances in which a society would rationally favor the currency of a prohibition of all abortions. Yet, first, under normal conditions, a society would have no need to prohibit early abortions, any more than to prohibit contraception. Because there is little tendency to see newly fertilized ova as relevantly similar to infants, society has little reason to worry that the currency of a permission of early abortions would put at risk the currency of a prohibition on infanticide. Second, it is reasonable to think that infants are members of society and that fetuses are not. Mothers are members of the society, whereas their fetuses are not yet members. Therefore, in cases of conflict, a moral code justified in terms of society's needs would give priority to the basic needs of a woman over the needs or welfare of a fetus she is bearing. Moreover, the needs of the mother can conflict with the needs of the fetus in ways that her needs cannot conflict with the needs of a newborn. Conflict between the needs of a fetus and the needs of the mother often cannot be resolved in favor of the mother except by means of abortion, but conflict between the needs of an infant and the needs of its parents can almost always be resolved without resorting to infanticide. If a society can meet the basic needs of its members with rough equality and to a decent minimal standard, it can also normally meet the needs of infants without compromising the needs of their parents. Hence, under normal conditions, a society would have reason to prefer a code that permitted abortion in cases where abortion is necessary to protect the needs of the mother.

Of course, certain societies may value morally the welfare of fetuses, but we cannot take into account the fact that fetuses are morally valued in a society in attempting to evaluate the society's moral values. If a society valued the welfare of fetuses nonmorally, as a matter of sentiment, let us say, in the way that societies value the welfare of infants, then the status of fetuses would be more closely analogous to the status of infants. Yet, abortion becomes a pressing political issue only where there is not a consensus in valuing the welfare of the fetus.

Because a blanket permission is not justified and a blanket prohibition is not justified, only the third, mixed standard remains a possibility. It seems to me that this standard recognizes the societal interest in the welfare of late-term fetuses while also recognizing the priority of the needs of the mother in cases of conflict. I therefore believe that society-centered theory supports a standard that permits abortion in the early stages of pregnancy but prohibits it otherwise, except where an abortion is required by the needs of the mother.

Amendment to the Theory: Overlapping Societies

Societies can be nested and can overlap, and most of us belong to more than one society. If our duties are given by the moral code justified relative to "our" society, then, since different moral codes can in principle be justified relative to different societies, we can in principle face conflicting moral demands. Call this problem the "overlap problem." To avoid it, I have said, a society-centered theory must be amended to introduce a coherence constraint on its account of justification.

To be sure, the significance of the overlap problem for society-centered theory depends on which theory of societal rationality is joined to the J thesis. However, the needs-based theory that I have proposed permits differences in the moral codes justified relative to different societies whenever the societies have different needs or nonmoral values. And given the qualifications introduced to deal with ties and to distinguish a justified code from an ideal code, the nature of an extant social moral code in a society can affect the content of the code that counts as justified relative to the society. Because different societies can be characterized by different social moral codes, the result may be that different codes qualify as justified relative to the different societies.

Traditional Inuit society may have had special needs due to the extreme conditions of life in the Arctic. If so, then according to the needs-and-values theory, the moral code justified relative to Inuit society at the time may have differed in significant ways from the code justified relative to the larger North American society. If some of the Inuit belonged both to the traditional society and to the larger society, then society-centered theory seems to leave open the possibility that they faced conflicting duties. Perhaps in some extreme cases elderly Inuit people had a duty under the code justified relative to Inuit society to let themselves die in the cold in order to save their family from starvation. But perhaps even in these cases, under the code justified relative to the larger society, they had a duty to try to live. Such a case seems possible in principle. Which duty should take priority in a case of this kind? This is the overlap problem.

One way to avoid the problem would be to argue that such cases show the existence of moral dilemmas at a deep level.[16] But I think a better way would be to offer an amendment to society-centered theory.

According to the amendment I propose, certain moral codes have priority over others, and the code with priority determines the actual moral requirements (or virtues, and so on) of the persons involved in an overlap situation. A justified moral code includes the implicit qualification that any code that has priority over it determines the actual moral requirements of people to whom it applies in overlap situations. In brief, my proposal is to qualify or weaken the moral code that would otherwise be justified relative to one society in an overlap situation in a minimal way, in order to ensure that conformity to it cannot prevent conformity to the moral code justified relative to a society in the situation that has priority over it.

And I propose to give priority to the code justified relative to the larger society. In overlap situations where some society contains all the overlapping societies, priority goes to the code justified relative to that society. In overlap situations where no society contains all the overlapping societies, I propose to give

---

16. This approach was suggested by remarks of Patricia Greenspan, in correspondence.

priority to the code that would be justified relative to the mereological sum of the overlapping societies—if it were a society.

Moral codes M and M' "conflict" in the relevant sense just in case conformity to M would prevent conformity to M'. For example, if M implies a duty to do A and M' implies a duty not to do A, the codes conflict. But if M' implies merely a permission not to do A, the codes do not conflict in the relevant sense because to do A would be to act in conformity with both codes. A situation is an "overlap situation" relative to a pair of societies if some people or collective entities in the situation belong to both societies (or are otherwise suitably related to both societies). My proposal is as follows: (1) For any moral codes M and M' and societies S and S', where M is justified relative to S, and M' is justified relative to S', if there is an overlap situation o relative to S and S', and if S has priority over S' in overlap situations, and if M would otherwise conflict with M', then if M implies a specific standard regarding the events or entities (or states of affairs) in o, then M' implies that that specific standard is justified, all things considered, notwithstanding any other standard in M'. (2) A group S has priority over a society S' in overlap situations just in case either S is a society and S' is a proper part of S or S is the mereological sum of societies that overlap and there is no society of which they are proper parts—in which case S is deemed a society for these purposes.

I should explain that a "specific standard" for an overlap situation is a standard that applies only to the event or entity (or state of affairs) at issue in the situation. In the Inuit example, the specific standard implied by the code justified relative to the larger society might be one that calls for Inuit who are members of the larger society not to sacrifice themselves for their families in extreme circumstances.

To fix ideas about this example, let us assume that Inuit society needs the currency of a code that, in some extreme cases, calls on elderly Inuit people to let themselves die for the sake of their family. Such a code is justified relative to the Inuit society, leaving aside overlap situations. Now it is unlikely that the larger society needs the currency of a code that *prohibits* people from letting themselves die in such extreme situations. On this assumption, the code justified relative to the larger society does not conflict in the relevant sense with the Inuit code, and the Inuit code is justified without amendment. However, suppose that the larger society does actually need a complete and unconditional prohibition on suicide and letting oneself die. If so, then, the code that would otherwise be justified relative to the Inuit does conflict with the code justified relative to the larger society. Hence, according to my proposal, the code justified relative to the Inuit is an amended version of the code that would otherwise be justified, and it does not actually imply that elderly Inuit people in overlap situations have a duty to let themselves die. It implies that they have a duty not to let themselves die. Elderly Inuit who let themselves die for the sake of their families would be doing something wrong, however admirable we might take it to be.[17]

The coherence constraint means, in effect, that a society's needs and non-

17. For discussion of "admirable immorality," see Slote, 1983, chapter 4.

moral values cannot generate moral requirements that conflict with the moral requirements generated by the justified code of a larger society in which it is embedded.

The coherence constraint is not merely an ad hoc device designed to avoid conflicting duties in overlap situations. For it can be defended on the basis of societal needs and on the basis of the intuitions that I invoked in chapter 6. Moreover, other solutions to the overlap problem are available, and there are independent arguments for some of these solutions. My proposal therefore is a substantive one, and it must be defended on substantive grounds.

Society-centered theory does, of course, give priority to societies over smaller social groups with specific purposes or objectives. The amendment I am proposing merely carries this priority over to cases in which smaller societies are contained within larger ones. The argument I gave in chapter 6 for giving priority to societies over other groups depended partly on the idea that a person who subscribes morally to a code desires that it have currency in her society. This means that she desires it to have currency in some society to which she belongs, and also, if I am correct, it means she desires it to have currency in every society to which she sees herself as belonging. We intend our moral conception for all the societies to which we belong.

One of the underlying ideas in chapter 6 was that any society needs a social moral code and that better codes are ones whose currency in a society would better facilitate coordination and cooperation among the members of the society. If a justified moral code is one that best contributes to making society possible, then the justified code for a society would not conflict with the justified code for another society that overlaps with it. For the conflicting duties in the societies' moral codes may create conflicting senses of obligation among the members and thereby reduce the opportunity for or the likelihood of successful coordination and cooperation among their members and across their boundaries. In cases where societies overlap or are nested in one another, to the extent that a moral code is justified, it should work to facilitate cooperation and make society possible throughout the group of overlapping or nested societies.

Societies have a need for peaceful and cooperative relationships with neighboring societies. Hence, in choosing a code to serve as its social moral code, a society would be rational to pay attention to the surrounding societies and to the moral codes justified with respect to them. And if a society overlaps with another society, then this is something it must take into account. It seems that a society would be rational to choose a code that is so qualified that it cannot conflict in overlap situations with the justified moral code of any larger society of which it is a part.

For these reasons, then, it is plausible to think that a justified code would be qualified so that it could not conflict in overlap situations with a code that is justified relative to the most comprehensive of the societies in a group of nested or overlapping societies to which it belongs. I do not think that my proposal can fairly be described as ad hoc.

I am, in effect, viewing the apparent existence of conflicting duties as showing that one of the codes giving rise to the conflict is unjustified as it stands.

Yet, one might object, moral dilemmas are part of moral life, and moral dilemmas are situations in which there are non-overridden moral requirements that cannot all be met.[18] Overlap situations are simply situations in which moral dilemmas can arise due to conflict between different justified moral codes.

However, needs-based society-centered theory provides a natural argument against the existence of moral dilemmas in that sense. Consider a moral code that can imply mutually incompatible non-overridden duties. Now imagine a moral code that differs from the first one only in that it implies a disjunctive duty where the first code implies conflicting duties. For example, if the first implied both that Alice ought to do *A* and that Alice ought to do not-*A*, and if it implied that neither duty is overridden by the other, then the second would imply that Alice ought to do either *A* or not-*A*. If a society had a choice between these codes, I think it would be rationally required to choose the second. For the currency of the second would better enable a society to meet its members' need for psychological integrity by eliminating a source of psychological tension. I think that societies would do well to choose moral codes that avoid overlap problems for the same kinds of reasons they would do well to choose codes that do not permit genuine moral dilemmas.

Moral Objections

Any proposal of the sort I am defending will be compared with our moral intuitions. I do not think that moral intuitions can be taken at face value, however, in cases where society-centered theory gives us reason to doubt that they are true and that the corresponding moral standards are justified.[19] Society-centered theory provides a criterion we are to use in evaluating our moral intuitions. Given that the theory is well-supported, intuitions that are unfriendly to it are suspect for that reason.

Yet there is some point where the weight of unfriendly intuitions would make any theory seem unacceptable. Moreover, it can be worthwhile seeing exactly which kinds of moral views conflict with a theory and why they conflict. I will therefore consider a number of moral objections to society-centered theory. There are many areas of conflict between the theory and well-entrenched moral views. I will argue, paradoxically, that this is a virtue of the theory.

Consider, then, that we share the view that caste societies are unfair and that societies in which there is slavery are unjust. I argued that any justified moral code would promote rough equality in meeting people's needs, and this does suggest that moral codes that require castes or that permit slavery are likely to be unjustified. Yet my argument set aside societal values. For all I have shown,

18. This definition of a dilemma is due to Sinnott-Armstrong, 1988.
19. In chapter 11, I argue that, by the lights of society-centered theory, the fact that a given moral standard has currency in society is prima facie evidence that the standard is justified. But it is not conclusive evidence of this. Hence, an intuition may be false even if it is very widely shared in society; the corresponding standard may fail actually to be justified by the lights of the theory.

a society that nonmorally valued a caste system in a stable and endorsed way might be rational to choose a social moral code that required castes. I have two tactical replies and a deeper strategic reply. First, I think that if a society valued a caste system, it likely would value it morally. Hence, the situation envisaged, where a society values a caste system nonmorally, is not likely to arise. Second, any society, except for the global society, is likely to overlap with a larger society. And the larger society is not likely to share with near unanimity the values of the original one. In nineteenth-century India, for example, the Hindu caste society and Moslem society overlapped each other and British society, and all of these parts were embedded in a larger entity that we can count as a society for our purposes. This larger society certainly did not value the caste system with near unanimity. Hence, if the norms that called for the caste system conflicted with standards justified relative to the larger society, then, given the amendment designed for overlap situations, it follows that these norms were not justified relative to the caste society.

More important, it is a virtue of the theory I am defending that there is no substantive moral standard that the theory shows to be necessarily justified relative to every society. It is a contingent matter whether a given moral standard is justified. This is a virtue of the theory, because it is what makes it possible for the theory to explain why standards are justified, when they are justified, on the basis of contingent facts about human nature and the nature of societies.

A different sort of objection turns on the possibility of situations in which incompatible moral codes are equally good candidates for the social moral code, from the standpoint of a society. It is unlikely that there would be exact ties between incompatible codes. An exact tie among codes would mean that the codes would do exactly as well at promoting the relevant society's needs and nonmoral values. They would therefore have to be equally teachable, equally likely to be widely complied with if incorporated into the culture as the social moral code, and equally likely, if widely complied with, to secure societal needs and values. This is possible, although unlikely.

Given my proposal about ties, if a number of codes are tied, and if none of them is in fact the social moral code, then none is justified. To be sure, any standards the codes have in common may be justified. Yet there may be little of interest that the codes have in common. For example, although my arguments suggest that a just society would ensure that its members are able to meet their basic needs with rough equality, no standard that actually calls for this to be done may be justified because all such standards could turn out to be equally eligible from the standpoint of the society.

Suppose that several different moral codes are such that, if implemented as a social moral code, they would be precisely equally effective at securing equality among the members of the society in their ability to meet their basic needs. One such code might say, in effect, that people have a right to be enabled to meet their basic needs. Another might treat equality as a virtue of society as a whole.[20] If these codes are tied as best, then no one of them is such that society

---

20. I have in mind a Rawlsian view; see Rawls, 1971.

is rationally required to choose it. Then, if no one of them is in fact the social code in the society, no one of them is justified. Yet the society is required to choose among them; in effect, their disjunction is justified. And this means there is a moral flaw in the society if it does not secure rough equality among its members. A morally good society would secure rough equality. Yet there is not in fact a right to be assured of the ability to meet one's basic needs, for example.[21]

This seems a plausible result. The theory says it is plausible because, ex hypothesi, there is no basis for choice among the different codes. And because of this, the theory can explain disagreement among people in the way they conceptualize the value of equality. The disagreement reflects the fact that the choice among ways to conceptualize the value of equality is underdetermined.

It may seem that society-centered theory allows the wrong kind of factors to count as morally relevant. Suppose, for example, that an evil genius would destroy our society unless it chose a social moral code that would promote inequality. Then such a code would be justified, and people would have corresponding duties. Yet the threat of an evil genius is the wrong sort of thing to be the basis of moral duties.

Yet I think that if an evil genius would in fact destroy a society unless a certain moral code were made the social moral code, then the society would be rational to adopt the code, and its members ought morally to comply with it. The argument may mislead us because of the fact that the genius is described as "evil." But if natural forces required a society to adopt an inegalitarian moral code in order to avoid destruction, then I think the code would be justified. And I think there would be little temptation to view this as giving rise to an objection to society-centered theory.

It may seem, however, that there is a relevant difference between the evil genius case and cases in which merely natural forces are involved. In cases of the latter kind, the character of the social moral code affects the ability of the society to meet its needs by affecting the behavior of its members, agents who subscribe to it. But in the evil genius example, the character of the social code affects the ability of the society to meet its needs in an indirect way, by affecting the behavior of an outside agent, an agent who does not subscribe to the code and who is not subject to its requirements.

The following example raises a similar issue. Suppose that a society is threatened with nuclear attack and the only way it can secure its safety is to threaten its adversary with unrestrained retaliation. Suppose, too, that if its social moral

---

21. To spell this out: Suppose that M and M' are tied as equal best for society S. If so, neither of the codes is justified, yet if neither is justified, the *disjunction* of the codes would be justified, for the society would be required to choose either M or M'. Suppose now that M contains a standard such that, if it were justified, it would be true that people have a moral right to be enabled to meet their basic needs. But M' contains no such standard, even though it does contain a standard such that, if it were justified, it would be true that equality in people's ability to meet their basic needs is a moral virtue of a society. Neither code is justified, yet M-or-M' is justified, and this means that the disjunction of the standards previously mentioned is justified. It follows that there is a moral flaw in society if it does not ensure that people are able to meet their needs. For the disjunction of the standards is still a standard that calls on society to ensure that people are able to meet their needs.

code prohibited retaliation, its adversary would not be deterred from attacking. In this case, it appears that the society would be rational to choose a moral code that permitted the society both to threaten retaliation and actually to retaliate, if attacked. Yet suppose that the other society *did* attack. In this circumstance, the society would not be rational to retaliate, let us assume, because doing so would only bring on further attacks. If the society were to choose a moral code in this new circumstance, it would be rational to choose one that prohibited retaliation. What is it to do? Which code is justified?[22]

Of course, a justified moral code would allow for changes in circumstances. Hence, although ordinary times differ from times of natural disaster, a society would be rational to choose a code that included standards that would tell us our duties in times of natural disaster. The deterrence example suggests, however, that even a *justified* moral code might sometimes fail to provide for foreseeable disasters. And it illustrates that a society's circumstances can change rapidly, with the result that a code that was justified becomes unjustified. Can our moral duties plausibly be thought to change in the same way, in tandem with the changed circumstances of the society? Can they plausibly be thought to change in this way, because of the behavior of outside agents?

If circumstances do change rapidly, then the character of the justified moral code could in principle change equally rapidly. So it may well be the case that prior to the attack by the enemy, retaliation would have been permissible even though, after the attack, retaliation was impermissible. However, prior to the attack, nuclear retaliation was, of course, impossible. This may be significant. It may be that if nuclear retaliation were possible, then any justified moral code would prohibit it. Yet I see no reason to conclude from this that nuclear retaliation would be prohibited by a moral code that is justified in a circumstance where retaliation is impossible.

This leaves the objection that the justification of a social moral code can turn on the effect its currency would have on the behavior of outside agents, such as evil geniuses and rogue societies. I am not worried by this objection. Consider, for instance, a moral code that prohibits interference in the internal affairs of other societies. Suppose that the currency of this code in a society would incline other societies to behave more peaceably than they otherwise would. It is surely no objection to society-centered theory that it would take this into account in evaluating the code. Yet in this example, as in the evil genius and deterrence examples, the code is being evaluated on the basis of effects that its currency would have on the behavior of outside agents.

Conclusion

In this chapter, I introduced four amendments to the *J* thesis of society-centered theory, amendments to deal with societal moral values, with ties, with the distinction between ideal and justified codes, and with overlapping societies. These

---

22. This objection was suggested by William Harper.

amendments are in addition to the amendment I introduced at the end of chapter 6 to deal with state-of-nature situations. These amendments are not ad hoc, but they are nevertheless optional, for it is possible to imagine alternatives to them within a society-centered theory.

In addition to introducing the amendments, this chapter developed an account of societal needs and used it in drawing substantive moral conclusions within the needs-based society-centered theory. The chapter also considered a number of moral objections to the needs-based theory.

Society-centered theory relativizes the justification of moral codes to societies. The normative consequences of this are mitigated by the fact that societies have the same basic needs, as well as by the amendment I introduced to deal with overlap situations. Yet differences in the cultures and nonmoral values of societies and differences in how societies can best meet their needs under different conditions can imply differences in the moral codes justified in relation to different societies. In the next chapter, I consider technical issues that arise from this and, more generally, from the relativism of society-centered theory.

11

Relativism, Realism, and Reasons

In this chapter I deal with a number of technical points that arise from the combination of the society-centered theory with the standard-based theory of moral judgment. These include points in the philosophical theory of normative language and judgment, metaphysical issues, issues in moral epistemology, issues in moral psychology, and questions about reasons to be moral. I will also address objections to the overall shape of the theory.

I have proposed four main doctrines: the standard-based theory of normative judgment, the attitudinal account of morality together with the account of moral subscription, the needs-and-values principle of agent-grounded reasons, and the society-centered theory of moral justification. These are four independent modules. Each could stand on its own or be combined with alternatives to one or more of the other modules.

Although these doctrines determine the fundamental nature of the needs-based society-centered theory, there are certain components that could be changed without changing the theory in a basic way. For example, there are alternatives to the amendments I introduced in the preceding chapter. Moreover, one could reject the proposals I made in chapter 2 about the detailed truth conditions of specific kinds of moral propositions, including propositions about moral wrongs and about moral virtues, without abandoning the underlying standard-based theory of normative judgment.

This chapter focuses on issues that arise from fundamental features of my account. I begin with the relativism that is implied by the combination of society-centered theory with the standard-based theory of normativity.

In Defense of Moral Relativism

According to the society-centered theory, if a moral code or standard is justified, it is justified in relation to a given society; that is, the status of being justified is in fact a *relation* between a code or standard and a society. It follows from this, given the standard-based theory of normative judgment, that moral propositions are relational.

Consider, for example, the proposition that slavery is morally wrong. If this proposition is true, then the relevant appropriately justified moral code precludes slavery. But, according to society-centered theory, if there is such a code, it is justified in relation to a relevant society. Hence, if slavery is morally wrong, it must be that it is wrong in relation to a society where the justified moral code prohibits slavery.

Bringing these ideas together, the conclusion to draw is that (paradigmatic) moral propositions are relational. A (paradigmatic) moral proposition entails that some moral standard is justified in relation to a relevant society, namely, the society relative to which the standard must be justified in order for the proposition to be true. Moral propositions are in this sense, at least in part, propositions to the effect that some given moral standard is justified relative to a given society. If slavery is morally wrong, then, it is wrong in relation to a relevant society.

It obviously does not follow from this that the sentences we use to make moral claims are relational in their *grammatical* form.[1] Nor does it follow that people who have moral beliefs and who are competent speakers of the language would realize, just in virtue of their competence, that the propositions expressed by these sentences are relational in the way I have been explaining. There are, in fact, many examples of sentences that express relational propositions even though people who accept the propositions and who are competent speakers of the language could fail to realize that they do.

The sentence "Elephants are big" expresses a proposition that is relational, a proposition roughly to the effect that, in comparison with things in a relevant comparison class, elephants are large.[2] The relevant comparison class would be picked out by the context in which the sentence is used. In one context, it might be the class of land mammals; in another, it might be the class of all mammals or the class of all living things. A competent speaker of the language presumably must realize that the sentence expresses a proposition that attributes a property to elephants, but she need not realize, I think, that that property is in fact a relation to a comparison class. To realize this, she would need more than simply competence with the language.

By way of contrast, consider the sentence "Edmonton is to the north." It expresses a proposition roughly to the effect that Edmonton is to the north *of this place*, the place determined by the context of use, which would typically be the place where the sentence is asserted or evaluated. This is something that a competent user of the language would recognize just in virtue of her competence. Yet "Edmonton is to the north" relates Edmonton not only to the place at issue in the context, but also to the north pole. It expresses a proposition to the effect that Edmonton is closer to the north pole than *this* place is, the place determined by the context of use. But this is not something that a competent user of the language would understand just in virtue of her competence. To understand this, she would need geographical competence, not just linguistic competence.

1. See Sayre-McCord, 1991, p. 175, n. 21. For further discussion, see Wiggins, 1988.
2. The example is from Harman, 1975.

Moral propositions are also relational. They are at least in part propositions to the effect that some given moral standard is (or is not) justified relative to a given society. Yet a person with moral beliefs might fail to realize that moral propositions are relational in this way, despite her competence in using the language. Consider again the sentence "Slavery is morally wrong." A competent user of the language presumably would realize that it attributes a property to slavery, but she need not realize that the property is in fact a relational property. It is roughly the property of being prohibited by the moral code that is justified relative to the society that is picked out in the context of the sentence's use. In order to realize that this is so, one would need more than linguistic competence.

Accordingly, it is not a consequence of my position that any competent speaker of the language, or any person with moral beliefs, should be able to see that it is correct. The relativism I have in mind is a thesis about the truth conditions of moral propositions. It is not something that we should expect to be known by everyone who is competent to make moral claims or who has moral beliefs.

I need to say something about how the relevant society is determined in given contexts. This is a pragmatic matter; it is a matter of the nature of the overall context, linguistic and otherwise. I will offer a proposal about this, but my proposal is not forced on me by the society-centered theory of moral justification or by the standard-based theory of normative propositions. It is independent of these theories and needs an independent defense. Before I explain my proposal, I will consider two alternatives to it.

First, one might think the relevant society is the society of the speaker, or of the person with the moral belief at issue. This hypothesis would have implausible implications in contexts in which people from different societies are discussing a moral issue. Let me assume that the French and the Germans constitute different societies. Suppose then that a Frenchman and a German are discussing (in English) the morality of capital punishment. The Frenchman says, "Capital punishment is morally unacceptable." The German says "Capital punishment is morally acceptable." In most contexts, of course, they would be in disagreement. But the first hypothesis implies that they are not disagreeing with each other. The Frenchman is saying that capital punishment is unacceptable in *his* society, and the German is saying it is acceptable in *his* society, and these are different societies. Since an acceptable account of the discussion between the Frenchman and the German must recognize that they are in disagreement, the first hypothesis must be rejected.

According to a second hypothesis, the relevant society is determined by the phenomenon being evaluated morally. Suppose the Frenchman says, "The execution of Louis Riel was morally unacceptable," and the German says, "The execution of Louis Riel was morally acceptable." The second hypothesis implies that they are expressing propositions that relate to the society of Louis Riel and his executioners, namely, late-nineteenth-century Canadian society. Because of this, it implies correctly that the two men are disagreeing with each other. But the hypothesis would make certain quite reasonable patterns of argument difficult to understand as reasonable. For example, suppose the Frenchman went on, "And so it would have been wrong, if Simón Bolívar's movement had failed, to have executed Bolívar. It is not acceptable for the victor to execute leaders of failed nationalist movements." On the second hypothesis, the Frenchman's reasoning would be seen as involving a leap from nineteenth-century Canadian society to nineteenth-century South American society, and then to some indeterminate contemporary society. Yet the Frenchman has given no reason to think that standards justified relative to the society in which Riel was executed were also justified relative to the society in which Bolívar lived or that these standards would also be justified in our own contemporary society. So the second hypothesis, combined with the society-centered theory, makes the Frenchman's reasoning seem unreasonable. This is why I reject the second hypothesis.

My proposal is that, in the *default* case, a moral claim expresses a proposition that relates relevant standards to the smallest society that embraces the person expressing the claim, as well as all the people in the person's intended audience and all the people otherwise referred to (or quantified over) in the context. The proposal is that the reasonable hypothesis in a context where a moral claim is made is that the society at issue is the one I have just described, although specific features of a context may alter the reference to a different society. Similarly, in the default case, a person with a moral belief is best taken to accept a proposition that relates relevant standards to the smallest society that includes her, all the people she is thinking of, and all the people otherwise referred to (or quantified over) in the context. However, specific features of the person's thinking may make a different hypothesis more reasonable. Let me illustrate my idea.

Consider again the dialogue between the Frenchman and the German. Initially, in discussing capital punishment, they are best taken to accept and to express propositions about the justifiability of standards that prohibit capital punishment in relation to Western European society. As I explained before, societies can overlap and can be nested. The sum of the Germans and the French probably does not constitute a society, although it is a part of Western European society. Hence, the smallest society embracing the Frenchman and the German is most likely the society of Western Europeans. The men are disagreeing about the justifiability of capital punishment in that society. Yet when they address Louis Riel and Simón Bolívar, they are best taken to accept and to express propositions of a wider interest, concerning the execution of nationalist leaders in European societies and colonies thereof. Accordingly, my proposal avoids the difficulties of the first and second hypotheses. It sees the Frenchman and the German as disagreeing about capital punishment, and it makes intelligible the Frenchman's reasoning from the case of Riel to the case of Bolívar and then to a general claim about political executions.

Specific features of a context may make the default hypothesis less reasonable than it normally is and suggest a different hypothesis as to which society is relevant. On the one hand, a person might intend to make a claim that is quite general. In this case, we should take her claim to be concerned with all societies or with a society that is much larger than the smallest one that embraces her and the intended audience. For example, someone might claim that capital punishment is not justifiable, "period," or that it is never justifiable. She might say, for instance, "Without any qualifications, capital punishment is not justifiable, period." If she were a philosopher and if she said this in a general philosophical context, she would evidently be intending to deny any variability from society to society. Even if she were an ordinary person without philosophical pretensions, she would likely be intending to deny any variability at all. Hence, in either of these contexts, it would be reasonable to take the sentence she uses to express a proposition to the effect that there is no society relative to which capital punishment is justified. On the other hand, a person might intend to make a quite restricted claim. For example, the Frenchman could say, "I don't know what to think about the situation in Germany or anywhere else, but I do think that capital punishment is unacceptable in the circumstances today in France." Here it would be reasonable to take the Frenchman to be expressing a proposition to the effect that the moral standards justified relative to French society prohibit capital punishment.

There may be some contexts in which the default hypothesis seems inapplicable because there is no society that embraces the speaker and the people in his intended audience. Suppose, for example, that an early-nineteenth-century European missionary says to a member of a Haida community that the potlatch is morally unacceptable. It may seem that there is not a society to which the Haida and the European both belong. In this context, I think there are two reasonable hypotheses. First, the missionary may intend to make a claim that is quite general. He could be interpreted as expressing a proposition regarding all societies to the effect that there is no society relative to which the potlatch can be justified. Second, the missionary may intend to make a specific pronouncement that takes into account the special situation of the Haida. He could be interpreted in this case as expressing a proposition regarding the Haida society.

There is normally no need for a person making a moral claim to refer explicitly to her society, for in the default case it is understood that, roughly, the society of the speaker is the one at issue. Therefore, a person who does refer explicitly to her society, by saying, for example, "Capital punishment is wrong in my society," implies that she does not mean to express the thought that she could express with greater economy by saying, "Capital punishment is wrong."[3] In many contexts, a person who said, "Capital punishment is wrong in my society" would imply that there may be societies in which it is not wrong, something that is not suggested in the default case where one simply says, "Capital punishment is wrong." In some contexts, a person who said, "Capital punishment is wrong in my society" would imply that she does not intend to convey a normative moral proposition at all; instead, she would imply a sociological proposition to the effect that capital punishment is considered wrong by people in her society.

There is nothing in the relativism I have proposed, or in the society-centered theory, to rule out the possibility that there is some moral code that is justified

3. For an explanation of such implications, called "conversational implications," see Grice, 1989, pp. 22–40.

relative to every society. In fact, as I argued in the preceding chapter, societies are sufficiently alike that, at a general level, they have the same needs. What a society needs is largely what determines the content of the moral code the society would be rational to choose as its social moral code. It is therefore reasonable to expect that the moral code justified relative to one society has pretty much the same content as the moral code justified relative to any other society. That is, the *ideal* code is pretty much the same, relative to any society. *Justified* codes may differ, given differences in the actual historical circumstances of different societies. The rational next step for one society may differ from the rational next step for another. But the goals of the different societies—the ideal codes they are ultimately to bring into their cultures—will be pretty much the same.

In Defense of Moral Realism

I take it that moral realism is the two-part thesis that, first, moral claims express propositions that are literally true or false and, second, some paradigmatic moral propositions are literally true.[4] So understood, the position I have developed is a version of realism.

The first part is easy to see. The standard-based theory of normative judgment implies that moral claims express propositions. In particular, a paradigmatic moral proposition is true only if some moral standard is justified. The second part is more difficult.

In chapter 2, I made independent proposals about the detailed truth conditions of paradigmatic moral propositions of certain kinds. According to one proposal, for example, a psychological trait, V-ness, is a moral virtue just in case there is a justified moral standard that calls for people to be V as a matter of their character. The proposition that charitableness is a virtue implies that justified standards for character call for people to be charitable. Now I am less interested in defending proposals of this kind than in defending most of the other components of my overall view. But something very much *like* this must surely be correct, if the standard-based theory is correct. So let us take it as given.

Consider, then, the standard calling for people to be charitable as a matter of their character. I think that any moral code that did not include this standard could be improved, from the standpoint of our society, if the standard were added to it. If so, then this standard is part of the best moral code, from the standpoint of our society, or, if two or more codes are tied as best, then the standard is included in them all. That is, any moral code that the society would be rationally permitted to choose would incorporate such a standard. Given the *J* thesis, as amended in chapter 10, it follows that the standard is justified.

Suppose I am wrong. Suppose any moral code that included the standard calling for charitableness could be substituted for—without loss from the standpoint of the society—by some moral code that did not include it. The substitute

---

4. Sayre-McCord, 1988, p. 5.

code might include a standard that gives people a right to charitable aid rather than the standard that makes charitableness a virtue. This would mean that any code that contained the latter standard would be tied with a code that would create a right to charitable aid. But I think that charity is regarded as a virtue in our own moral culture; that is, the standard calling for people to be charitable as a matter of their character has currency in the society. Given the *J* thesis, as amended in chapter 10 to deal with ties, it follows that the standard is justified.

Either way, then, the standard that calls for charitableness as a matter of character is justified, and so, given my proposal, it follows that it is true that charitableness is a virtue. This argues for the second part of the realist thesis, that some paradigmatic moral propositions are literally true.

The argument depends on a number of claims I have argued for in the course of the book, as well as on certain empirical claims about our own society in particular. For instance, the argument depends on the idea that the society would be better able to meet its needs if its social moral code included a standard calling for charitableness than if it did not. This is, of course, a speculative claim. But if the arguments I gave in chapter 10 about societal needs are accepted, then this claim also should be accepted. Charitable people will tend to help each other meet their basic needs, so a society of charitable people will be one in which people are better able to meet their basic needs than would otherwise be the case, other things being equal. And I argued that a society is better able to meet its needs if its members' basic needs are met. So a society of charitable people will be one that is better able to meet its needs than would otherwise be the case, other things being equal. Finally, a society in which the social moral code calls for people to be charitable will be more likely to be a society of charitable people than would otherwise be the case, other things being equal.

In any event, my overall position entails the first part of the moral realist thesis, and the second part seems likely to be true. Of course, it is compatible with my theory that no paradigmatic moral propositions are in fact true. But for this to be the case, the world would have to be such that no social moral code would contribute to any society's ability to meet its needs. This is a way in which moral realism might fail to be true, despite my theory, yet, of course, it is not a metaphysically interesting way for it to fail to be true. And I argued in the last chapter that any society is better able to meet its needs if it has a social moral code than would otherwise be the case.

Moral Properties, Queer Properties?

J. L. Mackie accepted the first part of the realist position, but he denied the second part, and for metaphysically interesting reasons.

> The ordinary user of moral language means to say something about whatever it is that he characterizes morally, for example a possible action, as it is in itself, or would be if it were realized, and not about, or even simply expressive of, his, or anyone else's, attitude or relation to it. But the something he wants to say is not purely descriptive, certainly not inert, but something

that involves a call for action or for the refraining from action, and one that is absolute, not contingent upon anyone's desire or preference or policy or choice, his own or anyone else's.[5]

What the ordinary user of moral language wants to say, Mackie suggests, is that the thing he characterizes morally has a moral property, such as the property of *being morally required*. But this property would be "utterly different from anything else in the universe." The property of being morally required, for example, would have *to-be-doneness* "somehow built into it," as it is in itself, independently of anyone's subjective psychological states. Moral properties would therefore be metaphysically queer, he maintains, and he concludes that there are no such properties.[6]

This argument raises two questions for my theory. The first is whether moral properties turn out to be metaphysically queer, according to the theory. The second is whether moral properties, according to my account, turn out to conflict in any interesting way with our pre-theoretical views about what we are doing when we make moral claims. Let me begin with the second question.

The relevant pre-theoretical views are things that any competent user of moral language or person with moral beliefs would believe about the properties expressed by moral predicates, just in virtue of his competence, or that he would have to believe in order to make sincere paradigmatic moral claims. I agree with Mackie that an ordinary competent speaker takes himself to be attributing something to things that he characterizes morally. For example, he takes himself to be attributing the characteristic or property of *being morally required* to things he characterizes as "morally required." Mackie may also be correct that the ordinary speaker does not think that such properties are relational.[7] Yet moral properties *are* relational in the way I have explained.[8] People do not need to have this in mind, however, in order to be competent and sincere in making moral claims, for the society and moral code at issue are fixed in any discourse by facts about the context, and the same point applies to moral thought.[9]

Mackie's fundamental idea is that competent speakers treat moral predicates as expressing properties that are "not purely descriptive" but in some sense involve "a call for action." Moreover, they treat this call for action as not being "contingent upon anyone's desire or preference or policy or choice." That is, I shall say, competent speakers give the appearance of believing that moral predicates express normative properties whose normativity is *categorical*, in the sense

5. Mackie, 1977, p. 33.
6. Mackie, 1977, pp. 38–40, 15.
7. Similarly, although a competent speaker of the language would presumably realize that the predicate "big" expresses a property, she may not realize that that property is in fact a relation to a comparison class.
8. For example, the property of *being morally required* is a relation among an action, a person or persons, a society, and a moral code. Simplifying somewhat, if we fix the society, an action stands in this relation to a person just in case the moral code justified relative to the society calls for the person to do the action.
9. The context of speech determines which society is at issue, and the moral code at issue is the one justified relative to that society. The idea of a context of thought is analogous to the idea of a context of speech.

that it is independent of any individual person's subjective psychological states. This idea creates no difficulty for the theory I have developed.

Consider, for example, the property of *being a moral virtue*. This is the property that a trait of character has, in relation to a society, just in case the moral code justified relative to the society includes a moral standard that calls for people to have the trait. This property, like the property of being morally required, is a normative property in the sense I explained in chapter 2. It relates things that have it to a justified moral code or standard. It is normative in that any paradigmatic proposition that attributes it to something is a normative proposition.

On the society-centered view, moral properties, such as the properties of being a virtue and of being morally required, are categorically normative. Moreover, justified moral standards that call for particular actions to be performed qualify as "categorical imperatives," in roughly Kant's sense. The account I have given of "the possibility" of a categorical imperative differs from Kant's, of course, but on my account, as on Kant's, the status of a moral code or standard as justified does not depend on any individual's subjective psychological states. It depends only on the needs and non-moral values of the relevant society. Changes in the psychology of any given person will not make a difference in which moral standards qualify as justified, for it will not alter the needs or values of society or the nature of the social moral code. Hence, if a justified moral standard calls on a person to do something, the requirement to do it does not depend on the person's desires or inclinations.

Let me therefore turn to the question of whether moral properties are metaphysically queer, according to my account. Mackie was primarily worried, I believe, about the intelligibility of the idea that certain properties could be categorically normative. The metaphysically queer idea was the idea of a property's being normative without being relational and psychological, relating things that have it to the motivations or other psychological states of relevant persons. For what else could the normativity of a property consist in? What is needed to escape Mackie's argument, then, is a non-psychological account of normativity, which is precisely what the standard-based theory of normative judgment provides, in combination with the society-centered theory. But I am not content merely to block Mackie's argument. In addition, I want to show that, on my account, the existence of moral properties raises no special metaphysical or epistemological problems. I attempt to do this in the next section, where I argue that the needs-based society-centered theory is a form of moral naturalism.

In Defense of Moral Naturalism

As I said before, I assume that a theory that postulates moral facts or properties counts as a form of naturalism only if it claims or implies that these facts or properties are *empirical*.[10] That is, moral facts are knowable (by humans) only

---

10. Recall that a moral fact is a true paradigmatic moral proposition.

a posteriori, or through experience, and every proposition that entails that a moral property is instantiated is knowable only a posteriori, or through experience.

Let us consider whether the needs-based society-centered theory counts as a form of naturalism. The answer to this question turns on whether my account of the justification of moral codes and standards is compatible with naturalism. There are two issues here, one concerning moral facts and one concerning moral properties. On my account, a moral fact entails a fact about the justification of some standard. This is the fact that might seem to be incompatible with naturalism. Similarly, on my view, a moral property exists just in case there is a justified moral standard. It is this that might seem to raise the question of whether my account of moral properties is incompatible with naturalism. The key issues, then, are two. First, what is the status, on my account, of the property a moral standard or code can have of *being justified*? Is this property a natural property? And second, what is the status of propositions to the effect that some standard or code is justified? If such a proposition were true, would this be a natural fact?

On the society-centered view, a moral standard is justified relative to a society just in case, roughly, the society would be rational to select the code as its social moral code. On the needs-based account, a society would be rational to select a code as its social moral code just in case, roughly, the code's serving as its social moral code would better serve the society's needs and nonmoral values than any alternative. Let us assume that these biconditionals hold exactly, because nothing here turns on the qualifications I discussed in earlier chapters. Then we can say that the property a moral code can have of being justified relative to a society is necessarily co-extensive with the property of being such that the society would rationally select it to serve as its social moral code. And the latter property is necessarily co-extensive with the property of being such that its serving as the society's social moral code would better serve the society's needs and nonmoral values than any alternative.

Let me begin by arguing that this last property is a natural property. My theory about the "grounding" of the basic needs of societies is not an empirical theory,[11] and partly because of this the issue of whether such-and-such is needed by societies may not be entirely an empirical one. Yet it is an empirical matter to determine whether a given moral code is such that its currency in a society would best serve the society's needs. Similarly, although the theory of the grounding of the basic needs of persons is not empirical, it is an empirical matter to determine whether I need a drink of water. And the property something can have of *being needed by me* is an empirical property. Moreover, given my account of societal values, it is an empirical matter to determine what a society values.[12] I maintain, therefore, that once we have identified a society's needs and nonmoral

11. Some philosophers might view it as empirical on the ground of a comprehensive empiricism, but I will not take comfort from their view.

12. In defending naturalism, Kitcher uses the idea of "the ends of the community" (1992, p. 112).

values, and once we have identified a set of moral codes, it is in principle an empirical matter to determine which of the codes would best serve the society's needs and values if it were to be the society's social moral code. This is analogous to determining which of a number of possible diets would best serve my needs and tastes, and there is no temptation to think that this is anything but an empirical matter. Hence, the property a moral code can have, of (roughly) best serving a society's needs and nonmoral values, is an empirical property.

I have already argued, in effect, that the property a moral code can have of being justified relative to a society is necessarily co-extensive with the property (roughly speaking) of best serving a society's needs and nonmoral values. Call the former property *J* and the latter *N*. Hence the property *J*, the property of being justified relative to a society, is necessarily co-extensive with the empirical property *N*. Does this mean that it *is* an empirical property?

Suppose first that necessarily co-extensive properties are identical. It would follow from this that the property *J*, of being justified relative to a society, *is* the property *N*, of best serving the society's needs and nonmoral values. Since *N* is an empirical property, it would follow that *J* is empirical.

Yet I think that there are distinct properties that are necessarily co-extensive.[13] Moreover, it may seem that although property *J* is evidently normative, property *N* is not. One might argue on this basis that *J* must be distinct from *N*. Similarly, one might argue that although any moral property is necessarily co-extensive with an "*N*-based property"—with a property that is some function of the *N* property—no moral property can be identical to that *N*-based property. For example, ignoring irrelevant details, the property an action can have of being morally required (relative to society *S*) is necessarily co-extensive with the propety of being called for by a moral standard that is included in the moral code with property *N* (relative to *S*). One might argue that these properties must be distinct. For although moral properties are normative, the fact that property *N* is not normative means that the relevant *N*-based properties are not normative. Now the key premise in this reasoning is the proposition that property *J* is normative while property *N* is not. This premise is false.

Recall that the *J* property, the property a moral code can have of being justified in relation to a society, is simply the status a moral code must have as a necessary condition of the truth of corresponding moral propositions. The main burden of my argument in this book has been that this status is the *N* property, the property of being such as to best serve the needs and nonmoral values of the relevant society. If I am correct, the *J* property and the *N* property are one and the same. And this property is normative according to the account of normative properties that I presented in chapter 2. For the property a moral code can have of being justified in relation to a society is the property of satisfying a standard calling for the social moral code of a society to best serve the society's needs and nonmoral values; this standard is justified in that moral codes that

---

13. Michael Jubien pointed out to me, for example, that the property of being an even prime number and the property of being a natural number greater than 1 and less than 3 are surely distinct, even though necessarily co-extensive.

satisfy it thereby meet a necessary condition of the truth of corresponding moral propositions. Hence, property *J* is normative, and, if *J* is identical to *N*, this implies that property *N* is normative. To be sure, there is an apparently non-normative sufficient condition for a moral code having property *N*, but, if *J* is identical to *N*, this condition is also sufficient for a moral code having property *J*. My thesis that *J* is identical to *N* increases the simplicity of my overall view and enhances its ability to explain the nature of normativity.

My claim that property *J* is identical to property *N* may nevertheless be controversial. For this reason, let me assume for the moment that *J* is distinct from *N*. The issue is whether *J* is empirical. However, given that property *N* is empirical, propositions to the effect that *N* is instantiated are empirical. This follows from the previous definition. But because *N* is necessarily co-extensive with *J*, a proposition to the effect that *N* is instantiated entails a proposition to the effect that *J* is instantiated and vice versa. Hence, propositions to the effect that *J* is instantiated are knowable through experience. Now the society-centered view is *compatible* with the idea that propositions to the effect that *J* is instantiated can be known by us in some other way as well. But, as far as I can see, they cannot be known in any other way. If I am correct, it follows that the *J* property is empirical; the property a moral code can have of being justified relative to a society is empirical.[14]

Let me turn to the issue of whether moral facts are empirical, on my account. This depends on whether propositions to the effect that some standard or code is justified are empirical. But that they are empirical follows from the fact that the property a moral standard or code can have of being justified relative to a society is empirical. For according to the definition I gave, if this property is empirical, it follows that every proposition which entails that it is instantiated—including every proposition to the effect that some moral code or standard is justified relative to a society—is empirical.

Taken together, the arguments I have given show that the needs-based society-centered view is a form of naturalism. Given the needs-based society-centered view, the property a moral code can have of being justified relative to a society is an empirical property. And propositions to the effect that a code or standard is justified are empirical. *Moral* properties are therefore natural properties, and *moral* facts are natural.

This last step in the reasoning may require some discussion. But the point is simply that, as I argued before, the only doubt about naturalism raised by my view is the doubt about whether the property of being justified is empirical and about whether propositions to the effect that a standard or code is justified are empirical. Indeed, I argued in chapter 2 that the standard-based theory of moral

14. It might be objected that the proposition that *N* is necessarily co-extensive with *J* is not empirical, and that this means that the conclusion that *J* is empirical does not follow from the premise that *N* is empirical. But compare this: The property of being an even prime number is necessarily co-extensive with the property of being equal to 2. Although this fact is not empirical, yet it is an empirical matter whether the number of books on my desk is equal to two, and it follows that it is an empirical matter whether the number of books on my desk has the property of being an even prime.

propositions is compatible with naturalism, if we assume a naturalistic theory of the justification of moral standards and codes. I have argued in this section that the needs-based society-centered view is a naturalistic theory.

The Open Question Argument

G. E. Moore's open-question argument aims to show, in effect, that no moral property is identical to a natural property. The argument is as follows: If we were to assume that some moral property *is* identical to a natural property, it would follow that certain questions are closed that we know to be open. For if property P is identical to property Q, then anything that is P is Q, and so it obviously is not an open question whether things that are P are Q. But, Moore thinks, no matter what natural property is thought to be identical to the property of goodness, it is an open question whether things with that property are good. More generally, for any natural property P and moral property M, it is an open question as to whether things that are P are M. Because the hypothesis that P is identical to M implies otherwise, it follows that P is not identical to M. Hence, no moral property is identical to any natural property.[15]

Of course, I am willing to concede for the sake of argument that moral properties are distinct from the corresponding N-based properties. But I have argued that, even if so, a moral property *is* a natural property. Since a property is identical to itself, it follows that any moral property is identical to a natural property. Moore is therefore incorrect to think that, for any natural property P and moral property M, it is an open question whether things that are P are M. For if M is a moral property, it is a natural property, and it is not an open question as to whether things that are M are M.

Unfortunately, Moore's argument has a close cousin that is not so easy to escape. Consider a moral property M and the corresponding N-based property, which we can refer to as the property N-*based*-M. Because these are necessarily co-extensive, it is necessary that anything that is N-*based*-M is M, and so it is not an open question whether things that are N-*based*-M are M. Yet, I think Moore would insist that this *is* an open question. Because my hypothesis that M is necessarily co-extensive with N-*based*-M implies otherwise, he would insist that my hypothesis is incorrect. A moral property is not necessarily co-extensive with a corresponding N-based property.

This argument trades on a shift in the notion of an "open" question. A question is "strictly closed," let us say, if a correct answer to it would be necessarily true.[16] Otherwise, the question is "strictly open." A question is "epistemically open" if conceptually and linguistically competent people might reasonably believe that it is strictly open. A question can be "strictly closed" while being "epistemically open."

Consider, for example, a pair of properties, M and N-*based*-M. On my ac-

---

15. Moore, 1903, pp. 7, 16–17.
16. That is, the proposition that would be affirmed by the answer is necessarily true.

count, because they are necessarily co-extensive, it is necessarily the case that things that are *M* are *N-based-M*. Hence, the question, whether things that are *N-based-M* are *M*, is strictly closed. Yet the question is not epistemically closed, for a conceptually and linguistically competent person could believe that it is strictly open without thereby making any epistemic error. She would be making a philosophical error, according to me, but not an error that indicates epistemic unreasonableness. That is, questions of the form "Are *N-based-M* things also *M* things?" are, in fact, strictly closed. Yet because a competent person may think they are strictly open, they are epistemically open. Accordingly, my account does not imply that questions of this sort are closed *tout court*.

I do claim that it is a necessary truth that if a moral proposition is true, some moral standard is justified. The following is therefore a strictly closed question: "Would it follow from the fact that some moral propositions are true that there are some justified moral standards?" But again, this question is not epistemically closed. Even though, as I think, it would be a conceptual or semantic error to accept a moral claim while denying that any moral standards are justified, this error is not precluded by ordinary competence with moral concepts. People with ordinary conceptual and semantical competence may have no beliefs at all that are explicitly about moral standards. Hence, a conceptually and linguistically competent person could believe that the question is strictly open without thereby being guilty of any epistemic unreasonableness.

I conclude, then, that Moore's open-question argument is not a threat to my position.

Indeterminacy and Virtue Theory

A moral code is a system of moral standards, and the nature of this system, together with relevant nonmoral facts, determines what things the code as a whole requires, prohibits, or permits. I have said nothing about how this works. I have treated moral codes as "black boxes." For all that I have said, even if there is a moral code that is justified relative to a society, the code may fail to yield specific prescriptions in situations where agents need to decide what to do. There may be significant areas of "indeterminacy" in which the code judges several actions to be equally acceptable, yet where a person who subscribed to it would not be happy to view them as morally innocent.

Vagueness is part of the issue here. For example, a justified standard calling on people to be charitable may fail to determine exactly what charity requires in certain situations. How much money should one give to those less fortunate than oneself? A variety of different actions may all qualify as charitable, and the code may fail to determine which of them is to be performed. Yet it may be unsatisfying to suppose that each of the charitable actions is equally acceptable.[17]

17. I want to distinguish indeterminacy arising from vagueness from a more common indeterminacy that is not at all troublesome. Whenever an action is morally required or otherwise called for, there will be a variety of ways that the action could be performed, and morality may not settle which of them is the way in which the action is to be performed. For example, suppose

More important, a justified moral code would presumably contain a variety of general standards, such as, perhaps, a standard calling on people to be charitable and one calling on people to be honest. For all I have shown, however, such a code may not contain a priority rule that would come into play when general standards give conflicting prescriptions. For example, charity and honesty conflict in situations where it would be uncharitable to express one's honest belief about someone's behavior. A code that calls for both honesty and charity may not determine which action is more appropriate in a situation of this kind, the honest act of expressing one's opinion or the charitable act of disguising one's opinion.

And there may be certain kinds of situation in which, for some other reason, a justified moral code would not decide among the options facing an agent. For example, suppose a trolley is hurtling toward five people, and it will kill them unless it is switched onto another track, but there is a person on the other track who will be killed if it is switched. You happen to be standing by the switch.[18] In some cases of this kind, the justified code might not settle what you ought to do, yet you might find it difficult to regard the options as equally acceptable.

The upshot is that even if there is a justified moral code in relation to every society, morality may still fail to give us the specific prescriptions that we often feel we need. We often feel torn by conflicting moral demands or by a sense of uncertainty about what to do, and there may be no underlying moral fact as to exactly what we ought to do. It may be unsatisfying to suppose that the alternatives in such situations are equally (un)acceptable. Yet morality may simply leave a good deal undetermined about how we are to act, setting general guidelines but leaving the specifics unfixed and a matter of choice.

These considerations lead me to ask the following question: Is it reasonable to suppose that a justified moral code would contain a priority rule, or some other mechanism for fixing exactly how we are to act in situations of the kind I have described in which a number of alternatives would otherwise be judged by the code as equally (un)acceptable? This is what I call the indeterminacy issue.

The answer to the question depends, of course, on the properties of the relevant justified moral code. The properties of such a code, including its internal structure and complexity, depend partly on the needs, nonmoral values, and circumstances of the society at issue. They also depend on the psychological capacities of people in the society. For moral codes are evaluated as candidates for society's social moral code, and a social moral code is the code that people in a society are brought up to subscribe to morally and that is transmitted from generation to generation in the culture. The nature of people's psychological

---

I am to repay a debt. Yet I could repay it in a variety of ways: in cash or by check, on Monday or on Tuesday, and so on. Indeterminacy of this kind is not troublesome in the way indeterminacy about charity may seem troublesome. For the issue raised by charity is not that there are different ways of performing (what is intuitively) the same charitable act. It is that there are (intuitively) different charitable actions, depending on different construals of charity and of the appropriate limits of charitable duties or virtues.

18. See Foot, 1978b; Thomson, 1975–76.

capacities would affect the impact a given social moral code would have on a society's ability to meet its needs and nonmoral values.[19]

Indeterminacy might not be an issue if some act-consequentialist principle were the unique justified moral standard. It is unlikely that this is so, however, for there are standard arguments which suggest that a society would not be well advised to select an act-consequentialist principle to serve as its social moral code. Henry Sidgwick argued, for example, that it would be best if ordinary people did not accept the act-utilitarian principle, for he thought it likely, "in the actual condition of civilized communities," that there would be bad results if the "vulgar" accepted the principle.[20] Many others have had similar worries, and act-consequentialists now typically defend act-consequentialism as an account of the "right-making" characteristics of actions rather than as a principle that people are actually to use in their reasoning.[21] According to the society-centered view, however, act-consequentialism cannot be correct as an account of right-making properties relative to a society unless the relevant society would be rational to select the principle as the unique moral principle that would be taught to people as the rule to subscribe to morally and to follow in their reasoning. Hence, given the society-centered theory, the standard arguments against the viability of act-consequentialism as a decision rule are arguments against its being justified. They are arguments, then, against the view that the right action is the action called for by the act-consequentialist principle.

It is common to suppose that even if act-consequentialism is justified, people might be well advised to use rules of thumb rather than attempt to calculate, at ˙ ery juncture, the expected value of the consequences of their options. These calculations would be difficult and costly of time and energy.[22] But then the society would be well advised to favor the use of rules of thumb, and it would be rational for the society to prefer that the better rules of thumb be taught to people in the course of their moral education, as part of the moral code they are to follow, so that they are brought up to subscribe morally to these rules. Then the justified moral code would include the so-called rules of thumb. It would not consist simply of the act-consequentialist principle.

The argument against act-consequentialism does, of course, rely on empirical claims. Hence, for all I have said, it remains *possible* that an act-consequentialist principle is justified. However, I think it is more likely that the justified moral code in most societies would be a code of general prima facie moral principles, much as was described by W. D. Ross.[23]

This still leaves us with the indeterminacy issue. But I think there is likely to be indeterminacy of the sort I described. Here I speculate, but I think there sim-

19. We considered an example of this when we discussed "psychological boundaries" in chapter 10.
20. Sidgwick, 1907, p. 490.
21. See Bales, 1971. Smart struggles with the issue (1973, pp. 42–46). Hare argues that people should not, in general, reason as utilitarians (1981, pp. 44–46). Compare Sumner (1987) on "indirect utilitarianism."
22. See, for example, Smart, 1973.
23. Ross, 1930.

ply are situations in which an agent faces a number of options, and the justified moral code does not determine that one of them is the option that is to be taken.

Technically, this means that each of the options is permissible, for the permissibility of an option can be understood as the absence of a prohibition against it. Yet if the situation is one in which a number of standards in the justified code give conflicting directions, it may well be that although several options are technically permissible, none of them is morally innocent; that is, it may be that each of them is spoken against by some standard in the justified code even though none of them is prohibited by the code as a whole. Because of this, an agent who subscribed to the conflicting standards might not feel at ease about choosing among the options. For, if he subscribes to these standards, he intends to comply with them and tends to feel guilty if he does not comply. For this reason, he likely would not feel at ease about performing an action that is spoken against by one of the standards. He may feel himself in a dilemma; even though he has options that are technically permissible, he has no option that seems morally innocent.

It might seem reasonable to suppose that a justified moral code would contain a rule that would settle conflicts between justified moral standards. And, in the spirit of the society-centered view, one might propose the rule that calls on us to do what will best serve the needs and nonmoral values of our society. Yet to defend this proposal, one would have to show that the currency of this decision rule would best serve the needs and nonmoral values of a society. It is not obvious that it would, as I explain in the next section.

It might seem that a virtue-theoretic approach could deal with the issue of indeterminacy.[24] People who have been brought up to subscribe morally to a justified code and to be virtuous by its lights would perhaps see clearly how to act or respond, even in situations in which the justified code leaves it indeterminate how they are to act. A virtuous person can see which aspects of a situation are morally relevant and in what way they are relevant and thus reach an overall appraisal of the situation. She is motivated appropriately by the aspects of the situation that she sees to be morally relevant so that, all things considered, she is motivated to do what is called for in her overall appraisal.

The chief problem with this suggestion, however, is that if the justified moral code does not determine which of a number of options is morally to be taken in a situation, then if a person reaches an overall appraisal to the effect that one of the options would be morally best, her judgment is not, strictly speaking, true. For, ex hypothesi, the moral code does not call for that option to be taken in preference to the remaining alternatives. Hence, people who have been brought up to be confident in reaching overall moral appraisals in such situations cannot be described as recognizing what morality calls for.

Certain ideas of virtue theory do, nevertheless, seem to be supported by society-centered theory. It seems plausible that the justified standards of virtue are sufficiently detailed to eliminate indeterminacy about character. But I doubt that

---

24. In what follows, I adapt to my purposes ideas proposed by John McDowell (1979) and Jonathan Dancy (1993, pp. 60–108).

the justified moral code would eliminate indeterminacy about actions. I suspect there are many situations in which a virtuous person will feel that there is only one morally acceptable alternative, but in which it is not true that she is morally required to take that alternative. In these situations, a virtuous person may "see" what to do, but it is not the case that she is morally required to do it.

Of course, it is possible for there to be indeterminacy about moral character, moral education, and upbringing, as well as about actions. I suggested that standards calling for honesty and charity can come into conflict. But then standards calling for people to develop secure dispositions to honesty and charity as a matter of their character may fail to determine precisely which complex behavioral disposition a virtuous person would instantiate. Still, I think it is reasonable to suppose that there are standards of virtue that would contribute best to the needs and nonmoral values of society, if they were part of the social moral code. We may not know exactly what they call for, but that is a different matter.

Rule Worship

If I am correct, a justified moral code would be a system of general moral standards governing behavior, character, social institutions, and the like. Suppose then that the justified code in a particular situation requires a person to perform a specific action. This means that this action is required by the code with the following property: Its serving in the society as the social moral code would contribute best to the society's ability to meet its needs and satisfy its nonmoral values. Yet even if the code has this property, it does not follow that every action that is required by the code would contribute better than any alternative to the society's ability to meet its needs and satisfy its nonmoral values. In some cases there may be some other action the agent could perform, other than the action required by the justified code, that would better serve the society's needs and nonmoral values.

This point may be familiar from the literature on rule utilitarianism. Suppose that a given action is required by the moral code whose currency in a society would maximize the social welfare. This is not necessarily the action that, of the alternatives available to the agent, would itself maximally contribute to the social welfare. J. J. C. Smart argued that this means that rule utilitarianism exemplifies a kind of irrational rule worship.[25] For the underlying rationale of utilitarianism is to promote social welfare. If a given action would best promote the social welfare, then it seems irrational—and an example of rule worship—to fail to perform the action simply because it is prohibited by a *rule*, even if the rule is one the currency of which in society would maximize the social welfare.

It may now appear that the society-centered view is subject to an analogous objection: The point of morality, according to the needs-based society-centered theory, is to enable society to meet its needs and satisfy its nonmoral values. Hence,

25. Smart, 1973, p. 10.

if a given action *A* would best contribute to the society's ability to meet its needs and satisfy its nonmoral values, it would seem irrational and an instance of rule worship to fail to do *A* simply because it is prohibited by a moral code, even if the code is the one whose currency would contribute most to the society's ability to meet its needs and satisfy its nonmoral values. For *A* is the action that the society would be rational to prefer to have done, and to fail to do *A* would be to fail to do the thing that would best enable the society to meet its needs and satisfy its nonmoral values. Hence, if the point of morality is to enable society to meet its needs and satisfy its nonmoral values, the morally best action must surely be the action that would best enable society to achieve these ends.

My reply is that, first, society-centered theory is not committed to denying this. It may turn out that the morally best action in every situation is the action that would best enable society to meet its needs and satisfy its nonmoral values. But neither is society-centered theory committed to accepting this. And second, society-centered theory says nothing about the "point" of morality. Rather, it specifies a standard for evaluating moral codes. Let me explain.

First, the rule worship objection can be understood as an attempt to argue in favor of an act-consequentialist moral code, a code consisting of the single standard calling on us to perform the action that would best enable society to meet its needs and satisfy its nonmoral values. It is, of course, true that the actions called for by this standard are all such that they would best enable society to meet its needs and satisfy its nonmoral values. It does not follow from this, however, that a society in which this standard served as the social moral code would be better able to meet its needs and satisfy its nonmoral values than would be the case if some more complex moral code were its social moral code. For perhaps people would violate the act-consequentialist rule more frequently than they would violate the more complex code, or perhaps the currency of the complex code would have beneficial indirect effects on the society's ability to meet its needs. Hence, it does not follow that the act-consequentialist moral code is justified by the lights of society-centered theory.

Second, society-centered theory proposes a standard for evaluating moral codes. The rule worship objection alleges that it is irrational to accept such a standard unless one applies it directly to actions. However, the idea of society-centered theory is that a justified moral code is a code that it is rational for society to choose as its social moral code. It does not follow that morally required actions are actions that it is rational for society to prefer. Furthermore, the standard a moral code must meet, to qualify as justified, is to be such that the relevant society would rationally choose it to serve as the social moral code. It makes no sense to think of applying *this* standard directly to actions.

It may seem, nevertheless, that there is a kind of incoherence in society-centered theory, an incoherence analogous to the "incoherence" David Wiggins saw in non-cognitivism. Wiggins said, of non-cognitivism, that it "depends for its whole plausibility upon abandoning at the level of theory the inner perspective that it commends" to the moral agent.[26] According to society-centered

---

26. Wiggins, 1988, p. 135.

theory, "at the level of theory" we are to evaluate moral codes on the basis of how well their currency in a society would serve the society's ability to meet its needs and nonmoral values. But, one might claim, successfully taking up this theoretical stance depends on abandoning the "inner perspective" that a moral agent would have toward a moral code if she had been raised to subscribe to it.

This claim is not correct. There is no reason why a person who accepted society-centered theory would automatically have to abandon the "inner perspective" she naturally takes toward the moral standards to which she subscribes. We are able to evaluate our moral standards on the basis recommended by society-centered theory without giving up the "inner perspective" of one who subscribes to them.[27] To suppose otherwise is to fail to see the close relation there is between the activity of theorizing about morality and the activity of reasoning morally. The activity of evaluating our standards is continuous with the activity of applying the standards in deciding how to behave or what kind of life to live.

Moral Reasoning, Moral Epistemology

Let me now turn to epistemic issues. There are three matters that I need to address. First, I want it to be clear that society-centered theory can vindicate the usual way we reason about moral issues. Second, I want to show that the society-centered theory does not undermine the distinction between the justification and the truth of a moral belief. Finally, I want to explain that although, as I understand things, the society-centered theory is not compatible with "particularism" in moral epistemology, it can neverless accommodate many of the insights that motivate particularism. Let me begin with moral reasoning.

According to society-centered theory, the best evidence for the truth of a moral proposition would include evidence that a relevant moral code or standard is appropriately justified. Further details depend, of course, on proposals about the detailed truth conditions of various moral propositions. In general, however, a paradigmatic moral proposition is true only if the moral code justified in relation to the relevant society has a corresponding property, such as the property of calling for acts of charity. I proposed, for example, that a person is morally required to perform a given action, relative to a given society, only if the moral code justified in relation to the society has the following (relational) property: It calls for the person to do the action. The best evidence for the truth of a moral proposition would therefore include evidence, first, that there is a moral code that is justified relative to the society in question and, second, that this code has the corresponding property.

When we are reasoning morally, however, we do not ordinarily take up this theoretical stance toward our moral standards. We do not question the justifi-

---

27. Unless, that is, the evaluation reveals that the standards we accept have socially unfortunate qualities. See Mullen, 1983, for an example of moral reasoning that includes reflection about the social consequences of the currency of particular moral rules.

cation of the moral code to which we subscribe, even if we are willing to recognize that some of our standards may be unjustified.

This does not mean that our ordinary moral reasoning is defective from the point of view of society-centered theory. The fact that we subscribe to a given moral code is at least some evidence that the code is justified, for few of us are complete rebels from the moral culture of our society. And the moral culture is the result of a very long historical process of adjustment to circumstances and pressures of various kinds. Given the continued existence of the society, it could hardly be the case that the code is socially non-viable. To be sure, it does not follow that the moral culture could not be changed in a way that would better enable the society to meet its needs and satisfy its nonmoral values. Given the arguments of the preceding chapter, for instance, sexism and racism in the moral culture are evidence that the moral code taught in the culture is not justified. Yet I think the fact that a code is part of the culture of a thriving society would be evidence that the code is justified, even if it is not conclusive evidence. And so, in the absence of direct evidence that the moral code in a culture is not justified, moral reasoning can begin with the local moral code. One can reason about moral issues by taking one's moral standards and convictions as a given, at least until they are undermined either by arguments internal to one's moral standards, or by arguments based in society-centered considerations of the sort we have considered.

Society-centered theory therefore vindicates the usual manner in which we reason about moral issues. We argue by analogy, and we construct thought experiments. We argue from principles or general standards. We attempt to reconcile our views on one topic, and the general standards they seem to commit us to, with our views on other topics, and the general standards they seem to commit us to. We aim to achieve a "local reflective equilibrium."[28] All of this is vindicated as a way to marshal evidence as to the truth of various moral claims, on the assumption that our moral code is by and large justified, or that its justification is not in question. On these assumptions, we can justify a moral belief by citing more general moral beliefs, and we can justify a group of moral beliefs by bringing them into coherence.

To be sure, a person may try to work from first principles, to discover the moral code that is justified relative to her society by developing a theory of societal needs and a sociology of the meeting of societal needs through the currency of a social moral code. She would need to resolve difficult philosophical and empirical issues before she could make real progress in this way. But we are not required to work from first principles in order to be justified in our moral beliefs any more than we must be chemists in order to be justified in believing that yeast causes bread to rise. It is typical for a person to believe what she was taught to believe. In many such cases, she is justified to believe it, if she is not aware of any reason to doubt its truth.

This brings me to the second matter, the distinction between the justification

28. See, for example, Daniels, 1979. Daniels explains a notion of "wide reflective equilibrium."

of a moral belief and the belief's being true. The standard-based theory implies that a moral belief is true only if a corresponding moral standard is "justified." Given this, it may be difficult to see how a true moral belief could fail to be justified. However, the issue of whether a person's moral belief is justified turns on whether the *belief* satisfies relevant *epistemic* standards. The issue of whether a person's moral belief is true turns on the different issue of whether the moral *standards* that correspond to the proposition believed by the person have the society-centered *J* property. Because of this, a person's moral belief may be true even if it is not justified, and a person's moral belief may be justified even if it is false.

Suppose, for example, that capital punishment is wrong; suppose a standard prohibiting capital punishment is justified by the lights of society-centered theory. Nevertheless, on the one hand, a person who believes truly that capital punishment is wrong may not be justified in her belief, for she may know that many people disagree with her, and she may not have paid any attention to their reasons for disagreeing with her. On the other hand, a person who was taught falsely that capital punishment is sometimes morally appropriate may be justified in believing this, for she may be unaware of any reasons to doubt it, and her lack of awareness may not be her fault. There are epistemic standards that we must meet, in order to have beliefs that qualify as justified, and the question of whether we have met these standards is different from the question of whether our beliefs are true.

Our moral beliefs would tend to be both true and justified if the social moral code in our society were justified. On this condition, the moral beliefs we would have as a result of learning the moral culture of our society would likely be true, by and large. There would be a connection between moral culture and moral truth, for learning and subscribing to the moral culture would tend to produce true moral beliefs. There might be a similar connection between moral culture and moral truth even if the social moral code were not entirely justified; it might be close enough to being justified that the moral beliefs produced in people who subscribed to it would tend on the whole to be true. In these cases, our moral beliefs would also tend to be justified, assuming the moral culture put us in a position to provide reasonable responses to people who disagree with us.

Let me now turn to particularism. It may seem that the account I have given is liable to objections grounded in particularist views about moral reasoning. I claim that an awareness of moral standards plays an active role in moral reasoning.[29] It may seem, however, that moral reasoning begins with specific instances, not with general rules. Moreover, moral reasoning does not always involve moral rules, and we can often simply "see" in a direct way, without inference, that a moral claim is correct.[30]

29. I defended this claim a moment ago when I discussed "the usual manner in which we reason about moral issues."

30. Dancy claims that our knowledge of the moral specifics is foundational and that the central issue in moral epistemology is to explain our knowledge of moral principles. (1993, p. 68; more generally, see pp. 60–108). See McDowell, 1979, pp. 332–33, 337.

But there is no problem here for society-centered theory. The account I have given of moral knowledge and reasoning does not commit me to the view that we learn the (justified) moral rules directly, without first learning how to act in specific situations. Nor does it commit me to the view that we always reason from moral rules. Moral beliefs can arise spontaneously, as a direct response to experience, without our being aware of any reasoning that involves the application of a rule.

Consider our knowledge of the grammar of our language. Competence with a language is plausibly viewed as dependent on a knowledge of relevant rules, for language is plausibly viewed as governed by a grammar. It is widely accepted that there are rules of syntax and that we have in some important sense internalized these rules and gained the ability to comply with them. Yet we do not generally *calculate* from the rules or use them as a decision procedure. And our initial learning of the rules depends on our having understood particular examples. But this is not incompatible with the idea that a knowledge of the rules is playing an active psychological role in the linguistic activity of a competent speaker.[31]

If we have rudimentary scientific knowledge, we may respond spontaneously to a flash of lightning by forming a belief about a discharge of electricity. Our belief may be justified even if we are unfamiliar with the science behind the electrical theory of lightning. If we learned our rudimentary science in the usual way, in school, and if none of our experiences has given us any reason to doubt what we learned, then we may have violated no standard of epistemic responsibility in forming the belief. In a similar way, if we subscribe to certain moral standards and view them as justified, we do sometimes respond spontaneously to events by forming a moral belief. Our belief may be justified in such cases even if we are unfamiliar with society-centered moral theory. For if our subscription to our moral standards is due to our upbringing in the usual way, and if our upbringing and subsequent experience have given us no reason to question our standards, then we may have violated no standard of epistemic responsibility in spontaneously forming the belief. None of this goes against society-centered theory or the account I have given of moral reasoning.

---

31. As I understand it, ethical particularism is the view that although there are certain particular act tokens that are morally required in specific situations, there are no correct general moral principles or rules. And moral virtue is simply a matter of getting it right. See Dancy, 1993, pp. 60, 66–71. An analogue of ethical particularism would be the view that although there are correct and incorrect uses of words, there are no correct general rules as to which specific sentence tokens are grammatical and which are not. And competence with the language is simply a matter of using it correctly. This radical view goes against the theorizing in linguistics about rules of syntax. It also goes against standard accounts of linguistic competence, which rely on the idea we have learned recursive rules. It implies that these accounts are mistaken, but it puts nothing in their place and suggests nothing *can* be put in this place. It makes linguistic competence more mysterious than need be. Moral particularism makes our moral competence similarly mysterious. It is psychologically unrealistic to suppose we can acquire an undifferentiated ability, which cannot be articulated, to judge what morality calls for. More to the point, moral particularism puts nothing in the place of the standard-based and society-centered theory of the truth conditions of moral propositions.

Justification, Belief, and Subscription

We have moral beliefs, to be sure, but it is part of my position that we also subscribe morally to corresponding standards.[32] Believing is a relation we can stand in to propositions, while subscribing is a relation we can stand in to standards and to codes of standards.

Moral belief and moral subscription are logically distinguishable. On the one hand, it is logically possible for one to believe that no paradigmatic moral propositions are true and yet subscribe morally to various moral standards, and there is no contradiction in doing so. For example, a moral skeptic might believe it is false that torture is wrong and yet subscribe to a prohibition on torture. On the other hand, it is logically possible for one to believe a paradigmatic moral proposition yet fail to subscribe to any relevant standard, and there is no contradiction in doing so. In chapter 2, I imagined the case of Alice. Alice believes that God has prescribed against abortions and that this means it is wrong to have an abortion, but she has no intention to comply with this prescription, which she views as hostile to women. She has the belief that abortion is morally wrong, but she does not subscribe to any standard that prohibits abortion.

Moral belief and moral subscription do nevertheless normally go hand in hand. On the one hand, the complex of attitudes that are involved in subscribing morally to a standard is normally accompanied by belief in certain corresponding moral propositions. There would be a psychological instability in combining these attitudes to a standard with the belief that none of the corresponding propositions is true. For example, moral subscription to a standard that prohibits torture cannot be combined in a stable way with the belief that torture is morally permissible. This would require combining the desire that people not torture, the tendency to blame people for torturing, and so on, with the thought that there is nothing morally wrong with torture. Such combinations of belief and attitude are normally unstable, even though they are logically tenable.

On the other hand, belief in a moral proposition is normally accompanied by subscription to a corresponding standard. There would be a psychological instability in combining belief that a given moral proposition is true—and so that some corresponding standard is justified—with a failure to subscribe morally to any corresponding standard. For example, the belief that torture is morally wrong cannot normally be combined in a stable way with an absence of a desire that people not torture, an absence of a tendency to blame people for torturing, and so on. Such combinations of belief and attitude are normally unstable even though, I claim, they are logically tenable.

Moral subscription entails moral motivation, as I explained in chapter 5, but moral belief does not. It is possible to have a moral belief but fail to subscribe to any corresponding moral standard. Yet because moral belief normally goes hand in hand with subscription to a corresponding standard, we are reasonable to expect a person with a moral belief to be appropriately motivated.

---

32. A proposition and a moral standard "correspond" to one another just in case the proposition entails that the standard is relevantly justified.

It is worth pointing out certain analogies between the justification of belief and the justification of moral subscription. First, there is, of course, a distinction between a person's being justified in believing a proposition and the *truth* of the proposition. Similarly, there is a distinction between a person's being justified in subscribing to a moral code and the code's being justified relative to a society. For a moral code to which a person is justified in subscribing may not be justified relative to the person's society, and the code that is justified relative to a society may be such that no one would actually be justified in subscribing to it. There may be no member of the society who realizes it is the justified code. The code may not in fact be accepted by anyone in the society, and people may have been raised to subscribe to a social moral code that is quite different from it. They might then be justified in subscribing morally to the actual social code rather than to the justified code.

Second, the issue of whether a person is justified in believing a proposition can be viewed in two ways. It can be viewed epistemically as, roughly, the issue of whether the person has met standards of epistemic responsibility in holding the proposition to be true. Alternatively, it can be viewed "practically" as, roughly, the issue of whether the person has adequate self-grounded reasons to accept the proposition. For example, belief in God may give a person a sense of security that contributes to his ability to meet his needs and satisfy his values. Similarly, the issue of whether a person is justified in subscribing morally to a given moral code can be viewed in two ways. It can be viewed, on the one hand, as the issue of whether the person has met standards of "responsibility for subscription" in subscribing to the code. Intuitively the issue on this construal is whether the person has adequate epistemic reason to suppose the code is justified. And, according to society-centered theory, this is the issue of whether the person has adequate reasons to suppose her society would be rational to choose the code to serve as the societal moral code. Call this the "epistemic" construal. On the other hand, the issue of whether a person is justified in subscribing morally to a given moral code can be viewed practically. On this construal, the issue is whether the person has adequate self-grounded reasons to subscribe morally to the code. According to the needs-and-values theory, this turns on the person's needs and values.[33]

Reasons to Be Moral

These ideas about the rationality and justifiability of a person's subscribing to the justified moral code lead naturally to a traditional worry about morality. If I am correct, it can be the case that a person would be justified in subscribing— and would also be rational to subscribe—to a moral code that is *not* justified relative to her society. And it can be the case that a person would *not* be justified in subscribing—and would not even be rational to subscribe—to the moral

---

33. The discussion in the preceding paragraph blurred the distinction between these two ways of construing the issue of whether a person is justified in subscribing morally to a given code.

code that *is* justified relative to her society. Because of this, it may appear that the justified moral code relative to a society is not necessarily of interest to a rational member of the society. So we face the question, Why be moral?

There are two interesting interpretations of this question. First, it may be interpreted as the question, Why subscribe to the moral code that is justified relative to one's society? This question can be construed both "epistemically" and "practically," in line with the distinction I drew in the preceding section. Suppose, for example, that the moral code *M* that is justified relative to Barbara's society is not in fact her society's social moral code. Suppose that a socially destructive code, *M'*, is the social code. Because Barbara was brought up in this society, her values have been shaped by *M'*. She subscribes in a stable and endorsed way to the standards in *M'*, and she has no conception of any other way of thinking of moral issues. In this case, to begin with the "epistemic" issue, Barbara may be justified in having moral values different from those that are in *M*. She may be aware of no reason to suppose that *M'* is not justified and she may not even be aware of *M*, much less of reasons to suppose it is justified relative to her society. Then again, turning to the "practical" issue, she may be fully rational even though she fails to subscribe to *M*. Subscription to *M* would not further her ability to satisfy her values, for her values reflect her subscription to *M'*. Moreover, it may well be that subscription to *M* would not enhance her ability to satisfy her needs. She may then have no self-grounded reason to subscribe to *M*, and she may be quite rational to subscribe to the local social moral code.

I might add that, in the case at hand, Barbara would presumably be justified in having moral beliefs that reflect her subscription to *M'*, even though *M'* is not the moral code justified relative to her society. For again, she was brought up to accept the moral standards of her community, and her community accepts standards and promulgates moral beliefs quite different from those reflected in the justified moral code *M*. The justified moral code is not even known to her community.

Why be moral? may also be read, in a second way, as the question, Why should one *comply* with the moral code that is justified relative to one's society? That code may not actually be the social moral code and may not even be known to the members of one's society, so there is no presumption that one would be rational to comply with it. Even if we assume it is known what the justified moral code requires, there is no presumption that one would be rational to comply with it. One is rational to pursue one's values, but since one may not in fact subscribe morally to the justified moral code, compliance with it may not actually further one's values, and so it cannot be assumed that one would be rational to comply with it.

It is hard to see why these results should be viewed as a problem, either for morality or for the society-centered theory. Even if we assume that Hinduism is the true religion, for example, it is hardly surprising if people raised in traditional Christian societies are entirely rational to be Christians and to worship in a Christian manner. It may seem that this is a poor analogy, however. For morality purports to be *action-guiding*, and because of this it may seem problematic if rational people can be indifferent to the justified moral code, and if there is not necessarily any good self-grounded reason to comply with the justified code.

The mistake here is to assume that "action-guidingness," or normativity, must be explained in terms of rationality. Reason purports to be normative or action-guiding as well. So if getting a "nice" answer to the "Why be moral?" question is crucial to understanding how morality can be normative, then getting a nice answer to the similar "Why be rational?" question must be crucial to understanding how self-grounded reason or epistemic reason could be normative. Yet this is simply to push the problem of explaining normativity back one step. In any event, the standard-based theory that I developed in chapter 2 explains normativity in an entirely different manner, one not dependent on getting a nice answer to the "Why be moral?" question.

In a well-ordered society, the actual social moral code is the justified moral code. In Barbara's case, the social moral code was not justified. Her society was not well ordered. Now it may seem important to ask whether rational people in well-ordered societies could be indifferent to the justified moral code and whether they would necessarily have sufficient self-grounded reasons to comply with the justified code. So consider Carol, who lives in a well-ordered society. Suppose that she was raised by a non-conformist family and that, as a result, her values are quite different from the standards that are part of the justified moral code. She presumably would not be indifferent to the justified code, for she would naturally view it as unjustified. Yet, in light of her values, she might have sufficient self-grounded reason to subscribe to the non-conformist code rather than to the justified code. And in cases where the codes give different prescriptions, she might have sufficient self-grounded reason to comply with her own code rather than with the justified code. In short, it is not necessarily the case, even in a well-ordered society, that rational people would subscribe to or comply with the justified moral code.

Again, however, it is hard to see why these results should be viewed as a problem either for morality or for the society-centered theory. Even if we assume that Hinduism is the true religion, it is hardly surprising if a person raised in a non-conformist Christian family in a Hindu society would be entirely rational to be Christian and to worship in a Christian manner.

It is important to realize, however, that I have been discussing the *logical* possibility of rational immorality. Rational immorality is not likely to be widespread in a well-ordered society. For in a well-ordered society, the justified moral code is the social moral code. It is the code that is embedded in the culture and passed on from generation to generation in the way people are brought up and educated. So in a well-ordered society, people's values are normally in line with justified moral standards. This means that people normally have self-grounded reasons to be moral, and their subscription to the justified moral code is normally rational because subscription to the code is subscription to the standards that are already among people's values. Moreover, given the arguments of chapter 10, the justified moral code would call for conditions to be created in which people are able to meet their basic needs. In a well-ordered society, then, there are not likely to be many situations in which there is conflict between a person's needs and his moral values.

In a well-ordered society, people are raised to be moral and to have moral values. Moral values are of central importance in the society at large, and they are of central importance in people's lives. People have values that give them self-grounded reasons to do what they have moral reason to do. And, if I am correct, these values call for people's needs to be met, so they call for decreasing the conflict there might otherwise be between people's needs and their moral values. And people are rational to be of moral character, for their values call on them to act morally and to subscribe morally to the justified moral standards for their society. Morality and reason walk hand in hand.

The Kingdom of Ends

In the *Grounding of the Metaphysics of Morals*, Kant writes:

> By "kingdom" [of ends] I understand a systematic union of different rational beings through common laws. Now laws determine ends as regards their universal validity; therefore, if one abstracts from the personal differences of rational beings and also from all content of their private ends, then it will be possible to think of a whole of all ends in systematic connection. . . .
>
> For all rational beings stand under the law that each of them should treat himself and all others never merely as means but always at the same time as an end in himself. Hereby arises a systematic union of rational beings through common objective laws, i.e., a kingdom that may be called a kingdom of ends (certainly only an ideal), inasmuch as these laws have in view the very relation of such beings to one another as ends and means.[34]

There should be no temptation to confuse the idea of a well-ordered society, under the needs-based society-centered view, with Kant's notion of a kingdom of ends. But the conception of a kingdom of ends can illustrate the idea of a well-ordered society. The needs-based theory tells us to abstract from the personal differences among the members of society and from the content of their private values. The moral acceptability of our individual ends is determined by the code that would be rationally chosen by the society as a systematic whole, with a view to realizing its basic needs or nonmoral values. In one way or another, this code will call on people to further each other's ability to meet their basic needs to a decent level and with rough equality. We have here an expression of the idea that each should treat everyone as an end in himself and never merely as a means. Pursuit of our private ends is morally acceptable only if we can realize them without failing to comply with the law that requires fulfillment of basic human needs, with rough equality.

This view expresses an idea of the kingdom of ends and a notion of respect for persons, inasmuch as none of our contingent ends has moral standing unless it can be or is a part of a systematic social union of ends. If serving a value

34. Kant, 1785, Ak 433.

is compatible with the requirements of the justified moral code and primarily with the moral priority of equality in serving basic human needs, it presumably is then permissible to serve it. Or if there is a stable and endorsed consensus in the society regarding a nonmoral value, it may be that the society would rationally seek to further the value by its choice of a moral code. Matters are complex. But in brief, we can say that our contingent ends have no moral standing unless they can be or are part of a systematic union of ends.

Moral progress has two dimensions. There is the progress we are morally required to seek, toward the ideal of a social moral code that ensures respect for human needs, on a basis of equality. But there is also the progress some of us may choose to seek, toward an ideal or value that we cherish. If we can secure a stable and endorsed consensus in our society regarding this value, then we may promote it to the status of a societal value. And if serving this value does not conflict with meeting societal needs, we can in this way alter the moral ideal. For we can in this way add content to the code that the society could rationally choose. The new options for the social moral code would be codes that respect our value. And movement of the culture in this direction would be progress toward a social union around our value, even if not progress toward a code that counts as rationally ideal right from the start.

References

Aberle, D. F., Cohen, A. K., Davis, A. K., Levy, Jr., M. J., and Sutton, F. X. (1950). "The Functional Prerequisites of a Society," *Ethics*, 60, pp. 100–11.

Ackrill, J. L. (1974). "Aristotle on *Eudaimonia*," *Proceedings of the British Academy*, 60, pp. 339–59.

Allison, Henry E. (1986). "Morality and Freedom: Kant's Reciprocity Thesis," *The Philosophical Review*, 95, pp. 393–425.

—— (1990). *Kant's Theory of Freedom*. Cambridge: Cambridge University Press.

Aristotle (1985). *Nicomachean Ethics*. Trans. by Terence Irwin. Indianapolis: Hackett.

Arrow, Kenneth (1963). *Social Choice and Individual Values*, 2nd ed. New Haven, Conn.: Yale University Press.

Baier, Kurt (1958). *The Moral Point of View*. Ithaca, N.Y.: Cornell University Press.

—— (1981). "Defining Morality without Prejudice," *The Monist*, 64, pp. 325–41.

Bales, R. Eugene (1971). "Act Utilitarianism: An Account of Right-making Characteristics or Decision-making Procedure?" *American Philosophical Quarterly*, 8, pp. 257–65.

Barwise, John, and Cooper, Barry (1981). "Generalized Quantifiers and Natural Language," *Linguistics and Philosophy*, 4, pp. 159–219.

Benedict, Burton (1968). "Societies, Small," in David L. Sills, ed., *International Encyclopedia of the Social Sciences* (New York: Crowell, Collier and Macmillan), vol. 14.

Benedict, Ruth (1934). *Patterns of Culture*. Boston: Houghton Mifflin Company.

Benn, Stanley I. (1967). "Society," in Paul Edwards, ed., *The Encyclopedia of Philosophy* (New York: Macmillan and Free Press), vol. 7, pp. 470–74.

Blackburn, Simon (1984). *Spreading the Word: Groundings in the Philosophy of Language*. Oxford: Clarendon Press.

Boyd, Richard N. (1988). "How to Be a Moral Realist," in Geoffrey Sayre-McCord, ed., *Essays on Moral Realism* (Ithaca, N.Y.: Cornell University Press), pp. 181–228.

Bradley, Raymond, and Swartz, Norman (1979). *Possible Worlds*. Indianapolis: Hackett.

Brandt, Richard B. (1979). *A Theory of the Good and the Right*. Oxford: Clarendon Press.

—— (1985). "The Explanation of Moral Language," in David Copp and David Zimmerman, eds., *Morality, Reason and Truth* (Totowa, N.J.: Rowman and Allanheld), pp. 104–19.

247

Bratman, Michael (1983). "Castañeda's Theory of Thought and Action," in James Tomberlin, ed., *Agent, Language and the Structure of the World: Essays Presented to Hector-Neri Castañeda, with His Replies* (Indianapolis: Hackett, pp. 149–69.

———— (1987). *Intention, Plans, and Practical Reason.* Cambridge: Harvard University Press.

———— (1989). "Intention and Personal Policies," *Philosophical Perspectives*, 3, pp. 443–69.

———— (1992). "Shared Cooperative Activity," *The Philosophical Review*, 101, pp. 327–41.

———— (1993). "Shared Intention," *Ethics*, 104, pp. 97–113.

Braybrooke, David (1987). *Meeting Needs.* Princeton, N.J.: Princeton University Press.

Brink, David (1989). *Moral Realism and the Foundations of Ethics.* Cambridge: Cambridge University Press.

Brower, Bruce W. (1988). "Virtue Concepts and Ethical Realism," *The Journal of Philosophy*, 85, pp. 675–93.

———— (1993). "Dispositional Ethical Realism," *Ethics*, 103, pp. 221–49.

Buchanan, James (1954). "Social Choice, Democracy, and Free Markets," *Journal of Political Economy*, 62, pp. 114–23.

Bunge, Mario (1974). "The Concept of Social Structure," in W. Leinfellner and E. Kohler, eds., *Developments in the Methodology of Social Science* (Dordrecht, Holland: D. Reidel), pp. 175–215.

———— (1979). "A Systems Concept of Society: Beyond Individualism and Holism," *Theory and Decision*, 10, pp. 13–30.

Campbell, Richmond (1984). "Sociobiology and the Possibility of Ethical Naturalism," in David Copp and David Zimmerman, eds., *Morality, Reason, and Truth* (Totowa, N.J.: Rowman and Allanheld), pp. 270–96.

Castañeda, Hector-Neri (1963). "Imperatives, Decisions, and 'Oughts,'" in Hector-Neri Castañeda and George Nakhnikian, eds., *Morality and the Language of Conduct* (Detroit: Wayne State University Press).

———— (1974). *The Structure of Morality.* Springfield, Ill.: Charles C. Thomas.

Copp, David (1979a). "Collective Actions and Secondary Actions," *American Philosophical Quarterly*, 16, pp. 177–87.

———— (1979b). "The Iterated-Utilitarianism of J. S. Mill," *Canadian Journal of Philosophy*, supp. vol. 5, pp. 75–98.

———— (1979c). "Do Nations Have the Right of Self-Determination?" in Stanley G. French, ed., *Philosophers Look at Canadian Confederation* (Montreal: Canadian Philosophical Association), pp. 71–95.

———— (1980). "Hobbes on Artificial Persons and Collective Actions," *The Philosophical Review*, 89, pp. 579–606.

———— (1984). "What Collectives Are: Agency, Individualism and Legal Theory," *Dialogue*, 23, pp. 249–69.

———— (1986). Review of Peter A. French, *Collective and Corporate Responsibility*, *Ethics*, 96, pp. 636–38.

———— (1990a). "Explanation and Justification in Ethics," *Ethics*, 100, pp. 237–58.

———— (1990b). "Normativity and the Very Idea of Moral Epistemology," *The Southern Journal of Philosophy*, supp. vol. 29, *Spindel Conference, 1990: Moral Epistemology*, pp. 189–210.

———— (1991a). "Contractarianism and Moral Skepticism," in Peter Vallentyne, ed., *Contractarianism and Rational Choice: Essays on Gauthier* (Cambridge: Cambridge University Press), pp. 196–228.

—— (1991b). "Moral Skepticism," *Philosophical Studies*, 62, pp. 203–33.

—— (1991c). "Moral Realism: Facts and Norms," *Ethics*, 101, pp. 610–24.

—— (1992a). "The 'Possibility' of a Categorical Imperative: Kant's *Groundwork*, Part III," *Philosophical Perspectives*, 6, pp. 261–84.

—— (1992b). "The Concept of Society," *Dialogue*, 31, pp. 183–212.

—— (1992c). "The Right to an Adequate Standard of Living: Autonomy and the Basic Needs," *Social Philosophy and Policy*, 9, pp. 231–61.

—— (1993). "Reason and Needs," in R. G. Frey and Christopher W. Morris, eds., *Value, Welfare, and Morality* (Cambridge: Cambridge University Press), pp. 112–37.

Dancy, Jonathan (1993). *Moral Reasons*. Oxford: Basil Blackwell.

Daniels, Norman (1979). "Wide Reflective Equilibrium and Theory Acceptance in Ethics," *The Journal of Philosophy*, 76, pp. 256–82.

—— (1980). "Reflective Equilibrium and Archimedean Points," *Canadian Journal of Philosophy*, 10, pp. 83–103.

Darwall, Stephen L. (1983). *Impartial Reason*. Ithaca, N.Y.: Cornell University Press.

Darwall, Stephen L., Gibbard, Allan, and Railton, Peter (1992). "Toward *Fin de Siècle* Ethics: Some Trends," *The Philosophical Review*, 101, pp. 115–89.

Devlin, Lord Patrick (l965). "Morals and the Criminal Law," in Lord Patrick Devlin, *The Enforcement of Morals* (Oxford: Oxford University Press), pp. 1–25.

Dworkin, Ronald (1986). *Law's Empire*. Cambridge, Mass.: Belknap Press.

Evans-Pritchard, E. E. (1940a). *The Nuer*. Oxford: Clarendon Press.

—— (1940b). "The Nuer of the Southern Sudan," in M. Fortes and E. E. Evans-Pritchard, eds., *African Political Systems* (London: Oxford University Press), pp. 272–96.

Feinberg, Joel (1970). *Doing and Deserving*. Princeton, N.J.: Princeton University Press.

—— (1973). *Social Philosophy*. Englewood Cliffs, N.J.: Prentice-Hall.

Foot, Philippa (1978a). "Moral Beliefs," in Philippa Foot, *Virtues and Vices* (Berkeley and Los Angeles: University of California Press), pp. 110–31.

—— (1978b). "The Problem of Abortion and the Doctrine of Double Effect," in Philippa Foot, *Virtues and Vices* (Berkeley and Los Angeles: University of California Press), pp. 19–32.

—— (1978c). *Virtues and Vices*. Berkeley and Los Angeles: University of California Press.

Frankena, William K. (1970). "The Concept of Morality," in G. Wallace and A. D. M. Walker, eds., *The Definition of Morality* (London: Methuen), pp. 146–73.

Frege, Gottlob (1988). "Thoughts." Trans. by P. Geach and R. H. Stoothoff. In Nathan Salmon and Scott Soames, eds., *Propositions and Attitudes* (Oxford: Oxford University Press), pp. 33–55.

French, Peter A. (1979). "The Corporation as a Moral Person," *American Philosophical Quarterly*, 16, pp. 207–15.

—— (1984). *Collective and Corporate Responsibility*. New York: Columbia University Press.

Gauthier, David (1984). "Justice as Social Choice," in David Copp and David Zimmerman, eds., *Morality, Reason, and Truth* (Totowa, N.J.: Rowman and Allanheld), pp. 251–69.

—— (1986). *Morals by Agreement*. Oxford: Clarendon Press.

—— (1988). "Moral Artifice," *Canadian Journal of Philosophy*, 18, pp. 385–418.

Geach, Peter (1958). "Imperative and Deontic Logic," *Analysis*, 18, pp. 49–56.

—— (1965). "Assertion," *The Philosophical Review*, 74, pp. 449–65.

Gert, Bernard (1988). *Morality: A New Justification of the Moral Rules*. New York: Oxford University Press.

Gewirth, Alan (1960). "Positive 'Ethics' and Normative 'Science,'" *The Philosophical Review*, 69, pp. 311–30.

—— (1978). *Reason and Morality*. Chicago: University of Chicago Press.

Gibbard, Allan (1990). *Wise Choices, Apt Feelings: A Theory of Normative Judgment*. Cambridge, Mass.: Harvard University Press.

Gilbert, Margaret (1989). *On Social Facts*. Princeton, N.J.: Princeton University Press.

—— (1990). "Walking Together: A Paradigmatic Social Phenomenon," *Midwest Studies*, 15, pp. 1–14.

Greenspan, Patricia S. (1994). *Practical Guilt: Moral Dilemmas, Emotions, and Social Norms*. New York: Oxford University Press.

Grice, Paul (1989). *Studies in the Way of Words*. Cambridge, Mass.: Harvard University Press.

Griffin, James (1986). *Well-Being: Its Meaning, Measurement, and Moral Importance*. Oxford: Clarendon Press.

Hardie, W. F. R. (1965). "The Final Good in Aristotle's Ethics," *Philosophy*, 40, pp. 277–95.

Hare, R. M. (1952). *The Language of Morals*. Oxford: Clarendon Press.

—— (1963). *Freedom and Reason*. Oxford: Clarendon Press.

—— (1981). *Moral Thinking: Its Levels, Method and Point*. Oxford: Clarendon Press.

Harman, Gilbert (1975). "Moral Relativism Defended," *The Philosophical Review*, 84, pp. 3–22.

Hart, H. L. A. (1961). *The Concept of Law*. Oxford: Clarendon Press.

—— (1968). *Punishment and Responsibility*. New York: Oxford University Press.

Hempel, C. G. (1979). "Scientific Rationality: Analytic vs. Pragmatic Perspectives," in T. G. Gereats, ed., *Rationality Today* (Ottawa: University of Ottawa Press), pp. 45–66.

Hill, Thomas E., Jr. (1985). "Kant's Argument for the Rationality of Moral Conduct," *Pacific Philosophical Quarterly*, 66, pp. 3–23.

Hobbes, Thomas (1651). *Leviathan*. C. B. Macpherson, ed. London: Penguin Books, 1968.

Hodder, Ian (1982). *Symbols in Action*. Cambridge: Cambridge University Press.

Homiak, Marcia L. (1985). "The Pleasure of Virtue in Aristotle's Moral Theory," *Pacific Philosophical Quarterly*, 66, pp. 93–110.

—— (1990). "Politics as Soul-Making: Aristotle on Becoming Good," *Philosophia*, 20, pp. 167–93.

Horwich, Paul (1993). "Gibbard's Theory of Norms," *Philosophy and Public Affairs*, 22, pp. 67–78.

Hume, David (1739). *A Treatise of Human Nature*. L. A. Selby-Bigge, ed. Oxford: Clarendon Press, 1968.

Hylland, Aanund (1986). "The Purpose and Significance of Social Choice Theory: Some General Remarks and an Application to the 'Lady Chatterly Problem'," in Jon Elster and Aanund Hylland, eds., *Foundations of Social Choice Theory* (Cambridge: Cambridge University Press), pp. 45–73.

Irwin, Terence (1988). *Aristotle's First Principles*. Oxford: Clarendon Press.

Johnson, Harry M. (1960). *Sociology: A Systematic Introduction*. New York: Harcourt, Brace and World.

Kagan, Shelly (1989). *The Limits of Morality*. Oxford: Clarendon Press.

Kant, Immanuel (1781). *Critique of Pure Reason.* Trans. by F. Max Muller. New York: Anchor Books, 1966.

——— (1785). *Grounding of the Metaphysics of Morals.* Trans. by James W. Ellington. Indianapolis: Hackett, 1981.

——— (1930). *Lectures on Ethics.* Trans. by Louis Infield. London: Methuen and Company.

Kern, Louis J. (1981). *An Ordered Love: Sex Roles and Sexuality in Victorian Utopias—the Shakers, the Mormons and the Oneida Community.* Chapel Hill, N.C.: University of North Carolina Press.

Kim, Jaegwon (1987). "'Strong' and 'Global' Supervenience Revisited," *Philosophy and Phenomenological Research*, 48, pp. 315–26.

Kitcher, Philip (1992). "The Naturalists Return," *The Philosophical Review*, 101, pp. 53–114.

Korsgaard, Christine M. (1986). "Skepticism about Practical Reason," *The Journal of Philosophy*, 83, pp. 5–25.

Kraut, Richard (1979). "Two Conceptions of Happiness," *The Philosophical Review*, 88, pp. 167–97.

——— (1989). *Aristotle on the Human Good.* Princeton, N.J.: Princeton University Press.

Kripke, Saul (1982). *Wittgenstein on Rules and Private Language.* Cambridge, Mass.: Harvard University Press.

Lehrer, Keith (1974). *Knowledge.* London: Clarendon Press.

——— (1977). "The Knowledge Cycle," *Noûs*, 11, pp. 17–25.

Leonard, Henry S., and Goodman, Nelson (1940). "The Calculus of Individuals and Its Uses," *The Journal of Symbolic Logic*, 5, pp. 45–55.

Lewis, David (1969). *Convention: A Philosophical Study.* Cambridge, Mass.: Harvard University Press.

Lyons, David (1976). "Mill's Theory of Morality," *Noûs*, 10, pp. 101–20.

Mackie, J. L. (1977). *Ethics: Inventing Right and Wrong.* Harmondsworth, England: Penguin.

Marshall, Thomas H. (1956). "Anthropology Today," *British Journal of Sociology*, 7, pp. 59–64.

Matthen, Mohan, and Levy, Edwin (1984). "Teleology, Error and the Human Immune System," *The Journal of Philosophy*, 81, pp. 351–72.

May, Larry (1987). *The Morality of Groups.* Notre Dame, Ind.: University of Notre Dame Press.

Mayhew, Leon H. (1968). "Society," in David L. Sills, ed., *International Encyclopedia of the Social Sciences* (New York: Crowell, Collier and Macmillan), vol. 14.

McDowell, John (1978). "Are Moral Requirements Hypothetical Imperatives?" *The Aristotelian Society*, supp. vol. 52, pp. 13–29.

——— (1979). "Virtue and Reason," *The Monist*, 62, pp. 331–50.

——— (1981). "Non-Cognitivism and Rule-Following," in Steven Holtzman and Christopher Leich, eds., *Wittgenstein: To Follow a Rule* (London: Routledge and Kegan Paul), pp. 141–62.

——— (1983). "Aesthetic Value, Objectivity, and the Fabric of the World," in Eva Shaper, ed., *Pleasure, Preference, and Value* (Cambridge: Cambridge University Press), pp. 1–16.

——— (1984). "Wittgenstein on Following a Rule," *Synthese*, 58, pp. 325–63.

——— (1985). "Values and Secondary Qualities," in Ted Honderich, ed., *Morality and Objectivity* (London: Routledge and Kegan Paul), pp. 110–29.

——— (1987). "Projection and Truth in Ethics," Lindley Lecture, University of Kansas. Lawrence: Department of Philosophy, University of Kansas, pamphlet.

——— (forthcoming). "Might There Be External Reasons?" in J. E. J. Althan and Ross Harrison, eds., *World, Mind and Ethics: Essays on the Philosophy of Bernard Williams* (Cambridge: Cambridge University Press).

McKerlie, Dennis (1988). "Egalitarianism and the Separateness of Persons," *Canadian Journal of Philosophy*, 18, pp. 205–25.

Midgley, Mary (1983). *Animals and Why They Matter*. Athens, Ga.: University of Georgia Press.

Mill, John Stuart (1863). *Utilitarianism*. London: Parker, Son and Bourn.

Moore, G. E. (1903). *Principia Ethica*. Cambridge: Cambridge University Press.

Moulin, H. (1983). *The Strategy of Social Choice*. Amsterdam: North Holland Publishing.

Mullen, Peter (1983). "What's Wrong Can Never Be Right," *Manchester Guardian Weekly*, December 4, 1983, p. 4.

Nagel, Thomas (1970). *The Possibility of Altruism*. Oxford: Oxford University Press.

——— (1986). *The View from Nowhere*. New York: Oxford University Press.

Neurath, Otto (1959). "Protocol Sentences." Trans. by George Schick. In A. J. Ayer, ed., *Logical Positivism* (New York: Free Press), pp. 199-208.

Nozick, Robert (1974). *Anarchy, State, and Utopia*. New York: Basic Books.

Parfit, Derek (1984). *Reasons and Persons*. Oxford: Clarendon Press.

Parsons, Talcott (1951). *The Social System*. Glencoe, Ill.: Free Press.

——— (1961). "An Outline of the Social System," in Talcott Parsons, E. Shils, K. D. Naegele, and J. R. Pitts, eds., *Theories of Society* (New York: Free Press of Glencoe), vol. 1, pp. 30–79.

——— (1966). *Societies: Evolutionary and Comparative Perspectives*. Englewood Cliffs, N.J.: Prentice-Hall.

Plott, Charles R. (1976). "Axiomatic Social Choice Theory: An Overview and Interpretation," *American Journal of Political Science*, 20, pp. 511–96.

Putnam, Hilary (1981). *Reason, Truth and History*. Cambridge: Cambridge University Press.

Railton, Peter (1986a). "Moral Realism," *The Philosophical Review*, 95, pp. 163–207.

——— (1986b). "Facts and Values," *Philosophical Topics*, 14, pp. 5–29.

Rawls, John (1971). *A Theory of Justice*. Cambridge, Mass.: Harvard University Press.

——— (1975). "Fairness to Goodness," *The Philosophical Review*, 84, pp. 536–54.

——— (1977). "The Basic Structure as Subject," *American Philosophical Quarterly*, 14, pp. 159–65.

——— (1980). "Kantian Constructivism in Moral Theory: The Dewey Lectures, 1980," *The Journal of Philosophy*, 77, pp. 515–72.

——— (1985). "Justice as Fairness: Political Not Metaphysical," *Philosophy and Public Affairs*, 14, pp. 223–51.

——— (1993). *Political Liberalism*. New York: Columbia University Press.

Ross, W. D. (1930). *The Right and the Good*. Oxford: Oxford University Press.

Russell, Bertrand (1905). "On Denoting," *Mind*, 14, pp. 479–93.

Salmon, Nathan, and Soames, Scott (1988). "Introduction," in Nathan Salmon and Scott Soames, eds., *Propositions and Attitudes* (Oxford: Oxford University Press), pp. 1–15.

Sayre-McCord, Geoffrey (1988). "The Many Moral Realisms," in Geoffrey Sayre-McCord, ed., *Essays on Moral Realism* (Ithaca, N.Y.: Cornell University Press), pp. 1–23.

—— (1991). "Being a Realist about Relativism (in Ethics)," *Philosophical Studies*, 61, pp. 155–76.

Schopenhauer, Arthur (1965). *On the Basis of Morality*. Trans. by E. F. J. Payne. New York: Bobbs Merrill.

Schwartz, Thomas (1986). *The Logic of Collective Choice*. New York: Columbia University Press.

Searle, John (1969). *Speech Acts*. Cambridge: Cambridge University Press.

—— (1990). "Collective Intentions and Actions," in Philip R. Cohen, Jerry Morgan, and Martha E. Pollack, eds., *Intentions in Communication* (Cambridge, Mass.: MIT Press), pp. 401–15.

Sen, Amartya (1970). *Collective Choice and Social Welfare*. San Francisco: Holden-Day.

Sidgwick, Henry (1907). *The Methods of Ethics*. London and New York: Dover, 1966.

Sinnott-Armstrong, Walter (1988). *Moral Dilemmas*. Oxford and New York: Basil Blackwell.

—— (1992). "An Argument for Consequentialism," *Philosophical Perspectives*, 6, pp. 399–421.

Slote, Michael (1983). *Goods and Virtues*. Oxford: Clarendon Press.

—— (1989). *Beyond Optimizing: A Study of Rational Choice*. Cambridge, Mass.: Harvard University Press.

Smart, J. J. C. (1973). "An Outline of a System of Utilitarian Ethics," in J. J. C. Smart and Bernard Williams, *Utilitarianism: For and Against* (Cambridge: Cambridge University Press), pp. 1–74.

Smith, Steven H. (1974). *Satisfaction of Interest and the Concept of Morality*. London: Associated University Presses.

Stalnaker, Robert C. (1984). *Inquiry*. Cambridge, Mass.: Bradford Books, The Massachusetts Institute of Technology Press.

Stampe, D. W. (1988). "Need," *Australasian Journal of Philosophy*, 66, pp. 129–60.

Stevenson, Charles (1944). *Morality and Language*. New Haven, Conn.: Yale University Press.

Strawson, P. F. (1974a). "Freedom and Resentment," in P. F. Strawson, *Freedom and Resentment* (London: Methuen), pp. 1–25.

—— (1974b). "Social Morality and Individual Ideal," in P. F. Strawson, *Freedom and Resentment* (London: Methuen), pp. 26–44.

Sturgeon, Nicholas (1974). "Altruism, Solipsism and the Objectivity of Reasons," *The Philosophical Review*, 83, pp. 374–402.

—— (1982). "Brandt's Moral Empiricism," *The Philosophical Review*, 91, pp. 389–422.

—— (1985). "Moral Explanations," in David Copp and David Zimmerman, eds., *Morality, Reason, and Truth* (Totowa, N.J.: Rowman and Allanheld), pp. 49–78.

Sumner, L. W. (1987). *The Moral Foundation of Rights*. Oxford: Clarendon Press.

Teller, Paul (1983). "A Poor Man's Guide to Supervenience and Determination," *The Southern Journal of Philosophy*, supp. vol. 22, *Spindel Conference, 1983: Supervenience*, pp. 137–63.

Thomson, Garrett (1987). *Needs*. London: Routledge and Kegan Paul.

Thomson, Judith Jarvis (1975–76). "Killing, Letting Die, and the Trolley Problem," *Monist*, 59, pp. 204–17.

—— (1989). "The No Reason Thesis," *Social Philosophy and Policy*, 7, pp. 1–21.

Trianosky, Gregory W. (1986). "Supererogation, Wrongdoing, and Vice: On the Autonomy of the Ethics of Virtue," *The Journal of Philosophy*, 83, pp. 26–40.

Tuomela, Raimo (1990). "What Are Goals and Joint Goals?" *Theory and Decision*, 28, pp. 1–20.

———— (1991). "We Will Do It: An Analysis of Group-Intentions," *Philosophy and Phenomenological Research*, 51, pp. 249–77.

Tuomela, Raimo, and Miller, Kaarlo (1988). "We-Intentions," *Philosophical Studies*, 53, pp. 115–37.

Turnbull, Colin M. (1972). *The Mountain People*. New York: Simon and Schuster.

Wallace, G., and Walker, A. D. M. (1970). *The Definition of Morality*. London: Methuen and Company.

Warnock, G. J. (1971). *The Object of Morality*. London: Methuen and Company.

Wiggins, David (1987). *Needs, Values, Truth*. Oxford: Basil Blackwell.

———— (1988). "Truth, Invention, and the Meaning of Life," in Geoffrey Sayre-McCord, ed., *Essays on Moral Realism* (Ithaca, N.Y.: Cornell University Press), pp. 127–65.

Williams, Bernard (1973). "A Critique of Utilitarianism," in J. J. C. Smart and Bernard Williams, *Utilitarianism: For and Against* (Cambridge: Cambridge University Press), pp. 75–150.

———— (1981a). "Internal and External Reasons," in Bernard Williams, *Moral Luck* (Cambridge: Cambridge University Press), pp. 101–13.

———— (1981b). *Moral Luck*. Cambridge: Cambridge University Press.

———— (1985). *Ethics and the Limits of Philosophy*. Cambridge, Mass.: Harvard University Press.

Wilson, Peter J., McCall, Grant, Geddes, W. R., Mark, A. K., Pfeiffer, John E., Boskey, James B., and Turnbull, Colin M. (1975). "More Thoughts on the Ik and Anthropology," *Current Anthropology*, 16, pp. 343–58.

Wilson, Robert (1972). "Social Choice Theory without the Pareto Principle," *Journal of Economic Theory*, 5, pp. 478–86.

Wittgenstein, Ludwig (1953). *Philosophical Investigations*. Oxford: Basil Blackwell.

Wong, David B. (1984). *Moral Relativity*. Berkeley: University of California Press.

———— (1994). "Moral Reasons: Internal and External." Paper presented to the Pacific Division of the American Philosophical Association, 1 April 1994, Los Angeles, California.

Index